A Day Apart

A DAY APART

How Jews, Christians, and Muslims Find Faith,
Freedom, and Joy on the Sabbath

Christopher D. Ringwald

OXFORD
UNIVERSITY PRESS

2007

OXFORD
UNIVERSITY PRESS

Oxford University Press, Inc., publishes works that further
Oxford University's objective of excellence
in research, scholarship, and education.

Oxford   New York
Auckland   Cape Town   Dar es Salaam   Hong Kong   Karachi
Kuala Lumpur   Madrid   Melbourne   Mexico City   Nairobi
New Delhi   Shanghai   Taipei   Toronto

With offices in
Argentina   Austria   Brazil   Chile   Czech Republic   France   Greece
Guatemala   Hungary   Italy   Japan   Poland   Portugal   Singapore
South Korea   Switzerland   Thailand   Turkey   Ukraine   Vietnam

Published by Oxford University Press, Inc.
198 Madison Avenue, New York, New York 10016
www.oup.com

Oxford is a registered trademark of Oxford University Press

Library of Congress Cataloging-in-Publication Data

Ringwald, Christopher D.
A day apart : how Jews, Christians, and Muslims find faith, freedom,
and joy on the Sabbath / Christopher D. Ringwald.
p. cm.
Includes bibliographical references and index.
ISBN-13: 978-0-19-537019-5

1. Sabbath.   2.   Rest—Religious aspects.   I.   Title.
BL595.S9R56 2007
203'.6—dc22
2006026028

Printed in the United States of America
on acid-free paper

To my children, Mitchell Furey, Jeanne Annemarie, and Madeleine Margaret, whose life, joy, and faith infuse this book and make our Sundays.

There is a realm of time where the goal is not to have but to be, not to own but to give, not to control but to share, not to subdue but to be in accord. . . . The Sabbath is a day for the sake of life.

ABRAHAM JOSHUA HESCHEL, *THE SABBATH*

Table of Contents

CHAPTER III

The Fight for the Sabbath: From the Monarchy to
Jesus and the Age of the Rabbis: 1000 BCE to 200 CE

CHAPTER IV

The Lord's Day: Easter to 1600

CHAPTER V

Islam's Day of Judgment

CHAPTER VI

Citizens and Sabbatarians: 1600 to 1890

Preface

On Friday nights and Saturdays in our neighborhood, the Jews walk to and from their Sabbath services along the sidewalks of the maple-lined streets. Well-dressed and at their ease, these families move inside a bubble of holy time. Their calm, happy mood conveys a belief that there is a God who loves them and has given them this day to worship and enjoy themselves. Here's the bargain: they keep the Sabbath and God keeps them. Who could not be attracted to such a deal? This covenant dates to Creation, almost six thousand years ago according to the Jewish calendar, and to the delivery of the Ten Commandments at Mount Sinai. More factually, evidence dates regular Sabbath observance to at least the eighth century and probably 1000 BCE, which gives us at least three thousand years of Jews walking to services on the seventh day as they still do in neighborhoods around the world.

Christians have their Lord's Day on Sunday and Muslims their Day of Assembly, Juma, on Friday. Though these are not Sabbaths, in the exact Jewish sense, each is a holy day that draws on Jewish tradition and theology. Christianity and Islam each developed a distinctive holy day whose features characterize their religion and distinguishes it from Judaism and each other. The common denominator is that the day is a gift that conveys and signifies God's love. The calm confidence, joy, and dignity of observant Jews, Christians, and Muslims on the holy day are striking. The mystery remains as to why only a minority in each monotheism accepts this divine gift. In the wider world, the secondary characteristic of the Sabbath is its general neglect and our relative ignorance. The Sabbath remains the dessert most people leave on the table.

So many of us say, "If only I could take a break, if only I could get away." Here's your excuse: God told you to. We often criticize ourselves, friends, or colleagues for acting as if the world rested on our shoulders, for thinking we are God, that the world spins around us, and that we have to take care of everything ourselves. In fact, the person who stops once a week imitates a God who made the world and then ceased.

This book tells a story that began at Creation and continues into the present. Along the way, it explores theology, philosophy, and practice of the day, notably in the lives of three families and my own reflections. The first chapter introduces these families and the basics of the Sabbath. Chapters 2 through 7 trace the history of the Sabbath, with much of the Muslim material concentrated in chapter 5. The implications and deeper nature of the Sabbath—time, eternity, sacred versus profane, salvation—is discussed in chapter 8, and the relation between work and rest is detailed in chapter 9. The final chapter looks at the prospects for common ground and at the ultimate aims of the Sabbath.

I write as a journalist and student of religion, but also as a Catholic. At times, I speak directly of my experience as a member of the Roman Catholic Church, notably on Sunday and at Mass. Rather than disguise this, I try to use my faith as a key that can help unlock the experience and beliefs of Judaism and Islam.

My method was to attend and be influenced by each religion and then report the effects on me and my life. This is an old journalistic tradition also known to social scientists as the participant-observer method. Thus I participated so far as possible in Shabbat and Juma without offending my hosts or violating my own faith. I usually attended services with one of my subjects, but both religious groups welcomed me, even when I appeared as an outsider without a guide. Jews as well as Muslims abide by the spirit of Muhammad's advice, "Better than the world and all it contains is that you bring guidance to one man." I can only hope that visitors to churches are greeted as warmly as I was at synagogues and mosques.

Quite literally, I would go through the motions. On the Jewish Shabbat, at the synagogue I would stand or sit with the congregants and read silently along in a translation. When visiting the Kligermans for lunch on Saturday, I or my family would dress well and try to walk the eight blocks from our house. At the two mosques I attended, I usually sat, stood, bowed, kneeled, and prostrated myself without saying the prayers. (These were in Arabic, and Muslims generally do not read along in books at their service.) Most of these gestures I have performed in my own prayers, and I did not recite any creed foreign to my own. The Sabbath can only be understood by participation. Since the Muslim holy day is concentrated in one short service, I followed the physical routine in order to experience it. The Jewish Sabbath involves 25 hours of meals, walking, and other restful activities and so I devoted more attention to those and less to the synagogue services. Christianity falls in between.

For the most part, I use the Bible, the Quran, and other scriptures literally and not refracted through the lens of interpretation and exegesis. In keeping with current custom, I refer to years in terms of BCE ("before the common era") and CE ("of the common era") instead of the more traditional if ethnocentric BC ("before Christ") and AD (*anno Domini*, "in the year of the Lord").

Naturally, I was most influenced by my own religion and my family's effort to make Sunday a day of rest and joy and faith, doing only those works of charity and necessity. I also conversed, so to speak, with the history and theology, the great lessons and debates over Shabbat, Sunday, and Juma. Again, I was, inescapably, most engaged and influenced by Christianity because of my membership and, equally so, because its literature on the topic is vast and contentious. For Christians, keeping the Lord's Day has always bound them up in social and political debates and conflict. Jews developed the most exhaustive theology and regulation for Shabbat, but did not fight over it among themselves as did Christians. Likewise, Muslims have elaborated on the day's meaning and practice without the same internal acrimony over its nature or obligation. However, the three religions have disagreed with each other over the day.

Belief appears in action. The most to be learned about the holy day is in the lives of the faithful. I thank the three families who opened their lives, homes and religions to me: Tom and Becky Kligerman and their children, Eli, Netania, Adina, and Ilan; Azra and Shamim Haqqie and their children, Naseem and Nadia; and my own family, Amy Biancolli Ringwald and our children, Madeleine, Jeanne, and Mitchell. Since religion is at once powerful and intimate, I appreciate their trust in me and hope this book repays that risk. I thank each family's congregation and their spiritual leaders: Rabbi Paul Silton, Imam Djafer Sebkhaoui, and Father Thomas Powers. They shared their ideas and religion with enthusiasm, conviction and generosity. Near the end of this project Father Powers retired. Our new pastor, Father Vincent Ciotoli, further inspired our Sundays.

This book would not have been without Jeanne Neff, president of The Sage Colleges, and Sally Lawrence, vice president, who sustained me with a room of my own. The Sage community provided a helpful and stimulating environment, from the librarians, notably Rosedelia Redwood, to the maintenance crew, especially Shirley Favreau, to the students and faculty. My neighbors in

West Hall on the Albany campus, Judy Waterman, Jeffrey Soleau, and Olivia Bertagnolli, cheered me on.

Many teachers, friends, and colleagues contributed. Early on, Dennis Gaffney helped immensely by envisioning the book I wanted to write. Lillian Thyssen donated invaluable research in Islam and translations from Greek, Latin, and Arabic. Mike Virtanen, John Dwyer, Tom Kligerman, Azra Haqqie, Rabbi Silton, Imam Sebkhaoui, and my wife Amy read and helped refine parts or all of the text. Tom O'Toole copyedited the draft and spared me many embarrassments. Fred Boehrer, Jane Gottlieb, and Bob Whitaker helped me hash out ideas and methods. Neighbors as the Stenard, Doody, Filkins, and Jeffers families attend our church and made Sundays more enjoyable. My colleagues at Advocates for Human Potential, a social service research and consulting firm where I work part time, tolerated a restless journalist in their midst. Friends and colleagues at the *Albany Times Union* helped in various ways, notably Rex Smith, Mark McGuire, and Paul Grondahl. Melvin Mencher, a former professor at Columbia, long ago convinced me of the merit of in-depth reporting on a subject's life via what he called a "live-in." Father Paul Ciofi, S. J., whose vibrant homilies at Georgetown elevated many a Sunday, offered several keen insights shortly before his death.

At Oxford University Press, my editor Cynthia Read liked this idea from the start and helped me deliver the best version. The copyeditor, Paula Cooper, was scrupulous; Lelia Mander brought the book to its final shape; and Aly Mostel helped present it to the world. My literary agent, Dan Mandel, was able to share his enthusiasm for Shabbat while ensuring my best interests.

I first lived the Sabbath, in the form of Sunday or the Lord's Day, as a child. I thank my late parents, Eugene C. Ringwald and Margaret Furey Ringwald, for their example on Sunday and all days. My siblings Marie, Carl, Anne, and Tom were part of those times and encourage me in the present. Ten years ago my interest in the topic was renewed by Alan Abbey, whose return to observant Judaism began with a Sabbath observed and led to his family's move to Israel. In 2001, I organized a day-long seminar on the Sabbath in Judaism, Christianity, and Islam and was overwhelmed by the response and greatly informed by the participants. Occurring a month after the attacks of 9/11, the event suggested that the holy day could be a bridge of peace among peoples and three very different religions.

Final thanks are due my wife and children who agreed to a more regular observance of Sunday, who shared their thoughts, reactions, and lives, and who helped me hash it all out onto the pages of this book.

A Day Apart

CHAPTER I

From Sinai to Sunday: The Holy Day in Three Religions and Three Families

Remember the sabbath day and keep it holy. Six days you shall labor and do all your work, but the seventh day is a sabbath of the Lord your God; you shall not do any work—you, your son or daughter, your male or female slave, or your cattle, or the stranger who is within your settlements. For in six days the Lord made heaven and earth and sea, and all that is in them, and He rested on the seventh day; therefore the Lord blessed the sabbath day and hallowed it.

TORAH, EXODUS 20:8–11

Then [Jesus] said to them, "The sabbath was made for man, not man for the sabbath. That is why the Son of Man is lord even of the sabbath."

NEW TESTAMENT, MARK 2:27–28

O you who believe! When the call is proclaimed to prayer on Friday [the Day of Assembly], hasten earnestly to the remembrance of Allah, and leave off business [and traffic]: that is best for you if you but knew. And when the Prayer is finished, then you may disperse through the land, and seek the Bounty of Allah, and remember Allah frequently that you may prosper.

QURAN, SURA 62:9–10

One Weekend, Three Sabbaths

Juma / Friday

On a cold blunt Friday in February, late morning, Azra Haqqie finishes printing out 20 letters to the editor at the *Albany Times Union* and stands up from her desk situated on the edge of the city newsroom. A slow gurgle of noise from telephone conversations and keyboards surrounds her. In quick, certain movements she reaches out to numb her computer, pick up her purse, and roll in her chair. Azra nods to another editorial clerk, who will cover the phones in her absence, walks out into the corridor, and enters the restroom. She is a slim woman of medium height with jet-black hair and a serious demeanor that is readily and often eclipsed by a bright, almost mischievous smile. She knows more than she's saying. Today, she wears burgundy slacks and sweater with a floral shirt of green, blue, burgundy, and off-white. Azra stands at the sink and washes her face and hands once, then again, then a third time. She is observing Juma, the weekly obligation to join with other Muslims on Friday for noon prayers at the mosque.

She leaves the building, a wide, squat structure by the side of a highway that heads north toward the Adirondacks, climbs into her Toyota Camry, and drives south, then west about four miles along wide avenues lined with stores, restaurants, and some empty lots. The landscape here in Colonie, halfway between Albany and Schenectady, stretches flat across what was once a vast pine barren. Azra turns right onto a small curving road and into a driveway that drops down toward the Islamic Center of the Capital District.

The building, with curves and spires along the roofline and a golden dome set at the middle, sits in a hollow shielded by a fringe of trees. Muslims, most on extended lunch hours from their jobs, shuttle their cars and vans into empty spots. Azra paces quickly into the building. In an alcove, she puts her shoes into one of a hundred or so cubbyholes that line two walls. Most people join the large assembly in the main room of the mosque. However she walks downstairs, to the overflow room where the *imam*'s sermon and prayers are broadcast. "I like it because you can get in and out without having to talk to a lot of people, which is important since I only have an hour and have to get back to work. I can get there and back in an hour and 15 minutes."

In each of the spaces, women sit in the back third, behind a rope strung knee-high across the room, and men in the front. Adult males are required to attend and women may; though it is considered a mercy from God that they are not so obligated. The crowd of the faithful contains smartly dressed professionals, college students in neat casual wear, older men with gray-flecked beards, mothers with young children, and some well-pressed blue-collar workers. Half or more are Pakistani, a large group in the Albany region, and the rest of African, South Asian, or Arab background. In the room, many people kneel back on their haunches and murmur some prayers in Arabic, and most eventually sit on the floor to wait. The upstairs room is carpeted. Downstairs the linoleum floor is covered with white sheets. Everyone faces toward Mecca, which is northeast from Albany following the shortest distance across the earth's curve.

The *imam*, or spiritual leader of the congregation, faces the congregation as he leans back on a stool-sized ledge in the pulpit or *minbar*, a wooden structure that resembles the back of a large lectern. At 12:30 PM, a man who serves as *muezzin* issues the Adhan, or call to prayer. All rise, then sit and listen to the imam's sermon or *khutbah*, which tells the story of Muhammad's first treaty with another power to coexist peacefully, after which thousands were converted and freely joined his ranks. "Regardless of what is being said today, Islam has always been spread by peace, not violence. Those who say otherwise, I say to them, show me the proof. Because we have the proof that you are wrong. We can show you how it was spread by peace."

After 25 minutes, the muezzin issues another Adhan. Everyone rises and forms tight lines from the north wall to the south wall. People shuffle in toward each other till shoulders touch and feet are inches apart from the neighbor's on each side in an ordered, solemn intimacy. Juma (or Jum'a) derives from the Arab verb, *jama'a*, to collect or unite, and means "Day of Assembly."

I found the actions of the assembly reassuring and also easy to follow. No one paid attention to my delayed reactions as I imitated the actions of others or my complete silence during the prayers, recited in Arabic. Performing any ritual in a large group feeds some deep human need. In this mosque on this Friday, I recall the medieval Christian leader who, when he heard that Muslims pray as one, shivered and predicted that they would achieve greatness.

"*Allahu Akbar*," the congregation pronounces, "God is great." Most members hold their hands to their ears as they declare this primary creed. The imam recites verses from the Quran. Azra prays along as do many others. Then she and all bend as one, putting their hands to knees. More verses, then people stand upright. "Allahu Akbar," and all prostrate themselves, with knees tucked in, and press their foreheads and noses to the ground. ("It reminds us that we bow only to God and only to the Creator," Azra tells me later.) At words from the imam, all sit back, then prostrate themselves again, and sit back again. Prayers and verses briskly recited accompany each movement. As a newcomer unaccustomed to sitting back on my heels for several minutes at a time, my knees and thighs burn with pain. This completes one *raka*, with a number prescribed for each of the five prayers required of Muslims. At this Friday service, the congregation performs a second.

When the imam is not praying, one hears only the friction of fabric and the slight exhalation of older members as all move forward, down, back, forward, back, and up. Azra moves lightly and reverently, her hair swishing softly back and forth over the temples of her eyeglasses. At the end, all sit and look to one side, then the other, greeting the neighbor on left and right with, "*Assalamu Alaikum*," or "Peace be upon you." Afterwards, many stay to pray privately. Azra does, and completes two more rakas. Then she slips out, dons her shoes, and avoiding entangling conversations—most people know each other—she drives back to the newsroom. "I like going, it's a little dose of religion."

During the same time, her husband, Shamim Haqqie, attended *salat* or prayers with about 20 others at the chapel in Albany Medical Center Hospital, where he is a senior physician. The Haqqies, both natives of Pakistan, are observant but not pious. Islam stipulates that though Muslims should return to their work, they should do so with a renewed consciousness of God. Shamim is a friendly man of medium height, black hair, and a serious if slightly distracted manner. Shamim may be thinking of his last patient, he may be zoning out—it's hard to tell.

Azra and Shamim say they feel renewed by Juma. The day is also suited for good works and family. "Ideally you should be doing that anyway," Azra says.

Shabbat / Saturday

Later that same Friday, as dusk creeps down, Tom Kligerman leaves his office at the New York State Department of Transportation, where he is a highway engineer. Tom, wiry and athletic, beams an intense energy from dark eyes set off by a sharp bearded chin and balding head. With him, a joke sinks in, a moment passes, and then he snaps up his face and laughs enthusiastically. He drives home to a 1926 house, cheerfully cluttered with scarves and boots and children's toys, on Van Schoick Avenue in Albany's Helderberg neighborhood. He and his wife Becky and their children—Eli, Netania, and Adina (another son, Ilan, was born later)—have already begun the weekly tidal shift from six days of work to one of holy rest. Their whole week tilts toward the Sabbath.

Becky, a professor of occupational therapy with a flexible schedule, may make desserts for the weekend on Tuesday or Wednesday. She cleans the house on Thursday, finishing up Friday morning. "If I start too early then it gets trashed all over again," Becky says. She is a lively woman with red hair who laughs readily, though her face can turn serious and is alternately reflective or attentive. Becky corrals the children, manages meals and the household and her job, purposely and without much ado. Minor things must be taken care of so as to attend to the larger purpose.

By Friday noon, the Kligermans have already cooked the main dishes for their Shabbat dinner, always a special occasion. Tom was up till 4:00 AM preparing his vegetarian lasagna, which he began after his Thursday night soccer game. "Sometimes I just skip going to bed and stay up to catch up and do everything." Friday morning, Becky ran errands with her infant, Adina. She picks up another daughter, Netania, at 1:00 PM from preschool. "That's really my deadline for finishing everything. I may chop vegetables or set the table in the afternoon, but that's about all I can do then. I honestly don't know how people who work eight to five and have children manage to keep Shabbat."

Since Jews are prohibited from making a fire, or setting a spark, during their Sabbath, the Kligermans have timers on bedroom and other lights so that these will flick off for bedtime. Other lights, as in the bathroom, are left on. The stove is set to turn off after warming the lasagna. Inside the refrigerator, Becky has taped down the automatic light switch for the duration so that it will not flick on when they open the door. Shabbat begins 18 minutes before sundown, when Becky lights two candles, one for each of the biblical commandments— in Exodus and Deuteronomy—to remember and to keep the Sabbath. An hour before that, she had the children put away their toys. Eli, their first child, is six and has a friend over this Friday. They roll off the couch wrestling, yelling, and watching a video. About 5:00 PM, Tom stops the last activity that belongs to the week but not to the day that ticks toward us. "Eli, off with the video." The boys fight on, bouncing off cushions and chasing one another. Now Tom speaks more sharply. "Eli, off! Shabbat!"

Then Tom and I put on our coats. He packs up Adina in a baby carrier and we set off to Temple Israel. Becky will light the candles at 5:07 PM, just before sundown. As with so much of Jewish law and practice, ancient decisions and interpretations dictate the Kligerman's observance. "The rabbis added extra time as a precaution against violating, so Shabbat begins 18 minutes before sundown Friday and it ends 42 minutes after sundown Saturday, which makes it 25 hours."

Just before I came over to the Kligermans, I read of the comfort of ritual in *Magic, Science and Religion* by Bronislaw Malinowski, the Polish anthropologist, who said ritual must be expressed through "the public concourse." And as we walk this evening along Helderberg Avenue, a quiet snowbound street that passes dark blocky homes glowing yellow through their windows, this one Jewish man, garrulously explaining the timing of the Sabbath as he steps lightly through the snow to synagogue with a baby on his back, embodies an ancient ritual in this byway of the public concourse.

"I was going to drive and leave the car there afterwards," Tom says, which would have been allowable since we left before sundown. Helderberg Avenue ends in a complex of garden apartments. We turn into a path between dumpsters, then climb over a 14-foot high pile left by the snowplows that cleared the parking lot in the rear of Temple Israel. Oddly enough, the synagogue does not have its front entrance cleared since most members arrive by car and enter from the back. Walkers must find their way there too.

Temple Israel is a low and wide brick building constructed in the 1950s, with many extra meeting areas and offices and classrooms and alcoves joined by an open staircase that stretches up three floors. The congregation and the Kligermans are Conservative, the progressive middle way in Judaism that developed in the nineteenth century in an effort to maintain tradition amid modernity. About a third of American Jews belong. The other main branches of Judaism are Orthodox—who believe the written and oral law are divinely inspired and worthy of exacting study and observation—and Reform—another post-Enlightenment adaptation that accepts only the moral laws as binding and rejects those rituals that do not accord with contemporary life.

We hang our coats and enter the small sanctuary where the service is under way. The rabbi, a dark-haired, intense man, stands to the side in the front. At the center, the cantor moves back and forth, side to side as he sings one of the infinite number of the melodious hymns of Judaism. To an outsider, Shabbat services are gloriously chaotic. The two dozen men there, most middle-aged and older, read along in the prayer book. Some wander up and down the aisle at will. A tall youth in front snaps back and forth vigorously as he prays, the fringes on his prayer shawl—the type worn under a shirt—bouncing and waving. A smiling older man comes over to play with Adina and touch her head. He and Tom talk. And the praying goes on in a boisterous rumbling.

It is as if these believers were so confident of their connection to God that nothing could interrupt it. Or perhaps God loves us so completely that, especially as they observe the oldest and first of the commandments, they feel nothing they do could change His mind. Hey, so what we talk—we're glad to see each other and to start another Sabbath. God won't mind if I take a break and chat with another of His people.

Later in the service, Tom brings Adina to the front and stands before a metal goblet full of wine. A tray holds some plastic cups with grape juice. He holds the goblet aloft and sings the Kiddush, or blessing, in a strong sure voice. The prayer begins with a passage from Genesis, in which "God blessed the seventh day and made it holy, because on it he rested from all the work he had done in creation." Adina looks blankly over the small congregation. Then Tom drinks and the young children are offered small portions in cups. After the service, some of the men linger and talk before heading home for their Shabbat meals.

We leave and arrive home for the Shabbat meal, for which every effort has been made. There is the lasagna, a dish of carrots, salad, and two loaves of *challah*, bread that is braided to beautify the commandment. The two loaves recall the double portion of manna that fell on Friday so the Israelites, who were wandering in the desert, would have enough for the Sabbath. We all sit. Eli and his friend yank at each other. Tom holds up a cup of wine, the children have juice, and he sings the Kiddush again. We eat. Becky explains some of the Sabbath customs and also the rules for keeping kosher, such as having separate sets of dishes for dairy and meat. Not everything has a reason beyond affirming traditions that acknowledge God. "A lot of the things in Torah, we don't know why. But we do it because it's in there or the rabbis have said we should." At the same time, she likes the perspective of their rabbi, Paul Silton. "He wants to make Judaism accessible."

The meal is not a time in the stillness of heaven. Eli runs off, comes back, pushes his friend and climbs halfway across the table to reach the juice, like many another six-year-old. The baby cries. Netania tells her father to make Eli stop. Later, after visitors leave and the baby sleeps, Tom curls up with Eli and Netania and reads the story of Jacob who worked for seven years to earn the hand of Rachel, only to have her older sister Leah substituted. This section is part of a children's schedule of readings to coincide with the weekly portion, or *parashah*, that Jews can read each week—outside of holidays—in order to complete the five books of the Torah each year.

"The kids like them because the stories are so human. Who can't relate to expecting one thing and then getting another? The stories are about people interacting, but also something much deeper." When Tom says this, in a flash I think, yes, the stories are about God interacting with us. And for the Kligermans, observing the Sabbath engages them in the oldest of Jewish practices. The Israelites were already keeping Shabbat by the time they arrived at Mount Sinai, before they received the Ten Commandments. God was the first Sabbath keeper, and by resting on the seventh day He made clear that Creation culminates in Shabbat. And on this Friday in dark, snowy Albany, the Kligermans have entered this oasis of time, this moment of eternity, where they feel the mighty presence of God, one that will not be disrupted by wrestling six-year-olds or a crying baby.

The Lord's Day / Sunday

The Sundays of my childhood were filled with sacred hours though no one called them such. The day was one of leisure though not laziness, of culture but not entertainment, of prayer but not piety, of fun though not foolishness. Sunday was a day of joy and order and simplicity and peace. Sunday was our Sabbath, our weekly Easter.

In our home in the Bronx, we rose and dressed in our best clothes, laid out the night before, in the cloud of controlled chaos expected from a family of seven. We walked down Bainbridge Avenue, crossed Fordham Road, and then up Marion Avenue to Our Lady of Mercy Church, its blunt gray concrete outline hovering over the families rushing in to Mass. Afterward, my father or one of the five children would make our only purchases of the day, the Sunday newspapers from a boy outside church and perhaps some salt rolls at Zaro's Bakery. We would walk home and eat a large breakfast, then go out for the afternoon to the Botanical Gardens or the Bronx Zoo, by subway to a museum in Manhattan, or to tour one of the city's neighborhoods. It was a day for culture, for higher enjoyments, for upright activities, and lots of walking. My mother would stay home for her own day of rest from cooking, cleaning, and kids.

The Sunday habit stayed with me in many ways: dressing up for Mass even as a bachelor during a wild period after college, seeking out cultural events or field trips or hikes in the afternoon, going to Mass and not working. On two jobs in which I had to work half the weekend, taxi driver and news reporter, I chose to work Saturday by instinct. Then, a Jewish friend, Alan Abbey, told me about his reconversion, which began when he spent the Sabbath with a girlfriend who was observant enough to not shop, a big deal in suburban New Jersey. Alan, a normally reserved man, glowed as he recalled that first Shabbat, for him, and the quiet pleasure of doing little other than walking around their town and having dinner, saying some prayers. And so it returned to me and my family.

Today on a Saturday in our home, the darkening windows signal time to finish up any final chores. Following the traditional Catholic schedule of prayers, with the first Sunday prayers the night before, we begin the Lord's Day at sundown Saturday. We try—valiantly if often in vain—to keep the day holy, happy, enjoyable, and restful. On one particular Saturday, relief washes over me as I put away the vacuum cleaner. Laundry that will be done, is done. The dryer spins on downstairs, but we will not unload it until Sunday night. No one will be rushing out to the store—we made our last purchase just earlier, of Italian sausage, hot and sweet, at Sainato's. We keep the television off, and the children gambol about. Jeanne puts her Barbies in their kitchen, Madeleine fans out her fantasy game cards, and Mitchell dumps a basket of toy trucks and stares at the clattering avalanche. Friends are coming to dinner, so I cook. Even without a formal beginning, we all sense the shift to a time apart, we hope, from work, bills, shopping, worry, and impatience.

Catholics who try to keep the Lord's Day beyond attending Mass can feel alone. Since 1960, neither Catholics nor most Protestants have made the holy day of rest a central practice beyond the communal liturgy, though interest appears to be growing. Still, compared to the Jews, we are at sea on the Sabbath.

The catechism of the Catholic Church, issued in 1992, spells out guidelines that would be familiar to most Christians and draw on 2,000 years of practice. We follow the basic rules: Mass, family, good works, play, culture, and, in the traditional phrasing, "to neither do, nor cause to be done, any servile labor." Since the early centuries Christians made exceptions for "works of charity and necessity." We don't discuss money or bills or our jobs. That last rule gets bent since Amy and I write and some of our topics—music, literature, religion, mental health—appeal to our better nature. So we may discuss issues but not the "servile" side, the salaries or office politics. We try not to gossip—maybe tomorrow, but we can always hold off for a day.

Normally, before dinner, we light a candle and thank God for the Lord's Day and ask that it be one of peace, rest, and joy. This night, after our friends Dennis, Kathy, and three-year-old Sophia arrive and we all sit for dinner, we try to pray. Self-consciousness restrains my prayer, the children strain at the pasta and bread and salad. Jeanne, my seven-year-old, burns her finger lighting the candle. But it's done and the Sabbath begins. Regardless of our hamhanded-ness, the Sabbath still comes.

These small rules bring outsized blessings. The Sabbath is a gift, and it is a gift that is confirmed in practice. The more we do in this regard, the more we want to do. Now Madeleine, at age nine, wants us to skip driving, except in severe weather and then only to go to church. These decisions call for a quiet awareness of God, one of the day's blessings. Any violation reminds us of that treasure to which we can return. For instance, once I was in the backyard in May and I leaned over instinctively to yank a weed from among the lettuce plants. One won't hurt. But then I saw another and another and soon I had spent 20 minutes weeding and was dirty and sweaty. Dirty and sweaty from tumbling with my children would be fine, but the work seemed wrong.

More recently, I shoveled a path to the firewood on a Sunday. We don't follow the Jewish law against fire, which makes all of us happy and warm as we spend our time on games and reading together in the living room. But I spend a few moments wondering if the shoveling is wrong before I go ahead in favor of the greater good of a warm hearth.

The next day we dress up, attend Mass, have a large breakfast, sit and read the papers or books, and sink into a relative stillness, insofar as we can with three children. Later we rouse ourselves and drive—no other choice in winter—to the Albany Institute of History and Art, a gem of a museum now showing George Benson's photographs of the Beatles. I remain in my suit and tie since it's comfortable and seems right. The calm propriety of the day appeals to me. Among the museum goers, I sense the week's tedium washing away and a peaceful dullness, prior to true serenity but still a blessing, creeping upon us all. We're in it together. Sunday afternoon blesses us all.

We hearken to the example of our Puritan forebears, as described by the historian Alice Morse Earle in 1909. "Sweet to the Pilgrims and to their descendants was the hush of their calm Saturday night, and their still, tranquil Sabbath—sign and token to them, not only of the weekly rest ordained in the creation, but of the eternal rest to come."[1] Though the Pilgrims could return to work on Sunday night, we generally don't. The Lord's Day extends its hold fore and aft, temporally, and into the household and world spatially. At dusk we light the candle again, pray, read the Magnificat, or Canticle of Mary, bless each other with holy water, and smell some sweet spices and herbs I keep in a wooden box, something we borrowed from the Jews, to remind us of the sweetness of the Sabbath in the days ahead. The Lord's Day is over. God holds us yet.

The Fight for the Sabbath

We fight for the Sabbath, it comes not easily. We fight for the Sabbath, our day of peace and rest and divinity. We fight for the Sabbath: against ourselves, perhaps against other believers, and certainly against the claims of the world. The Haqqies, Kligermans, and Ringwalds struggle to keep the day holy in their ordinary ways. They are not exemplars, just families trying to live their faiths

All three religions set apart one day from the others—Jews and Christians have a day of rest and worship, Muslims a time for communal prayer and good works. Time, rather than space or material, becomes sanctified and an avenue to the divine. Aside from time, all three religions share other elements in observing their day apart: community, a balance between public and private, ritual, participation in Creation, special access to eternity, and regular, observable behavior that shows one's faithfulness. The Puritans taught that good Sabbaths make for good Christians and the Jews believe if all of Israel keeps one Shabbat properly, the Messiah will come.

Today many Jews, Christians, and Muslims are rediscovering the Sabbath. Some nonreligious people also value a day of rest as a hedge against the pace and demands of modern life. A handful of how-to books tracks this development.[2] Latter-day adherents who prefer flexibility face the challenge of adding the ballast of ritual and tradition, a likely area for personal and social conflict. Modern Sabbath keepers may find, as did their predecessors over the centuries, that the cause is popular with the laity but not religious leaders. The Sabbath, notably among Christians, has more often sprung like wheat from the soil than from the precincts of hierarchy.

Shabbat, Sunday or the Lord's Day, and Juma have God as their end and serve the purposes of religion. The day apart pits the believer against all his or her worldly intentions. The train set to running the other six days does not slow down or halt easily at the border of the seventh. You can't just skid to a stop at sundown. "That is why the Puritan and Jewish Sabbaths were so exactingly intentional, requiring extensive advance preparation—at the least a scrubbed house, a full larder and a bath," writes Judith Shulevitz. "The rules did not exist to torture the faithful. They were meant to communicate the insight that interrupting the ceaseless round of striving requires a surprisingly strenuous act of will, one that has to be bolstered by habit as well as by social sanction."[3] In order to have a holy day of rest, we have to work at it.

Believers have often fought over the Sabbath. Among the monotheisms, it has been a point of contention and dependence. Christianity and Islam broke away from Judaism and define themselves against Judaism. They did so in terms of the Sabbath most of all. Each changed the day and formed new rituals. Both derived essential ideas from Judaism, the Sabbath included. All three share a basic formula of faith and practice known first to the Israelites: keep the covenant and prosper, break the covenant and suffer. Consistently in Judaism, and intermittently in Islam and Christianity, the Sabbath embodied a formula: keep the day and live, break the day and die. We even disagree on numbering the Ten Commandments. Jews, Orthodox Christians, and most Protestants count the Sabbath as the fourth, which I retain, while Catholics and Lutherans count it as the third.

Within religions we also fight over the Sabbath. During the Dark Ages, the Reformation and the nineteenth century, Christians argued and even fought over the holy day and its requirements. Today the Seventh-day Adventists and Seventh Day Baptists who rest on Saturday, the "seventh day," castigate their fellows for changing the fourth commandment, which they say Jesus never authorized.

Observance pits one against society, commerce, and even neighbors. My boss may agree that I never work on the Sabbath, but time passes and the needs of the firm press in. "How strict are you about Sunday? Could you leave Sunday night for the trip to Washington?" Our children may be invited to a play date that requires a ride in the car. Friends may ask you to help them move a sofa. To be *shomer* Shabbat, Hebrew for Sabbath observant, pits one against time itself, or at least our limited notion of time. We think we need that time, those 24 hours, for chores and errands and work, for the self-important duties of real life. Get to it, man!

To what are we attending? To the things of this world, to mammon, to our desires and wants and appetites. Sabbath calls us away from our counterfeit reality, Sabbath calls us to God. We say "no" to regular time. For on that day, we say no to the press of the clock and its urgencies, its demand that we act on the timetable of seconds and minutes and hours. Time rushes on till the morrow and inclines us to the workbench where we hunch and hammer. Time inclines us to work for the future. Time urges us to lay aside for tomorrow by laying waste to the present.

When we keep the day we stand off from society and with our fellow believers. We join another team. To keep the day apart is the most obvious sign of religious membership. Jews head to synagogue, Christians to church, Muslims to the mosque. We do that and, thus, not the other. The observant in all religions worship together and, to some extent, cease creative activity. Other commandments may be kept, or broken, privately. The fourth commandment requires public action, or inaction. Failure to observe can remain private. The ancient Hebrews and the Puritans punished, usually, only those who profaned the day publicly and contemptuously.

Attendance is the quickest measure of devotion, especially extreme devotion, and especially given the fragile nerves of the twenty-first century. In Islamic nations, crowds kneeling in prayer outside certain mosques at Friday worship may indicate a surge in fundamentalism. People in Saudi Arabia, Iraq, or Pakistan are not, after all, rushing to hear the moderates. In other eras, crowds at fundamentalist revivals in the United States or at Catholic churches run by firebrand Jesuits in El Salvador also tipped us off to a shift in religious sentiments that would ignite political fires. In watching Iraq, for instance, political analysts and journalists deploy this shorthand, to wit: "On January 2, 2004, the 3rd Platoon was roused early. It was a Friday, the Muslim Sabbath, a day when clerics in Mini-Vietnam were known to preach mischief."[4]

Sitting in his living room one night, Shamim Haqqie contemplates this type of danger. "Here the imams are educated. In the old country, they can exploit people for political causes. The mosque on Friday is a great place to influence people."

In the same way at other times, Catholic priests were believed to have set their mobs of believers off to rampage against the Jews for having killed Christ, or Protestant hate mongers incited their flocks to persecute their Catholic cousins. Since the faithful gather on Friday, Saturday, or Sunday, those days are the occasion for preaching a religion's message in all its ideals and distortions.

The Blessings of the Sabbath

Does it really matter how we spend that one day in seven, be it Juma, Shabbat, or Sunday? Yes. We keep the day holy, and the day changes us such that we want more. Living the Sabbath, we understand the great gift of the Sabbath, a treasure given us by the Jews, the first of the monotheists. Living the Sabbath reveals its many dimensions and gifts. As with the three families, these joys and satisfactions come to any who follow some basic rules in the company of their fellows.

On the Sabbath, heaven beckons. The day apart opens onto the ultimate concerns of God and humanity: creation, eternity, judgment, time, meaning, work, leisure, necessity, and charity. Yet it opens from here on earth, joining the concrete with the transcendent, the material with the ineffable, and the profane with the sacred.

We ask for only that which God offers that day: everything of import. In a Shabbat prayer, Jews ask, "On this, the Sabbath day, give us rest. . . . On this, the Sabbath day, give us time. . . . On this, the Sabbath day, give us understanding and peace."

On the Sabbath we are all equal, for the commandment relieves all—slave, child, master, animal—from work that day. In Deuteronomy, Yahweh reminds us that we were once aliens ourselves. We are enjoined to ensure that no one serves another. Rich and poor are that day equal. Ralph Waldo Emerson called the Sabbath "the jubilee of the whole world; whose light dawns welcome alike into the closet of the philosopher, into the garret of toil, and into prison cells, and everywhere suggests, even to the vile, the dignity of spiritual being."[5] Religion should be observed or ignored freely, but a social consensus often protects society's least powerful members. Personal habit may need social sanction.

On the day apart we are free. We are not pack animals, day by day trudging wearily through the world of gain and loss. The Sabbath liberates the entire world from the claims of the material. We consecrate time. Sabbath is our time with God, with eternity, reminding us of Eden, and giving us a taste of heaven here on earth.

The day apart is a day of remembrance. "Remember the sabbath," begins the commandment. We remember God, we remember ourselves, we remember family and friends and those in need, we remember the joy of life.[6] Though we work not, in all three religions it is a day to help others. The Kligermans usually have friends over for Shabbat lunch. We Ringwalds tend more to our children, try to visit sick or elderly friends and sometimes have guests to dinner. The Haqqies return to work after Juma services with a renewed consciousness of God and ready to help others, such as Shamim's patients at the hospital and Azra's colleagues and the newspaper's readers.

The day apart gives meaning to our earthly labor. It completes our work, but not by allowing us to finish the tasks of the previous six days. We complete our work by stopping. As did God at Creation, we are called to cease and see of our handiwork that "it is good." In this way, the day apart created culture by creating leisure. Historians and economists often regard leisure and its offspring, art, as products of wealthy societies that can afford to stop working periodically. But the Sabbath was instituted and observed when life was a grim struggle for survival. Commanded to cease each week for a day, men and women had time to let loose the mind and spirit. This is hedged by the Jewish ban on any creative labor. But music was a part of the earliest Jewish Sabbaths. And today, many people—believers or not—find Sunday a fine time to play instruments or sing or paint. There is a blessed reciprocity in the Catholic teaching for families to visit museums or hear concerts. A weekly day off from work ensures that all people, and not just the rich, can enjoy art and music. Through these many of us find God.

For Muslims, the benefits of Juma, and salat in general, are many, with some similar to those of the other faiths. Beyond Azra and Shamim Haqqie, my guide to Muslim practice was Imam Djafer Sebkhaoui, a family friend who leads a Muslim school and mosque, Masjid Al-Hedayah in Troy, New York. He is the Muslim chaplain at nearby Rensselaer Polytechnic Institute, where the Haqqie children, Nadia and Naseem, have been students. Tall and thin with a narrow, bearded face and a steady manner, the Algerian-born scholar combines humility with scholarship and conviction.

"Juma tends to focus people inward," Sebkhaoui tells me. "It reminds them that they are first and foremost servants of God. We should not allow ourselves to be absorbed by daily routines. What also helps is that there are the five daily prayers, at dawn, noon, middle of the afternoon, sunset, and evening. Second, it reminds us of other duties. Juma makes the heart always focused on God, and reminds us that we will meet him one day and to be ready. Third, Juma reminds us of our duty to others, that our humanity is foremost in service to others. We go back and keep remembering God. That's where the Muslim links the holy with the mundane in life. There's no separation."

Sadly, the Sabbath exemplifies our knack for converting a blessing into a burden, as did both Pharisees and Puritans. We have a knack for ignoring the day altogether, and leaving the gift unopened. It is observed most in the breach.

In the living we know the Sabbath. A man may believe in God, at least by habit and hope, but let him need and find God in a crisis or near death, and he will believe in a new way. He will be convinced there is a God by the blessings thereby bestowed, through the window his faith opened, as surely as he knows gravity by the weight he carries or by his failure to fly. So too the day apart. None but the extraordinary could arrive at a conviction in the practice other than by the practice. I only know the Sabbath to the extent I take my small steps into this holy time. I knew it as a child, thanks to my parents, and I know it again now. In a way, I always knew it, and ceasing—the basic command of God—calls up a knowledge, a feeling, a spirit from deep within.

In writings on the topic, one invariably comes to a passage full of sweet gratitude for the gift of the Sabbath. And mixed with this the author often expresses a surprised awe that this prosaic custom, even when kept sketchily, transforms us for that day and for all days. Once we know the Sabbath, it never leaves us. At the same time, the day can feel oddly unfamiliar, a sense related to our exile from Eden. Are we ready to go back?

The Sabbath is an experience, not a creed. Divine reality breaks in when we participate, when we cease as God ceased. The day rescues us from the sterile rationalism toward which theologians often aspire. Any religion, over time, systematizes its beliefs into dogma and doctrine. Almost always we are lured too far in this direction, and divest our faith of all nonrational elements. We lose the awe before an unknowable God, the humble excitement of discoveries yet to be made.[7] There is an equal danger to emotionalism; religion needs both faith and reason. The day apart confirms our faith by allowing us to experience God in our actions and inaction of the day as guided by tradition and community. On the Sabbath, we know God in a way that intellect or emotion alone can never provide.

From Creation

Where did it start? At the beginning of time. All three monotheisms explain the day by reference to the Creation. For Jews, Shabbat repeats the rest that God took after six days of making the world. For Christians, Sunday may be the day of the Resurrection but it is also the first day of Creation. For Muslims, Friday is the day set aside by Allah since it is when he made man and woman.

The nature of Sabbath "rest" has been much debated. The Jewish Torah recounts, "On the seventh day God finished the work that he had been doing, and he ceased on the seventh day from all the work that He had done." Though typically translated, especially in Christian Bibles, as "rested," the Hebrew verb, *sbt*, has the primary meaning of cease, with "rest" a secondary notion. Throughout time, the theology of both Shabbat and the Lord's Day emphasize cessation of normal labor rather than rest per se.

The Israelites received two commands to keep the Sabbath. The first, in Exodus, justifies the Sabbath in terms of creation. At Sinai, Yahweh told Moses to remember to keep holy the Sabbath day just as He did. In the second version, in Deuteronomy, Yahweh enjoins the Jews to remember their time of slavery and redemption, and to keep holy the Sabbath day, and to have their slaves rest as well. From these directives, an entire lexicon of rules evolved for observance, including the 39 types of labor to be avoided. Many Jews regard the Sabbath as the most important element of their religion and lives. As Asher Ginsberg, an early Zionist leader and thinker, observed in a now-universal sentiment, "It is not so much that the Jews have kept the Sabbath, but that the Sabbath has kept the Jews."

Though it celebrates time, Shabbat does not denigrate the space and matter made by God that He declared to be good. Time and space, Abraham Joshua Heschel tells us, are entwined. "What we plead against is man's unconditional surrender to space, his enslavement to things. We must not forget that it is not a thing that lends significance to a moment; it is the moment that lends significance to things."[8]

For Christians, Sunday was the day on which Christ rose from the dead, three days after his death. By the middle of the second century, the early Christians were meeting regularly on Sunday to celebrate the Eucharist and pray, take a collection, and eat. Church fathers also justified it as the first day of Creation when God "let there be light." They saw Jesus as the Sun of Righteousness. They appropriated the pagan day of the sun, with the Catholic Church's genius for converting the holidays and deities of other peoples to its own purposes.

Christians adapted the Sabbath to their faith. Sunday became the new Sabbath. It also became the law of the land in the Roman Empire, centuries later in England and parts of Europe, and then the United States.

Sunday, or the Lord's Day, deserves our attention because "of its close connection with the very core of the Christian mystery," Pope John Paul II wrote in his encyclical *Dies Domini*.[9] The Resurrection is the central event of Christianity, and on Sunday we are invited to know the joy of the women who discovered the empty tomb. We can experience that "our hearts burn within us," as did the disciples who met the resurrected Christ on a Sunday on the way to Emmaus. This first day of the week celebrates the new creation brought about by Jesus that points us toward the world to come. By the fourth century, St. Jerome would cry out, "Sunday is the day of the Resurrection, it is the day of Christians, it is our day."[10]

For Muslims, Friday is the day set aside by Allah for congregational prayer in Sura 62. The verse refers to the Day of Assembly, *yaum al-juma*, which appears to have been Friday in Mecca and much of Arabia even before the time of Muhammad. This history gives Juma an ancient lineage, much as Islam—and Judaism and Christianity, for that matter—converted preexisting practices and devotions to its own ends. Even though the Quran refers to Creation only briefly, Juma commemorates Creation in several ways.

Imam Sebkhaoui's mosque is housed in a former funeral home, an old Victorian frame house now camouflaged behind an angular, tan stucco front. The quiet intensity of children and adults there contrasts with the nearby group homes of RPI students and fraternities. ("No ball playing from balcony," reads one sign on a house.) On one of my pilgrimages to his *masjid* (mosque) Sebkhaoui speaks about Juma.

"We believe God created this day to celebrate," Sebkhaoui tells me. "We believe God ordained Friday from the beginning. It was the day Adam was created, and the day he entered Paradise. It is the day he was kicked out of Paradise, and it will be the Day of Judgment. And in that day, there is one hour when Allah will grant any prayer of the Muslim."

The day evokes the blessings of Creation, with the promise "that you may prosper." This refers more to the health of spirit and mind, rather than wealth and otherworldly reward. Sura 62 concludes with the pledge that "Allah is best to provide (for all needs)." Muslims should not be distracted by fears and appetites since Allah will provide for them better than they could imagine.[11]

Role of Decalogue

The Ten Commandments are the foundation for law and morals in much of the world and especially in the West. All three religions refer to them, though with varying degrees of absentmindedness. The Ten Commandments have been seen as both a basis for civilization's conduct and as a guide for a religious life. Of course, the universal law that makes up most of the Decalogue was given, in whole or part, several times: to Adam and Eve, to Noah after the flood, and to the patriarchs, notably Abraham, revered by Jews, Christians, and Muslims alike.

Christians believe Jesus gave us a new law or at least the Gospel, the "good news." Paul, while saying that Christ delivered us from the Jewish law, also taught that we have a law "written on our hearts" that, theologians later concluded, accords with the revealed law (Rom. 2:15). For Muslims, Muhammad follows, succeeds, and completes these prophets as the final Messenger of Allah.

In the first three of the Ten Commandments we worship God. In the last six we turn to our fellow man. All nine make sense, that is, they are part of the natural law. We could discern them by reason and faith without the Decalogue. Not so the fourth commandment. In a state of nature we would rest but not for a full day every week. With the Sabbath, however, we are ordered to rest exactly after six days of work, as did God. And in that we are "in His image and likeness."

The Ten Commandments are a covenant and much more than a set of ethical rules. Human obedience to God's commands involves both sides "in a cosmic drama and a historic narrative."[12] The Decalogue involves us in the cosmos and God in history, us in the holy and Him in the profane, most of all on the day apart.

Historically, Sabbath keeping revealed the temper of various times and peoples. Nothing evokes the dour side of Puritanism so much as our image, however inaccurate, of their dour Sundays. Even earlier, in the Middle Ages, the Catholic teaching that sins against God outweighed all others was distorted such that killing a thousand people was considered a lesser offense than working on Sunday. I prefer the calm joy of Tom and Becky Kligerman as they corral their children and attend Temple Israel and have guests back for lunch, revealing a deep confidence in a loving Creator.

The Basics of Each Day Apart

For observant Jews, Shabbat begins at sundown on Friday. This keeps with the ordering of days at Creation, "And there was evening and there was morning, a first day" (Gen. 1:5b). One of the women in the house lights two candles, one for each of the commands: to remember, in Exodus, and to keep, in Deuteronomy, the Sabbath. She recites the blessing, "Blessed are thou, O Lord our God, King of the Universe, who has sanctified us by the laws and commanded us to kindle the Sabbath light." The family or, more often, the husband, will attend services at the synagogue on Friday. It includes the song of Shabbat, Psalm 92, which expresses the joy and release of the day:

> It is good to give thanks to Yahweh
> to play in honor of Your Name, Most High
> to proclaim your love at daybreak
> and your faithfulness all through the night
> to the music of zither and lyre,
> to the rippling of the harp.
> I am happy, Yahweh at what you have done;
> At your achievements I joyfully exclaim:
> "Great are your achievements, Yahweh,
> immensely deep your thoughts."

Usually the whole family attends the main liturgy on Saturday morning and then some or all may attend a third time on Saturday afternoon, about an hour before sunset, for the Minhah, or afternoon prayer service. This service ends with the Havdalah, Hebrew for "separation," which formally closes Shabbat. The service can be conducted at home or the synagogue and involves three blessings—of wine, fire (usually a candle), and spices. "It separates the holy day from the rest of the week," Tom Kligerman tells me.

Despite the numerous regulations, the Jewish practice of Shabbat has an endearingly human quality. In the Conservative Judaism commentary on the

Torah, after a discussion of the twin commands to "remember" and to "keep" the day, it is written, "Those whose circumstance make it impossible to keep Shabbat as they would like to, should at least find ways to remind themselves that it is Shabbat."[13]

For Christians, Sunday is a day of rest that accords with the fourth commandment but also that memorializes the Resurrection of Jesus on that day. Some Christians begin Sunday with vigil prayers on Saturday evening, but most begin on Sunday morning by attending a liturgy. For Catholics, the Mass is Sunday's centerpiece.

The Eucharist is more than a reenactment of the Last Supper. At the Mass, God through Jesus comes into our midst. Aside from my faith and hope, I am convinced that there must be a miracle in the Mass for a simple reason: Catholics keep coming, week after week, despite frequently bad homilies, weak music, and a general gracelessness to the proceedings. We in the pews are guilty as well: barely responding, ready to rush out after Communion, tuning out the prayers, not bothering to know when we should stand, sit, or kneel. But we do come, and we come for God. And God comes through Christ.

One Sunday in Lent, our pastor, Father Thomas Powers, reminds us of the communal meal at the heart of the Mass, the Eucharist, the sacrament instituted by Jesus as he shared the Last Supper with his disciples. "When you gather round the table for Sunday dinner, look around you," he says. "That's community." Fittingly, the three readings from the Old Testament, Epistles, and Gospel, cover the entry of the Israelites into the Promised Land, Paul's announcement that we are made new in Christ, and the parable of the prodigal son, taken back by his loving father. Powers challenges us to see ourselves as the resentful brother who never left home and wonders why the fuss is being made over the reprobate. All are lessons about God's providence and that we worship as a people, together, in this case, on Sunday.

After church Christians generally do not work for pay, though they often perform chores and tend to family. (Admittedly, financial need, the 24-hour workplace and jobs such as police, fire, and medicine cause others to skip the Sunday rest.) Those with children may have Little League or soccer games. Others hike, bicycle, visit museums. Far too many visit stores and malls. Many have a large meal together with relatives and friends. The day winds down with anticipation or dread of the week ahead.

In the Quran, Muslims find only one direct reference to Juma. There are many other teachings about the day and its observance. These are recorded in the Hadith (Arabic for "narrative" or "report"), the accounts of the teachings and actions of Muhammad from his contemporaries. Each hadith consists of the teaching itself and then the chain of authority, or *isnad*, by which the tradition was passed on.

A related body of Muslim authority is collected in the Sunna (custom), which records the habits and religious practice of Muhammad and his Companions. These two sources are crucial since the Quran enjoins us to follow Muhammad's example, much as Jesus directed his disciples to follow— or imitate—Him. The Hadith and Sunna alike are marked by the depth and magnitude of detail. "Sunna is our second reference after the Quran," Imam Sebkhaoui told me. Most of the guides, restrictions, and revelations about Juma are recorded in the Sunna and Hadith.

Juma epitomizes Islam, a religion whose name derives from the Arabic verb, *aslama*, for "submit." All of Islam leads and encourages the believer in this submission, and on Friday Muslims bow in unison. They bow to one God, whose unity is also stressed, as in Judaism. The Quran rejects the Christian Trinitarian conception of God. Muslims recite the creed, "There is no god but God and Muhammad is His Prophet."

But Islam—like Judaism and most of Christianity—is a religion of faith and works. On Friday, Muslims submit in faith and they show that submission by attending salat and bowing as one to the one God.

The Friday assembly unites Muslims on a regular basis. They hear the imam review the events of the past week or recent past, either generally or within the community, and then advise and exhort them on the duties of a Muslim in the world. Juma fits within the concentric circles of worship. The believer prays five times a day. The mosque community gathers each week. The larger community from several mosques may gather twice a year for the major feasts— Id al-Adha during the annual pilgrimage, or *hajj*, to Mecca and Id al-Fitr at the end of Ramadan. And once in a lifetime, at least, all Muslims join the international hajj. All promote the collective understanding and action that are the heart of the *umma*, the idealized Muslim community.

Muslims keep Friday special in several ways: ablutions, assembly, prayers, and good works. Even their secular work is transformed by the day's devotion. But it is not a day of not working, as with Jews and Christians. Muslims assert that God never feels fatigue nor needs to rest. Muslim scholars note that the Jewish command in Exodus stipulates rest without mentioning prayer or worship. By contrast, writes A. Yusuf Ali, "Our ordinance lays chief stress on the remembrance of Allah."[14]

Invisible and Ubiquitous as Time

Now began long ago. We love the present, it is our home. In the here and now we live; we cannot break free. Yet one day we step into forever. The Sabbath we celebrate began at Creation and leads into heaven. Perhaps it really directs us into the deepest sense of the day, of time, of every moment, since there we find eternity in each tick of the clock. We participate in eternity. The Sabbath frees us from the clock and releases us into a type of time, duration, that creates because it unfolds always. Time rolls rather than clicks. This is the same sense of time that the Greeks called *kairos* and that Christians see as God's truth breaking into time. The Jewish philosopher Henri Bergson, credited as the first to take time seriously, said that each moment of duration allowed new qualities to emerge.[15] And the Christian theologian, Paul Tillich, considered time as opportunity rather than mere transition.[16]

We stop and are in time, God's presence in space and matter. We are closest to God on the Sabbath since we do as He did. We stop, we cease, we let be. Thus God is time, in a sense, and the Sabbath is the pinnacle of time and the Sabbath is God. Hence the power, hence the holiness, hence the grace of the day. But also hence the fighting. When Muhammad corrected the Jews on the day apart, or when Jesus violated Shabbat, the Jews felt their very existence threatened. It was the sign and guarantee of their pact with Yahweh. Break it and all is at risk.

Despite these and many other attacks, the Sabbath endures. The Jews kept it for millennia despite persecution and dispersal. Muslims keep it around the world in native and foreign lands. After the French Revolution in 1789 and the Russian Revolution in 1917, the new governments abolished Sundays with new weekly calendars. These sought to make labor more efficient and, simultaneously, diminish religion. Sunday outlasted both schemes.

God's Hand on Our Clock and Calendar

God's commandment to keep holy the Sabbath was the stone tossed into the water of time whose ripples continue to shape our daily and weekly lives. Rest is an instinct. Among humans, however, the weekly day of rest was unique to the ancient Hebrews. Much of the world still responds to its gravity.

In America, more than half of us attend services weekly or at least once a month. But the sabbatarian cycle shapes all our lives, be we religious or secular. Monday starts the workweek. Wednesday is for many a matter of getting over the hump. Friday we relax and cut loose. Saturday is more work, often at home or in the yard, but also a day for recreation and usually the more strenuous or organized forms—team sports, children's games, rock climbing, fishing, and so on. Come Sunday, we settle into a deeper state of rest. Even the nonreligious relax. They may play pickup football in the morning or nosh on their bagels and read the newspapers.

The day apart occurs on earth. The holy day is at once transcendent and terribly profane. It is a sacrament—a visible and effective sign of God's presence according to Catholic definition—that manifests the ideal in the real. The Sabbath is tied to this planet, where rotation and orbit of earth and moon demarcate all days, including this holy day. Thus divinity blesses us in this encounter, and the exact conduit for the grace depends on matter, space, and the things of this world. It would be different on another planet, or anywhere else unmoored from the 24-hour clock and the rising and setting of the sun.

The Sabbath even regulates death. For the Cold War spies Julius and Ethel Rosenberg, Shabbat brought the end a few hours early. They were convicted of passing atomic secrets to the Soviet Union and were to be executed on June 19, 1953, at Sing Sing, the imposing granite prison in Ossining, 30 miles up the Hudson River from New York City. Normally, prisoners were killed at 11:00 PM, which "would have pushed the executions well into the Jewish Sabbath." Judge Irving R. Kaufman said the timing caused him "considerable concern." The Justice Department agreed, and so the time to die was moved up, into profane time. "Killing the couple was one thing," columnist Clyde Haberman writes. "But to do the deed on the Sabbath, apparently, was quite another."[17]

Research into Israeli mortality rates find a definite dip/peak pattern in deaths, which subside on the Jewish Shabbat and rise again on Sunday, as if to make up for the lag. This is not an entirely unknown phenomenon. Other researchers have found that deaths often decline for holidays and then resume, presumably because people near death rallied for the occasion or due to the nearness of family and friends.[18] I tell a colleague about this weekly fall and rise in deaths. After a moment she replies, "Then if every day was Sabbath, we'd never die."

The week revolves around the Sabbath. On a Tuesday in January, I sense the pivot ahead on which the week spins, the axis of eternity from which time spirals out centrifugally into the dissected minutes and hours of our now-now-now lives. Four days before Sunday I wait, like a Jewish mystic freshly bathed and in white robes, for the Queen of Time, the promise of heaven. The Sabbath is our weekly heaven, our day apart. And if we profane it—with anger, anxiety, or gossip; with labor, money grubbing, or worry; with some act or attitude—then we can still rejoice that God gave us a day so pure and peaceful that any divergence reminds us to what we can always return. As Amy says when we discuss our failings to keep Lenten vows, "The paradox of human frailty is that it reminds us of the ideal."

Rituals Toward God

In the Sabbath, we participate in God's life. We live as he lived, resting after our days of creation. Though the day is an experience, it is also a symbol into which we pour our spiritual aspirations. "Religious emotions always tended to transform into lively images," Johan Huizinga writes in his *Autumn of the Middle Ages*.[19] To understand mystery, we transform it into matter or space or ritual. Through tangible signs we come to understand the inexpressible. The Sabbath is that sign par excellence. In it and through it, we honor and worship Yahweh, Allah, God. Thus, we cannot overestimate the value and impact of our Sabbaths. What we do on that day apart always means more than we realize; we never plumb its depths.

The day is both private and communal. Worship emanates from both the person and the group. "When each of you performs his prayer, he is in intimate communication with his Lord," Muhammad told his followers.[20] In Sufi Islam, the mystical brand, the importance of salat lies in reciting the words of worship and, simultaneously, thinking of its meaning.[21] These devotions unite each Muslim with all others in space and time.

A God of love invites us into the day. We are admitted by our humanity, not our perfection. We may miss this fact, distracted by the avalanche of rules and regulations in all three religions. But in the Quran, God promises over and over that the person who strives with good intent "to urge what is right and denounce what is evil" can count on God's mercy even if he or she fails in other ways.[22] Both the Jewish and Christian scriptures convey, over and above and around the other material, the same message. We are so convinced of God's love that mistakes are overlooked. No Jew in the world could ever keep Shabbat perfectly given all the rabbinical stipulations. Who could live a whole day perfectly? The day calls us to a banquet of time, not a prison of gestures and abstinence. An omnipotent God needs not our perfection.

The Sabbath is ritual toward God. Through rituals the community joins to worship, but not as end in itself. On the Sabbath, we unite to participate in divine life. Together we ascend to a God who is already near. "Frequently recite salat on Friday," Muhammad told his followers, "for the angels are present on that day."[23]

One Christmas I relax in the wake of family and presents and love and a meal at the Connecticut home of Anne and Bob, my sister and brother-in-law. God abides despite a too-full belly and a surfeit of material. Time crunches under the weight of space crystallized. I think of Einstein's theory, $e = mc^2$. Energy is mass multiplied. So does energy—always spent or displaced over time—become mass when slowed or stopped? Does time, fleet and fast and free, congeal into matter? Into physical space? We revere time on the Sabbath. It is a festival in and of time, freeing us from the shackles of clock time and thrusting us into the freedom of divine time. On the Sabbath, we stop, we rest, we rescue some part of time from the death of matter. We rescue our unfinished selves from world of concrete substance.

Without God, the day makes no sense. Modern men and women hope, desperately, that they can justify and secure a day off—quiet time, down time, time for me, family time—without reference to religion. It would be handy in a democracy. But here is the fatal flaw of such humanitarian schemes: unless justified on a transcendent basis, they often collapse. The U.S. Supreme Court ruled in 1961 that a Maryland ban on Sunday labor originated in religion but was constitutional since such blue laws, perhaps named for the paper these were printed on or for the color of fidelity, promoted a day "of relaxation rather than religion."[24] That was the beginning of the end. Forty-three years later, the Virginia State Legislature rushed into special session to undo a new law that, inadvertently, restored workers' right to take Sunday off.

The question is whether the biblical injunction of relief from labor for all, poor and rich, can be translated into a secular and communal rest day. When we take different days off, the day of rest becomes a purely religious, even private affair. Rest is harder if most others are working. Without social sanction, the working poor and aliens have little protection against employers who demand they keep going. But who wants a government-enforced Sabbath? The best answer would be to guarantee each person the right to their holy or secular day of respite.

The practices and habits of the Sabbath reveal God. These promote belief, awaken our souls, enforce worship, dispose our hearts, and conform us to the religious norm. The day apart directs us beyond. Huizinga writes that medieval Europeans always knew "that all things extend in an important way into the world beyond," a conviction that fills us "with that calm and strengthening certainty that our own life shares in the mysterious meaning of the world."[25]

This takes preparation, and each religious action primes us for a payoff. We keep the Sabbath, and enjoy its blessings. We eschew work, save those actions of charity and necessity, and we are rested. We do this in the name of God, and then we credit Him for these rewards.

To the nonbeliever or scholar, observance confirms that which motivated us in the first place. We may not know the first mover, but we know what we feel. Belief is the condition for ritual, and the prescribed words and acts merely release the dispositions we already had within. The experience "proves" faith to the faithful. As a social reality, religion is charged with "such an aura of factuality that the moods and motivations seem uniquely realistic."[26] For the believer, treating faith as a "social reality" profanely drops God from the equation. And ritual is an entirely appropriate means of building resolution and fidelity in faith. Ritual creates an internal certitude just as etiquette breeds respect. Today, when many people don't participate in symbolic religious activity, worshipping in tight rows or refusing to carry an umbrella in a rainstorm on Shabbat seems arbitrary or nutty. To the practitioner, faith expresses itself in acts that, in turn, build faith. These direct us into the depths of the Sabbath where we find eternity in the ticks of the clock.

Sabbath-keeping by Three Families

Kligermans

For the Kligermans, Shabbat came with marriage. Becky grew up in a nonreligious Christian family in Battle Creek, Michigan, and Middletown, New York. As a young adult, Judaism drew her attention and admiration. While in college, she became friendly with a Jewish professor and dated her nephew. They invited her to Shabbat meals and other holidays. "I liked the heritage, I liked the rituals, I liked that they had something to look forward to," Becky says. She later worked as an occupational therapist at Jacobi Hospital in the Bronx. Some colleagues kept kosher and her interest was revived. She found a synagogue in Cos Cob, near her home in Westchester County. Becky studied Reform Judaism with the rabbi there, who encouraged her interest.

When she met Tom at a Sierra Club conference, Becky may have been more immersed in Judaism than he was. Tom's parents were of the assimilationist variety, those Jews eager to fit into America in the decades after World War II. Becky and Tom talked over the phone for six months, dated and then lived together in Albany. "I learned he was Jewish when we were dating, and it was intriguing to me because my key relationships in the past were with Jewish men."

Growing up in Springfield, Massachusetts, "I had a typical left-of-center Conservative [Jewish] upbringing," Tom says. "My parents divorced when I was little, and they communicated very little about religion to me."

He attended the United Hebrew School, which educated children from all three branches of Judaism. The synagogue featured organ music at services, an innovation rejected by both Conservatives and Orthodox. "You're not supposed to hear music from electronic instruments on Shabbat," Tom says. His father, a pharmacist, worked every day. His four grandparents, immigrants from Russia and Lithuania, worked most days in the typical struggle for survival. His mother's parents attended synagogue and influenced the Kligermans in this regard when his grandmother lived with them.

"It was my mother who took me to *shul.* On Friday she lit the Shabbat candles and we attended services on Saturday. We'd go to the temple and then go shopping for groceries." She also insisted that Tom had to marry a Jewish woman. "And I didn't get married to a non-Jewish girl," Tom observed. But a year after Tom's *bar mitzvah,* the Jewish ceremony for a boy's attainment of adulthood at age 13, he stopped attending services. "I was raised moderately Jewish, and then for 15 years, I did nothing. Then in my midthirties I met Becky, and I became religious, much more than before."

Marriage, and the prospect of offspring, moved Tom to consider ultimate issues. "As I got ready to be married I asked myself, 'What do I have? What can I bring to a marriage?' And after Eli was born I asked myself, 'What will I give my son?' My father, he didn't give me anything in terms of religion." He saw a gift and legacy in the religion he had neglected. "I said to myself, 'The Jews must have something, they've survived for more than 3,500 years.'"

Becky and Tom started attending Temple Israel before their wedding and came under the influence and example of Rabbi Paul Silton, his wife Faye, and their seven children. Becky expressed her interest in converting, and certainly had a track record of interest to show her sincerity. "It's a Jewish custom, if someone wants to convert, that the rabbi should reject them three times to test them. It was funny, but Rabbi Silton didn't, maybe because we were getting married and this way the children would be Jewish." Becky attended classes for six months, taught by Faye Silton, the rabbi's wife. Her conversion culminated in her immersion in the *mikveh,* the ancient Jewish ritual bath.

Becky and Tom were not fully there yet. They met with Rabbi Silton to plan the wedding and Becky asked, "Does it have to be kosher?" Yes, it did. And, she says now with amazement, "While we were planning the wedding, we would drive on Shabbat to plan the wedding." Going all the way would be marked, most of all, by keeping Shabbat and also by having a kosher home and observing the holidays.

"Within six months of the wedding, I was expecting Eli. We decided to make the change before kids arrived to avoid confusing them. After Eli was born, Rosh Hashanah and Yom Kippur were so much more poignant because we were a family."

Ringwalds

For Amy and me and our children Madeleine, Jeanne, and Mitchell, the day continues to unfold within our faith, our marriage, our family. It was already love at first sight with Amy, but on our first date she told me she had converted just two months before. That sealed it. Once married, we kept Sundays by attending Mass and then reading the papers, walking, running, playing, hiking, wandering about, maybe a movie. With children, Sundays became both more routine and chaotic. And with this book, of course, we began to tend to the day more carefully. It has been a blessing; it has been difficult. We have had to sort things out, argue things out, bend and compromise and, often, drop the topic. But we keep on, because the day apart draws us in, as it does with anyone who glimpses the expanse of heaven within the Sabbath. We go it alone, in many regards. Catholics are not known for observant Sundays. Amy and I are most inspired by the Kligermans and other Jews, especially those we see in our neighborhood walking, walking, walking on Friday nights and Saturday mornings.

In observing the fourth commandment, Christians often find their leap from the seventh day to the first day difficult to justify. When New England Puritans debated the issue, their deliberations turned on this issue: "The true questions is whether the Sabbath is one of those laws commanded because it is intrinsically good and of perpetual and universal obligation or a Jewish ceremonial precept from which Christians are exempt. All agree that the law of the Fourth Commandment is moral; the real controversy is how and in what respects this is true."[27] Of course, the real basis for Sunday is Easter, which the early Christians and, today, Catholics claim as sufficient justification for making the switch.

In the Catholic Church, despite our complacent nonobservance, our readings of scripture reinforce the forgotten importance of the day. One April Sunday at our parish church, St. Teresa of Avila, we read from Revelation. John, the author, writes from the island of Patmos and begins his passage by telling us, "I was in the spirit on the Lord's day, and I heard behind me a loud voice like a trumpet." John turns and sees "the Son of Man" who announces, "Do not be afraid; I am the first and the last, and the living one. I was dead, and see, I am alive forever and ever" (Rev. 9:10, 17–18).

This is the first use of the phrase "the Lord's Day" for Sunday. And we immediately notice its importance, for Jesus appears and confirms his divinity on that day. Then the Gospel reading, from John 20:14–30, reiterates the importance of Sunday. "When it was evening on that day, the first day of the week, and the doors of the house where the disciples had met were locked for fear of the Jews, Jesus came and stood among them and said, 'Peace be with you.'" He then commissions to disciples to preach the good news, making that Sunday the birthday of the church.

Thomas was not there and he doubted. And so, the reading continues with the next Sunday. "A week later his disciples were again in the house, and Thomas was with them. Although the doors were shut, Jesus came and stood among them and said, 'Peace be with you.'" Thomas is soon convinced of the Resurrection.

As I sit here in our parish, far from the centers of world power and religious gravity, I realize we, too, are being commissioned on a Sunday. Just a few weeks earlier, on Palm Sunday, we read the Passion from Luke and were reminded that Jesus and his followers were faithful Jews. After Christ is dead, his disciples rush to bury the body since it was late on a Friday, "the day of Preparation, and the sabbath was beginning." Then, we hear, "On the sabbath they rested according to the commandment" (Luke 23:53–56). Father Powers emphasizes the present tense of the Gospel and our role. "Luke always puts us in the story!" he says.

Here we are, believers in a Savior whose burial was timed to finish before Shabbat, and whose Resurrection gave us reason to switch to a new day, Sunday. And as we walk home—the girls dragging behind to finish a talk with their friends, Mitchell insisting on a perch on my shoulders—in our Sunday clothes, the world silent around us, a sense of purpose upon us, and the five of us sealed up in a holy happy bubble, I feel a special kinship with our Jewish neighbors.

Haqqies

Azra Haqqie was born in Karachi, in what was then West Pakistan. She grew up in Dacca, in what was then East Pakistan, where her father, a civil servant, was assigned. In 1971 when East Pakistan, which became Bangladesh, rebelled against West Pakistan, her father sent the family home to Karachi on an emergency flight while he remained to work. He was later imprisoned along with thousands of other West Pakistanis by Indian forces, which backed the rebellion. After almost two years, he rejoined the family. Azra attended Catholic schools, prized for the quality of education. In 1980, she married Shamim, already a doctor, and they moved to the United States.

As a child, her family was moderately religious, with her mother the devout parent and her father more worldly. "He saw the big picture. He would always say, 'God will be pleased with people in the West because they use their brains and they do good for their fellow man.'" The men always attended Juma, and were given two hours off from work to do so. Following the British influence of colonial times, Friday was a workday while Sunday was a holiday. Afterward, Azra's father would talk about the sermon and "if he liked it or if the imam went on and on. Or if people were inconsiderate with parking their cars." Her mother, for her part, "did extra prayers at home." The children always bathed or showered, cut their nails and dressed well. "We learned that we had to make an extra effort to make ourselves clean." Azra recalls the day as somber.

Shamim recalls his childhood in Karachi, where he lived until age 21 when he moved to England. His mother, who lives in Karachi, was and remains very religious. His father was a lawyer and civil servant who died at 40 when Shamim was boy. On Fridays, he and his father always bathed, "put on nice clean clothes," and attended the mosque, as did most men they knew. "I knew Friday was a special day, and I was supposed to be on my best behavior."

At one point Juma became a national holiday in Pakistan, at least after 1:00 PM when government and businesses closed in time for the Friday assembly at 2:00 PM. However Sunday remained a full holiday, a colonial legacy. As that withers, Juma has advanced. "I was in Pakistan three years ago and when it was time for prayers, the roads closed and people would be outside the mosques, squatting on the road and in the streets," Shamim says.

Before the congregation began at Albany Medical Center, Shamim would drive 45 minutes to the Islamic Center in Schenectady and back every Friday. Now it is easier with Juma in the chapel downstairs. But the command is not absolute. "If a patient is very sick, or there's an emergency, you don't go," he says. "Our religion is very flexible."

Does the service influence the rest of his day? Shamim is blunt about his shortcomings. "I go back to work like usual and then, I forget." He laughs humbly. He values the sermon. "It is a process of education. We all have difficult times, sometimes I get down and depressed, and if you learn something from the khutbah, then you are not going to give up."

A friend of the Haqqies, Haider Khwaja, who has joined us, responds when I ask why Juma is obligatory. "In Muhammad's time, people would meet to discuss their problems at that time. And God is the Supreme Being, and he asked us to pray and go to services. Self-pride goes down when we do that." Shamim picks up this thread. "We are closest to Allah when we are on the ground, with our head on the ground." Azra adds that the social occasion is also important in bringing people together regularly to unite and strengthen the community. "I like going, even if I only get there for the sermon. It wakes up dormant feelings that are important." Haider concludes, simply and humbly. "Spiritually, it gives you a lift."

The Birth of the Sabbath: From Creation to Mount Sinai and into the Promised Land in 1100 BCE

Man, when left to the guidance of his own inner persuasions, searches after the Author of his being, and seeks to comprehend the purposes of his existence, and his final destiny.

LEWIS HENRY MORGAN, *LEAGUE OF THE IROQUOIS*

Heaven on Helderberg

The Sabbath is among the oldest continuously celebrated, regular religious rituals, and almost certainly is the oldest weekly one. Scholars estimate that the Israelites left Egypt to wander in the wilderness during the thirteenth century BCE, and had arrived, by conquest and settlement, in the Promised Land of Canaan at the start of the twelfth century BCE.[1] By biblical accounts, they received God's revelation of the Ten Commandments between those events, by which point they were already keeping the Sabbath. It was well established probably during the monarchical period, which began in 1025 BCE, the time of Kings Saul, David, and Solomon, and certainly by the eighth century.[2] Thus the Sabbath has been known and kept for about 3,000 years, or 156,000 weekly holy days. What could explain such longevity? Was it force or fidelity? Was it fear of God or love of God?

At some level it may have been a gift, a joy. The order to imitate God by ceasing work had an innate appeal that enabled the Israelites to overcome their fear of losing livestock, of starving, of falling behind their neighbors or the other tribes that threatened them. The joy of the Sabbath seized them. It has never let go. Each Jew has learned from and taught the others, and each generation has received and passed on Shabbat through a strict observance of the law coupled with personal lesson and example.

And so the day came to the Kligermans near the end of the twentieth century as they began to embrace Judaism. They gave up to gain. Shabbat meant selling their beloved camp in the Adirondacks, the rugged green mountains 60 miles north of Albany. Tom bought the place, a former summer camp, before he married Becky and they spent weekends renovating it. The two of them love the outdoors: hiking, canoeing, skiing, climbing. They met at a Sierra Club event. Both are licensed Adirondack guides. But after they became shomer Shabbat, or Sabbath observant, their American weekend was cut in half.

"We had a weekend camp that became a Sunday camp," Tom says. "It's not that we couldn't keep Shabbat at the camp, it's that we would have to get up there way before sundown on Friday. And we would be keeping it by ourselves but not with the community. It's not a requirement to keep Shabbat with your neighbors, but it is an extra *mitzvah*," he adds, using the Hebrew word for commandment that commonly refers to a good deed. "The kids wouldn't see their friends; we wouldn't go to the pond with the other families." Of course, the main part of the Saturday morning service is the Torah reading, which a Jew must do as a community.

For her part, Becky had been an even firmer advocate of Shabbat after they wed. She also knew it would cost her the weekends in the Adirondacks. "I did think to myself, 'There goes our outings.' " But the day drew them in when they began attending services at Temple Israel and then lunch at Rabbi Silton's home. "Once you commit to going every Saturday, that's about it," said Tom with a shrug. He says that the children adjust and enjoy the day. They grow up learning that come sunset Friday, the television goes off, the parents are home, demands are few, and life is full of slower, simpler pleasures like reading and talking. Shabbat has survived because it is a gift. But only by participating do you receive.

One Saturday the Kligermans invited my family for the Shabbat lunch. We dressed well and walked to their home along Helderberg Avenue, a quiet, leafy side street with few cars. In several spots, there are dead ends connected by footpaths. We pass Jewish families returning from the six synagogues in the neighborhood—two Orthodox, two Conservative, and two Reform. Some smile familiarly at us, perhaps not noticing that our children are on scooters and bicycles, a clue that we are probably not shomer Shabbat. We see, or notice, few other pedestrians. We walk in a holy zone. The houses, the yards, the trees, that lawn, this garbage can—all seem peaceful, still, luminous. The world glows. Time slows and stops.

We have a lovely visit, one that reminded me of Sundays with my family visiting relatives in the afternoon for dinner and then playing in our church clothes afterwards. Back then, the men I knew wore dark suits, fedoras, white shirts, thin ties, and gleaming shoes; the women hats or scarves, dresses, thick nylons, and conservative pumps. The boys wore pressed pants, polished shoes, and shirtsleeves; the girls mirrored their moms minus the nylons and hats. At the same time, we were at ease, relaxed, unhurried, unguarded. We walked through a world where for 24 hours there were no bosses, no trains to catch, no quarts of milk to pick up, no evening hours painting the bathroom. The fathers would banter about sports or travels, the mothers about children or their jobs, and all about the church and the demands of faith. My parents exemplified the oft-forgotten sophistication of lay Catholics in the 1950s and 1960s. They watched Bishop Fulton Sheen on television and read Thomas Aquinas, G. K. Chesterton, and Sigrid Undset. With the Doyles, Foleys, Flanagans, and other members of the Catholic Family Movement, they debated church teachings and social justice in our living room.

As on those Sundays of my youth, the Jewish men gather in the Kligermans' kitchen while clearing dishes to debate theology. Tom and two guests explore the derivation of Hebrew words before moving on to a fine point in Sabbath regulations. They cite competing scholars and interpretations. They argue with joyful gusto.

Franz Kafka wrote in his diary that, for a Jewish man, discussions of Talmudic matters are the "very core of his life."[3] He lamented the exclusion of women, which Becky and other women have broken through. Such discussions double as observance on the holy day. Tom and Becky and their friends affirm their practice through words, and the words affirm their resolve and faith.

Kafka also observed that his fellow Jews "come together at every possible opportunity, whether to pray or to study or to discuss divine matters or to eat holiday meals whose basis is usually a religious one. . . . They flee to one another so to speak."[4] The Kligermans routinely have another family or other adults to lunch on Saturday. Today Rich and Amy Drucker are here with their children Reed and Michal, as is a bachelor friend. "We invite each other," Tom tells me. "That way, you know you'll be eating at a kosher home if it's within your community. It's easier that way. That's also why the rabbis made kosher more restrictive than what's in the Bible." One can be Jewish alone, but it's easier together.

The community of fellow believers, walking from home to home, helps one avoid the minor transgressions that lead to more serious ones, Becky says. "If you drive on Shabbat, it's easy to go to Crossgates Mall, it's easy to go to the store, it's easy to let it all fall apart."

We step outside to play whiffleball on the front lawn. Rich pitches to his son. "Reed, don't keep your feet flat when you swing. Pick up your back foot, like this!" Rich shows him, Daddy DiMaggio pivoting at the plate as he swings a small red bat. The other children—Eli, Netania, Madeleine, Jeanne, Mitchell—take their labored turns at bat. Amy Drucker and Becky—both wearing hats—and Amy, my wife, stand in their long dresses near the porch and talk. I wonder what the Christian evangelists Paul or John, those Jewish converts who were so harsh toward the Jews they left behind, or even the Pharisees who criticized Jesus for violating Shabbat, would think. That world-shattering split, the millennia of enmity and now, here we are, back together, batting a white plastic ball across a patch of grass. Eli, swing!

The sun lowers. Tom mentions that taking a nap is another Shabbat tradition, which seems like a good idea about now. We Ringwalds gather our bicycles and walk home with a lowered metabolism. The Sabbath has cast its spell on us. We meet Andrew along the way, a Russian immigrant Madeleine knows from school. He gazes in on us in our terrarium of peace. We are still in this world, this special time, the anointed time of Shabbat, our little heaven on Helderberg Avenue.

Creation

Readers of the Bible may miss the fact that Creation culminates not with the making of Adam and Eve on the sixth day, but with the first Shabbat on the seventh day. We are not the whole point of God's effort.

On the third day God separated sea from land and created vegetation; on the fourth, the stars, the sun, and the moon; and on the fifth day, the birds and the sea creatures. On the sixth, He first created animals. After each of these bursts of creation, "God saw how good it was." Later on the sixth day, "in the divine image . . . male and female He created them." And at this point, "God looked at everything that he had made, and he found it very good." The rest of Creation is "good," we are "very good." There is one more day, the seventh, when Creation is finished because God stops.

Thus the heavens and the earth were finished, and all the host of them. And on the seventh day God finished his work which he had done, and he rested on the seventh day from all his work which he had done. So God blessed the seventh day and hallowed it, because on it God rested from all his work which he had done in creation. (Gen. 2:1–3)

Remember here that "rested" derives from the Hebrew verb *sabat*, which means to cease, not to rest or relax. Of course God stopped! Had He gone on and on, Creation would have multiplied itself like a cancer into self-destruction. Too many animals, too much sea or dry land, too much firmament, too many creatures "in our own image" rather than just the first man and woman. Order is the first law of heaven. Creation is marked throughout by its order, pace, and divisions. Contrary to the chaotic and conflicting forces in other creation accounts from the Ancient Near East, in Genesis, "Creation follows effortlessly from God's mere word."[5]

On that seventh day, God ends Creation. He ceases and He divides this one day from the others by marking it as holy. After blessing things that He has created over six days, God now blesses time, the seventh day.

The divine order of actions or observance—complete, rest, bless—eventually shapes the Sabbath. At God's order, we finish our work, we cease from further labors, we bless the day. "The Israelite household at rest recapitulates the celebration of God at the moment of conclusion and perfection of creation."[6] And like Creation at the end of the sixth day, with the onset of Sabbath the Kligermans are removed from the profane world and distinguished as God's own.

Only after God rested on the seventh day did He bless and sanctify it. He inaugurates the Sabbath; then, *ipso facto*, it's holy and set apart because of His act. At Sinai it is likewise justified, "For in six days the Lord made heaven and earth, the sea, and all that is in them, but rested the seventh day; therefore the Lord blessed the sabbath day and consecrated it" (Exod. 20:11). Interestingly, at Creation, God does not name the "Sabbath," nor does He command its observance, and the day of rest is omitted entirely from the second, and much older, Creation story in Genesis 2:4b–25.

From a naturalistic perspective, without Genesis before us, Sabbath springs logically from the idea of a Supreme Being. We ask who made us and seek them out. And we would first assume, as humans always have done, that God would be like us but also different. Similarly, ancient religions assumed that things of earth corresponded to things in heaven. Since we work, God must work, primarily creating and sustaining us and our universe. But unlike us, at least unlike our ancestors in the primeval struggle for existence, God must not have to work all the time. Being omnipotent, God could choose when to call it a day. Thus we do likewise.

The first version of the Decalogue recalls Creation. Exodus 20:8–11 tells us to keep the Sabbath holy and to not work because then God rested. However, God did not tell Adam and Eve to rest once a week. Likewise, the Bible is mute on whether the patriarchs kept the day, though their stories in the Torah refer often to seven days of waiting or mourning or even pursuing an enemy. Later Jewish sages decided that Adam's descendants must have kept Shabbat.[7] The blessing for the Sabbath afternoon services thanks God for the day of rest and holiness that "Thou hast given thy people—Abraham was glad, Isaac rejoiced, Jacob and his sons rested thereon."[8]

This topic arose during the Sabbatarian debates of the Reformation. Martin Luther taught that Adam must have kept the day and passed it on to his children and grandchildren.[9] The debate continues today among Seventh-day Adventists and other Christians who keep the Sabbath on Saturday. Regardless, to Jews, Christians, and Muslims, the commandment-by-example in Genesis dates the Sabbath "to the foundation of the world."[10] Before they reached Sinai and heard the Ten Commandments, the Israelites were already a Sabbath-keeping people.

Before Mount Sinai

The Sabbath appears unique to the Israelites in the ancient Near East. It derives from no other festival or ritual, and has no parallel among the other religions of the time. There are several candidates worth considering.[11]

One was the Babylonian *sapattu*, a "day of rest of the heart" on the fifteenth day of the month when the full moon appeared. There were also evil or taboo days (*ume lemnuti*) when work was prohibited, on the first, seventh, fourteenth, nineteenth (the most important), and twenty-eighth days. But these were not a civil schedule and did not fit into a seven-day cycle. Despite past enthusiasm, there is "no compelling evidence in the Old Testament for an alleged transfer from a pre-exilic monthly sabbath to an exilic/post-exilic weekly sabbath."[12]

Another supposed origin was with the Kenites, metal-working nomads the Israelites met in Sinai and who left their ovens cold on Saturn-day, which did not occur weekly. No documents support this inheritance. Biblical citations used as evidence have other explanations. For instance, Exodus 35:3—"You shall not even light a fire in any of your dwellings on the sabbath day"—reinforces rest, and has since been interpreted also to prohibit anger.

Some have argued the Sabbath derived from ancient Arabs who worshipped the moon on the four days each month when the moon entered a new phase. But the lunar month has 29 days and the weekly Sabbath cycles never coincide with the moon's phases. Others wonder if the Sabbath derived from a market day, though there is no evidence of a weekly market day in the Ancient Near East. More likely it is that the weekly Shabbat led to a weekly market day, such as Friday in Mecca at the time of Muhammad.

Without clear evidence, some scholars assume some connection to pagan antecedents for the Sabbath. But even these credit the Israelites with a "radical break from the past," one that made the Sabbath rest an expression of divinely ordained sanctity.[13] Thus, even if the Israelites adopted the Babylonian monthly, lunar taboo, or rest day, they "detached it from its connection with the moon, extended it and generalized the abstinence associated with it, stripped it of superstitions and heathen associations and made it subservient to ethical demands."[14]

There was an eventual confluence of the Sabbatarian week of the Israelites and the planetary or astrological week. The seven-day week, in place by the beginning of the Israelites' monarchical period, was unknown among the ancient Greeks, whose holidays were held on various days in various regions. The Babylonians had already spotted and named the seven heavenly bodies—the sun, moon, and five planets. In the second century BCE, the Egyptians assigned the planetary names to the days of the week and Rome adopted the system after Julius Caesar conquered Egypt. Eventually the Jewish and astrological weeks were joined and spread through the world by Christianity. Constantine set the week in the Roman calendar; in 321 CE he made Sunday its first day.[15]

Despite its astrological undertones, the week exists oblivious to nature. The lunar cycle is 29.5 days, not 28 days or four weeks. The solar year is 365.25 days, not the 52-week year of 364 days. Only with a week that is seven days, rather than some portion of the lunar month or solar year, could humans have "the temporal regularity" that underpins civilization. Though other societies have weeks of three, five, six, and eight days, in the ancient world the Jews became known for their distinctive week defined by the Sabbath.[16]

Lacking proof of an outside source, we can best look for the origins of the Sabbath in the primary Hebrew scripture of the Torah. Also known as the

Pentateuch, this consists of the first five books of the Bible: Genesis, Exodus, Leviticus, Numbers, and Deuteronomy. The Torah traces the history of the Jewish people from Creation to the death of Moses at the threshold of the Promised Land. For Jews it is the written law as revealed to Moses at Sinai and the basis for the oral law. When the Kligermans and Rabbi Silton—and most devout Jews—refer to scripture to explain their beliefs and actions, they usually cite these books.

A final confusion can arise since the weekly Sabbath is mentioned together with the day of the new moon (Isa. 1:13, 66:23, Amos 8:5). But one is weekly and the other every lunar month. The new moon is greeted and blessed to this day by Jews as a sign of God's presence and symbol of nature's renewal, but is a separate event.

After Creation, the Bible does not mention the Sabbath until the topic is raised in a scene just before the Israelites arrive at Sinai, when they were six weeks out of Egypt. After entering the Desert of Sin, hunger and despair led them to curse God and Moses and to wish they had remained in captivity where at least they were fed.

This temptation reverberates throughout our history. In a parable told by a character in Dostoyevsky's *The Brothers Karamazov*, the Grand Inquisitor tells a latter-day Jesus, who has returned to sixteenth-century Spain, that men and women will gladly trade freedom for food. They yearn, he says to the silent Christ, "to lay that freedom at our feet, and say: 'Enslave, but feed us!'"[17] Who among us has not taken a leap away from security and into the unknown, following some dream or vision or divine urge, and then bitterly regretted the chill discomfort of a new clime?

In Exodus 16:4–5, Yahweh takes pity on the Israelites but not overmuch. God gives but also expects.

> Then the Lord said to Moses, "I am going to rain bread from heaven for you, and each day the people shall go out and gather enough for that day. In that way I will test them, whether they will follow my instruction or not. On the sixth day, when they prepare what they bring in, it will be twice as much as they gather on other days."

Then, as if this were not enough, He says He will give "you meat to eat in the evening and your fill of bread in the morning." But they must let each day's portion of manna, the bread from heaven, suffice unto itself; those who keep some overnight find it rotten and full of worms in the morning. Thus those who gathered too much manna ended up with nothing and those who gathered too little had enough, a point raised by Paul in his Second Letter to the Corinthians (8:14–15). This egalitarianism also marks the Sabbath commandment later revealed at Sinai. They were also told to stay in their homes on that day, perhaps as a way of enforcing the ban on gathering manna (Exod. 16:29).

God's directions regarding manna affirm His insistence that the Israelites depend utterly on Him, that they live in faith. This, too, is the spirit of Sabbath, when we rest and trust that our needs will be, or have been, filled even without continued effort and labor.

After they gathered the double portion on the sixth day, the leaders reported back to Moses. And he said to them, in perhaps the oldest biblical reference to Sabbath:

> This is what the Lord has commanded: "Tomorrow is a day of solemn rest, a holy sabbath to the Lord; bake what you want to bake and boil what you want to boil, and all that is left over put aside to be kept until morning." So they put it aside until morning, as Moses commanded them; and it did not become foul, and there were no worms in it. Moses said, "Eat it today, for today is a sabbath to the Lord; today you will not find it in the field. Six days you shall gather it; but on the seventh day, which is a sabbath, there will be none." (Exod. 16:23–26)

Oddly, God mentions the day of rest in an off-handed fashion, as if He were referring to a known fact rather than a new order. Indeed, it is "proclaimed as something which is already in existence."[18] Later, the prophets believed so as well. Nehemiah wrote that God at Sinai "made known your holy sabbath to them," as if it were well established and not new (9:14). And in Ezekiel 20:13, God laments that Israel "rebelled against me in the wilderness . . . and my sabbaths they greatly profaned."

If it was well known, nevertheless some disobey again. Who at that time could not do so? Growing or getting enough food to eat was the major activity of each day, especially for nomads crossing a wilderness. Then they hear from Moses, whose bright idea launched them on this idyll, that they are to kick back on the seventh day and not worry. I am sure they grumbled, even yelled at this idiocy. And some followed their instinct out the door and into the field. They are rebuked and relent.

On the seventh day some of the people went out to gather, and they found none. The Lord said to Moses, "How long will you refuse to keep my commandments and instructions? See! The Lord has given you the sabbath, therefore on the sixth day he gives you food for two days; each of you stay where you are; do not leave your place on the seventh day." So the people rested on the seventh day. The house of Israel called it manna; it was like coriander seed, white, and the taste of it was like wafers made with honey. (Exod. 16:27–31)

Several verses later, God rewards their fidelity. "The Israelites ate manna forty years . . . until they came to the border of the land of Canaan."

At Mount Sinai

By the parting of the Sea of Reeds, the Israelites escaped Pharaoh's armies. But in the desert they still are far from the Promised Land. They set camp at Mount Sinai. Moses goes up the mountain. The Lord speaks, "If you hearken to my voice and keep my covenant, you shall be my special possession, dearer to me than all other people, though all the earth is mine" (Exod. 19:5). They agree. Then on the third day God came down in fire, amid thunder and lightning, and delivered the Ten Commandments, or Decalogue (ten words).

The first commandment is that the Israelites are to worship God, the one who brought them out of Egypt; the second that they are to not worship false gods; and the third to blaspheme not. Then came the longest, the fourth commandment.

Remember the sabbath day, to keep it holy. Six days you shall labor, and do all your work; but the seventh day is a sabbath to the Lord your God; in it you shall not do any work, you, or your son, or your daughter, your manservant, or your maidservant, or your cattle, or the sojourner who is within your gates; for in six days the Lord made heaven and earth, the sea, and all that is in them, and rested the seventh day; therefore the Lord blessed the sabbath day and hallowed it. (Exod. 20:8–11)

"Remember" confirms that Israel already knew and was keeping the Sabbath. This version uses the example of Creation ending with God's rest as justification. The other version of the commandment, in Deuteronomy, cites a different reason.

> Observe the sabbath day and keep it holy, as the Lord your God has com-
> manded you. Six days you shall labor and do all your work, but the seventh
> day is a sabbath of the Lord your God; you shall not do any work—you, your
> son or your daughter, your male or female slave, your ox or your ass, or any
> of your cattle, or the stranger in your settlements, so that your male and
> female slave may rest as you do. Remember that you were a slave in the land
> of Egypt and the Lord your God freed you from there with a mighty hand
> and an outstretched arm; therefore the Lord your God has commanded you
> to observe the sabbath day. (Deut. 5:12–15)

While the first version, in Exodus, justifies the Sabbath as freedom from labor in the memory of God's rest after creating the world, the second offers freedom from slavery in memory of the Israelites' bondage in Egypt and their release or exodus. Now, we are told to keep, rather than remember, the Sabbath. This presentation has a timeless immediacy. "Not with our ancestors did the Lord make this covenant, but with us, who are all of us here alive today. The Lord spoke with you face to face at the mountain, out of the fire" (Deut. 5:3–4).

This note resounds through Jewish and Christian scripture, which address the reader regardless of time or place. God speaks always anew to His people, here and now, through the Bible. In Exodus 31, we learn that the Sabbath is a "perpetual covenant" and "a sign between you and me," one that binds God's protection to a people's obedience.[19]

The Sabbath Covenant

The Sabbath is a sign of the covenant with God, as was the rainbow shown to Noah after the flood, and circumcision, as revealed to Abraham. (Circumcision takes precedence, even today, and must be performed on the eighth day after birth even if on Shabbat.) The Sabbath signifies God's consecration of Israel, and Ezekiel singles it out from among all divine law (20: 12ff). Over time, the Sabbath rose to paramount importance; proper observance could wipe away other sins and neglect would outweigh other fidelities. Israel alone received this revelation. Later, the prophet Isaiah and others over the centuries broadened the covenant to all people. The Jewish philosopher Philo (20 BCE–50 CE) called the Sabbath "the festival not of a single city or country but of the universe . . . belonging to all people."[20] It is the birthday of the world. Christians, especially, have since concluded that the covenant applies to them as the religious descendants of the Jews.

The Sabbath command was one of the first expressions of human equality. King and slave alike had a day off. In the same spirit, my German immigrant grandfather would dress on Sundays in his best suit and straw boater, attend Mass and then march the family over to Central Park to promenade, row boats, and picnic. Secure in his day off, he would proclaim to his children, "Today, no one knows I work in a brewery." And in pictures he is not a foreign-born wage slave but a free American and Catholic, framed by his upright son and daughter, all of them comfortable in their leisure and doing as God did, ceasing from their labors.

The Exodus and Deuteronomy passages on the Sabbath both include children, animals, slaves or servants, and strangers or aliens among those who must rest. They enjoy God's favor as much as Israel and Israel benefits from having their observance reinforced by outsiders. Both these impulses drove later attempts, from the Roman emperor Constantine to the Puritans, to require a Sabbath rest among all residents of an empire or community.

The Sabbath commandment makes the day both holy and social, which echoes two aspects of the Decalogue as a whole, which opens with "your God" and concludes with "your neighbor." The first three commandments stipulate reverence and obedience toward the Lord, the last six command respect for parents and neighbors. The fourth commandment, set in the middle, concerns both by ordering rest in imitation of God and also as a rest for all people. "In that sense," writes Francine Klagsbrun, "it spans the ideals of all the others; like Jacob's ladder, it spans heaven and earth." Our duty toward others—humanitarian, egalitarian—originates in our faith and religious obligation.[21] In another claim for the unity of the two Sabbath commands, the Jewish sages of the first centuries CE taught that the first key word of each—"remember" and "observe"—were uttered by God in a single breath.

A Law Above Others

For good reason did the rabbis of the first century, and since, teach that the Sabbath precept is more important than the other laws. The fourth is the longest of the Ten Commandments and it is the most frequently repeated of the 613 divine laws found in the Torah. For Jews ever since, these laws and all the others given at Sinai became a central concern. "They tried to arrange every detail of their lives to accord with these divine laws, and the laws themselves were studied down to their tiniest particulars."[22] An important reiteration occurs in Leviticus. Here we read that the Lord told Moses, "Six days shall work be done; but on the seventh day is a sabbath of solemn rest, a holy convocation; you shall do no work; it is a sabbath to the Lord in all your dwellings" (Lev. 23:3).

The word "convocation" highlights an important distinction. The Sabbath at Creation established a moral aspect to the command, while the order at Sinai gave the day a ceremonial aspect. Later, during the Reformation and after, many Christians said that they were free to dispense with the Mosaic justification, which applied to the Jews alone. Christ freed us from the law, and thus using a "one day in seven" version, the church could switch the moral obligation to Sunday.

The "holy convocation" that is Sabbath marks the seventh day as sacred, an important element in Jewish life today. Then, as now, servile labor is banned and, toward that end, so is fire and cooking. But at that time, place or space could be equally important. Witness the elaborate construction and guarding of the sanctuary, God's place of presence on earth. Space also matters on the Sabbath. Exodus 16:29–30 instructs Israelites to stay in their homes on that day. This order could merely enforce the day's rest, but by my reading it elevates home and hearth as the place where the Sabbath is observed. Similarly, Jacob Neusner observes that the structure and order of the Israelite household mark "the confluence of time, space and circumstance." A wall descends at sundown Friday to separate the private domain from the public. They neither work nor cook, only eat and rest "in perfect repose."[23] Like God.

At its core the Sabbath symbolized the covenant by which the Israelites were saved by God. Individual violations threatened this relationship and thus Israel's existence. So it was particularly heinous when a man was found collecting firewood, presumably in preparation to light a fire.

> While the Israelites were in the desert, a man was discovered gathering wood on the sabbath day. Those who caught him at it brought him to Moses and Aaron and the whole assembly. But they kept him in custody, for there was no clear decision as to what should be done with him. Then the Lord said to Moses, "This man shall be put to death; let the whole community stone him outside the camp." So the whole community led him outside

the camp and stoned him to death, as the Lord had commanded Moses. (Num. 15:32–36)

The stick gatherer may have been stoned for his presumption and as an example. But it did not scare everyone into devout observance. We read in Ezekiel that God swore to the Israelites in the wilderness that He would not bring them to the Promised Land "because they rejected my ordinances and did not observe my statutes, and profaned my sabbaths; for their heart went after their idols" (20:16). Again, the sin is presumption. Nevertheless, God relented and brought them to Canaan after all.

After Mount Sinai: The Monarchy and the Divided Kingdoms of Israel and Judah

The Sabbath regulations date to the earliest period of Jewish history (Exod. 23:12). On that day all were to cease working. Religious activity occurred, but the texts don't specify beyond certain sacrifices in the Temple (Num. 28:9–10). Additional sacrifice was required on the Sabbath, two unblemished he-lambs and some flour mixed with oil, which by the time of Ezekiel was increased to six lambs and a ram, and even more flour and oil (46:4–5). Keeping the Sabbath is coupled with reverence for parents and for the sanctuary (Lev. 19:3, 19:30, 26:2).[24]

Other precepts emerge in Exodus. The Sabbath is not violated even to plant or harvest crops, a high price to pay for an early society (Exod. 34:21). God's instructions on building the tabernacle end with an admonition to keep the Sabbath, and Moses' repetition of these directions begins with another reminder (Exod. 31:12–5, 35:1–3). Thus, even work on the tabernacle was to halt for the Sabbath. From this juxtaposition, the rabbis later derived 39 categories of forbidden labor, all of which are associated with building the tabernacle. (These are spelled out in the volume Shabbat in the Mishnah, the oral law accumulated over the ages and compiled by the third century CE. The better-known Talmud consists of the teaching, commentary, and discussion of the Mishnah. A Jerusalem Talmud was completed in 500 CE and the Babylonian version in 600 CE.)

The Sabbath figured in the arrival of the Israelites in the Promised Land. Shortly after crossing over the Jordan River into Canaan, they came to the fortified city of Jericho. The Lord tells Joshua to march around the city once a day for six days. Then on the seventh, they are to circle it seven times, then blow their horns and shout. So they did, and the walls came tumbling down (Josh. 6:1–21). Though the story reflects the Israelite, and ancient Near East, obsession with "seven," it does not mention Shabbat. Perhaps the ban on rest is not violated since God does the work here, although the Israelites promptly slaughter all the inhabitants of Jericho. Still, that the first major conquest in Canaan occurs on the seventh day carries deep meaning. For Jews today, however, on the Sabbath it is time rather than space that is conquered and brought to God's ends.

For the time of the monarchy and divided kingdoms, from 1000 to 586 BCE, the Bible reveals more details. The Sabbath was being observed regularly in ninth- or eighth-century Israel (2 Kings 4:22–23, Hosea 2:13). The king provided the 12 loaves of show bread that were kept on the Temple altar and then eaten by the priests, and the Levites sang in a chorus during ceremonies (2 Chron. 31:3, 1 Chron. 9:32, 30–31). People visited holy men and consulted prophets. After the kingdom split, the weekly day of rest continued in both the Northern Kingdom, Israel, and the Southern, Judah, during the eighth century (Amos 8:5, Isa. 1:13).

Sabbath practice was not perfect compared to after the exile. The queen mother Athalia, who usurped the royal family, was captured and killed on the Sabbath in a Sabbatical year (2 Kings 11:5–16). (This may have exemplified the principle, elaborated in later centuries, that violations may occur if these advance the common good.)

The Psalms, half of which were traditionally attributed to David, were mostly composed for liturgical worship. Only one, Psalm 92, is assigned to a particular day. The first verse labels it a "Sabbath song," but there are no other direct references. Its "chiastic" structure—parallel phrases with words in reversed order—evinces an order and equilibrium that, to some scholars, characterize the Sabbath. The psalm celebrates Yahweh's works, the recompense of the wicked, and the reward of the righteous who shall flourish forever. Conceivably, it celebrates the eternal and the weekly Sabbath when we rely on God's providence rather than ourselves.

Hosea, in the eighth century, counts the Sabbath among the joys that God may take away from Israel as punishment. Even at this early point, Sabbath observance may have begun to shift from the moral toward the ceremonial, away from people and into the Temple. Prophets such as Isaiah, Ezekiel, Hosea, and Jeremiah lambaste empty rituals and hypocrisy. "New moon and sabbath and the calling of assemblies—I cannot endure iniquity and solemn assembly"

(Isa. 1:13). They also cite the greedy merchants who cannot wait for the day to end so as to resume their trade. Jeremiah 17:19–27 puts the Sabbath within the covenant and thus its observance guarantees Israel's survival. It permeates all of Judaism. The book of Chronicles ties the Sabbath to the covenant, land, rest, the temple, redemption, and restitution.[25]

The Israelites were known as Sabbath keepers, and their enemies put it to good use. Sennacherib, the Assyrian ruler, writes of his attack on Judah in 701 BCE during King Hezekiah's "seventh time," believed to be the Sabbath when the Israelites would be at rest.[26] Scholars have synchronized Babylonian records with biblical dates to show that the capture of Jerusalem in 597 BCE, a later assault in 588 and its complete fall shortly thereafter all came on the Sabbath. Later, during the Greco-Roman period, from 200 to 500 BCE, the writers Horace and Ovid and the Emperor Augustus all attested to the strictness of Jewish Sabbath observance and Philostratus describes the Jews as "a people that devises a world apart."[27]

Surprised by the Joy of Sabbath

One day I bend over to stretch on the campus lawn and a gem's light of gold catches my eye. As I stand up, the color—sun's refraction in a dewdrop—switches to bright blue and back to gold. One earth-bound drop of water unfurls the sun's blinding light into a dozen colored banners.

Similarly, the Sabbath dissects the light of life into its parts. The light of six weekdays, at the workbench or the office or the farm field, now unfolds and reveals to us all its unseen blessings. And I imagine the moment when the ancient Hebrews must have discovered this joy as they struggled to keep Shabbat. When ceasing to work or fight would invite starvation or defeat, they must have wondered at the seeming stupidity of this commandment.

Picture a family stopping, ceasing, and even resting in that harsh climate. Likely they are unhappy about this order from on high. "Now what does Yahweh want of us?" And then, in a twinkling, one of the family relaxes into the forced leisure, perhaps a child plays. A smile spreads. They settle into God's presence in space. Heaven reveals itself.

This is the great legacy of the Sabbath, given to us by God's example and by His commandment at Sinai. We deserve rest not because of our labor and thrift but because providence dropped it in our lap. Perhaps because of our stubborn nature, the gift was pressed upon us by the threat of death for neglect.

Shabbat, Sunday, and Juma come for all of us, believer and heathen, found and unfound.

Sitting in our front yard one Sunday in August I try to let enough be enough, as did God, "who looked at everything he had made" and "found it very good." Around me the black-eyed Susans reach for the sun, erect and bright. Purple phlox waver stiffly in a breeze, the goldfish in the pond hides in the shade of lilies, and the stalwart Norway maple breaks up the heat. And despite a war in Iraq, poverty and crime, despite our slim bank account and big dental bills, despite all I've not done and all I need to do, despite death and chaos and evil afoot, it is good, good enough to let be for the day.

A Day of Happy Salvation

The Sabbath varied in importance in different times and for different writers of scripture. It mattered most to the writers of Exodus 16–20, Leviticus 6–26, Deuteronomy 5, Nehemiah 10 and 13, Isaiah 56 and 58, Jeremiah 17, Ezekiel 22–23, Maccabees, and Jubilees. These show, in sum, a faithfully kept and revered day of rest.

Joy and gratitude are consistent themes in the ancient Sabbaths, although with a sterner note than we moderns associate with those feelings. But this is a joy of a people who on the seventh day celebrated and kept the covenant with a God who had delivered them from bondage, brought them to a Promised Land, and sustained them daily and against their enemies. In the days of the Jerusalem Temple, a shofar or ritual horn was blown to announce the call to rest.

Later observers saw the joy. Wrote Plutarch, "Their feast of Sabbath is not without reference to Dionysius."[28] The early ban on sex, in Jubilees, was reversed by the rabbis of the first century CE and later, with some Orthodox sages eventually suggesting a couple make love three times. The ancient ritualistic use of sex on festivals survives in these suggestions, which early on envisioned the wife as "light of God." Most Jews would probably say they are consecrating their love, making the day one of pleasure and obedience to God's command to "be fruitful and multiply."

Sabbath bounty is so great that it spills fore and aft. The books of Judith and Maccabees extend the blessed quality of the Sabbath by excusing people from fasting or other obligations in the days before and after. Today, some Jews, during the Havdalah service concluding Shabbat, scrape off a speck of spice to carry under a fingernail into the profane days ahead. Jubilees, a noncanonical book, extends the Sabbath into the cosmic realm (but also widens use of the death penalty for violations). Much later, near the time of Christ, Philo imagines that plants and trees must rest as well on the Sabbath.[29]

Isaiah 58, though from a section of the chapter written after the Babylonian exile, suggests that the Sabbath was originally a happy time for the obedient people of God. Early verses decry fasting and rituals in favor of freeing the oppressed and feeding the hungry. Then comes this blast of joy in verse 13–14.

> If you refrain from trampling the sabbath,
> from pursuing your own interests on my holy day;
> if you call the sabbath a delight
> and the holy day of the Lord honorable;
> if you honor it, not going your own ways,
> serving your own interests, or pursuing your own affairs;
> then you shall take delight in the Lord,
> and I will make you ride upon the heights of the earth;
> I will feed you with the heritage of your ancestor Jacob,
> for the mouth of the Lord has spoken.

Over time and especially in the first centuries of the Common Era, the Sabbath emerged as we know it today. It is more the joyous vision of Isaiah 58, than the death threat from the early teachings, that sustains Shabbat. So too for Juma among the Muslims and the Christian Sunday—more are drawn by the day's blessings than by fear of punishment. But the balance in these religions is always between God's gift and His demand, between our freedom and the law that preserves this freedom. It is the restrictions that transform this one day into "a sabbath of solemn rest, holy to the Lord" (Exod. 31:15).

Friday Night and Saturday Afternoon

On a Friday we Ringwalds eat dinner at the Kligermans. Tom cooked the main dishes on Tuesday, the only way to juggle work, family, and religion. "It's not for nothing that even secular Jews have a love affair with food because food," says Tom, "is so important to all our rituals."

Before we sit, the Kligermans wash their hands, right hand first, at the kitchen sink then come to the table in silence. Tom picks up two loaves of challah and sings out a blessing to "you God, who bring forth blessings from the earth." He puts the bread down, sprinkles salt on it, and breaks off a chunk to chew and swallow while waving off a question of mine. "The washing of our hands and the blessing are considered one blessing, so you can't talk until you eat the first piece," he explains later. The salt recalls that used on the animal sacrifices of the Holy Temple to season the meat and also to draw out its blood, a purification required by Jewish law. After the final destruction of the Temple, prayer—including that said on Shabbat—replaced the sacrifices. The Temple altar was replaced, symbolically, by the Sabbath table in Jewish homes.

We eat the meal and discuss children and the balance between genetics and our influence on them. Amy notes that if their makeup is determined 90 percent by nature, then the 10 percent role of nurture becomes all the more important. Tom says that, "When I look at their religious education, that will always be a part of them." He notes his own 15 to 20 year hiatus from Judaism before meeting Becky, when his early training helped him renew his faith. Our six children play Twister in the living room. Eli still wears his embroidered *kipa*, or yarmulke. Jews, mostly men and boys, wear a skullcap, Tom says, "to remind us that there is something above us."

Becky wonders why anyone who had a religion would forsake it so readily, as did her forebears. "My parents told us we could choose for ourselves," she says and shakes her head. Tom mentions several *shlichim* or emissaries from Israel who are here on extended visits. "They're here to educate and serve the Jews of Albany and to encourage some make *aliyah* to Israel." Aliyah is the ultimate step for a Jew and involves emigrating to the Holy Land.

Before we leave, Tom leads the family in *zmira*, a traditional song sung during Sabbath meals, to the tune of the Beach Boys' "Sloop John B." The song's yearning melancholy matches our mood at the evening's end. Later, he offers a rough, partial translation: "God invites his children to partake of Shabbat; to rest from labor, enmity and strife. / Shabbat restores the heart and inspires wisdom; and restores dignity to life."

The next day, I walk the mile to Temple Israel and meet the Kligermans and their friends Rich and Amy Drucker and their children, who are having us over for lunch at their house. The ten of us strolled there, a good two miles, with babies in strollers and children dashing about and rain threatening to fall from wooly grey clouds. The conversation veered from the sublime to the mundane. The couples discuss leaving the bathroom light on from Friday afternoon till Saturday night. Making a fire or lighting a candle is forbidden on Shabbat, and initiating electrical activity is considered to fall under this prohibition. Becky tells me that her family questioned her observance since Shabbat and kosher,

for instance, involve special efforts. "They do things because they're convenient. So they ask me, 'Why would you do it the hard way?'"

Soon we are discussing families and congregations that keep the Sabbath to
varying degrees. But no one speaks with censure; they merely observe. Who's
perfect? Rabbi Silton told me that, as a boy, his son Akiva asked why so many
Jews drove to Sabbath services. "I told him that while driving is forbidden, we
should not look at what they don't do but at what they do. If they drive, at least
they are going."

Still, if the Sabbath brings such joy, so why aren't more Jews like the
Kligermans? American Jews come back from Israel and express wonder at the
calm of Shabbat there, the complete halt to secular life. "If only everyone kept
it like that!" they say, as if unable to change their lives. The command speaks
to each person—today, now, this week—and not only to an entire people.
"Happy is the mortal who . . . holds it fast, who keeps the sabbath."

Tom and Becky don't wait for every Jew to be observant; they start with
themselves, each Friday at dusk, one untouched light switch at a time. By the
time I collect my jacket and umbrella, the skies have opened and the rain is
falling in gusty torrents. Providence did hold off till the Jews were safe at the
Shabbat lunch, but I have less luck. The Kligermans will stay until dark, when
the Druckers can drive them. Rich and Amy insist I take their car and leave it
at the synagogue.

Now, several years later, I still remember the enforced languor of that afternoon walk as we laughed and talked and chased the kids before eating lunch in
the Drucker's immaculate apartment. And how the rain held off while we
strolled without rushing, confident God would protect those keeping his law.
And how no one said, we better get there before it rains.

The Fight for the Sabbath: From the Monarchy to Jesus and the Age of the Rabbis: 1000 BCE to 200 CE

But if you do not listen to me, to keep the sabbath day holy, and not to bear a burden and enter by the gates of Jerusalem on the sabbath day, then I will kindle a fire in its gates, and it shall devour the palaces of Jerusalem and shall not be quenched.
JEREMIAH 17:27

Thus says the Lord:
   Maintain justice, and do what is right,
for soon my salvation will come,
   and my deliverance be revealed.
Happy is the mortal who does this,
   the one who holds it fast,
who keeps the sabbath, not profaning it,
   and refrains from doing any evil
....
All who keep the sabbath, and do not profane it,
   and hold fast my covenant—
these I will bring to my holy mountain,
   and make them joyful in my house of prayer.
ISAIAH 56:1–2, 6–7

The Sabbath, announced in a time when survival depended on constant toil, probably aroused rebellion from the start. Why else such strict penalties for offenses? Interpretations differed. Some considered the Sabbath a sign of their covenant with God, others as a means to uphold that covenant. Observance and regulation passed through cycles. One simplistic version has it that the

Sabbath was at first a day of joy that was later ruined by the high priests and legalistic Pharisees. If observance waned for a time, the Sabbath reemerged as paramount during and after the Babylonian exile. Rules multiplied under the threat of death. Later, Jesus debated with his fellow Jews over permissible Sabbath activities. The sages of this time and the first centuries of the Common Era further interpreted the law while emphasizing the joy of Sabbath and allowing a large measure of compassion and accommodation. The Jews had already decided that they were not supposed to die over it. As the oral law was compiled and interpreted, it made the Sabbath a prime ingredient of the recipe for Jewish survival. Ever after the Jews, out of duty and love and self-preservation, have moved between observing Shabbat and making Shabbat observable. Generally, the observant have preserved it for the rest.

A Simple Law Elaborated

Two elements strike an outsider about the Sabbath in the Torah: there are few specifics and God now treats his people like grown-ups.

There are the commands to remember and to keep the day, to not work, to stay at home and not start a fire, to neither plow nor harvest a field. The Torah provides the basic rules, and a dense and complex oral law unfurled over centuries as rabbis posed and answered questions and case studies. The elaboration began early when Moses asked God for directions on dealing with the wood gatherer.[1] The prophets, upset at disregard for the day, enforced the ban on work by restricting trade and the carrying of goods.

Jews traditionally believe that God at Sinai gave Moses the written law or Torah and the oral law. The latter was memorized and passed on until it was written as the Mishnah, beginning in the early third century CE. This is the second source after the written law. The Mishnah acknowledges no other sources, basically ignoring all biblical texts written after the close of the Pentateuch in 450 BCE. This approach allows for the oral law to have been authoritatively revealed at Sinai but also to continue unfolding today.[2]

Sabbath was also unique in that it required our consent, unlike earlier covenants. The first covenant involved God's pledge never again to flood the world and was marked by the rainbow. In the second, God promises that Abraham will father a nation that will possess Canaan, and whose men will be marked by circumcision. The third covenant is with Moses and his people, who are given the Sabbath as a sign. But while the rainbow issues from heaven

and circumcision is performed on a newborn, it takes an adult acting volun-
tarily to keep Shabbat and uphold the covenant.[3] Now Israel grows up, so to
speak, as God makes it—and us—a conscious partner in the love that sustains
the world.

In the earlier phase among the Israelites, the cessation of labor followed as a
consequence of the religious observance. Then the humanitarian justification
emerged. The land lies fallow in the seventh year so that the needy and animals
may eat of it, and Israelites must rest on the Sabbath "in order that your ox and
your ass may rest, and that your bondsman and the stranger may be refreshed"
(Exod. 23:10–12). So too Deuteronomy 5:14 directs none to work "so that your
male and female slave may rest as you do." So too with the early Christians,
who found they needed time off from work in order to attend the weekly Lord's
Supper and Easter remembrance. Later Christians developed, or borrowed
from Judaism, the idea that the divine rest was granted to humanity as a blessing in itself.

God's high regard for humans is exemplified in rules for Sabbath, and Jewish
law generally, in that there is plenty of room for thought and judgment. It is not
as if religious law is a simplistic matter of do or die. The most cursory observer
of Jewish life notes the enormous range and ingenuity of exceptions and circumventions in observance. God's law may be absolute, but its interpretation
and application provide plenty of room to wiggle. More importantly, it allows
us to grow into worthy creatures of the divine. "The Shabbat rules also include
exceptions, for laws without exceptions shut out morality and conscience."[4]
The room for interpretation is great since there are so few rules regarding the
Sabbath in the first five books of the Bible. By contrast, there are long, detailed
instructions on building the tabernacle, the portable sanctuary that the
Israelites carried through the wilderness. (In its inner part the ark of the
covenant contained the tablets inscribed with the Decalogue. In synagogues
today the ark refers to the niche that contains the Torah scrolls.) The first three
verses of Exodus 35 concern the Sabbath—rest or be executed, no fires—but
the remainder and the next four chapters involve the Tabernacle.

Amy, my wife, considers this a healthy approach. "If Catholics had an absolute rule about resting on Sunday, the priests would preach it and everyone
would nod then just go out and ignore it," she says. "The Jews have these harsh
laws, but then they find all these smart ways to live with them."

So imagine the Israelites standing at the foot of Mount Sinai. They are
grateful to be out of Egypt, but they wonder where all this wandering will lead.
They are tired, hungry, and mystified by their leader who is up the mountain

in a cloud of smoke and fire. Then Moses comes down. The first two or three commandments make sense. Yahweh wants all our love, attention, and respect.

Then comes the next commandment. "Remember the Sabbath day, to keep it holy. Six days you shall labor, and do all your work; but the seventh day is a sabbath to the Lord your God; in it you shall not do any work." To a people scrambling for survival, trying to get home, the order to cease and desist from work must have been a bit much. To any people of the second millennium BCE, a day off from farming, hunting, gathering, or tending cows or sheep could have been disastrous.

I'll wager that some Israelites said, "You're kidding!" It must have been hard, or nearly impossible, to keep Shabbat. That's why the Lord instituted the death penalty shortly after handing down the Ten Commandments and why the Israelites killed the first person to break Shabbat. But after the man who gathered firewood was stoned, we never read in the Bible of another person so executed. (The Mishnah records a case where a court had a man executed for riding a donkey, a common offense at the time. A third was in Puritan New England. And in the early 1900s a New York policeman fired his gun at workers who tried to flee after he found them violating the Sunday closing laws.) For the average believer, the example at Sinai may have served for all time.

The Ten Commandments rivaled the deliverance from Egypt as an event central to ancient Israel. The commandments disclosed the fact, meaning, and purpose of God's word for Israel and the world.[5] The covenant was not of Israel's choosing, it was imposed by God. The Israelites obeyed out of gratitude for past deliverance and in hopes of future provision. Their world depended upon it. It was a gift, but also the key to their existence. Hence, the priests and later the rabbis erected a hedge about the law and surrounded Shabbat with protective restrictions.

Hubris was the biggest danger. After some time in the desert, the Israelites arrived near the Promised Land and 12 scouts had reconnoitered Canaan. Rebellion was in the air. The Israelites worried that they could not defeat the "veritable giants" then living in Canaan. They suffered defeats after disobeying Yahweh's instructions. Then God warns them against sinning defiantly, against making themselves into gods who control their own destiny.

"But anyone who sins defiantly, whether he be a native or an alien, insults the Lord, and shall be cut off from among his people" (Num. 15:30). Violations of Shabbat are never seen as minor or inadvertent. It is "a perpetual covenant" that all must keep, now and forever.

You shall keep the sabbath, because it is holy for you; every one who profanes it shall be put to death; whoever does any work on it, that soul shall be cut off from among his people. . . . It is a sign for ever between me and the people of Israel that in six days the Lord made heaven and earth, and on the seventh day he rested, and was refreshed. (Exod. 31:12–17)

The fourth commandment soon evolved in a strict direction. Those who profane it should be killed, and lands that violate it will be rendered desolate. By chapter 35 of Exodus, it is "a sabbath of complete rest." A change was underway in the continuing cycle in which a religion consolidates its doctrine and power but then decentralizes, grows strict then flexible, turns authoritarian then liberating, and so on.

Hezekiah, King of Judah from 715 to 687 BCE, reformed worship and revived the Code of Deuteronomy. He changed the mystical basis for Shabbat to a rational one. Previously the Sabbath was justified by Creation, now it was a memorial of Israel's liberation from slavery. Later, King Josiah (640–609 BCE) promoted the sacred covenant with Yahweh and centralized worship in Jerusalem, leaving many to do without formal religious ceremonies. Jews in distant locales were left to observe the Sabbath on their own. Coming only 40 years before the exile, Josiah's move was almost prescient in preparing Israelites who lived far from Jerusalem to keep the Sabbath on their own.

Embracing Judaism and Shabbat

Shortly after Tom and Becky began dating, she found out he was Jewish and he discovered that she was halfway to Judaism.

"We were living together and I decided to do what Tom was doing. I mean, first of all I had nothing and, second, I was interested in Judaism because it was reasonable. There was nothing mystical where you idolize something. They were respectful people with good families. The religion was family oriented. I liked that it was predictable. In my family, growing up, there wasn't a consistency. We didn't celebrate Easter in the same way every year. In Judaism there seemed to be a lot of consistency and predictability. During Hanukkah you have the eight days and you light the candles the same way every year," Becky says.

"Judaism in general focuses on the family and children and passing these rituals and beliefs on to the children. I like that whole concept." She pauses and thinks back. "Obviously I was looking for something."

In her children's lives, Becky sees an ancient faith being passed on pre-
dictably and consistently by their parents and the larger Jewish community of
Temple Israel and Albany. "They need that in a world where there are too many
choices. They have something that is bigger than their parents. That gives
people the strength to get through the good times and the bad times. Early on
I decided that Judaism would be the path we followed because of the path that
I had followed even before I met Tom." Her parents, though puzzled, were not
horrified at her choice and they helped walk Tom and Becky down the aisle.

Soon after the nuptials, Rabbi Silton came to their house and showed
Tom and Becky how to keep kosher. Becky studied with Faye Silton. And they
continued attending on Sabbath and holy days. "We gradually stopped driving
on Shabbat," Becky says. As it has for thousands of years, the seventh-day habit
passed from one generation to the next. "The rabbi and his wife are captivating
people," she continues. "They raised seven kids and each turned out successful
—smart, respectful, good colleges." That all seven are shomer Shabbat greatly
impressed her. "The Siltons made Shabbat easy for families, and it seemed
like Shabbat was a good way to stay connected."

I ask Becky if she ever wants to step off the path toward greater observance.
"No, I don't," she replies firmly and quickly. "And now there are even more
things pulling us in different directions. Eli has Little League games and practices, but it's easy to say no to the ones on Saturdays. It's the same with Netania's
dance recital. It was hard to find a class that didn't require a Saturday recital."

On another occasion, Tom tells me that it was Becky who first said that they
would have to raise their kids Jewish. Long before that, however, she felt called
toward the divine. "I remember telling my mother that my sister and I wanted
to go to church. So on Sunday my mother got us dressed and dropped us off at
the Presbyterian church and gave us change to drop in the basket and picked us
up afterward. We did that for a season and then stopped."

At Temple Israel, invitations came from fellow members and Becky was
drawn to the familiar rituals and habits, the loaves of challah and the chicken
soup. "You could expect the same flow of events at different people's houses,"
she says.

Within this community they keep the fourth commandment. Though the
number of observant Jewish families nearby is not that of 40 years ago, Becky
says there's one family on Sycamore Street, another on Turner, several more on
South Main.

"A new family with a Jewish father moved into a house on Oakwood. We're
well connected in this neighborhood. There's Temple Israel, Ohav Shalom,

B'nai Sholom, Beth Abraham Jacob and the *shteibel* on New Scotland, the house synagogue that's Lubavitch. It's small and intimate. They do outreach to other Jewish families. It's amazing to see how these large families cope."

For their part, the Kligermans have influenced and encouraged other families in being shomer Shabbat. Rich and Amy Drucker, for instance, were not religious when first married. After their first child was born, Rich became more involved in his Judaism and Amy took Faye Silton's conversion classes.

Becky said she feels her Judaism most "when we're with this Jewish community and we have this common bond. It's the little things. Going to Temple Israel can be a nonspiritual experience due to the mechanics," she says, referring to chasing the children and changing diapers and taking them out for breaks or snacks. "But I see the long-range effects as well, such as experiencing the holidays and the rites, the bris and the baby-naming ceremonies, the bar and bat mitzvahs. There are rituals at death and for funerals that give a certain structure to grieving. I love the holidays; it's fun to plan and prepare, especially for Passover, to have the whole family involved in cleaning the house." (Before Passover, Jews must remove every speck of leavening or leavened bread.) Becky tells me that the joy of the Sabbath infects even the children. "Every day this week Adena asked me, 'Is it Shabbat yet? Is it Shabbat?'

"They get to spend that day with their family and friends. They know they have both parents for 25 hours. I hope they realize it's not TV or video games and tapes that make life valuable but people. You know, a mother of Eli's classmate said to me, 'We could never turn off the TV for a whole day' and I said, 'Oh, you'd be surprised.'"

Exile and Return: 597 to 539 BCE

Three themes of the Sabbath that characterize Becky's observance emerged during the theological ferment of Israel's exile and restoration 2,500 years ago. Her Shabbat habits exemplify the successful shifts in Jewish observance. Participation moved from the Temple to the family; the locale shifted from place to time; and the ritual was changed from sacrifice to prayer.

The Sabbath, and the Judaism we know today, were refined and defined in the Babylonian captivity. In 597, the Babylonians captured Jerusalem and took King Jehoiachin, the prophet Ezekiel, and other leaders back to their homeland in an effort to subdue Judah. The Jews revolted again, so in 586, the Babylonians looted and destroyed the Temple, razed much of Jerusalem and exiled the country's remaining elite to Babylon where they joined the earlier contingent. The captivity ended after Persia rose as a power under King Cyrus II and defeated Babylon in 539. The next year Cyrus released the Jews. Many returned to their shattered Promised Land over a long period and began to reconstruct their society and religion.

During the exile, alone in a foreign land, they had time to reflect on what had gone wrong. Ezekiel had foretold the destruction of Judah and now, in exile, he urged the people to turn inward toward a separate holiness. He was equally harsh toward the elders of Israel for breaking the Sabbath while wandering in the desert after the Exodus (Ezek. 20:10). The prophets and wise men concluded that through the Babylonian captivity, God had punished the Jews for their failure to obey His laws. Once they learned that lesson, it was time to go back and God brought forth the Persians to release the people of Israel.[6] They also pondered the role of Jerusalem and the Temple in a time of exile and diaspora. Genesis 1–2:4 offered one answer. The whole world, rather than just one place, was God's sanctuary. He would be worshipped in time—Shabbat—rather than in a place.[7] Another group of exiles in Egypt included the prophet Jeremiah and developed a similar theology of strict observance coupled with a more expansive notion of God's presence.[8] In this theology of exile, contrition led to the ritual acts that could be performed anywhere.

On the other hand, one could argue that the proof for Sabbath revival among the exiles is weak. Ezekiel discusses the Sabbath but usually with reference to Jerusalem and the Temple. Perhaps the reforms of Josiah and Hezekiah, before the exile, had more of an impact than the exile. But we do know that within a century of their return to Judah, the Jews came to see the Sabbath as central to their relationship with God. If nothing else, the biblical books they wrote are full of reflection on the Sabbath and its meaning. These writings tell us far more about why, rather than how, to keep holy the seventh day.

Restoration: 539 to 322 BCE

When the Jews returned from Babylon to the Promised Land, they were eager to return to life as lived by previous generations. Since few living witnesses could guide them, they turned to their collective memory, largely embodied in their holy texts and expressed in the law. Now back in Judah, the Israelites took "an oath to walk in God's law, which was given by Moses the servant of God, and to observe and do all the commandments of the Lord our God and his ordinances and his statutes" (Neh. 10:29). So now they scrutinized the law. Beyond a failure to obey, perhaps they had not understood it fully.

If they were to cease working on the Sabbath, what exactly did that mean? Were they to remain immobile? Could they walk? Eat? Carry a child? Lift a plate? Any burden? If servants were to rest as well, did that mean the master and mistress were to clean up after meals? You couldn't work with your cattle, but could you milk them to avoid causing them the pain and risk of full udders? As James Kugel writes, this culture of bookish scrutiny and a fervent desire to do things right this time led to the rise of the interpreter or sage and ultimately yielded the vast body of oral law and commentary that makes up the Talmud.[9]

For example, Isaiah 58 seems to ban "speaking a word," in some translations, but in a context that really concerns doing God's will rather than one's own. Then there was the more serious issue of the death penalty, set clearly in Exodus 35:2. Who would know exactly when a person's actions constituted a sufficient violation to merit death? Passages in the Bible were often obscure and contradictory. People and authorities needed guidance.[10] Hence the scribes and sages began working it all out in an effort that lasted into the first centuries of the Common Era.

The exile and Restoration promoted family observance and emphasized clear marks of allegiance such as circumcision, Passover, and the Sabbath, as well as the laws of diet and purity. The Sabbath became the defining sign of Israel's covenant with God and of the individual's participation in that agreement. The priestly writers of the Torah, one of the four traditions discernible in those books, exalt the Sabbath by making it the climax of Creation and a ritual inaugurated by God. Its sanctity would be guarded by regulations—a habit that flourished under the rabbis who compiled the Talmud—and its violation punishable by death. But the obligation to rest, to cease creative labor, shifts from a sacramental act to an end in itself, and "the whole of the subsequent legislation proceeds from this point."[11]

Some scholars, and certainly those who see God's law as unchanging, believe that the exile experience did not transform the Sabbath so much as consolidate Jewish teaching and practice.[12] Ezekiel, it could be argued, promoted the traditional Sabbath. The passage that grounded Sabbath in Creation, Exodus 20:11, may predate the Creation account in Genesis. In either case, the Judaism of today was forged in the flames of the Temple's destruction.

In this period, the Sabbath became the supreme religious obligation, a condition for the coming of the Messiah. The prophet Jeremiah, often a scold, promises death to those who violate the Sabbath by working or bearing burdens, a new obligation added to hedge temptation (17:19–27). If you can't carry anything, work is even less likely. Such prohibitions usually prove that a practice, in this case working on Shabbat, was common.

Misdeeds were easy. Exodus 16:29 tells Jews to stay home on the Sabbath, an absolute rule that must have been hard to observe. Worse than just going out, the prophets lamented that Shabbat deteriorated into a market day. Amos ridiculed those who could not wait for Sabbath to end so as to return to commerce (8:5). And Nehemiah lambasted merchants in Jerusalem for making wine and transporting and selling wheat and figs on the Sabbath. He then barred the city gates on the seventh day to prevent the carrying of burdens. Jeremiah elaborated:

> Thus says the Lord: "Take heed for the sake of your lives, and do not bear a burden on the sabbath day or bring it in by the gates of Jerusalem. And do not carry a burden out of your houses on the sabbath or do any work, but keep the sabbath day holy, as I commanded your fathers." (19:21–22)

Immediately, the prophet complains this was ignored. But the rule, and its elaborations, govern—or bless—the Kligermans today.

"The initial interpretation was that you couldn't even leave your house. The rabbis reinterpreted that as [meaning] you couldn't carry anything from your house. The modern interpretation is you can't carry anything from a private space to a public space," Tom says. "For example, you can push a 300-pound sofa around your living room, that's okay, but you can't carry a tie pin out of the house."

This restriction gave birth to the *eruv*, one of Judaism's trademark accommodations between law and life. An eruv is any of several symbolic manners of circumventing Shabbat restrictions. It consists of a perimeter that converts the enclosed space into a private domain, within which carrying is allowed on Shabbat.

"Traditionally, in a walled city like Jerusalem, the whole thing is considered private and you could do what you want within the walled city," says Tom. "In Albany we have an eruv. It's checked every week to be sure it's not broken. It uses fences and telephone wires to create a defined perimeter." In the days before Shabbat, local Jews can telephone to hear a recorded message confirming if the eruv is unbroken. "I usually don't, since I'll hear if it's broken the night before at Temple Israel. That's the nice thing about the Friday service and services in general; it's a networking thing for the community."

The eruv makes the Helderberg neighborhood, and the larger New Scotland Avenue area, one big Jewish household. Within that, the Kligermans can push Ilan in his baby stroller to the synagogue or carry a whiffleball and bat outside to play afterwards. "Without the eruv," Tom adds, "you can't even carry your *tallit* [prayer shawl] bag."

The Sabbath Unites a People

During the Restoration the Sabbath promoted Jewish solidarity in other ways. The seventh year became a time when farm fields are not planted and debts are forgiven. Some saw this as one act of worship too many. The Roman historian Tacitus was later to write that the Jews ended their toils on the seventh day, "but after a time they were led by the chains of their indolence to give over to the seventh year as well." His remark also proves that the Sabbath day and year distinguished Israel as a whole. In this way, it became the only nation in the Ancient Near East to see itself as acting and suffering and worshipping together.[13]

Early on, making or extinguishing a fire was banned to prevent cooking or working or other creative acts, another hedge about the law of Shabbat. God gave them a double portion of manna on the sixth day so they would not have to go out or cook on the seventh (Exod. 16:29). Today, since an internal combustion engine involves making a spark, essentially a small fire, driving is out. So is riding a donkey or other animal, since these were to rest as well and for other reasons. These bans kept Jews within walking distance of their synagogues, as they were before automobiles and as Orthodox and many other Conservative Jews remain.

"This whole neighborhood was built by Jews who walked to Temple Israel," says Tom. But while it was shaped by millennium-old laws, so has the area been reshaped by a change made just decades ago. Reform Jews have long permitted driving on Shabbat. And a contentious 1950 ruling by the Conservative movement's Committee on Jewish Law and Standards allowed members to drive to synagogue for services. Between the ruling and the suburban exodus of the 1970s, many families moved to the suburbs. "It's why my son doesn't have any Jewish playmates on this block," Tom says. The Kligermans drive their kids to most play dates on the other days of the week. "Without that ruling, my kids would probably have more playmates nearby, two or three times the families we have now."

On the Sabbath, those still here walk and talk and visit with other families who have children, and in the fair weather they all meet at Buckingham Pond after lunch. The kids gambol on a playground, the adults talk, play basketball with older children, or chase infants. It's a joy derived from a restriction. So, too, do kosher laws push Jews into each other's dining rooms.

Sometime after the exile, the Jews decided that they were allowed to walk no more than 2,000 cubits on the Sabbath. Exodus 16:29 prohibits journeys on Shabbat. Joshua 3:4 specifies that the Israelites keep 2,000 cubits between their tents and the ark. (The cubit is an ancient linear measurement based on the distance between the elbow and middle fingertip, usually from 17 to 21 inches.) The sages concluded that was the permissible limit, since the ban on journeys was obviously not a ban on walking to the ark to worship on the Sabbath. The notion of a "sabbath's day journey" was well established by the time of Jesus. After His ascension into heaven from Mount Olivet, for instance, we read that the disciples returned to Jerusalem, a trip of that same distance. The Damascus Document, which dates to 100 BCE, refers to these limits as well.[14]

Another post-exilic rule that still affects the Kligermans is the ban on erecting a tent, one of the 39 prohibited categories of work that were elaborated by the ancients. As a result, Tom and Becky don't carry umbrellas on Shabbat, even on long walks in the rain. "It's not the carrying, it's the opening," he says. "When they were carrying the ark, they were also carrying a portable tent." Both were prohibited on the Sabbath, when the ark was laid to rest. Thus the Kligermans walk in the rain. They live in the day set at Creation, reinforced at Sinai, and reinvigorated by Nehemiah, the leader, and Ezra the scribe in the time after the exile.

Time Becomes Holy

Goodness and Sabbath keeping go hand in hand. So too do the Sabbath and God go together. Holy time begins to embody holiness, even the source of holiness itself. For Ezekiel, violation of one violates both. "They pay no attention to my sabbaths, so that I have been profaned in their midst" (22:26).

The renewal of faith along traditional lines accelerated 100 years after the exile, when Persia sent Nehemiah to serve as the secular governor of Judah after 445 BCE. He restored the city walls of Jerusalem and the laws that protected their covenant with God. Ezra emerged as the lawgiver who revived Judaism, by reading the Torah to the assembled in Jerusalem, and gave it its modern form by basing the religion in the living word of God.[15]

The perimeters erected by Nehemiah and Ezra, one in stone and the other in law, protect the holy city from its profane surroundings and the chosen people from their nonbelieving neighbors. The Jews stood apart by keeping Shabbat. They stayed apart by the era's restrictions on inter-marriage, arguably a social version of the eruv. Later, a writer in the apocry-phal Book of Jubilees, written 135 to 100 BCE, held that Israel alone has the right to keep the day (2:28–31). Nehemiah took all measures necessary to ensure holy Sabbaths, notably shutting the gates of Jerusalem on that day (13:15–22).

These practical acts resonated in the spiritual and secular realms. "It is the single happiest moment in Judaism, and, coming as it does every week, the Sabbath sheds its light on every day," Jacob Neusner writes.[16] Tom and Becky cease their labors, devote themselves to sacred acts, attend the synagogue, study, and debate Torah. They play, feast, entertain, visit, walk, and go slow. They are distracted only by their children, one of the main blessings of the day. Like so many Jews, they find in the Sabbath the meaning of their lives.[17]

No degree of restriction can cover the liberating and egalitarian throb of the Sabbath laws. Early on, the Sabbath concept was extended to the seventh year, when the land should lay fallow, and to the jubilee after seven cycles of seven years, or every fiftieth year. In these, slaves would be freed and debts canceled. The poor could glean from the farmer's idle fields and family lands sold—perhaps to forestall a crisis—would revert to the original owners. These rules provided relief to individuals and also helped equalize wealth across a society, avoiding the rich-poor disparities that rend our world today.

Amid the welter of regulation and crackdowns, some voices soothe. Second Isaiah predicts the rebirth of Israel and urges the Jews to keep the covenant, observe the Sabbath, refrain from evil, and shelter the alien.[18] Thus would God's blessings spread to all. In Isaiah 56:4–7, written after the exile, God tells the Israelites that even the eunuchs and foreigners who keep the Sabbath and God's covenant will have a place of honor and be more than sons or daughters. This marvelous book ends with the promise that all these will be brought to the holy mountain and made joyful, "for my house shall be called a house of prayer for all peoples."

Joy is a consistent theme from the earliest days, when God delivered a dou-ble portion of manna just before Shabbat, an automatic grocery delivery. It was celebrated as a festival with temple visits, songs, and special food (Hosea 2:13, Isa. 1:13–14). It is included in the list of "festivals of the Lord" (Lev. 23), which begins a tradition of rich diets and leads to the rabbinical bans on fasting and outward expressions of grief and mourning.[19] Eventually, three meals were suggested instead of the normal two.

Centuries later, the Sabbath was so well known that outside observers such as Juvenal, Persius, Martial, and Seneca noted and even criticized this profligacy as well as the "waste" of a seventh of one's life.[20] The Sabbath rest and joy proved contagious. In the first century of the Common Era, Josephus observed, "There is not any city of the Grecians, nor any of the barbarians, nor any nation whatsoever, whither our custom of resting on the seventh day hath not come."[21]

It is the orthodox who bear the ark through the desert and into the Promised Land. The moderates are left behind debating some perceived inequity. Who invigorates the laggard and attracts the unbeliever; who emboldens the faithful? The true believer and not the one busy fitting God to our world. Thus Isaiah promises, "Happy the man . . . who keeps the sabbath free from profanation and his hand from any evil doing" (56:1–8).

Limits to Remembering: The Maccabees

By the time of the second century, the people of Israel were scrupulous about the Sabbath even in war. In one sequence, after soldiers pursued an enemy "for some distance, they were obliged to return because the hour was late. It was the day before the sabbath, and for that reason they did not continue their pursuit" (2 Macc. 8:25–26). During this time, the Seleucid rulers suppressed the Jews. Antiochus Epiphanes conquered Egypt, then Israel. He ordered its residents to worship Zeus and to profane the Sabbath and other feast days. Mattathias led a group of Maccabbean rebels who were "zealous for the law" into the hills. The Seleucids followed the example of the Assyrians and neo-Babylonians before them and attacked one group on the Sabbath, who refused to profane the day by fighting. "Let us all die without reproach." And so they did. The Maccabees later wised up:

> And all said to their neighbors: "If we all do as our kindred have done and refuse to fight with the Gentiles for our lives and for our ordinances, they will quickly destroy us from the earth." So they made this decision that day: "Let us fight against anyone who comes to attack us on the sabbath day; let us not all die as our kindred died in their hiding-places." (1 Macc. 2:40–41)

Rather than simple self-preservation, they also wanted to continue the praise and honor of God. Happily, the two impulses coincide. "Yeah, if we all got killed, there would be no Shabbat observers left," Tom Kligerman says to me on the telephone one afternoon, confiding in a low, growly voice from his office. "It's like that episode of Star Trek, when Captain Kirk deliberately provokes Spock into a fight to break him from a spell caused by a plant. After the fight, Spock mentions that striking a fellow officer is a felony offense, to which Captain Kirk replies, 'If we're both in the brig, who's going to save the rest of the crew?' "

Over and over in the two books of Maccabees, the Sabbath is suppressed in order to suppress the Jews. But they turn the tables and those who keep the Sabbath are ultimately victorious. Judas and his troops succeed on the offense, which they halted for the Sabbath. After collecting the arms and spoils of Nicanor's troops, "they observed the sabbath with fervent praise and thanks to the Lord who kept them safe for that day on which he let descend on them the first dew of his mercy" (2 Macc. 8:26–27). Later, they win on the defensive.

Nicanor then attacks on the Sabbath, thinking he will win handily. The Jews plead with him to respect the day that God has exalted. He declines, saying that he is ruler on earth, and attacks, not knowing that the Jews had reinterpreted their teachings to allow self-defense. Nicanor loses, dies, and his head is hung on the wall of the citadel. He had, after all, profaned both God and the Sabbath simultaneously, a reminder that the two are, in some mystical manner, one.

As with the wood gatherer at Sinai, the Israelites kill those who deny the Lord by denying His day. And God delivers those who exalt the Lord by keeping the day. A century later when the Jews were fighting Rome, they would even attack on Shabbat, according to the Jewish historian Josephus.[22] The doctrine of self-defense was firmly established and later informed the traditional Christian allowance for acts of charity and necessity on the Sabbath. But the Romans kept the habit of attacking on Shabbat, perhaps presuming that the Jews would still be easily surprised.

After Rome annexed Syria in 67 BCE, civil war broke out in Judea and General Pompey invaded. He attacked Jerusalem in 63 BCE. For three months, he laid siege to the Temple Mount, where a group of holdouts had retreated, before overwhelming the Israelites on the Sabbath. Pompey entered the Temple but rather than profane it he ordered it cleansed. His action embodied the characteristic respect granted Jewish practice by the civil laws of the empires that governed them.

This pattern began under the Greeks, continued under Caesar and Augustus, and lasted until the Near East was Christianized in the fourth and fifth centuries CE. Generally, Jews were exempt from military service, did not have to appear in court on the Sabbath, and could collect their share of grain on another day if authorities handed it out on the seventh day. Sabbath fidelity came from below as much as from above. "With little or no reference to the rabbis, the devotion of Jews in the diaspora to the Sabbath (and other Law) continued unbroken, and forced itself for recognition even into Roman law."[23] In coming centuries, a similar grassroots phenomenon drove the Sunday habit among lay Christians despite the countervailing rulings of church leaders and councils.

There was pressure as well from on high in Judaism. In the last two centuries before Christ, religious authorities continued to mandate Sabbath observance. The Damascus Document, a set of rules and instructions for a sect of Jews who had escaped from Judea, dates to about 100 BCE. It enjoins strict observance without threat of the death penalty. Restrictions multiplied. People could not wear perfume, lift stone or dust at home, have sex in the city of the sanctuary, or rescue an animal from a pit or a person from a pool of water. Joy remained important, however, and fasting was prohibited.[24]

The book of Jubilees retells the history of Israel from the Pharisee point of view and is even stricter. It confirms the seventh-day Sabbath and bans fasting, working, riding, or traveling. Violators should be killed to preserve the day among the children of Israel, again tying Sabbath to the covenant that preserves Israel. At the same time, Aristobulus, a Jewish priest who wrote a commentary on the law, developed more esoteric notions of the Sabbath. He relates Shabbat to the cosmos, wisdom, and the sevenfold structure of all things.[25] This appears to be an attempt to reconcile the practice to Greek thought. Such ideas were developed further in the Middle Ages by the Jewish mystics who wrote the kabbalah. And both Aristobulus and some of the kabbalists displayed the recurrent tendency to accommodate Judaism to prevailing philosophies, or vice versa. Such reforms had a practical side. The Sabbath has always been one of Judaism's most appealing aspects.

The passages in the Damascus Document and Jubilees of the fourth commandment presaged the welter of regulations to come in the Talmud. But the rabbis, while adding rules and explanations, also mitigated harsher elements. They opened windows in Jewish law to accommodate the reality of people's lives.[26] Now the average believer had some guidance in making decisions about keeping the Sabbath. Brilliantly, the sages yoked creativity to devotion.

Were the loopholes in the spirit of the law? Or did these send Judaism sliding down a slope so that today only a small fraction of Jews follow the law and keep Shabbat? But these few faithful, such as Tom and Becky and Rich and Amy, know the delight and triumph promised in the final books of Isaiah, written after the exile by disciples of the great prophet. Isaiah envisions a day when, "From new moon to new moon, and from sabbath to sabbath, all flesh shall come to worship before me, says the Lord." While joy comes to the faithful, death visits the apostates. "And they shall go out and look at the dead bodies of the people who have rebelled against me" (66:23–24).

The Lord of the Sabbath

Christians believe that Jesus, a Jew, perfected the covenant between man and God. He fulfilled the law, though he also said he ended the law. He criticized his fellow Jews for overloading Shabbat with so many restrictions as to obscure its divine nature, that of a gift to sick and weary humanity. If he came to fulfill the law, Jesus also "found that human interventions had set aside what is essentially divine and spiritual in it."[27]

Overall, Jesus was a faithful Jew who kept the Sabbath. Luke 4:16 records that at the start of public life in Galilee he "went to the synagogue, as his custom was, on the sabbath day." Other Gospels confirm this habit through his life (Mark 1:21, 29, 3:1, Luke 4:44, 13:10). Christians are left with the uncomfortable truth that Christ did not tell his disciples to switch the Sabbath to Sunday. He did, however, heal and liberate on the seventh day to the dismay of the Pharisees, who appear in the Gospels as rhetorical straw men to be knocked down by Christ's compassion. In all, there are seven accounts of miracles. Luke, my favorite, has six stories that illustrate Christ's approach, which was either shockingly new or a return to the original spirit of the Sabbath.[28]

Early in his ministry, Jesus teaches in the synagogue and assumes the mantel of divine authority in the words of Isaiah—"The spirit of the Lord is upon me" (Luke 4:16–30). He lays out, also in Isaiah's words, that on the Sabbath he will relieve the poor, liberate captives, bring sight to the blind, free the oppressed, and "proclaim a year acceptable to the Lord." The Sabbath is subordinate to Christ, as he later teaches, because he fulfills these pledges. These actions also embody the spirit of the Sabbath presented in Genesis, Exodus, and Deuteronomy: rest, bounty, equality, and liberation.

Soon thereafter, in Capernaum, Jesus teaches on the Sabbath and exorcises an evil demon from a man possessed (Luke 4:31–37). Before departing the spirit first cries out, "I know who you are—the Holy One of God." Jesus can heal and on the holy day precisely because of his special relationship, son-ship, to God. In Luke 6:1–5, Jesus declares that "The son of man is Lord of the Sabbath." This would mean he is also above the law, which to the Jews is a blasphemy that could topple their whole enterprise. Blatant disregard for the Sabbath tramples on the covenant that sustains Israel. These events coincide with others detailed in Mark—Christ forgiving and eating with sinners, his disciples not fasting or washing as prescribed by Jewish law—that make the Jews apprehend his rejection of the law.[29]

Like an intelligent but tiresome child in Sunday school, Jesus presses the point on another Sabbath. After teaching under the eye of scribes and Pharisees, he calls up a man with a withered hand. He asks the assembled, "Is it lawful to do good on the sabbath rather than to do evil, to save life rather than destroy it?" Though this story reassures Christians with the hypocrisy of Christ's opponents, it is a piece of sophistry. Jesus was about to heal an arm, not save a life. The Jews had long taught that it was lawful to save life on the Sabbath. Their response was that Jesus could heal on any of the other six days. An objective observer may wonder why he chose the Sabbath, other than to pick a fight. By the end of the story, "the Pharisees were filled with wrath."

Here Luke's story differs from Matthew, who has the Pharisees, irate at the disregard for their beloved Sabbath, plotting to destroy Jesus. After a point in Luke, the Pharisees drop out of sight and are not implicated in Christ's demise. By making the Pharisees the bad guys in his telling of the story of the man with the withered arm, Luke criticizes the first-century Jewish Christian Pharisees who were rigorous about continuing the Sabbath in its strict Judaic form despite the message of Jesus.[30]

In Luke 13:10–17, Jesus heals the woman who had been crippled for 18 years. Here the synagogue elder rightly observes, "There are six days when work should be done. Come on those days to be cured." Jesus responds that if one could untie an ox so it could drink water, as allowed by rabbinical law, why not untie a person—"whom Satan has bound," Jesus says—from their handicap? Again, Jesus fulfills the promise of Isaiah by freeing the captive. This healing recalls also the Exodus from Egypt, an early justification for the Sabbath.

In Luke's last story, Jesus eats at a Pharisee household on the Sabbath, in the great Jewish tradition of good food and hospitality that continues at Tom and Becky's house. Jesus cures a man of dropsy, which certainly seems a breach of etiquette for a guest at an orthodox home. Jesus then asks his tablemates, "Who among you, if your son or ox falls into a cistern, would not immediately pull him out on the sabbath day?"

The Sabbath miracles were part of Jesus' larger challenge to his fellow Jews since he performed miracles on other days as well and always in the name of God. The Pharisees reply that saving a life is fine, but other actions—healing or picking grain—could be postponed without harm. They felt, most of all, that Jesus undermined the Torah by justifying his actions on his own terms. Though he did cite the Torah, ultimately Jesus acted as the Son of God. In this way, his enemies saw the truth before Christ's own disciples did, and on this basis the Pharisees realized they must eliminate the threat he posed. Any violation of the Torah put all of Israel at risk, just as perfect observance of the Sabbath would bring the Messiah.

If Jesus broke Shabbat, his followers did not always follow suit. The Gospel of Mark tells that after Jesus healed a demoniac and Simon's mother-in-law on the Sabbath, people brought others who were ill or possessed (1:21–34). But they did so, "When it was evening, after sunset . . ." that is, when the holy day was over.

One could say that Jesus abolished not the law but the petty enforcement of its subsidiary rules and regulations, which were then being developed by the rabbis. In the Gospels, we see the Pharisees characterized by this strict mindset. Jesus was not always provocative and often told the people he healed to tell no one about it. And he showed a certain fidelity to Jewish law by challenging the scribes, in Mark 7:1–23, in their terms. Here Jesus does not reject the Torah, but argues that the Jews had nullified its spirit by traditions of their own making. Jesus defends his authority in John 7:23 by pointing out that the Pharisees would circumcise an infant on Shabbat if that was the eighth day of his life, thus using their own judgment to place one covenantal law above another.

Interestingly, Jesus does not perform creative work on the Sabbath, which is the primary activity banned on the seventh day. Jesus does, however, claim divine authority, hence the harsh reaction. "For this reason the Jews were seeking all the more to kill him, because he was not only breaking the sabbath, but was also calling God his own Father, thereby making himself equal to God" (John 5:18).

Nevertheless Jesus did not reject the Sabbath. One of his principle sayings, "Sabbath was made for man," affirms devotion to the commandment and also repeats the Jewish teaching later recorded as, "The Sabbath is given over to you, you are not delivered unto the Sabbath."[31] From its earliest days, the Sabbath was celebrated as an equalizing boon to man and slave alike, just as today the Kligermans revere and celebrate the day as a gift. Jesus did say that his fellow

Jews went too far in laying on burdens, which was his perspective on the "hedge about the law" that the rabbis were creating at that time around the Sabbath.

Close kin best see each other's depth and weakness in the truth they share and over which they fight. By a more political interpretation, it was not the teachings of Jesus that led to his death but the fear that his messianic claims would alarm the Romans, who would remove the scant privileges and independence granted to and treasured by the Jews of Palestine.

In either case, Jesus anticipated that his disciples would remain faithful to the law of Moses and continue shomer Shabbat: "Pray that your flight will not be in winter or on the sabbath" (Matt. 18:20). This could simply acknowledge that flight would be difficult on days when the Jewish majority was at rest. More likely, it also confirms that Matthew's community of Jewish Christians in Antioch was still keeping the Sabbath when the Gospel was composed, about 80 CE. But their time was to be short, and soon was surpassed by the age of Gentile Christians. Meanwhile, they had to struggle with one question. Could they remain good Jews and still follow Jesus? The question remains for Christians yet. Can we keep the Sabbath but on Sunday?

Despite their bad press as narrow-minded martinets, the Pharisees sustained Judaism at a time when it was under siege. "Pharisaism, with all its faults, was the heart and soul of the nation, the steward of its treasures, the Holy Scripture, the trustee of its vitalizing hope."[32] The Sadducees, generally rich and powerful, were the real heavies, so to speak, who promoted an older, more legalistic approach to Jewish law. Jesus clashed with the Pharisees since they both taught and lived among the common people. Only when Jesus threatened the peace of Jerusalem and thus the prevailing order did the Sadducees pay attention.[33] Later, when the Resurrection made Sunday so important, Jesus' argumentative example emboldened the early Christians to use the choice of another day to further split off from their Jewish brethren.

The Rabbis and the Mishnah

The Judaism that emerged during and after the Babylonian exile, with its themes of prayer and teaching, became more relevant at the time when Jews scattered after the final destruction of the Temple by the Romans in 70 CE. Now the rabbis, each with their own attentive congregation, encouraged an even greater obedience of Torah and its daily demands. The Jews had to work harder to keep what they had in the diaspora; they also sought through fidelity to avoid the tragedies of earlier generations. Shabbat was their ideal religious luggage: portable, immediate, weekly, family centered.

By 200 CE, the Jewish oral law or Mishnah had been collected and arranged in an authoritative form. In the next few centuries, more than 2,000 scholars in Palestine and Babylon, generally known as the rabbis or sages, discussed and interpreted the Mishnah to produce the Gemara, or commentary. This and the oral law were compiled as the Jerusalem Talmud, by 500 CE, and the Babylonian Talmud, by 600 CE. As Jewish law was codified and elaborated, so were the rules for Shabbat.

Given the terse command to keep holy the Sabbath, interpretation was often not enough.[34] The rabbis had to develop and apply the law, sometimes with scant basis in the Bible. They acknowledged as much in a famous passage, "The established practices [*halakhot*] of the Sabbath are like mountains hanging by a hair—there is little that is written but numerous halakhot."[35] Put another way, the law of Shabbat "articulates in acute detail only a few generative concepts. But these encompass the whole." The concepts are presented in exemplary cases to inform and illustrate correct observance.[36]

Rabbinic literature abounds with regulations and detailed instructions that aim, above all, to protect the day from profanation. As one guards a child or puts away a treasure, the sages erected a "hedge about the law," in the words of Rabbi Akiba, who died in 135 CE. By adding regulations and applications, they built a fence around the house of God's law to preserve it. By respecting the fence, Jews would be much less likely to violate the house itself. (This saying first referred to the literal fence of commentary that surrounds the excerpt of oral law that appears on the typical page of the Talmud. Some call this layout an early version of hypertext, the computer software that allows users to click on a highlighted word and jump to another entry.[37])

The sages thought long and hard about work as a prohibited activity for Shabbat. The Torah orders a cessation of ordinary toil, specifically fires, wood or food gathering, leaving home, and a few other activities. Later, the rabbis noted that Exodus 35 prohibited "work" on the Sabbath just before using the same word in a list of tasks needed to build and maintain the tabernacle. From these specified or implied labors they drafted a list of 39 categories of banned labor—sowing, plowing, reaping, etc.—that some later interpreted to yield 1,521 forbidden activities.[38]

In the oral law, the Shabbat tractate, or volume, begins with a long explication of carrying, even though it is last on the list of 39. Why? The great sage, Maimonides, offered three reasons. Work often involves carrying and people easily err here. We forget that carrying is an activity. And carrying is among the activities prohibited close to nightfall.[39] The list of pre-Shabbat prohibitions ensures that people will begin the transition Friday afternoon, or sooner, and are not caught unawares at sunset as the holy day begins. The Shabbat volume opens with a densely reasoned set of rules applying to a man who hands or takes an item from a private to a public area or from a public to a private one. The interpretation of carrying lays out four domains: public, private, neither, and exempt. Though one cannot carry between public and private, it is allowed to carry between an exempt domain and the public or private domains.

While the full lesson eludes me, the elaboration displays Judaism's relentless division and subdivision of time and space into public and private and into sacred and profane. It also features the perennial effort to discern exactly how God wants us to live. The effort is part of worship. By debating the rules in his kitchen, Tom and his friends tacitly acknowledge that the rules point toward God.

The sages of Jerusalem and Babylon meditated on God's promise in Isaiah 58:13 to reward them if they sought not their own interests on the Sabbath nor engaged in "speaking a word."[40] The rabbis decided that this referred not to all speech, but to talking about work. Similarly, modern translations of the Bible render this passage from Isaiah to read "pursuing your own affairs" instead of "speaking a word."

But the sages decided that God meant us not to work and therefore to neither plan nor discuss work. Jubilees had already prescribed death for anyone even "who says anything about work on it" (50:8).[41] They had decided that, as Rabbi Levi declared in the third century, "The Sabbath is equal to all the laws." Keep it, you kept all; break it, you've broken all. Therefore, they worked hard to protect, elevate, and observe the day. In its rituals, ethics, social justice, and divine assurance, Francine Klagsbrun writes, Shabbat encompasses the Torah's fundamentals.[42]

The basic one remained God's love. Compassion weaves throughout the Mishnah. On the Sabbath, a Jew can extinguish a lit lamp if "he is afraid of the Gentiles, a bad spirit, or it is so that a sick person might sleep."[43] Hillel, a leading sage of the Second Temple period who lived from the late first century BCE into the Common Era, emphasized leniency as well. As a poor child who could not afford religious lessons, he listened in from a rooftop on a Friday evening. He was discovered in the morning, half frozen. The rabbis brought Hillel inside and made a fire: the Sabbath could be violated to save the boy's life.

God's love is also cause for celebration. Amid the rules, the rabbis preserved the joy in the Shabbat tractate of the Mishnah. One did not have to die keeping Shabbat. One could flee, save life, or assist in childbirth. The Mishnah advises that to better appreciate the three meals of the Sabbath, people should eat sparingly on Friday. Certain methods for keeping food warm are allowed. The Jews are to welcome the Sabbath with a lamp, today a candle, lit by the wife before sundown. The husband blesses the wine and the day by reciting the Kiddush or sanctification. He also sings a song to his wife and blesses each child, an affecting and tender practice. The two loaves of challah recall God's generosity with manna in the desert. Each person pays homage to God and dignifies herself by wearing special clothes and even walking or talking in a different manner.[44] These practices embody the concept, and guarantee the experience, of *oneg* Shabbat, or Sabbath joy or delight, as articulated by Isaiah.

At the same time, the rabbis sought to preserve the Sabbath as the exclusive birthmark of Israel. It was made for the Jews and not others, according to interpretations of scripture. During the third century CE, Rabbi Simeon ben Lakesh taught that Gentiles who were shomer Shabbat deserved death.[45]

The Fight for Peace

One Sunday I speak briefly with Tom Kligerman on the telephone and he discusses his family's Shabbat. I sense ours is awry. After I hang up, I talk with Amy and we cut off the TV, which was playing a videotaped musical, and rouse the children to play. Then I assemble the dinner, a roast with potatoes and onions in the pan, and let it cook while we walk the neighborhood. Thus the Jews save another Gentile family.

Even in breaking away, Christians have always been tempted by the promises of Judaism and, in particular, the Sabbath. Even our discussion of how to keep the day echoes a central goal of Shabbat for Jews. The Jerusalem Talmud declares that Sabbaths and all festivals were instituted "for the sole purpose of Torah study."[46] In the first century the Jewish historian Josephus observed, "The 7th day we set apart from labor; it is dedicated to the learning of our customs and laws, we thinking it proper to reflect on them, as well as on any good thing else, in order to our avoiding of sin."[47]

Regardless of how we resolve it, the debate confirms that we have turned toward God for the day. I may think this or that exception to the fourth commandment is only reasonable, but then I remember that no religious ritual is reasonable. If it were, what good would it be? If it were, how could faith vault us over the abyss to God?

One Sunday in late June we begin our Lord's Day before dusk on Saturday as Amy goes out to shop for food. We crowd the sunset. I do chores, small and self-contained, but conscious of each and weighing the gain in order versus the loss in peace. (I spent Saturday writing a magazine assignment and so had no time for housework until day's end.) Will this domestic tidiness enrich Sunday enough to make the chores, pushing into holy time, worthwhile? Is the chore, this or that or any or all, a must? We sing and Jeanne lights the two candles.

The next day, after a lazy morning, we walk to our parish church for Sunday Mass at 11:00 AM. Father Bob Longobucco delivers a good homily based on Paul's epistle. The letter boldly proclaims that when we are weak, we are strong through God's grace, that our sin is God's opportunity. I now see the unfolding opposites of the day. We do less and are more, we stop earning and grabbing and have more, we cease from making and make more, we let Creation be and in our repose we see it to be more than ever we knew.

Brunch at home, then off to Crystal Lake across the Hudson in Rensselaer County, where we meet Jane and her son Maxim. A green wet hot sunny day. All to our home later for dinner in the yard: barbecued London broil, corn, and broccoli.

The contented languor of Sunday, this heavenly preserve fenced in by the sunsets fore and aft, the fence that though we crowd and press and even breach remains to protect us within the time that needs no protection. But I am haunted, then and now, by a fear that we're inserting Jewish elements in our Catholicism—an odd fear, since we descended from Judaism—or that I am elevating the practice of Sunday into an object of worship. Zealots are always pressing their case against a stubborn tide, and they can easily become dogmatic and make the rules foremost rather than the means to the end.

Jesus criticized the Pharisees for their hand washing and kosher laws. The disciples ate with unwashed hands and Jesus tells us that nothing from without can pollute us, that we contaminate with the evil within us. Here the endless temptation, to replace God with law, which is hubris, really, a matter of casting our own golden calf out of our rules and regulations. But do we resolve this dilemma by shedding the tradition? Or by putting these to proper use?

This drive for control stains my own Sunday urges, as when I lose patience with distracted children who won't sit still for a hymn and prayers. "Be at peace!" I may as well yell at them—and at myself. The urge to control, to ensure a liturgical order, coincides with another aspect of Sabbath: it's when the id comes out. The normal schedule and outside disciplines fall away, thank God, and we are cast free. This may be welcome, this may be a curse. Since my weakness is God's chance, I see it as natural and useful to have all the faults shine early on Sunday. Then God can clean them up.

Yet another weekend, Anna and Martin Seigel were here for their annual summer visit. They witnessed our nasty exchange this morning before Mass. It concerned the dreary perennial—a child's footwear or apparel—but also my opinion that we yell too much rather than punish and blah-blah-blah. I apologize to our guests. Martin bluntly replies, "It seems to happen every time I come up."

But then the Mass at St. George's, the eucharistic meal, and the gathering of joyful believers and our two Jewish friends, transform us. I have no idea how much until I spot a pal on Livingston Avenue. I pull over. A tall, dapper, garrulous man, he leans in with a joke, compliments "these nice people" I'm with. I tell him, "We're a whole lot better after church then we were before." And he shouts back laughing, "I know what that's like!"

Be it Sunday or the Sabbath or Juma, God is always there, ready for us. Jeremiah promised destruction to Sabbath breakers but he also promised heaven to the faithful.

> "But if you listen to me," says the Lord, "and bring in no burden by the gates of this city on the sabbath day, but keep the sabbath day holy and do no work on it, then there shall enter by the gates of this city kings who sit on the throne of David, riding in chariots and on horses, they and their princes, the men of Judah and the inhabitants of Jerusalem; and this city shall be inhabited for ever." (Jer. 19:24–25)

Heaven comes in the keeping of the Sabbath, not later. We follow these small rituals and the door to heaven opens for a spell till, distracted, we look away and slam it shut. But we can always relax, drop our insistent rationality, and welcome the divine. In our feelings toward God we apprehend God or at least the clues to God's existence. The Jews conceive of *shekhinah*, God's presence in the world, and in Islam, the Arabic term *sakina* refers to "supreme peace" sent by God that dwells in the ark of the covenant (Quran 2:248). Without the ark we have the Sabbath, and there dwells God's presence. We sanctify time and by these small steps we wander into the cloud of divinity.

CHAPTER IV

The Lord's Day: Easter to 1600

After the sabbath, as the first day of the week was dawning, Mary Magdalene and the other Mary came to see the tomb. And behold, there was a great earthquake; for an angel of the Lord descended from heaven, rolled back the stone, and sat upon it. . . . Then the angel said to the women in reply, "Do not be afraid! I know that you are seeking Jesus the crucified. He is not here, for he has been raised just as he said."
MATTHEW 28:1–2, 5–6

Easter changes everything. Because their leader rose on that day, the disciples realized the day's importance and soon met regularly then to worship and reenact the Last Supper. Some church fathers, those thinkers of the first few centuries who mapped the contours of Christianity, elaborated on Sunday's justification and grace. This grace arrives most powerfully during the Mass, which Christians celebrate most regularly and fully on Sunday.

Despite its origin in Judaism, the Lord's Day soon divided Christians and Jews, or at least became a sign thereof. Earthly authority sanctioned the move to Sunday. In 321 CE, the Roman emperor Constantine declared Sunday a day of rest across the empire and furthered the enduring entanglement of church and state. Some thinkers denigrated the move to a Sunday Sabbath, since every day should be holy. But the populace disagreed. By the sixth century, grassroots support led to the codification of church rules for Sunday. For Jews, scattered and often persecuted, the Sabbath rose in importance as a domestic, even private ritual that could be practiced and nourished on the basis of the Talmud. In the sixteenth and seventeenth centuries, the choice of day became a battleground among Protestants, who also bashed Catholics for lax observance. In order to keep holy the Sabbath day, the Puritans set sail for the New World.

Sunday with the Ringwalds

One week in March our day apart began Saturday night, the vigil of Sunday, after Jim and Darryl's St. Patrick's Day party, an afternoon of excellent food and spirited talk among journalists, politicians, and writers. Home we come full and happy and vital. We light a candle, sing "Come Holy Ghost" (the ancient *Veni Spiritus*) and Madeleine reads the Gospel passage from the Breviary. This prayer book, also known as the Divine Office or the Liturgy of the Hours, prescribes a set of psalms, hymns, New Testament readings, petitions, and responses for each of the various times for prayer.

Saturday evening serves as the vigil of Sunday, as was kept by the early Christians in keeping with the clock of Genesis—"evening came and morning followed, the first day"—just as Jews begin the Sabbath on Friday evening.

The vigil habit keeps us tilted forward to the day ahead, but in a pleasant, unhurried way. We pray that it be a day of joy and family and fun and worship and gratitude. The children and Amy mention their requests or blessings— time to play with friends, patience, no bad dreams, family. And so to bed. Each piece builds into the next. After such an evening, Sundays are more peaceful, perhaps only marginally so given the hubbub of getting dressed and out the door to church.

Normally we walk to church, our local parish, St. Teresa of Avila. Leaving the car behind magnifies the day's calm and joy. If we leave the house with some of us in a foul mood, we are usually at peace once we arrive. We enjoy the exercise, fresh air, the sight of neighbors' houses—though rarely the neighbors themselves, who keep other schedules or habits. Unlike the Puritans of New England who marched to church in a growing procession of dark-clothed families, we promenade in our own universe. Leaving the car or van behind frees us from 2,000 pounds of steel, rubber, and plastic, from a ton of matter we otherwise lug from place to place. We are free from Ralph Waldo Emerson's dictum that, "Things are in the saddle and ride mankind."

Simone Weil, the Jewish French intellectual who converted to Catholicism during World War II, believed that God created the universe then withdrew. Likewise, we should withdraw from material concerns in order to rejoin God. In leaving the vehicle behind we relinquish one possession, temporarily. Gravity eases and we float up.

When we walk to church, I sense a righteous calm radiating before us and to the left, right, and rear. Peace trails in our wake along the sidewalks. But often enough we drive, in deep winter or to attend a more distant church. This

Sunday, we attend Mass at St. George's, the Black Catholic Apostolate. It was created as a home for African Americans from across the sprawling Diocese of Albany and is open to all. We loved the warmth and joy of the apostolate, a spirited mix of Africans, African Americans, Caribbeans, Hispanics, and Caucasians. Many members and the choir came to our wedding and the pastor, Father Kofi Amissah, witnessed the nuptials, baptized our children, and helped bury Amy's mother and sister. (We belonged for years before joining St. Teresa's.) Mass at St. George's is a long happy affair with gospel music and clapping and the warmth of old friends.

Sunday proceeds from the Mass. Pope John Paul II called us to mark the day, from start to finish, "by a grateful and active remembrance of God's saving work." Thus all elements—family, society, relaxation—should be shaped "so that the peace and joy of the Risen Lord will emerge in the ordinary events of life."[1]

After, we drive over to see Sister Liquori, an elderly nun we know at an old folks home, an "assisted living facility" in the bloodless phrase of the healthcare bureaucracy. At her lunch table we begin bouncing a blue balloon for Mitchell. Sister Liquori, who is bright eyed but moves little and barely speaks, lunges for it. Soon she is poking and slapping it in our round robin, smiling fiercely like Lazarus woken from his sleep. Then upstairs to see Sister Jackie, a friend from St. George's whose sharp wit is wrapped in Irish warmth. The girls dance for her and we all laugh. Amy drives off with Mitchell, who's still a toddler, and I walk home with Jeanne and Madeleine. The sun shines and our earth warms from winter's lingering grasp. Under the trees of New Scotland Avenue, where yesterday the Jews walked to and from their synagogues, we meet and chat with friends. We stop for a bagel, coffee, chocolate milk. Together, the girls and I walk through these 40 minutes of life.

Similarly, on a Sunday in May, we drive to Mount Greylock on the western Massachusetts side of the Berkshire Mountains. The ghosts of Thoreau and Melville haunt the woods. Thirty feet into the forest along a trail near the summit, I inhale deeply the pine- and hemlock-rich air. I stop. Divine air, our oxygen, fills me, renews me, and I, withered by the six days of work and self, expand to fill the soul God gave me.

A similar realization must have startled the first disciples, who were stumbling into a new religion as they broke away from the old. But then that business of separation and distinction immediately plunges us back into the profane world of doctrine and dogma. We are us by being not you. Yuck! Maybe the Seventh-day Adventists are right to say that all children of Abraham can be unified in the seventh-day Sabbath, instead of the Muslims meeting on Fridays, and the Christians on Sundays, which promotes their distinction from the Jews and division among God's many children. Fittingly, a Jewish friend reawakened my Sunday devotion.

Alan Abbey, a former colleague I profiled in a book on writers and faith, told me the story of his return to Judaism after growing up in the assimilationist atmosphere of post–World War II American Jewry.[2] It began when he spent a Saturday with a friend who showed him the basic mark of Shabbat: cessation. Then came to him, "the realization that you are part of something bigger than yourself," Alan told me. "We didn't go to the malls as everyone in New Jersey did. We spent this lovely spring day walking around the streets." They ate dinner together, said some prayers—and he was captured by the spirit that first animated the Israelites on the seventh day. Years later, the radiant calm of that day spread across Alan's generally sober and composed face. "I was at peace; it was a very peaceful day." He said that the Sabbath may have been Judaism's greatest gift to humanity. "The awareness that life and people are cyclical, that there are times for resting and sitting back and taking things as opposed to trying to make things."

I saw the gift in my own religion that had been there all along. Sunday came anew, Christ rose again and the sun shone on our life and family. I realized the great gift of my parents, who kept the day holy, restful, and special by example. And so the faith passed from one generation to the next in the living. In our home and family, a tone and habit has emerged or been imposed on the day Christ opened the door to eternal life. "This way," he whispers to us. "Hurry, now."

After Easter

Sunday was an innovation of the early Christians. Jesus did not institute the day. He went to the synagogue on the seventh day and spent much effort demonstrating the proper approach to Shabbat, to the consternation of his fellow Jews.

We can imagine the disciples, most of them Jews, slowly realizing that Sunday was now the important day of the week. More than other passages in the Gospels, the stories of Jesus' passion and resurrection specify Sunday in relation to the Jewish Sabbath. Mary finds the empty tomb and hears that Jesus has risen "after the sabbath, as the first day of the week was dawning" (Matt. 28:1–2).

The Gospels of Mark, Luke, and John all attest that Jesus rose on "the first day after the Sabbath." On the same day, the Risen Lord appeared to the two disciples who were walking to Emmaus and to the Apostles (Luke 24:13–35, 24:36, John 20:19). A week later, he appeared to them and showed his wounds to Thomas to prove his risen reality (John 20:26). And the Holy Spirit came upon the disciples on Pentecost, the Jewish festival that fell on a Sunday at that time (Acts 2:1, Luke 24:49). Pentecost, now also a Christian holy day, marks the birth of the church, when Peter overcame his fears and announced to the crowds of many nations that had gathered in Jerusalem that Christ was risen and that those who received his word were saved (Acts 2:41).[3] Salvation from sin and the "new life" in Christ now embody the promise of Creation. "The seventh day completes the first creation. The eighth day begins the new creation. Thus, the work of creation culminates in the greater work of redemption."[4]

As the central event in Christianity, Christ's resurrection from the dead also emboldened the disciples—scared and scattered after their leader's execution—to shift their attention to Sunday. Practically, they also needed a time to meet regularly to worship and preach the good news.

Early Christians continued to keep the Sabbath. Paul and others preached in synagogues then but also met among themselves the next or first day. For several centuries, in some areas, Shabbat and Sunday coexisted. It appears that some Jewish Christians would observe Shabbat and then, after sundown, rush to meet their co-believers in Christ. At dusk they would leave one religion to join another, if only to repeat the pattern the following week. But even this activity shows the different nature of the Lord's Day. First of all, traveling was allowed beyond the Jewish Shabbat limit of 2,000 cubits. And on Sunday, Christians met for the Eucharist but seemed to have followed their normal routines during the remaining hours.

Thus the weekly cycle of life for the disciples began to spin around this first day of the week. They began to gather for the breaking of the bread, in memory of Christ's Last Supper, on that day. Though this meal took place on Passover, the disciples shifted it to the newly prominent Sunday. "Now on the first day of the week, when the disciples came together to break bread, Paul, ready to depart the next day, spoke to them" (Acts 20:7). Paul tells the Corinthians to collect money for the poor on "the first day of the week" (1 Cor. 16:2).

The church's great missionary and first theologian, St. Paul, challenged this weekly habit. In his letters to early Christian communities, Paul combines an exuberant joy at being released from the demands and strictures of Jewish religious law with near contempt for its application in myriad rules and regulations. Paul dismisses all holy days or times and places; he spurns the idea that we earn salvation by punctilious observance; he declares that Christ Jesus redeems us by grace and regardless of our works or worth. If freed by Christ, why should Christians oppress themselves with man-made religious laws? Who are we to fetter God's love?

Christians are freed even from the Sabbath, the primary obligation of Jews then and now. Those who still keep it have not truly heard the good news. "You are observing days, months, seasons and years," Paul laments. "I am afraid on your account that perhaps I have labored in vain" (Gal. 4:10–11). Against his colleagues who were imposing Jewish law on Gentile converts, Paul carried the day at the Council of Jerusalem in 49 CE. Here the new church abolished the seventh-day Sabbath along with other festivals and purifications. But Paul has compassion and envisions a truly catholic church with room for all. He advises that we not judge each other, "For one person considers one day more important than another, while another person considers all days alike." But still, Paul continues, "Whoever observes the day, observes it for the Lord" (Rom. 14:5–6). This remarkable compassion should inform our practice today.

He and other disciples evangelized with a rash confidence, driven by the urgency of the kingdom of God.[5] Jesus healed on the Sabbath because God's time was and is now. "We must work the works of him who sent me while it is day; night comes when no one can work" (John 9:4).

Already in Paul's time, however, Sunday was the day. He visits Troas, where Christians were already in the habit of gathering for the Lord's Supper on Sunday. Also on that day while there, Paul heals a man just as Christ healed on the Jewish Sabbath (Acts 20:7–12). The man, Eutychus, fell from a window after he dozed off "while Paul spoke on and on," still a liability for homilists and church goers.

As Paul and other disciples spread the good news, Christianity spread beyond the Holy Land into areas where the Greek and Roman calendars and festivals predominated. Given their minority status, the disciples would meet before dawn on Sunday.[6] In Jewish areas, the end of the Sabbath at sunset Saturday enabled them to travel without suspicion on the eve of Sunday. As in Judaism, the church has always considered a day to begin the night before. Thus do Christians celebrate the Easter vigil and Christmas midnight Mass, and Catholics have vigil masses on Saturday evening.

But the Jews also prepared the way in non-Jewish areas. By the end of the first century, Josephus could brag that the Sabbath rest had spread to all cities and realms, Greek and barbarian. They assumed that a weekly cycle with one day off for rest was the natural order, which made easier a switch to Sunday. "The synagogue on Saturday, the church on Sunday," went the popular summary of practice even into the 390s when it was condemned in sermons in Antioch.[7]

In one of the church's many recyclings of pagan practices, the choice of Sunday Christianized it and drew people away from worshipping the sun.[8] Now Christ is the light of the world, the new dawn. Luke 1:78–79 echoes the promise of Isaiah in referring to Christ as the "light to those who sit in darkness and in the shadow of death." Similarly, Simeon greeted the infant Jesus as "the light to enlighten the Gentiles" (Luke 2:32).

In Gentile areas, ironically, the Christian cycle helped spread the Jewish seven-day week, another Jewish heritage carried forward and transformed. The "Lord's Day" itself is first referred to by John in the Book of Revelation. Though not repeated in scripture, the title is picked up by others. The Sunday habit was codified in the Didache, an early church manual composed from 80 to 140 CE. In 105, Ignatius says Christians should observe the Lord's Day and not the Sabbath.[9] It emerged among believers before the canon of the New Testament was accepted in the fourth century, much as Shabbat was observed by the Israelites well before the Torah was written.

Those who followed Jesus, the Jew who declared himself "the Lord of the Sabbath," felt free to make these changes. Their theological struggle was part of the larger process to codify the Jewish oral law through the writing of the Talmud. We glimpse in the Gospels the rabbinical debate of the time over the meaning and application of religious law. And just as the Christian Sunday emerged from Judaism, the emergence of Christianity, by and among Jews, helped shape the Talmud. Jacob Neusner makes this same point when he writes that "Judaism as we know it . . . was born in the encounter with triumphant Christianity, just as, in its formative century, Christianity had come into being in the encounter with an established Judaism."[10]

Meanwhile the Jewish sages were developing two notions of the Sabbath. In Palestine, Jews eager to preserve their identity under persecution interpreted the Sabbath as exclusively Jewish. They tied its inception to the origin of Israel at the time of Moses. But among the Hellenistic diaspora, the Sabbath is a universal ordinance established at the Creation. Philo calls it "the birthday of the world."[11]

In a way, Jesus taught the same idea but more broadly. For he was not arguing the details; he was recasting the entire institution. Love was the ultimate command, leading him to heal nonfatal illnesses or injuries on the Sabbath, which was subservient to God and His son. Jesus demonstrated an urgent love that cannot ignore suffering. "Come unto me, all who labor and are heavy laden, I will give you rest" (Matt. 11:28).

By the fourth century when the church chose the books that would make up the New Testament, it also instituted the Lord's Day. Christians came to consider the day divinely ordained.

Today in Catholic teaching, the commandment to rest on the seventh day originated at Creation. Christ changed and extended that concept by rising from the dead on the first day. Sunday then becomes, John Paul II wrote, "the full revelation of the mystery of the world's origin, the climax of the history of salvation and the anticipation of the eschatological fulfillment of the world."[12] Sunday celebrates the "new creation" of the Risen Christ. The rest promised to the Israelites as they entered the Promised Land is reread in the Gospels and Epistles of the New Testament as the definitive "Sabbath rest" that Christ enters through His resurrection[13] (Heb. 4:9). And so at the start of the fifth century, Pope Innocent I declared, "We celebrate Sunday because of the venerable Resurrection of our Lord Jesus Christ, and we do so not only at Easter but also at each turning of the week."[14]

The first Christians constantly wondered if they could follow Jesus and Moses. The Gospels of Matthew and John were written by Jewish Christians to convince other Jews that the Mosaic Law was fulfilled in Jesus. It was this divide, over the law and not the crucifixion of Christ, that led to the final split with the Jews and the emergence of a distinctly Christian religion. The abandonment of the Sabbath and the emergence of Sunday as the Lord's Day most clearly marked this divide.

Early Fathers

The leading thinkers and teachers of Christianity's first centuries, known as the church fathers, sought to interpret and apply the teachings of Jesus, much as the Jewish authors of the Talmud had done with the Torah. With regard to the Sabbath, the fathers strained to recognize the first-day practice of the common believers—those independent-minded laity!—and especially to justify the Lord's Day without reference to the fourth commandment as understood by the Jews.

Only a century after Christ's death, in about 140 CE, Justin Martyr observes that "On the day called Sunday, is an assembly of all who live either in the cities or in rural districts, and the memoirs of the Apostles and the writings of the Prophets are read." Particulars of the day include prayer, Eucharist, collection of alms. He lists the reasons. "It is the 'First Day,' on which God dispelled darkness and the original state of things, and formed the world, and because Jesus Christ our Savior rose from the dead upon it . . . therefore it remains the first and chief of all the days."[15] Justin speaks of life as a perpetual Sabbath, but that does not abrogate Sunday itself.

However, many also taught that Christ liberated us from the law and freed us from sin. The only Sabbath is a spiritual one. Clement of Alexandria taught that Christians should celebrate the Lord's Day through purity and self-knowledge. Origen extended this point and called Sunday a concession to weak believers. Such people, Origen wrote, "being either unable or unwilling to keep every day in this manner, require some sensible memorials to prevent spiritual things from passing altogether away from their minds."[16] Though church leaders could not disconnect it entirely from the Jewish Sabbath, they certainly tried. The Council of Laodicea in 363 condemned Judaizing the Lord's Day but also declared it was a festival and a day of worship.

During the first century, Ignatius of Antioch taught that Christians should not mar Sunday's joyful character by kneeling or fasting.[17] Justin Martyr tied it to the first day of Creation, in contrast to the Jewish Sabbath, which falls on the seventh. Other theologians associated Sunday with the Trinity and with the descent of the Holy Spirit on Pentecost.[18]

Fissures opened due to the uneasy balance between Christ's liberation and our all-too-human love of regular ritual. In the third century, Irenaeus, like Origen before him, called the Lord's Day a temporary and symbolic aid to devotion. But Iranaeus and other bishops acknowledge Sunday as the Lord's Day in practice. Under him the churches in Gaul, modern France, designate Sunday as the proper time for the Lord's Supper or Paschal Feast.[19]

At the start of the third century, Tertullian writes, "Sunday, we give to joy."[20] Penance is prohibited. Interestingly, some recommend fasting on Saturday, for penance but also to increase the joy of Sunday—much as the rabbis urged Jews to fast before the Sabbath so as to better enjoy that day's meals.[21] Yet Tertullian also makes clear that, "we have nothing to do with Sabbaths, or the other Jewish Festivals, must less those of the heathen."[22] Origen says that it is the sign of "the perfect Christian to keep the Lord's Day," but also that the Sabbath obligation is past.[23]

In these centuries after the death of those who knew Christ, the pressure for a weekly and sacred first day came from below. "While the leaders of the

Church gave no sanction to the idea that Sunday was the heir of the Sabbath, that idea was all the time gaining power among the mass of the Christian people in the West," writes one scholar. "Theologians long resisted it, but at last yielded, and sought for reasons to justify a practice which the people had adopted."[24]

Christians thus obligated themselves to Sunday as a holy day set apart from the profane world. The *Didascalia*, a third-century church catechism, urged on Christians. "Leave everything on the Lord's Day and run diligently to your assembly, because it is your praise of God. Otherwise, what excuse will they make to God, those who do not come together on the Lord's Day to hear the word of life and feed on the divine nourishment which lasts forever."[25] The first sentence echoes the spirit and structure of the Quran, wherein Muslims are told to leave their business and "hasten to the remembrance of Allah." While Muhammad likely did not read the *Didascalia*, he urged the same spirit of devotion.

The split between the Jewish and Christian obligation continued for centuries. In 538, the Third Synod of Orleans condemned limits on cooking as Jewish superstition. It was not until Charlemagne, and his numerous regulations, that the full Sabbatarian spirit was applied to Sunday. Among the church fathers, only Eusebius claimed that Jesus Christ himself instituted the switch to Sunday. The others, for the most part, preached the day as a spiritual Sabbath, sign and token of our new life free of sin.[26] This tension has yet to be resolved, most clearly in my life and my family's keeping of the Lord's Day. We yearn for God, but cannot stand too much divinity.

Meeting the Lord on Sunday

We encounter a manageable portion of divinity on Sunday. So before more history, a word about the day's centerpiece, the encounter with God through Jesus Christ in the Eucharist.

It seems simple enough: one dresses well for Mass. The instinct is deeply ingrained in society. We all know the phrase "Sunday best," and we certainly recognize people who are going to or coming from worship services by the clothes they may wear: the Jews on Friday night or, more likely, Saturday morning; Christians on Sunday morning. Muslims attend on a workday and so do not necessarily stand out beyond the tidy, scented, and dignified comportment inspired by Muhammad.

Yet my children seem unaware of this great juggernaut of tradition rolling into their lives. We appear past the worst struggles, but still it is often a challenge one to get out the door nicely groomed and dressed for church. Not that other Catholics always inspire in this regard. During the hair-down, post–Vatican II era 30 years ago, my Aunt Mary lamented the tendency of young adults to dress "like lumberjacks" for Mass. The affront seemed greater, no doubt, since her immigrant father found in his restful, well-dressed Sundays the fulfillment of the American egalitarian promise.

These deeper issues are often hidden by the perennial quibbling over attire and demeanor. In the late Middle Ages, a French observer captured the Sunday scandal in verse:

Earlier people were
Very pious in church,
On their knees in humility
Close to the altar,
And meekly uncovering their heads,
But at present like beasts
Too often they come to the altar
With hood and hat on their heads.[27]

Many of us look back yearningly to some mythical time when people carried themselves with a dignified joy at Mass. Perhaps they did so for a few years in the 1950s, or the 1890s, or during the Puritan rule in colonial New England, or back at the Last Supper. If so, it came and went, over and over. We always return to the old days to reinvigorate and reinvent religious rituals.

In our time, the Second Vatican Council renewed the ancient lineage of the Christian Sunday. "Every seven days, the Church celebrates the Easter mystery. This is a tradition going back to the Apostles, taking its origin from the actual day of Christ's Resurrection—a day thus appropriately designated 'the Lord's Day.' "[28]

Ideally for Catholics and Orthodox Christians, the Eucharist is the center of Sunday and their entire faith. For most Protestants, scripture and preaching may be paramount. Both schools share an inheritance from the early Christians and their Greek neighbors, who understood truth as an existential truth that lifts us out of this distorted world and up toward "the immovable One." Through the Eucharist, the reenactment of the Last Supper, and the lessons, the early Christians shared in the truth, the good news, of Jesus.

Jesus blessed bread and wine and shared it with his Apostles on the Jewish feast of Passover, which commemorates the meal of lamb, a traditional sacrifice, that the Israelites ate the night they fled Egypt. Catholics believe that the great saving act of God now shifts from the Exodus to the death and resurrection of Jesus.[29] Like Jews at Shabbat services, we also use bread and wine. The priest's preliminary blessing over these paraphrases that of the Jews. "Blessed art Thou, O Lord our God, King of the universe, who creates the fruit of the vine." The bread and wine, transformed into the body and blood of Christ, make believers immortal. Out of context that sounds odd, but we Catholics repeat it in our prayers at Mass every week. Death is the wages of sin because sin removes us from God. Christ reunites us through the Eucharist.[30]

Jesus is always present but on Sunday in a special way, at least by virtue of our heightened attention. One spring Sunday at St. Teresa, we stand outside under the magnolia and pine trees and we talk with Father Bob Longobucco, with Celine and Nicholas, a lively French couple from Lourdes, and others. Peace drenches us like a weightless rain. Amy turns to me with a laugh. "We should go to Mass every minute of every day."

For Christians, the Eucharist shapes Sunday and the week that follows. Christians participate in the truth that saves them by imitating God's rest after Creation, doing good works, enjoying this world, and feeding our souls. The Eucharist is the fountainhead "that feeds and forms the church," John Paul II wrote.[31] Further, at Sunday Mass, we relive the experience of the Apostles when Christ appeared to them on the evening of that first Easter, and again a week later (John 20:19, 26). "Peace be upon you," Jesus said, inaugurating the Lord's Day, when we have gathered ever since.[32] And so, the Catholic catechism teaches, "The lives of the faithful, their praise, sufferings, prayer and work, are united with those of Christ and with his total offering, and so acquire a new value."[33]

The earliest detailed account of a liturgy comes from Jerusalem in the late fourth century. The journal of a Spanish pilgrim named Egeria describes services that "on the seventh day, the Lord's Day," the people gathered before dawn for almost eight hours of scripture readings, hymns, prayers, sermons, and processions.[34] This corporate exercise was the focus of the day; no work or other activities were possible.

Thus, "the Eucharist makes Sunday and Sunday makes the Eucharist."[35] Worship was primary. Today Christians sanctify the day by abstaining from servile labor, which frees them to worship God with fellow believers around the world. On Sunday they are united across space. On Sunday they are one across time with all the Sundays stretching back to Easter and to the first day of Creation, as well as into the eternal future.

Sunday is not the Christian Sabbath but the Lord's Day, distinct and justified though trailing proudly spiritual and social vestiges of the Jewish Sabbath. On Sunday morning at Mass, I sense nothing if not the rightness of what the early church set in motion on the first day, when Jesus rose from the dead.

Goodbye to the Synagogue

For Christians, especially Jewish Christians, their new religion fulfilled the hopes and prophesies of Judaism. But most fellow Jews of the time felt otherwise. Despite efforts to harmonize conflicting beliefs, the break came. At the Council of Jannia (Jaffa) in 91 CE, the rabbis of Palestine expelled the Jewish Christians. As our opponents often see the truth of our position more clearly than do we, the rabbis realized there was no reconciling Christianity with Jewish law. Paul, almost alone among the early disciples, shared this insight. Within a hundred years, by the middle of the second century, Christianity was a separate religion.

Easter elevated Sunday and the disciples began to celebrate the Last Supper then. They then wrestled with the question of how to support this celebration. Time, or an entire day off made sense for practical reasons but also to protect the sacred from the profane. But would this be in the name of the Lord's Supper, or would they invoke the fourth commandment? What emerged was a bit of a muddle. God ordered rest, Jesus ordered the Lord's Supper. But at the time, Jesus also questioned the prevailing observance of the Sabbath. Thus the Christians felt free to switch the day in order to keep both God and Christ's commandments. Sunday remained preeminent by recalling, every week, the Resurrection. Indeed, the annual Easter holy day was not established until well after, perhaps by a hundred years, the Lord's Day.

Jesus returns to the commandment over and over, always reinterpreting it in light of his life and mission. But Jesus commanded only that the disciples celebrate the Last Supper. He said nothing about rest, nothing about the first day becoming the Sabbath. But as God sustains Creation every day, including the seventh, so Jesus declared himself able to heal on the Sabbath. "My Father is at work until now, so I am at work" (John 5:17). He was the Lord of the Sabbath.

The Sabbath/Sunday conflict embodies these tensions. These debates were, basically, internal disagreements between most Jews and those who now followed Christ. Here we see the choked, intimate hatred possible only between relatives.

On this basis were written some of the strongest passages regarding the Jews, some of which were later used to justify anti-Semitism. Given the fundamental disagreement, the divide only grew. Over the period when the Gospels were written—60 CE to about 100 CE—the animosity between Jewish Christians and Jews worsened. Mark was written first, then Luke and Matthew. Even among these, the tone was hardening. In Luke, John the Baptist calls the multitudes that come out to be baptized "a brood of vipers." Matthew has the same story but John applies the phrase to "the Pharisees and Sadducees" who come to be baptized. The Gospel of John was last, and contains some of the strongest language in this regard. Christians asserted an identity apart from and against Judaism especially in terms of the Sabbath.

God ordered rest but Jesus ordered the Lord's Supper. So Christians switched the day of worship and rest in order to keep both God and Christ's commandments. The contours were set by the middle of the second century when Justin Martyr wrote his famous description of Sunday in the early church. "On this day called Sunday, there is an assembly in one place of all who dwell either in towns or in the country; and the Memoirs of the Apostles or the writings of the Prophets are read, as long as time permits." Then comes a discourse from the presider and the congregation stands to pray. Bread and wine are consecrated and eaten. A collection is taken for orphans, widows, travelers, prisoners, and those who are ill.[36]

"We all of us assemble together on Sunday," Justin explains, "because it is the first day in which God changed darkness and matter, and made the world. On the same day also Jesus Christ our Savior rose from the dead. For he was crucified on the day before that of Saturn; and on the day after that of Saturn, which is the day of the Sun, he appeared to his apostles and disciples and taught them what we now submit to your consideration."[37]

However, Justin does not use the name Lord's Day. Neither does he mention resting nor cite the law of Moses. In fact, none of the church fathers quote Jesus to support the idea that Sunday has become the "Christian Sabbath," a phrase not used widely until centuries later. Only Chrysostom cites Moses in proposing that the church reserve one day a week to assemble for worship.[38]

A small sect of Jewish Christians who lived east of the Jordan River were declared heretics for following the Torah by keeping Shabbat. In about 135, Emperor Hadrian suppressed the Jews and their Sabbath keeping. This spurred Christians to differentiate their Lord's Day in practice, by settling on Sunday to avoid confusion with Shabbat, and theology.[39] As a result, the church developed a theory of Sunday that has, ever since, neglected or distorted its Jewish patrimony and confused Christ's relation to Jewish law. Among the Jews, their persecution by Hadrian confirmed the value of a portable, family-centered ritual that could be observed anywhere.

For Christians, the day remains built upon—or mired in?—the fourth commandment and Jewish law, just as Christians emerged from and still draw upon Judaism. It is a relationship as rich and tense as between father and son, or between an older and younger sibling. We are as familiar and as foreign to each other as cousins, as spouses, as believers in the same God who also seem to be from different planets. The relationship between a new religion and its parent always bears an Oedipal cast.

After the Jewish Christians died off, their Gentile successors made the break. They had to assert their own beliefs, the positive motivation, by distinguishing these, often negatively, from the Jewish beliefs. To follow Christ, they could no longer be Jews. The Sabbath provided a natural place to draw the line, just as Muhammad would a few centuries hence. The split that began with the Council of Jerusalem widened when Christians refused to participate in the Jewish rebellions in 67 and 130 CE.[40]

By the third century, Jews and Christians were legally distinct but a war of words continued, with each side slandering the other and trying to win converts. But the conflict was one between siblings, especially since many families had relatives in both camps. Judaism continued to influence Christian practice. In 306, the Council of Elvira required Christians to rest on Sunday, not Saturday, presumably so they could attend services. Similarly, they changed the direction of their prayer away from Jerusalem, that of the Jews, to the east, that of the rising sun, the symbol of Christ.[41] Centuries later Muhammad redirected his followers from Jerusalem to Mecca.

Today, the Catechism of the Catholic Church justifies the Lord's Day as an extension or transformation of the Sabbath. "The sabbath is at the heart of Israel's law. To keep the commandments is to correspond to the wisdom and the will of God as expressed in his work of creation." Then it declares, "But for us a new day has dawned: the day of Christ's Resurrection."[42]

Sunday Triumphant: Constantine and Augustine

Three centuries after Easter, the Lord's Day was enshrined in government edict and social consensus as Sunday triumphed in both the legal and theological realms.

Jews suffered through the conquests of the Greeks and Roman armies
and their public observance of the Sabbath waned, though most continued
the practice on their own. Christians had also suffered persecutions by the
Romans. But their lives had eased in Britain and Gaul under the rule of
Constantine, the future emperor. In 312, he won a major battle seemingly with
help from the Christian God and became emperor of the West. The next year,
he and Licinius, in the East, restored the rights of Christians and granted
religious liberty to all in the Edict of Milan.[43] As sole emperor in 324 CE, he
established the first day as an imperial holiday.

> On the venerable day of the sun let the magistrates and people residing in
> cities rest, and let all workshops be closed. In the country, however, persons
> engaged in the work of cultivation may freely and lawfully continue their
> pursuits; because it often happens that another day is not so suitable for
> grain-sowing or for vine-planting; lest by neglecting the proper moment for
> such operations the bounty of heaven should be lost.[44]

Constantine's motive remains unclear. The Lord's Day was well established
in practice but still lacked formal teaching by church leaders. Most likely,
Constantine sought to create time for worship in his newfound religion. Soon
enough, church thinkers such as Eusebius forwarded the theory that Sunday
fulfilled the Sabbath, which endures to this today.

Constantine also had a civic and commercial impulse. People can only work
if they rest, and we rest best if we do so regularly. And whether for Christian zeal
or imperial ambition, Constantine was only baptized on his deathbed but
apparently wanted all nations to unite in worship on the Lord's Day. He and
later emperors magnified the Sunday habit, from granting Christian soldiers
time to rest and worship to banning legal action on Sunday. Here Rome followed the Christians who had already stopped legal and business proceedings
on Sunday. Church and state support for Sunday continued for the next 15 centuries in a nasty cycle. Christians were first given time to worship, then church
and state required they do so.

Theologians of the age began to elaborate on Sunday as a portal to and
foretaste of eternity. Saint Basil said it symbolized the day without end that will
follow this time, and thus gives us hope and encouragement. Augustine
(354–430), the leading thinker of the church's first millennium, says precious
little about the Lord's Day until the final chapter of *The City of God*. Then
he describes heaven by evoking the Lord's Day and its Jewish heritage. "There

will be the Great Sabbath which has no evening, which God celebrated among His first works, as it is written, 'And God rested on the seventh day.' "[45]

Augustine seems to endorse the Lord's Day when he postulates that the sixth age of humanity is ending. "And the seventh shall be our Sabbath, which shall be brought to a close, not by an evening, but by the Lord's day, as an eighth and eternal day, consecrated by the resurrection of Christ, and prefiguring the eternal repose not only of the spirit, but also of the body."[46]

At the same time, he diminished the concrete practice by casting the Sabbath as an allegory. It signified not rest from work but rest from sin. If the Sabbath was a type, so to speak, it had been replaced by the Lord's Day. But the nature of this replacement developed into a controversy that continued into the Reformation and beyond.

Regarding the importance of Sunday, the church hierarchy tended to exhort rather than prescribe an obligation that average Christians, apparently, felt so strongly. Only later, when some neglected the day, did the church adopt specific canonical requirements from the fourth century onward. The Council of Elvira of 300 calls for penalties after three absences from the service, a three-strike leniency that appears in Judaism and Islam. By the time of the Council of Agde, in 506, these decrees were shaping a universal norm and tradition that became church law in 1917.[47] Today, Catholics are obliged to attend Mass on Sundays and other holy days.[48]

Church councils in the fourth and fifth centuries enforced church attendance and participation in prayers and the Eucharist. The Fourth Council of Carthage banned Judaizing and asceticism as a refutation of the joy of the Resurrection. The bishops also prohibited attending games or public circus as a distraction from the joy of worship.[49] During the same era, the Apostolic Constitutions, a compilation of church teachings, sponsored the Sabbath and the Lord's Day. "Keep as Festivals the Sabbath and the Lord's Day," they ordered. "Let the servants work five days, but cease from labor and be at church on the Sabbath and on the Lord's Day."[50] (As the theologian John Dwyer pointed out to me, this may be the first endorsement of the five-day workweek and the two-day weekend.) The leaders may have only acknowledged popular custom. Just as many non-Jews had already adopted the Jewish day of rest, so the masses must have liked the idea of two days off even more.

By then, and into the fifteenth century, the Lord's Day contributed to multiplication of festivals. By the time of the Reformation, by some counts, there were more than 200 holy days or holidays. Many of these were justified by

Jewish law and custom, just as the Lord's Day was often identified with the Jewish Sabbath.

Church councils veered back and forth in their teachings. The trend toward Sabbatarianism spread in Spain and France such that the Third Council of Orleans warned against popular beliefs that it was wrong to use horse or oxen, to prepare meals, or to clean house or even bathe. It was, the bishops said, an erroneous temptation to make Sunday the Christian Sabbath. Gregory the Great, in 603, inveighed against a too-strict observance.[51] He tried to steer the church back to the spirit of Paul's Epistles and the habits of the early Christians.

The Second Council of Macon in 585 displayed these twin impulses: Jewish precedent but Christian holiday. "For this is the day of perpetual rest," the council declared. "This is shadowed out to us by the seventh day in the law and the prophets."[52] The bishops threatened to punish violators. Even monks who transgressed the holy time would be shut out of their community for a spell. Still, the council recalled the happier side of the day. "Keep the Lord's Day, whereon we were born anew, and freed from all sins."[53] Nevertheless the Christian's joy at salvation appears incompatible with the burden that was increasingly being laid upon on the faithful.

The Letter from Heaven: A Yoke Descending

In the gathering mists of the Dark Ages, there appeared a mysterious document that surfaced in various forms over the next thousand years and shaped attitudes toward Sunday that endure to our time. In 584 or so, the "Letter from Heaven on the Observance of the Lord's Day" landed in the hands of Bishop Vincentius on Ibiza, a Mediterranean island off the coast of Spain. The author was unknown and many believed it fell from heaven on a wayward church. (In a marvel of sleuthing, German theologian Robert Priebsch pieced together the document's record.)

Christ's Epistle, as the letter came to be known, taught that people should keep or guard the Lord's holy day—"*custodire diem sanctum dominicum.*"[54] It demanded that priests preserve and protect the law "since there are pagans within the land who do not observe the law." One version specified that observance was binding from Saturday evening to Sunday evening, an echo of the Jewish Sabbath. Similarly, Christ's Epistle demanded complete bodily rest on Sunday and is the oldest church document to clearly replace the Sabbath with the Lord's Day.

The letter criticized the noisy behavior of people during Mass. Rather than attending Mass, people spent their Sundays in quarrels, in the market or forest, and in idle chatter. It also condemned the magic arts and the worship of field and forest.[55]

Christ's Epistle found sympathetic ears among bishops, who were in the habit of convening local synods to contradict their opponents. Meeting in Burgundy, the Second Council of Macon in 585 complained that "the people rashly profane the Lord's Day and, as on ordinary days, give themselves up to unceasing labor thereon." Comments Priebsch, "This was the sore that somehow had to be healed."[56]

From the pulpit came dire warnings. Sixth-century preachers in France and Spain, such as Bishop Gregory of Tours, told of calamities that befell those who profaned Sunday by working: the man who yoked his oxen and was paralyzed; the woman who gathered vegetables and her arm shriveled; others who were struck by lightning.[57] (A thousand years later such stories were a staple of the English Sabbatarians.) Many Europeans of the time admired the fidelity of the Arian Visigoths and their King Theudis. Christians all, these Visigoths were defeated by the Romans in Africa in 543 because it was a Sunday and they would not draw their swords[58]—just like the Maccabees.

In fact this stern spirit contrasted with the joy of the Jewish Sabbath during the same era. Augustine and other Christians wondered how their religious forebears could mark the day as holy and yet dance in their homes and eat and drink so well.[59] It was as if many Christians followed the rules but ignored the joy of Judaism.

A divide between sacred and profane opened up due to the early Christian emphasis on bodily purity. For the Gnostics and other Christians, the Sabbath was now contained within each believer, a nice idea that soon became a heavy burden for the human among us. (Among my Jewish friends, I sense that their sanctification of an entire day releases them from any obsessiveness about earning God's love in other ways.)

As usual with the Lord's Day, these bishops and rulers were following their flock. In France and Spain, many Christians had Jewish neighbors and in-laws. Many considered Sunday their Sabbath and adapted Jewish practices to it. More moderate voices prevailed, at least in the hierarchy. After reading Christ's Epistle from his pulpit, Vincentius sent the letter over the sea to his boss, Licinianus of Cartagena, who dismissed the tract and ceased its publication. Licinianus began preaching a more spiritual and tolerant version of the Christian's Sunday duty, as did others.

In 745, Pope Zacharius retired the "Letter from Heaven" to the Vatican archives. But that was his copy. People continued passing around the tract. Other seventh- and eighth-century councils continued the Judaizing of Sunday practices. Emperor Charlemagne hit back. His legal code, influenced by the church law collected under Pope Hadrian, forbade Christians from resting on the Jewish Sabbath.[60] In 789 he denounced the substitution theory and Christ's Epistle, but this only seemed to fire popular sentiment for the Jewish approach.[61]

Other civil rulers followed their subjects. In the spirit of Constantine they buttressed religion with civil law. In England in the late 600s, the king of West Saxon forbade all work on Sunday. In 743, the Archbishop of York did the same. The juggernaut gathered speed. During the tenth century, Edgar the Peaceable declared that the Lord's Day began at 3:00 PM Saturday and lasted until Monday at dawn.

Priebsch finds the Letter from Heaven cited in an Irish sermon of 884, which claimed it was given from heaven to an Irish pilgrim visiting Jerusalem. Much of the letter is repeated in an eleventh-century Anglo-Saxon homily, and its stern precepts appear in a Norse poem in Iceland in the thirteenth century.[62]

By this time, the Lord's Day is considered special for reasons beyond the Resurrection. On the first day, Christians then believed, God created the angels and will sit in judgment, akin to the later teachings of Muhammad regarding Friday.

By the Middle Ages, the church was waist deep in a quagmire that it first stumbled into centuries earlier. The Lord's Day stood alone as a holy day until the Council of Nicea in 325, when Christians began to develop a liturgical calendar and holidays multiplied and the special quality of Sunday declined. In response, church and state spewed minute regulations to bolster the Lord's Day, much as the rabbis had created "a hedge about the law" for Jews. But the church's effort backfired.

Strictness triumphed over love by the fourteenth century, when Tostatus, bishop of Avila, declared unnecessary labor a mortal sin.[63] What had begun as a proper demand among the faithful for a day of rest and worship had evolved into an institution supported by obscure theories with draconian rules enforced by kings and other rulers. This was far from the early Sundays dedicated to joyful worship and good works.

Jewish Joy and Persistence

The hectic changes in Christian practice contrasted with the more private, sober, and joyful habit of the Jews. Since they could not enforce their rules with civil authority, the Jewish people relied more on moral and theological suasion. In its obedience to rules that often have an otherworldly sense, Judaism often hints at the mystical.

Moses Maimonides, who lived from 1135 to 1204, taught that a Jew does not have to understand each command, since each inculcates some truth.[64] So, too, does Tom Kligerman often explain that many of the Sabbath and other rules his family follows are beyond his ken. He frets not. He simply obeys. Obedience bears a reward that confirms practice. Jewish law has a meaning beyond this world. To know and understand the law leads to obedience, and obedience leads to immortality. Rituals such as Shabbat, circumcision, and kosher diets enmesh Jews in three cycles: that of the year, the week, and of the believer's life.

Since the final destruction of the Temple in 70 CE, the Sabbath had deepened and evolved or, we should say, the sages had explored and charted its depths and riches. (As in Christianity and Islam, God is unchanging but we learn more about Him as time passes.) In the first century, Philo argued that Moses banned physical labor but allowed study and teaching. After six days of bodily effort, the soul has its turn on Shabbat. Abstention from labor sanctifies the day, but also leads the Jew toward a higher spiritual state.[65] A story from the Talmud tells of a man who decides to fix a crack in his garden wall on the Sabbath. He repents of that mere thought of labor by never doing so. Instead, he memorializes the change of heart by, later, planting a caper tree in the wall. It flourishes and supports him with its fruit for the rest of his life.[66] One lesson: the seemingly impractical discipline of rest bears rich rewards.

On the Sabbath, we accept God's love by not grabbing for it. This view of the law, as a discipline that deepened the experience of Shabbat rest by opening one further to God's blessing, is a far cry from Paul's view of Jewish regulations as a burden that obscured God's love.[67]

The sages bequeathed two happy themes of the Sabbath to the centuries of practice that stretched into Middle Ages. One was a joy in the experience. The Talmud tells of Caesar asking why Sabbath food was so fragrant. A rabbi says there is a special spice called Sabbath, and the emperor asks for some. Alas, the rabbi replies, the spice only works for those who keep the Sabbath. The other blessing, presented by Isaiah and repeated by Philo, was that Shabbat transcends nations and graces all humanity.

This aspect has remained in tension with the idea of the Sabbath as a gift to Israel alone. I sense it too, when I consider our haphazard Sunday practice, often kept in contrast to even other Catholics, with the certain habits of the Kligermans and other families at Temple Israel. In one painful moment, I

described our Saturday evening prayers to a Jewish friend. Though not observant, she still gasped at what seemed to her a grab-bag approach. Every Jew
to some extent has some idea of what to do for Shabbat. Medieval Judaism
persisted among families and local communities without a hierarchy or even
regular rabbinical assemblies.[68] "When you're scattered around the world,
you really are on your own," Tom Kligerman tells me.

Medieval Jews turned back to the Talmud's Sabbath teachings and elaborated on these. Shabbat receives 38 chapters in the Code of Maimonides and
175 sections in Joseph Caro's 1565 code of Jewish law, the Shulhan Aruk.
Maimonides urged Jews to remember the purpose of the Law, which was given
not "to bring austerity into the world, but compassion, mercy and peace."[69]
Also at this time, some Jews developed the mystical school of the kabbalah,
which elaborated the mystical glories of Shabbat. In 1540 or so, the kabbalist
Solomon Alkabetz composed the poem "Lekha Dodi," still sung in synagogues
and homes to welcome the Sabbath on Friday evening.[70]

> Come, my friend, to greet the Bride, let us receive the Sabbath!
> The One God declared "Observe" and "Remember" as one word
> The Lord is one and his name is one; name, glory and praise
> ....
> Come forth to greet the Sabbath, for she is the fount of blessing
> Cast for ever from the beginning, final deed in pristine thought
> ....
> My people, shake free of the dust, don your beautiful robes,
> Draw near to my soul.

This mystical joy both suited and contrasted with the underground nature of
Jewish life, made such by the growing persecution by church and civil authorities.
Jews kept the cycle of the week and year in tight-knit communities led by rabbis.
Many in Europe died as martyrs rather than convert during the Crusades in the
eleventh and later centuries. There was a great slaughter of Jews in the period
from 1348 to 1400. Survivors moved into special Jewish quarters or ghettos, but
even there they kept their customs and took "a special delight in Sabbath strolls."[71]

Jews fared better in Islamic lands, notably Andalusian Spain, where their
culture and faith flourished. It worsened when radical Muslims assumed control then improved under the Christian Reconquista of Spain. Then, in 1391,
thousands of Jews were killed in riots and others forcibly baptized, before all
who refused conversion were banished after 1492.[72]

During the Spanish Inquisition, many Jews were forced to convert but continued Sabbath habits such as lighting candles and preparing food, albeit secretly, on Fridays. These *conversos* display the persistence of Jewish practice, and especially Shabbat, when subsumed in a hostile religion. Centuries later and even today, many descendants of conversos in Spain, Portugal, and, by some reports, Mexico and the American Southwest, repeat these habits. In his wonderful book, *Diaspora: Homelands in Exile*, French photographer Frederic Brenner depicts some of these descendants in Belmonte, Portugal, lighting Shabbat candles inside a cupboard in 1989.

Their secret practice bespeaks the Sabbath instinct of Jews. It also serves as an analogy for the persistence of Jewish influence on the Christian Sunday and the Muslim Juma. The Inquisition records show that women were more likely to be persecuted for Sabbath practices, indicating the domestic nature of the practice. Once they lost the synagogue or community life, men had fewer outlets for practicing Judaism discretely.[73]

The Christian taste for the Sabbath arose, in part, from proximity. In many areas Christians and Jews socialized, dined together, and even married (as in my and many American neighborhoods today). Many Christians respected the Jewish Sabbath. In 500, the Council of Agde sought to stymie Judaizing among Christians by requiring that they fast during Lent on Saturdays, when Jews were having their weekly feast.[74]

Maimonides, whose best-known work is *Guide of the Perplexed*, brought the endlessly adaptable nature of Judaism to new heights. Influenced by early Greek and also Muslim philosophers, he taught that spirituality or faith can be supported by reason, a popular medieval idea. Wisdom begins with our recognition of God. Maimonides deeply influenced Thomas Aquinas, Meister Eckhart, and others who in turn shaped Christianity into and beyond the Reformation. But there, alternating strictness and laxity prevailed more often than reason.

The Medieval Circus: Let the Good Times Roll

The internal tensions between the Lord's Day and its Jewish patrimony and the external debates over its nature and requirements worsened during the Middle Ages and came to a head during the Reformation.

Medieval church courts adjudicated violations of Sunday rules, notably attendance at services, but with some flexibility. In England, for example, the

Council of Clovesho in 747 banned work other than preparing food. Travel was allowed "on the condition that he hear his mass and neglect not his prayers."[75] The rules promoted worship first, and rest as a means to that end, much as among the first Christians but now with the force of law. In 1448, markets were banned on Sundays and other holy days. Activity for the commonweal was allowed, in the spirit of the Maccabees. Under Richard II in 1388, a law required laborers on Sunday to have ready their bows and arrows for defensive action.

The strict conditions established over these centuries were absent from the life of the early Christians. The Eastern Churches continued in that more liberated spirit and by the end of the fourth century, their Sunday had become a festival day with a divine service. Christ's Epistle did not achieve universal acclaim.

The Council of Orleans encouraged rest and worship, but declared that Sabbath restrictions are of Jewish not Christian religion. In some lands or regions, Sunday was given to worship, rest, and recreation, despite periodic complaints that many believers resumed their labors after church services.

At another extreme, some sects followed the message of St. Paul rigorously and rejected all feasts and special days such as the Lord's Day. These included the Petrobussians in the Pyrenees in the twelfth century, the Waldenses in thirteenth-century France, and the Lollards in fourteenth-century England.[76] All these were condemned as heretics.

In the mainstream, Sunday was firmly ensconced, overloaded with rules, and often neglected. Ecclesiastical Sabbatarianism grew as believers turned away in frustration. As the Reformers later observed, the devil sometimes undoes by overdoing. "The profanation of daily religious practice was almost without bounds," writes Johan Huizinga.[77] Sunday suffered as other holidays proliferated. Civil authorities and landowners began demanding the church cut back since the peasants were too often away from the fields.

The trend toward such strict regulation of the Sabbath produced some schizophrenia: plenty of rules, plenty of exceptions. Even public devotions, while popular, were often too popular and overdone. Cause for scandal was all around. One anonymous homilist in 1560 intoned that, "God was more dishonored, and Deveil better served on the Sunday, than upon all the days in the week beside."[78] The rules for Sunday must have been neglected if the church councils had to reiterate these over the centuries.

Abuses of the Lord's Day grew. "From 900 till the Reformation there was practically no limit set to the amusements of the people on Sunday," Huizinga concluded.[79] Contemporary observers recorded a return to business and re-creation after services, if these were attended at all, in England as well as most of Europe. And after the thirteenth century, church authorities began to grant more and more dispensations from all the strict rules they had made, such as attendance at Sunday Mass. Teaching and practice swung back and forth. The term "Christian Sabbath" was finally coined in twelfth-century England. In 1201, the abbot Eustace of Flay campaigned for its strict keeping.[80] Kings were quick to follow, banning markets in 1237, bodily labor during the mid-1500s, and various sports and amusements in 1625. (The Lord's Day law of the late 1600s, which mandated observance and banned commerce and labor save acts of charity or necessity, was carried to the American colonies.)[81]

During the 1400s and early 1500s, many in England skipped church but attended games, fairs, dances, church fundraisers that sold local ale (church ales), and blood sports such as bear baiting in which dogs were set against the larger mammals. Devout souls complained that even those who attended services wandered in and out before rushing off to their entertainments. Some of this makes sense, since most people worked long hours for six days and had only one to rest.[82]

The divide between social and religious obligations among believers persists. Today, when most in the developed world, and many even in poorer nations, have adequate leisure, a good number of us run from services to a Little League game or shopping or even to our coffee and newspaper.

In such a climate, a reaction was building. First came evolutions in theology. Thomas Aquinas tried to smooth out the contradictions and uncertainties regarding the Lord's Day. He argued that the fourth commandment required time set apart from labor, the moral element that was also rooted in natural law, but that the choice of the seventh day was merely ceremonial. With the law ended by Christ, the church could choose another day. He acknowledged the long precedent, which justified continued observance.[83] This position was further developed by others, but first came the break with Rome and the Sunday of the medieval church.

The Reformation

The Protestant Reformation began in 1517 when Martin Luther, a German priest and professor, produced his "ninety-five theses" questioning church authority and doctrine. The movement to reform Christianity, and the subsequent Catholic Counter-Reformation, convulsed Europe until 1648. Reformers emphasized the primacy of faith and scripture and devalued the role of church tradition and hierarchy. In this process, some Protestants transformed Sunday from a casual combination of Mass and relaxation to the Sabbatarian Lord's Day of the Puritans.

The theology of the Lord's Day evolved as a test case. Some early Reformers extended Aquinas' reasoning that the day could be any of seven. William Tyndale in England argued that Christians could move it further, to Monday, or double the days, or abolish it altogether. In this uncertain atmosphere, public practice and civil laws fluctuated from extreme to lenient. In 1542, servants were allowed to play cards or tennis. Five years later the king ruled that the day was to be given wholly to God.[84] Later Anglican Church leaders called Sunday "our Sabbath" and tightened the rules while Queen Elizabeth and James I encouraged lawful amusements.[85]

To correct the errors of Rome and live by God's word, the Reformers turned to the Bible. Led by Luther and John Calvin, they taught the entire Bible as true and binding. Scripture became the measure of faith and the church.

By and large, Christians consider the Bible as a whole. The Jewish scripture or Old Testament leads to and is fulfilled in the New Testament. Christ is the Messiah, and his love succeeds the law. But different schools of scriptural interpretation shaped how the Sabbath was considered and observed.

Luther was more Catholic than others in his approach to Sunday. He considered it part of the law that Christ had ended. But tradition and the practical need for a day of worship made the habit a useful one. Calvin preached a stricter Lord's Day, and deeply influenced the Puritans.

The Puritans arose in England, frustrated with the slow pace of change. Henry VIII split from Rome but was succeeded by the Catholic Mary Tudor. Protestants fled to Switzerland and studied Calvin's doctrines. They returned under Elizabeth I, who ushered in the Anglican age. Those who favored local church rule, also called Presbyterianism or Congregationalism, relied on the Bible while the queen and her bishops remained loyal to many Catholic traditions.[86]

The Puritans used the Bible, notably the Jewish teachings in the Old Testament, to justify the Sunday Sabbath. Their opponents, however, relied on church authority and tradition, saying the Lord's Day was instituted by the early Christians and lacked divine pedigree other than a loose connection to the fourth commandment. Both arguments contained internal contradictions that plague Christian teaching to this day.

Some resolved this doctrinal conundrum, surely enough, by blaming the laity. These spiritual weaklings could not live in the good news all the time, and so needed a special day. Martin Luther denied Sunday was the Christian Sabbath but said it was a convenient day "ordained by the Church for the sake of the imperfect laity and the working class," which needed the time to rest and attend Mass.[87]

The Sunday debate highlighted the Puritan reliance on scripture as the ultimate source of doctrine and the moderates' reliance on church authority and tradition. To the stricter Puritan minds, the Sabbath commandments in the Decalogue and throughout the Old Testament were simply true. The Sabbath became for Christians the sign and guarantee of their election by and covenant with God. Their model community was both the Israelites and the early Christians. To the Puritans at least, scripture made clear that the Sabbath had to be enforced as doctrine.

To those who argued against the shift to Sunday the Puritans responded in this way. The moral component of the fourth commandment was established at Creation. It is a day of rest and worship, but this could be any day. The seventh-day requirement applied only to the Israelites in their historical setting. If St. Paul, a favorite of the Reformers, objected to Sabbaths, he must have meant the Jewish or ceremonial aspect thereof. Thus, the Puritans glided to a Christian Sunday observed with the rigor of the Jewish Pharisees.

"All obstacles vanished before these zealous men," Peter Heylyn later wrote. "It was nothing to them that the New Testament distinguished the Lord's Day from the Sabbath. . . . Nothing that the early Church never appealed to the Fourth Commandment as a ground for observing Sunday."[88]

These hard-liners referred to Jesus' observance of the Sabbath while ignoring two points: he did so without proscribing recreation or socializing, and he moderated the strictness of Sabbath at the time. The Puritans called it the Sabbath, and often used Lord's Day, but disdained "Sunday" as a heathen term that evoked pagan sun worship.

In 1548, John Hooper was the first Reformer to espouse Sabbatarianism. Two major letters were issued on the topic in 1554, which became the birthday of the Puritan Sabbath. By 1570, Sabbatarianism was widespread in rural England to the dismay of church leaders.[89]

This was yet another instance of the grassroots support and hierarchical uneasiness toward the practice found in Christian and other religious history. Leaders uphold traditions but discount rituals and emphasize intellectual routes to God. Lay people, unmoved by such methods, embrace rituals that engage the emotions and the body. Essentially, the two sides differ on the best route to the spirit or soul. Yet believers often turn to rituals in reaction to their own perceived infidelity to God. For a time, popular preachers predicted tragedy for Sunday transgressions, an old theme. In 1578, John Stockwood promised God's judgment on such as those who attended bear baiting and other blood sports in London's Paris Garden. Five years later, while the bears and dogs were fighting, a gallery collapsed and seven persons died.[90] The penitent masses clamored for strict Sundays and Parliament assented. Queen Elizabeth held them off, but only for a time.

On the Continent, the Catholic Church worried over the neglect of Sunday. The sixteenth-century councils of Milan, Rheims, and Narbonne lamented the day's profanation by markets, dice, sports, witchcraft, theater, dancing, and singing.

From the ferment of the Reformation erupted the book that created the Puritan Sabbath and shaped Sunday for centuries. Nicholas Bownd, a Cambridge-educated minister, published *The Doctrine of the Sabbath* in 1595, with a later edition in 1606.[91] This work consolidated and renewed, rather than pioneered, the relevant scripture and tradition regarding the Lord's Day. The major flaw was in his tortured case, based solely on scripture, for switching from the seventh day to the first. He here conflicted with Calvin, who respected Sunday but taught, with St. Paul, that Christ abolished the Sabbath. Nevertheless, Bownd persuaded many to strictly keep a 24-hour Lord's Day as the Christian Sabbath.

The Lord's Day, Bownd wrote, "is to be consumed and spent" in "the ministry of the Word, sacraments, prayer, and all other parts of his holy discipline and government."[92] One cannot do this alone, but must join with others in the sacred assembly where there must be preaching. "We must be present also at the reading of the Word, common prayer, and administration of the sacraments from the beginning to the end," Bownd insists, in a rebuke to legions of Jewish, Christian, and Muslim latecomers. (Some latter-day Catholics, I must confess, consider a sufficient Mass to last from the Gospel to communion.)

Bownd's book consolidated the Sabbath as a system. His major points were as follows: the commandment is moral and perpetual; other things Jewish fell away but this remained as changed; rest is required but must be careful and exact; scholars and lawyers should not pursue their books and arguments; government officers and judges are to rest; churches should ring one bell only; no feasts nor weddings should be held; all recreations were forbidden; and the faithful should not speak of pleasure or worldly matters. It is, however, a day for the Eucharist and baptism.[93] For all his rules, large and small, Bownd exhaustively cites scripture, the church fathers, and early Reformers as John Calvin.

Bownd's conviction, that to profane the Sabbath was to profane God, gave rise to the seriousness with which Puritans and their descendants, into the twentieth century, prosecuted violations. The book's impact was dramatic, especially in reaction to the laxity of Late Medieval Catholicism. In England and then elsewhere, Sabbatarianism seized the populace. After a ban on Puritan publication ended in about 1640, a flood of similar works followed Bownd's.[94] The laity embraced the fourth commandment as if for the first time.

Later thinkers considered it incredible that the Lord's Day, so quickly and thoroughly, "began to be precisely kept, men becoming a law to themselves, forbearing such sports as yet by statute permitted."[95] Soon churchmen were preaching that to work on the Sabbath was as great a sin as to kill or commit adultery.[96]

The fate of John Trask illustrates the era's severity. A traveling preacher ordained in 1611, Trask was convinced by a follower's epiphany to keep the seventh day. He soon insisted on all Jewish holidays and diet and, as if to drive home his point, demanded followers work on Sunday. He was arrested in 1618 for making "the people of God, his majesty's subjects, little better than Jews." They whipped Trask, nailed one ear to a pillory and branded him as a Jew. He was released, then whipped on his way to another pillory, to which his other ear was nailed. Imprisoned for life, he recanted and was released. His wife, Dorothy, however, remained firm and spent 25 years in jail keeping Saturday, the seventh day of the week, as the Sabbath and refusing nonkosher foods.[97]

The Trasks were not the first or last Christians to keep the Seventh-Day Sabbath. Their successors in today's Seventh-day Adventists and Seventh Day Baptists claim a pedigree dating from the early church and through the German Anabaptists of the sixteenth century, against whom Martin Luther inveighed. Such contingents have remained a minority, though their faith and embattled consciousness have produced some of the best scholarship and theology on the topic.

Those pressing a joyless cast on Sunday aroused resentment. During a royal tour, commoners complained to King James who defended Sunday amusements. In 1618, James issued his *Book of Sports*, allowing Englanders to pursue athletic games, parish parties, and lawful pastimes after Sunday services. James ordered the tract read in churches, but dissenters refused and it was not enforced. Positive commands—do good, love your neighbors, enjoy God's creation—are invariably more difficult to enforce than the negative ones. The *Book of Sports* did, however, help drive some Puritans to Holland.

As for the Trasks, King James likely approved their persecution in order to signal his displeasure with the Puritans.[98] But the reformers, and some part of the populace, carried the day, often using Sabbatarianism to express their anti-Catholicism. They legislated their strict views through the Long Parliament and the Westminster Standards. In 1657, even necessary labor was banned. With the Restoration of Charles II, this law was nullified. But then the Act of 1677 once again restricted Sunday labor.[99]

Was the observance of the Sabbath impacted by politics? Yes. But even more so it was emblematic of the clash of positions on fundamental issues in any religion: God's law versus ours, discipline versus love, sin versus salvation.

Strict laws multiplied. Soldiers were sent out to catch idlers and strollers out of house or church on Sunday. Rules and exactitudes flourished, even more so in Scotland. Debates continued. Hundreds of books issued forth with the same arguments, pro and con, repeated and elaborated. For such tracts there was an endless appetite, as is the case for diet manuals today.

In a sign of the times, there is an amusing tale of John Knox, the Scots Reformer, who on a visit to Geneva allegedly finds John Calvin engaged in a game of bowls, a lawn game with balls that resembles the Italian game of bocci. This story shocked other Reformers and, yet today, some Presbyterians deny its veracity (thereby reinforcing the dour reputation of the Calvinist Sabbath).[100] After all, the Puritans knew that recreations on Sundays impeded their service of Christ and filled the heart with "froth and vanity."[101] As Calvin wrote, "If we spend the Lord's day in making good cheer, and in playing and gaming . . . is it not a mockery, yea, and a very unhallowing of his name?"[102] Instead, Christians were to worship God all the day long.

To the Puritan Sabbath, there were three reactions among Christian thinkers: some people embraced the doctrine as ancient truth, some thought it poorly grounded but to good effect, and others condemned the burden of Jewish law being laid on the backs of Christians.[103]

But to the Puritans, the Sabbath was the sign of a covenant between God and his people, they thought, for the Jews previously and now the Christians. They found England under King James hopeless and their pastors were often overruled and even silenced. To establish a New Jerusalem that would preserve the Sabbath in its integrity, the Puritans sailed off to the Americas, much like the elves heading to the Grey Havens at the end of the *Lord of the Rings* when their day in Middle Earth had passed.

"Some of our early Puritans who had taken refuge in Holland, after ten years in vain pressing for the observance of the Sabbatic Sundays, resolved to leave the country, where they had been kindly received and went 'to the ends of the earth' among the wilderness of America, to observe 'the Lord's day' with the Jewish rigors."[104]

CHAPTER V

Islam's Day of Judgment

Juma at the Hospital

One Friday in February, the world raw and bright outside, Shamim Haqqie appears just before noon in the lobby of Albany Medical Center Hospital. He nods a greeting and we shake hands. He turns and strides low and quick and tilted forward down a corridor crowded with patients, dazed visitors, maintenance workers with ladders and tool belts, secretaries making lunch plans, and doctors checking their beepers on the fly. "I've been running all morning seeing patients. I must cover a mile." We arrive at the congregation room, actually the lower level of the hospital chapel. Half the ceiling is open to the upper level in a seeming oversight that achieves an architectural transcendence.

White sheets cover the floor. A dozen men pray while others stand to the side removing their shoes. Several women kneel in their section off to the left rear, and three chairs are set aside for infirm members. Individually, some pray in the universal cycle of movement: they stand facing toward Mecca, and cup their hands behind their ears and say, "Allahu Akbar," or "God is great," then bend with hands on knees while saying, "*Subhanallahi-Lazeem*," or "Glory to God," then prostrate themselves to press their heads on the floor, sit back on their heels, prostrate again, and then stand. It is Juma, the day Muhammad singled out as "the Master of the days."

Asgar Saleem, a slight, bearded man in a lab coat, appears at the last minute and calls our attention. He issues the Adhan, or call to worship, all in Arabic.

He says, "Allahu Akbar," four times, then the *shahada*, or profession of faith, "There is no god but God and Muhammad is His Messenger," and then "Come to prayer," "Come to success," and "God is great," each two times, and finally but only once, "There is no god but God." (At dawn prayers, the Adhan contains a seventh phrase, inserted in the middle, "Prayer is better than sleep.") People then sit.

He then delivers a sermon on the hajj, the annual pilgrimage to Mecca by Muslims that is currently underway. Saleem is a doctor-in-training who is considered the most learned among this gathering, so he often leads the Friday prayers. "For ten days, our brothers and sisters have been performing the rites of the hajj. Last week, we spoke of *say* (the running) which is an affirmation of faith."

In the main event of the hajj, the believers circle the Kaaba ("cube" in Arabic), a small square building said to have been built by Adam, under an equivalent Kaaba in heaven, and rebuilt by Abraham, known as Ibrahim to Muslims. Muhammad cleansed it of pagan idols and directed daily salat toward it. Located in the center of the great mosque, the cloth-covered Kaaba is entered only once a year. Afterwards, pilgrims leave the mosque, left foot first, to perform say. They climb the hill of Safa, pray, and then run across a valley to Mount Marwa, where they again pray facing toward the Kaaba. The ritual recalls the ordeal of Hagar, Abraham's wife according to the "sound tradition" of Muhammad, and their son Ishmael, who were sent into the desert by Sarah, Abraham's wife according to Jewish scripture. According to Islamic tradition, Hagar's water ran out and she feared for her son's life. She ran between the two mountains seeking water, which later began to flow from a well at Zamzam.

Saleem tells me later that Hagar ran seven times from one to the other. "She knew that God would provide, but she also acted." During the service, he tells the congregation the lesson. "True faith follows with action." He asks us to remember the pilgrims, then making *dhikr*, or the nightlong vigil of supplication to Allah, on the Plains of Arafah. "There are so many things for us to be doing." At this point, I sag inside. Saleem speaks in such a breathless and earnest manner that I feel worn out with duties unfulfilled, duties never to be fulfilled, and duties never even contemplated. He continues. "But how many times in our lives do we forget?"

Shamim sits attentively in the congregation of 21 men and 4 women, the senior physician being instructed by the medical resident. It affirms the stern egalitarianism of Islam: all bow to Allah and listen to those who spread His message. This small group in a hospital chapel worship in concert with their proxies who have traveled to Mecca to reenact the rites instituted by Muhammad.

Asgar Saleem tells us that the pilgrims are on the tenth day of the hajj, Id al-Adha, when they throw stones at a rock called Jamrat al-Aqaba, in Mina, that represents Shaitan, or Satan. "Not only are they stoning the devil but things in them that hold them back . . . Abraham was willing to sacrifice his son because Allah asked him. . . . How are you going to connect with the whole world and the situation of Muslims if you are not able to get up early and make dhikr, to make sacrifices?"

He folds his hands and looks down for a moment, then ends by reciting some prayers in Arabic. We line up, foot to foot, shoulder to shoulder. The solitude of contemplation now shifts to the physical reminder that we are in this together. "Allahu Akbar," he says, then recites the seven verses of the first chapter of the Quran, the Al-Fatiha. "Praise be to Allah, the Cherisher and Sustainer of the Worlds; Most Gracious, Most Merciful; Master of the Day of Judgment. You do we worship, and Your aid we seek. Show us the straight way, the way of those on whom You have bestowed Your grace, those whose [portion] is not wrath. And who go not astray." The imam then adds another portion of the Quran.

We bow with our hands on knees, kneel, and prostrate ourselves, then sit back on our heels in a half-kneeling position, then prostrate again, and sit back.[1] This is one raka, "bending" or unit. Normally, noon prayers involve four rakas (or *rakatin*). But the communal prayer on Friday involves only two, perhaps to leave time for sermon or because of the special merit of group worship. Individuals typically perform more on their own before or after the service, much as Catholics may arrive early or stay late after Mass to pray in silence or to say the rosary in a small group. After the final raka, and while still kneeling back on their heels, the men and women profess their faith once again, say a prayer upon Muhammad, then look to their neighbors on each side and say, "*Assalamu Alaikum*," or "Peace be upon you." The service has lasted about 40 minutes.

About half the worshipers stay on to pray, while the others rise and quickly slip on their shoes and jackets or lab coats as they catch up with one another and then rush back to patients or clinics or offices. Shamim says goodbye with a brief nod that also asks if we are done. There are sick people who need his attention.

Muhammad Gathers the Community

In breaking his workday, Shamim follows the direction of God and the example of Muhammad who, 15 centuries ago, put Friday at the center of a religion. As he told his followers, "The best day on which the sun rises is Friday. [On Friday] Adam was created and on that day he entered paradise and on that day he was expelled from paradise. And the Hour will come to pass on Friday."[2]

Muhammad was born about 570 CE to a family prominent in the culture, history, and commerce of Mecca, but one that had come upon hard times. Their clan belonged to the tribe of the Quraysh, who later posed a challenge to the Prophet.

The harsh climate of Arabia matched the stark terms of survival, which required loyalty to one's clan and tribe. This solidarity resounds today in the internal discipline of Juma, when the faithful kneel, bow, and stand in unison, "foot to foot and shoulder to shoulder." Their moral and ethical code fulfilled the functions of a religion and required courage, patience, endurance, loyalty, and a willingness to defend the weak and defy the strong.[3] Other practices of the time were fulfilled later in Islam. Once a year, in a tradition dating to Abraham, pilgrims visited Mecca and circled the Kaaba, as did local Arabs on other special occasions; kept vigil on the plains of Mount Arafat; and threw pebbles at the pillars in Mina. Even before Allah spoke to Muhammad, these rites "seem to have been re-creative, helping Arabs to centre themselves and discover in symbolic gestures an eternal dimension to their lives," Karen Armstrong writes.[4]

Arabia was a hinterland to the imperial struggle between Persia and Byzantium. An ancient polytheism was practiced, often devoutly, centered on the Kaaba at Mecca. There was almost no Jewish or Christian presence in the city and little beyond. Arabs admired the sophistication of these religions—both monotheisms and both set in motion by Abraham—and were acutely aware that no such revelation had yet been given them. At the same time, they suspected these faiths as potential tools of the warring empires, used to reduce southern Arabia or Yemen to a vassal state.[5] At the top of their divine pantheon, the Arabs worshipped a high god, *al-Llah*. By the early seventh century, some began to believe this was the same God as of the Jews and Christians.

Muhammad's childhood was dotted with propitious moments, prophecies fulfilled, and recognition by holy men as the Promised One, much as the early life of Jesus and other religious founders as recounted in sacred texts. At the same time, Muhammad was orphaned twice, and then raised by a grandfather and an uncle, perhaps inspiring his lifelong teachings to care for orphans and destitute people. He grew up to be a successful and respected merchant. By the age of 40, Muhammad had begun making an annual retreat to the Cave of

Hira, on Mount Nur. Here he prayed and gave alms in accord with religious practices of the time.

On the twenty-seventh night of Ramadan in 610 CE, an angel appeared and ordered him, "Recite!" At first he responded, "I have nothing to recite," which suggests the sad loneliness of a new religion yet being born.[6] Despite Muhammad's protests that he was neither holy nor a scholar, and only after two years passed, he began to preach publicly as the revelations continued.

The God revealed to Muhammad was loving, and the earliest chapters of the Quran vibrate with a grateful joy. But Allah could also be impersonal, inscrutable, more like the God of the later Jewish prophets and less like the deity who walks through the Garden of Eden in Genesis, or yells at Moses in Exodus over Israel's infidelity. Muhammad had little exposure to practicing Jews or Christians, and he developed his monotheistic spirituality in near isolation. Later, he sparred more directly with the Jews of Medina, first with the attitude that he was correcting their errors and later in a rebuke that they resisted the truth of the revelation.

Muhammad presented a revelation, not a creed. It was to be accepted in a surrender that was confirmed in prayer and alms giving. Due to Allah, there is order instead of chaos. Muslims submit to His Law and have their lives similarly ordered. Rather than assent intellectually, one practiced the faith. As in Judaism and Christianity, orthopraxy or correct practice often matters more than orthodoxy or correct doctrine.

Despite the picture we have of desert-wandering Bedouin falling to their knees in *islam* (surrender), the religion was more a product of the city than of the desert, and specifically a city of commerce and finance. The first Muslims, largely drawn from Muhammad's relatives, met for prayers morning and night. Their break from custom and community became more apparent as Muhammad told his followers to abandon the old religion, an act that seemed to threaten the common welfare. Hostility and retribution mounted as the people of Mecca recognized the nature of Muhammad's bold mission.

In 620, Muhammad experienced his mystical Night Journey to Jerusalem accompanied by the angel Gabriel. On the Temple Mount, Moses, Abraham, Jesus and other prophets greeted them. Muhammad then ascended to heaven and conversed with God. His visions cemented the idea that Islam was the correct version of Abraham's monotheism and put the Holy City into the pantheon of sacred sites.

During this *miraj* to the divine throne, by some accounts, God told Muhammad to worship, or perform salat 100 times a day. On his way home he met Moses, who thought that was excessive and sent Muhammad back for leniency. After several such returns, God settled on five times.

In the same year, Muhammad met and converted six pilgrims from the settlement that later became Medina. These converts returned to Medina with Muhammad's instructions to meet on Friday afternoons.[7] Historically, this was when the Jews were preparing for the Sabbath. Some outside scholars argue that Muhammad retained a connection with Judaism or chose the day for practical reasons. Muslims reject the idea that the Prophet had any say in the matter since they believe the Quran to be the word of God. (By contrast, Muslim scholars claim that Jewish and Christian scriptures cannot be traced to Moses or Jesus and thus, while instructive, lack divine authority.[8])

But other Jewish habits seemed to follow. Muhammad ordered a fast, known as Ashura, on Yom Kippur. The Muslims, who were already praying in the morning and evening and sometimes at night, began to pray in the middle of the day, as did the Jews. And they prayed facing Jerusalem, which the Night Journey had revealed as holy. This was the first *qibla*, or direction for prayer.

By 622, Muhammad had 70 Muslims and their families escaped the hostility of Mecca by moving to Medina, and he followed shortly thereafter in a providential escape. On the way they stopped in the vale of Beni Salim and performed the first Juma. Thereafter, Friday was set apart for the weekly celebration of public worship.[9] Tradition has it that Muhammad also entered Mecca on a Friday, June 28, 622, and immediately performed the worship.[10]

Within a year, the first mosque was built, though with a niche in the northern wall indicating qibla toward Jerusalem. Muhammad began to preach that Islam was a return to the faith of Abraham, a faith free from the later divisions of Judaism and Christianity.

But one inheritance did appeal to him. Just as the Jews believe they are descended from Isaac, Abraham's son by Sarah, Muslims believe Arabs descended from Ishmael (or Ismail to Muslims), Abraham's other son with Hagar. In Muhammad's time, Arabian Jews believed that Hagar and Ishmael were left near Mecca, and that later Abraham visited and built the Kaaba with his son. The legend may have reassured Muhammad that his people, rather than spiritual orphans, were part of God's plan from the beginning. Later Muslim tradition has it that Abraham was ready to kill Ishmael, not Isaac, in the famous story of the sacrifice that God ordered and then aborted.

Juma figured again in the final break from Judaism. In January 624, Muhammad was leading Friday prayers when a new revelation led him to abruptly have the congregants turn from Jerusalem and face Mecca and the

Kaaba, the shrine that preceded all religions and became Islam's physical center of attention. It was a revolutionary move, albeit so prosaic. It was "a declaration of independence."[11] Imagine a small group of people in an oasis town little noticed by their neighbors or the world beyond. At a word from their leader, and reportedly after completing two prostrations, they stopped facing north and turned to the south.

The rotation returned Muslims to their pre-revelation focus on the Kaaba, which had no relevance to Judaism or Christianity. It returned them to the pure monotheism of Abraham, to the time before the Torah or the Gospels, to the time before God's religion had been split apart by fractious humans.[12] Certainly some must have objected. Maybe all but a few hesitated to change direction from that favored by all their ancestors and relatives. "Indeed it was a change momentous except to those guided by Allah" (Sura 2:143).

Yet, as they shifted their gaze to the new qibla, the world tilted toward a new monotheism. The Muslims found their own route, the original path, toward God. And the shift, a half turn for each person, embodied the discovery of a new way to God in a religion where a bow and a prostration encouraged and expressed spiritual submission.

The Quran presents these changes in direction—from Mecca to Jerusalem and back—as tests of discipline that would weed out the weak and obstinate. In Sura 2:144, Allah speaks in mercy and kindness, "We see the turning of your face (for guidance) to the heavens: now shall We turn you to a Qibla that shall please you. Turn then your face in the direction of the Holy Mosque." Jerusalem remained sacred to Islam, but the new qibla "enabled it to shake off the tradition of a dead past and usher in the era of untrammeled freedom dear to the spirit of Arabia," A. Yusuf Ali writes in his commentary on the Quran. Both the rediscovery of the primordial message given to Abraham and the founding of a new umma, a new Muslim community, under God made new ordinances necessary.

To the Jews of Medina, this act of defiance was too much. They made plans to get rid of Muhammad, much as the Pharisees found Jesus' take on the Sabbath to be an apostasy that imperiled the covenant with Yahweh that preserved them. For his part, with the change in qibla Muhammad acknowledged that he would neither attract most Jews nor fuse the two groups into one umma. By some reports, the Jews taunted the Muslims over the change. If so, it was the last thrust of the spear by a cornered warrior.

The confidence and identity of the Muslims grew apace. After Muhammad and his followers defeated the forces of Mecca at Badr, he instituted the month-long observance of Ramadan as a memorial of their victory and salvation. In the most violent conflict with the Jews, one that still reverberates, Muhammad ordered the massacre of 700 men of the Banr Quraysh, an ancient Jewish tribe near Medina. The women and children were sold as slaves. Karen Armstrong compares this act to those of the Jewish King David, equally merciless and also done in God's name. Though a millennium apart, the eras were similar within the development and history of each people.

But after 627 and into the twentieth century, Jews and Christians enjoyed religious liberty throughout the Islamic empire.[13] Despite the harsh criticisms of Jews in the Quran, the book still has many—some say more—positive passages compared to negative ones. By this time, in 628, Muhammad could be magnanimous. Only five years after their arrival in Medina, he and his followers and their faith were supreme in Arabia as converts flocked to their sides and into the mosques. For most, attendance at Friday prayers proved their allegiance and practiced them in the faith of surrender to God. Then and there, they bowed as one to Allah.

The Sources of Faith: The Person of Muhammad

Muhammad is the first and ultimate Muslim. Inspired by God, his life serves as a source of religion after the Quran.[14] The Sunna, Islamic custom and practice based on Muhammad's words and deeds, teaches that Muslims should imitate the way he spoke, ate, washed, ruled, and worshipped, thereby reproducing his life and presence.

One day I sit with Imam Sebkhaoui in his modest study: a four-shelf bookcase, two office chairs, a stuffed wing chair, a Formica-topped desk, and a window facing west toward the Hudson River. I ask why Muslims attend to the smallest acts and sayings of the Messenger. Sebkhaoui looks to the side, in a reverie, and quotes Sura 3:31, "If you do love Allah, follow me: Allah will love you and forgive you your sins." Then there is Sura 59:7, which reads in part, "So take what the Messenger gives you, and refrain from what he prohibits you, and fear Allah." And finally he cites Sura 33:21, "You have indeed in the Messenger of Allah excellent exemplar for him who hopes in Allah and the Final Day."

Sebkhaoui had been perched forward and now leans back slightly. "These three tell us that, A, Islam cannot be practiced without the example of Muhammad. The people of Quraysh said, 'Why would God send a human as a messenger?' and He answered them, 'If you were angels, he would have sent an angel.' B, Muhammad is a source of legislation. He understood from the beginning that Islam is a way of life. Muhammad served as a soldier, a trader, and a leader, which means that every action of his must be watched so we can follow. And C, Muhammad knew that you are responsible to convey what you have learned. You have to be careful—of course, he had no private life. Everything was reported about him."

Muhammad's teachings, acts, and personal bearing served as the basis for the mores and norms developed in Islam in the centuries after his death. These became the Muslim way of life. Faithful practice, and imitation of Muhammad, produced a distinctive Muslim identity. I have seen this repeatedly in the serene and gracious manner of Muslims from upstate New York to Manhattan to Amman, Jordan, and the Iraqi cities of Baghdad and Basra.

All his life, Muhammad led the congregational prayers on Friday, even when he was fatally ill and two companions had to help him walk to the assembly. (Suitably, tradition has it that Muslims earn a special merit if they walk to the mosque, just as Orthodox and many Conservative Jews still do.) This is another of the vividly human pictures we have of the Prophet, as an old, frail man submitting to God by keeping the weekly Juma.

He also left a legacy of benevolence and self-discipline, of being hard on himself but fastidiously concerned with the community's well-being. Muhammad urged those who lead prayers to keep it brief out of concern for the weak in the assembly. "When one of you leads people in worship, he should keep it short, for among you are the feeble, the sick, and the aged. But when one of you worships by himself, he may extend it as long as he likes."[15]

Benevolence brands Muhammad's practice of Islam. For while the Hadith, the accounts of the teachings and actions of Muhammad by his contemporaries, and subsequent jurisprudence govern all aspects of worship, intention counts most of all. "Every ritual action, including ablution, must be attended by a conscious expression of the worshiper's intention to perform the duty well and in purity of heart and mindfulness of what is being done."[16] Our intention validates each and every of our actions, even if those actions are also designed to shape our disposition. Thus, the Prophet himself appears to soften the volumes of restrictions and directions that accumulated since His death. What lies within also counts. As the Quran reveals, "God knows what is in your heart" (Sura 33:51). Similarly, Paul wrote to the Hebrews that God's word discerns "what is in the heart" (Heb. 4:12). Imam Sebkhaoui reminds me that both actions and intentions are important; faith must be expressed in actions.

The opening lines of al-Bukhari's collection of hadith recall the words of Muhammad on this note. "Actions are [judged] according to [their] intentions, and every man gets what he has intended." Perhaps this is why many Muslims, such as the Haqqies, seem accepting of disagreement. They take others at their word, for only God sees within and can judge. I have heard many Muslims, devout and casual, say the same thing. "Only God will judge, who am I?"

The Sources of Faith: The Quran and Hadith

In the Quran, God tells Muslims that He has spoken to them through the pen. Islam is foremost a religion of the book, as with Judaism and Christianity. The Quran is a work of poetic prose in 114 suras or chapters, not always arranged in the sequence of revelation to Muhammad. The first words given are Sura 96, "Proclaim in the name of your Lord and Cherisher, who created, Created man, out of a leech-like clot. Proclaim!" After a silent six months or a year passed, the rest was revealed to Muhammad over 23 years until he died in 632. The earlier, shorter suras tended toward ecstasy and gratitude, the later-revealed, longer suras were more practical and, toward wayward Muslims and obstinate nonbelievers, harsh. The passages were memorized and recorded by Muhammad's followers, then assembled into a canon under the Third Caliph, Uthman ibn Affan, who ruled from 644 to 656. The Quran has remained unchanged for 14 centuries.[17]

The Quran culminates a long line of messengers, stretching back through Jesus, Moses, and Abraham. Since its words are God's, reading and reciting the Quran provides the most direct possible contact with the divine. Many Muslims memorize some and youths often memorize it all as a rite of passage. The Quran generally provides principles, not specific guidance. The early Muslims needed more. So they collected in the Hadith (tradition or narrative) the sayings and actions and pious examples of the messenger, Muhammad's way or Sunna (custom). Saleem explains that the Sunna were passed along orally and then compiled 70 to 80 years after Muhammad's death. To be accepted, each teaching must conform to basic rules such as correspondence with other teachings and accounts and a documented chain of transmission. The words and actions of Muhammad elaborate the special nature of Friday and its observance.

The Quran has few specifics on when and how to worship and does not mention the five daily prayers, which later evolved. It does prescribe prayers "at the two ends of the day and at the approaches of night" (Sura 11:114). And it does mandate the gathering for prayers on the day of assembly, Friday. Hadith makes up for this seeming gap with long chapters on principles, details and practice.

The Practice of the Faith: The Five Pillars

Juma is embedded among the famous Five Pillars of Islam. First, the believer must profess *shahada*, that there is no god but God and Muhammad is His prophet. Then, Muslims must perform salat five times a day facing Mecca; give *zakat* or alms, a fixed percentage of savings; fast during the days of Ramadan; and, finally, make the hajj or pilgrimage to Mecca at least once if possible.

Salat is the second most important of the pillars, and Juma is its weekly, public, communal form. But whether private or public, salat has a prescribed form and is recited in Arabic. The five daily prayers—dawn, noon, afternoon, sunset and late evening—each involve two, three, or four cycles, or rakas. Each raka involves seven steps: facing Mecca and saying "Allahu Akbar"; reciting the Fatiha or the opening lines of the Quran; bowing while praising God; prostrating in submission to God; sitting back and continuing prayer; another prostration; then sitting back and praying silently. After the final raka, Muslims turn to the right (the favored side) and then to the left and wish peace upon their neighbors.[18]

Salat derives from an Aramaic or Syriac word that means to bow or bend. Imam Sebkhaoui notes its relation to an Arabic word for "connect." Worship is an act of connection and surrender. The body worships, the mind recites, the whole person partakes. Salat is the universal sign of being a Muslim. Sura 2 tells us, "Do not confuse truth with falsehood, nor conceal the truth knowingly, perform the salat and give the zakat, and bow with those who bow."

Further, "Prayers are enjoined on Believers at stated times." These times are not specified in the holy book, but they are practiced by tradition and custom at dawn, midday, afternoon, evening, and night. The exact times vary according to the changing times of sunrise and sunset. Importantly, prayers are expressly forbidden at the exact time of sunrise and sunset, as well as high noon, when the sun is at its meridian, right overhead. The reason: the first Muslims did not want their religion confused with sun worship.

There is also a way to worship. One evening, I ask Sebkhaoui about the order of prayer at Juma. We get no further than the word. "It depends on what you mean by 'prayer.' Prayer in Christianity is more like supplication. But salat is more than just prayer."

Salat is worship and differs from *dua*, personal prayer or supplication. The other type of devotion is dhikr, acts of remembrance of God. All three—salat, dua, and dhikr—are based on the example of Muhammad. Over time, these developed a formal pattern, especially the communal worship of Juma.

Sebkhaoui continues and leans in to me with his inquiring, certain expression. He looks to see if I am open to this marvelous truth of Allah. He has a long face with a sparse beard, light brown. He wears a white head wrap and robes of white and brown. "When do I pray? Anytime, anyplace, but I cannot perform salat at any time when I want to. I pray when I want to [but] *salat* has to be prepared and conducted at certain times."

Friday services follow a standard order, with minor variations based on locale, congregation, and imam. Believers who arrive early may perform several rakas alone, and then sit on the floor as they wait for the service to begin. It begins at noon, or 1:00 PM, or at a time that changes with the year's cycle if the congregation follows the official times for prayers.

After the call to prayers, the imam or other leader begins with a brief prayer that includes the phrase, "The prayer has started." Then everyone sits for the khutbah, which often has two parts, one in the standard language on living as a Muslim, a practical application of Islam, and the other a recitation of divine praise, often passages from the Quran in Arabic. The imam typically sits between these portions. Afterwards, he leads the congregation in two more rakas.

The opening prayer after the sermon is the first chapter of the Quran, which begins, "Praise be to Allah, the Cherisher and Sustainer of the Worlds; Most Gracious, Most Merciful; Master of the Day of Judgment. You do we worship."

All prayers are preceded by the Adhan, whose opening phrase is "Allahu Akbar," "God is great." The call is a vestibule leading into the worship of Allah. "It is said to enter the state of prayer, which is like a sanctuary, a sacred place," Sebkhaoui says. "Then, to exit the sanctuary, at the end of salat, we say 'Assalamu Alaikum.'" This greeting of peace ends the communal Friday prayers.

Clean for God: Ablutions

Intent can be shaped by actions. With ablutions, the Muslim purifies his or her attitude and spirit so as to be ready to surrender in word and deed. Before salat, the believer must wash with water three times the hands, face, forearms, top and back of head, neck, and feet. Right side goes first. An ablution remains effective, even for subsequent prayers, unless one has broken it by urinating, defecating, sleeping, bleeding, or touching another person with desire. After sexual intercourse or menstruation, a full bath is required.[19] The site for prayer must be clean. Most people wear nice clothes.

On Fridays, a complete wash is required, a special requirement in water-scarce Arabia at the time of Muhammad. As Azra points out, most people today bath daily. Still, Muhammad said, "Anyone of you coming for the Juma prayer should take a bath." This is repeated in several hadith, though others have it that a bath is required at least once a week.[20] On Fridays Saleem showers in the morning and puts on cologne that he reserves for this day.

Muhammad also told his followers to clean their teeth with the *miswak*, a stick with one end frayed that comes from the branch of an arak tree, which grows in Arabia. Muhammad used it during fasting and to freshen his breath before prayers. (Modern research confirms that its antiseptic qualities prevent decay and promote healthy gums.)

Some habits emerged from local practice rather than the word of God or Muhammad. The removal of shoes, Sebkhaoui told me, is a technical issue rather than a religious law. "At the time of the Messenger, peace be upon him, they prayed with their shoes on. When they built bigger mosques with beautiful carpets, it was unfit to wear shoes."

He refers back to the ultimate aim of the rites. A proper ablution, Sebkhaoui says, begins with the proper intent, that is, to purify oneself inside and out for worship and, ultimately, submission to Allah. Then, "You wash your hands, your nose, your mouth, your arms to the elbow, right hand then left. Almost in everything there is a certain order. To enter the bathroom, you enter with the left foot. To enter the mosque, you use the right foot, and you leave with the left."

"Ablution is not just a physical act, but a symbolic preparation for the act of worship, to be in the presence of God. You don't have to be extravagant in the use of water. If there is only enough water for your donkey or you to drink, to keep your car running on a hot day, then it is recommended that you use a dry ablution, with clean sand or a rock, that you touch with both your palms. You then rub your palms together, touch your face, and so on. The intent is spiritual cleaning, so that you go before God with a clean spirit."

One washes with prayers as well as water. Before Juma, "You should be in a state for prayers, from reading the Quran and reciting words of remembrance,"

Saleem tells me. Sura 18, The Cave, is recommended for reading. This chapter is a lesson on the brevity and mystery of life, which can be understood only through patience and knowledge and vigilance.[21]

The Assembly of Juma

Over sandwiches in the hospital's low-ceilinged, sprawling cafeteria, Saleem tells me about his embrace of Juma. "Some people tend to underestimate the importance of it," he says. Gathering weekly is critical, he said. "The scholars teach that we were created to worship."

Saleem traces a steady increase in his devotion to the ritual. He repeats the Quran's injunction that the believer is unaware of the full benefit of the day and points out the importance of being early. Saleem cites the hadith that an angel stands at the door of mosque recording names of those who enter until the imam begins, when the angel closes his book. Muslims believe that there is an unknown hour on that day when God will answer prayers.

In addition to Allah's command, some scholars say the choice of Friday made sense for other reasons. There are reports that the day had been one of congregational worship long before Muhammad.[22] Sura 62 does refer to the "Day of Assembly" as if it already was such, though ancient Muslim sources state the opposite.[23] The choice would fit new religion's pattern of reaching past Judaism as it developed to older indigenous rites, such as facing the Kaaba instead of Jerusalem. To this day, the man who leads Juma may, while delivering the khutbah, hold a lance or stick, an insignia of the pre-Islamic judges who would resolve disputes on market days in many communities of the ancient Near East.[24]

In any case, Muhammad told his followers to meet "on the day when the Jews prepare for their Sabbath."[25] Though Muslims began gathering to worship on that day from early on, by some accounts before they arrived in Medina, it was not revered by all even after they were more settled. One Friday during Muhammad's sermon, a Syrian caravan arrived in town and many of the believers ran off. Hence the Quran's admonition, "But when they see some bargain or some pastime, they disperse headlong to it, and leave you standing." This counts as one of the more humanizing pictures of the Prophet, founder of a great religion, standing alone at the pulpit abandoned by his distracted flock. Soon rules were added: ablutions, sobriety at prayers (and later total abstinence at all times).[26]

Over time, Muhammad became more severe regarding Juma. The day was paramount. He eventually preached a mandate stretching from the present until the end of time. "Beware of it that Allah has enjoined upon you as duty here in this place, on this day, this month and this year, till the Day of Judgment the Friday prayer."[27] In another sermon, the Prophet told Muslims that they "should give up the practice of discarding Fridays otherwise Allah will seal their hearts and they will be included among the slacks."[28] Yet a humanity prevails. Aside from women and children, also excused from Juma are the sick, travelers, slaves, cripples, blind people, those who fear oppression, and those hurt by the cold or heat.[29]

The mosque, or masjid, evokes the sanctity and the civil haven of Mecca, where combat was prohibited long before Muhammad. It also recalls the courtyard of Muhammad's house in Medina where the believers would gather to learn of their new religion. It is not church, but a building where the faithful gather. Muhammad told his followers that any place they stop to pray is their masjid. "For most of my life, most Friday prayers were not in a mosque," Saleem tells me at lunch. "When I was at [college], we held them in the student union, then in the armory."

Muhammad's square courtyard, open to the sky except for some palm branches to break the sun, was the first mosque. Most mosques are simple, open spaces with the eastern wall serving as the front wherein a niche or plaque indicates the qibla or direction of Mecca. There are no pews or places of honor. Everyone lines up in rows behind the imam by order of arrival. Muhammad instructed that no one was to step over others by moving to the front. When it is time for prayer, people fill in the empty spots.

For teaching, Muhammad used a palm tree stump as a podium. This was later replaced with the minbar, the open-fronted lectern. Imam Sebkhaoui told me that the minbar is generally used only for the Friday sermon.

Sects differ regarding the gathering. Some require a minimum of 40 worshipers. Shiites, as in Iran, believe that it should be held in only one location, usually a mosque, in each community. Though primarily religious, Juma was also political from the start. (Of course, Islam does not separate the two realms, and sees the religious fulfilled in the civil and Allah's will revealed in history.) Attendance showed a person had joined the fledgling Muslim community, and so it is today. Also, in the first millennium of Islam, attendance was a show of allegiance to the caliph or governor who conducted the service.[30]

Teaching the Faith on Friday: The Khutbah

From the start, Friday was an occasion for Muhammad to reveal Islam as it was revealed to him. He would also explain the implications of the Quran and the lessons for living in submission to Allah. The event allowed full scope for his oratorical skills as he established his personal authority and the claims of Islam. The sermon soon was established as a Sunna.

After the Prophet's death, the local leader or caliph, who also led the prayers, typically delivered it. Later, some leaders who recognized their lack of learning used trained scholars to deliver the khutbah. Most large mosques have an imam, learned in the Quran and Arabic, to lead and preach. If not, the community could pick one of their own, as did the doctors at Albany Medical Center, who chose a young medical resident for his devotion and insight. Still, the leader is not a priest and he relates to God the same as the others. He has no special power, sacramental or ritualistic, beyond the confidence the congregation invests in him either by election or response.

The khutbah continues as the medium for teaching the message of surrender to Allah. It is delivered in the standard language, or vernacular, of the community, though the prayers and passages from the Quran remain in Arabic.

The khutbahs that I heard at the Islamic Center resembled some of those recorded in Egypt by Patrick Gaffney, a scholar of Islam.[31] Certain themes recur in both sets: Islam's strength, unity, and harmony; the believer's eternal gratitude to Allah; the resentment of Islam by its enemies both named and unnamed; and a bemused wonder at the obstinate refusal of nonbelievers to see the truth and glory of Islam.

After the sermon, people rise for worship. Quickly and smoothly they align themselves in rows spaced so that they can kneel and bow without bumping into those before and aft. People fill in any openings in the lines before them. Women are typically segregated, since bowing and bending could be awkward in mixed company. Though the Quran appears silent on the issue, social custom and tradition also dictate segregation in most Islamic communities. Some countries exclude women altogether, and they pray at home.

Asgar explains that the choreography of service—shoulder to shoulder, foot to foot; the movements in precise unison—"is a physical representation of the unity of God but also the physical unity of humans. The idea is also for us to help each other in the worship of God." The movements of Juma repeat those of Muhammad when he led prayers nearly 14 centuries ago. "There is a spiritual benefit to following the Prophet's example."

For Sebkhaoui, "Salat involves all the senses of the body." He lifts his head and swivels it from side to side, as if to demonstrate. "You listen, you look exactly where your forehead is going to be, and since you are praying with others, you have to think of other people. We are one line. Everyone else prays as we do. We emphasize the importance of the collective. That's why performing congregational prayer is 25 degrees better than doing it alone."

Sebkhaoui observes that many, if not most, of his adult congregants arrive late, "very very late," for Juma. He understands the struggle to rush out of offices and hospitals and classrooms in the middle of a workday. "People are living in a land where they don't have control over their time. They don't get all the benefit of Juma, because they don't have time to meet with other people. The sermon reminds them of their duty to Allah, to their wives and children."

Sebkhaoui talks about the Day of Judgment, always invoked by Juma. "Any good Muslim wishes not to be alive for that day. There will be calamities and trials that I am not sure I could pass. Being alive, I have to keep myself"—he searches for a word—"checked. I try to always rejuvenate my faith. What determines the end is how you lived your life all the way to the end."

Even if he died before judgment day, and avoids the earthly disruptions, Sebkhaoui knows his life will be scrutinized as if in a divine court of law. "The judgment is horrible. Everyone I did something wrong to will be coming for their rights." God will see our acts and, more chilling, our motivations. "We can do things in the right form, but what must also be there is sincerity." Much like the other monotheisms, the last judgment grew in importance as Islam developed. The earliest chapters of the Quran mention the Day of Judgment only briefly.

The teaching that the Day of Judgment will come on a Friday, "reminds me that this could be the day, and I want to remain in a state of remembering God. Our attitude, that's the faith." He tells a story about the proud man who comes to the mosque and butts through the lines of worshipers to achieve a spot in the front. "The question is," Sebkhaoui says with a smile, pointing one index finger up toward heaven, "are you doing the prayers for God or other people?"

Solidarity

The practice of Juma displays the nonhierarchical nature of Islam and its fundamental unity. Islam remains, to many, the lay religion par excellence. As many have observed, "there are no monks in Islam." At the mosque on Friday, all are one. To fall out of line, to choose one's motions, to do your own thing, to pray "in my own way," as many people today say they do, would recreate the divisions of mankind born of disobedience to God, in whom all is one. The Muslim does not attend Juma to fulfill herself, to feel better, but to obey Allah in word, deed, and thought. Islam folds in all human endeavors under divine principles.[32]

At congregational salat, the men and women line up in their tight rows. As Sebkhaoui describes it, "You feel the body heat of the persons next to you, you feel strengthened and united. Everyone is united, rich or poor. We forget all that separates us. And this is done every week. If Juma is done properly, it should change people."

"In some places, Juma became an empty ritual," Sebkhaoui says. How can Muslims avoid that danger? "We struggle. The whole value of prayer is to struggle that it not becomes just a habit. That is why we do it as a congregation and not alone," he says. "These things are a supporting system. If we do them right, if we do the five daily prayers, then the whole day is connected to God."

Jews and Christians

To an outsider, the most striking difference of the Muslim Sabbath is its allowance for work. The day is not, Imam Sebkhaoui says, a day of rest, "because we don't anthropomorphize God, who is beyond fatigue." Sebkhaoui recalls that the Jews were given a day, and then the Christians another, but that the Muslims, as the last to receive the revelation, were given the correct day. As the Hadith has it:

> We are the last [of the people to come] but the first on the day of resurrection. They received their books before us and we got ours after them. This day was obligatory upon them, but they differed concerning it, and Allah guided us. The people, therefore, follow us: the Jews tomorrow and the Christians the day after tomorrow.[33]

To the Muslim, the correct day for worship was originally Friday, as it must have been for Abraham. Jews erred in choosing Saturday as did Christians with Sunday. Allah steered Muhammad back to the divinely appointed Juma.[34] In the Quran, the Jews are made to rest and obey other rules as a punishment for their infidelity to God (Sura 16:124). Muslim scholars have applied this lesson to the strict Sabbatarianism of Reform Protestants. Given its lengthy treatment in the Torah, the order to cease work on the holy day is conspicuously absent from the Quran.

At the same time, Allah inveighs against the Jews for not keeping their Shabbat. Sura 7:163–167 tells the story of a Jewish community where the fish would rise to top of the ponds on Shabbat, secure in their instincts that no one would be fishing. Thereby Allah tested them; some Jews failed and fished. Soon enough, "they transgressed all prohibitions," in the way that sin often leads to more. Here the Quran reiterates a point made in Jewish scripture, namely that for Jews, Sabbath breaking leads to moral collapse.

But religious antagonism may not have caused the final split with the Jews. More than one biographer of Muhammad reports that he was generally on friendly terms with the Jews "and inclined to adapt their institutions."[35] As for the change in Sabbath, Muhammad likely had before him the precedent of Christians who switched to Sunday. By moving to Friday, the new religion retained some connection to the Jewish Shabbat while also distinguishing itself.

Perhaps Muhammad sought to attract Jews, who conceivably could follow the law of Moses within Islam. And there are instances recorded of rabbis visiting the first mosques just as the Prophet and his followers visited synagogues.[36] Both religions share restrictions on usury, a criminal code that follows the law of retaliation, and ceremonial purification with water or sand, among others.[37] Further, Islam mandates that all men above puberty attend prayers on Friday and exempts women and boys, just as the Talmud excuses women, slaves, and boys under 13 from reciting the Shema and wearing phylacteries.[38] Other, Western scholars suggest that Muhammad chose the day out of spite toward those who rejected Islam, so that the shops would be closed at midday when Jews would be stocking up for Shabbat.[39] Of course, Muslims believe Allah chose the day and so told Muhammad as recorded in the Quran. It is God, not a sociological historical force, that commands them, "hasten to the remembrance of Allah."

But perspective is all. These sacred rituals of Islam, seemingly similar, could also evince a clear break from the preceding monotheisms: Friday instead of Saturday or Sunday; a verbal call to prayer rather than the use of bells or trumpets; Ramadan, a lunar month of fasting during daylight, instead of the 24-hour Day of Atonement or Christianity's 40 days of Lent. Like Jesus before him, Muhammad's break with the Jews' Shabbat struck at the core of their religion, the core of their very being. On the other hand, Judaism and Islam share one feature in that their fasts are absolute—no food, no water. Azra told me that she found much more in common in discussing Ramadan with Jewish friends, rather than with Christians who may give up sweets or alcohol but otherwise barely cut back. (The fast has been stricter in other times and places.)

One Friday I arrive early for Juma at the Albany Medical Center chapel, which is also used for Christian and Jewish services. I help some of the men move aside the chairs and a lectern and spread the sheets on the floor. The actions struck me as richly symbolic as well as practical. Is this not the first task of any religion, and especially Islam, to clear away the artifacts of the old religions? Muhammad often framed his message as a return to the faith of Abraham and his son, Ishmael, the traditional ancestor of the Arabs. Now, at the hospital chapel, with the chairs used by the other monotheists out of the way, the Muslim can kneel on the ground, close to earth, and submit himself to God.

The Shiites Across Town

Sunnis and Shiites on the other side of the world may be at odds, but here they sit together in the Haqqie living room. Haider A. Khwaja stopped by one night when I was there. A scientist at the University at Albany School of Public Health, he and Shamim are longtime friends. The differences between Islam's two main branches lie more in tradition—specifically succession, governance, social organization and leadership—than theology. (Of the world's billion or so Muslims about 90 percent are Sunni and 10 percent are Shia. Shiites constitute the majority in Lebanon, Iraq, Iran, and Oman.[40]) Shia awards more importance to the imam. And in Shiite countries, such as Iran, Friday prayers are often only held in a single location.[41] As such, Shia Islam seems inherently more hierarchical than Sunni Islam.

Neither the Haqqies nor any of their friends at the Islamic Center ever spoke of the specifically Sunni aspect to their faith. To see the other side for myself, I visited the Al-Fatima Islamic Center, the mosque for the region's Shia Muslims, which is about three miles southeast of the Islamic Center.

It stands off of South Family Drive in an open raw area beyond the subdivisions of Colonie, where institutions tend to relocate from the cities. Next door is a new Russian Orthodox church, which the Muslims once rented for Juma. Up the street is Christian Brothers Academy, with two black iron military cannons flanking the driveway.

Al-Fatima is the name of Muhammad's daughter, who married Ali bin Abi Talib, his cousin. Ali was later assassinated during the Islamic state's first civil war, and it was his son, Al-Husain bin Ali, who was martyred at Karbala, in today's Iraq. The violence done to the family of the Prophet caused a profound rethinking of Islam and became the focus of the Shia faith.[42]

At 12:50 PM, I find only a deserted parking lot and locked doors. Then, minutes later and all at once, cars and vans and SUVs swarm in and discharge people fresh from their homes and schools and offices. Khwaja greets me. We tour the building. Men and women have separate entrances, with alcoves for shoes and socks, and separate passages as well. "We kept the women's and men's side separate all the way through the building for their privacy," said Imdad Imam, a research scientist and president of center. "We learned from the 'best practices' of other mosques," he adds with a warm smile. The halls continue into a lobby, illuminated by a glass chandelier. There are two sets of double doors leading into the women's and men's sides of the mosque. Unlike many mosques, these are of equal size and each has a minbar.

On the west side of the divide, eight women and four girls kneel behind a tan cloth and metal office partition that divides the sections. The president, Imdad Imam, serves as muezzin, the person who issues the Adhan. (They favor a translation of the Quran by Muhammad Sarwar.)[43] On the other side there are about 20 men and boys. Inside the door, to the left, a table bears a box of prayer beads and clay tablets. The tablets resemble tabletop hockey pucks, though some are heart shaped. These *turba* are made of clay from the plain of Karbala, Iraq, where Husain, the grandson of Muhammad, was slain by Islamic opponents along with his family while they were marching from Medina into Iraq in a vain campaign for Islamic unity. Aside from being a memento of Husain's martyrdom, the clay tablets provide a place for worshipers to touch their heads during prostrations. In the front, a small golden frieze of double doors, modeled on Husain's tomb, marks the qibla, or direction of Mecca.

"Principally, it is to put our head on a natural thing. If you were praying outside, you could use the grass. Some people use a piece of wood, or a leaf, so long as it is not man-made." Haider adds, with a squirm, that at other (Sunni) mosques, people press their forehead to the carpet "where people have walked with their feet." Imam continues, "If it's a dirt floor, you don't need it. But we don't worship the clay. It makes it easier for you to focus on Almighty God."

Shakil Virjee, a dentist, arrives to lead the prayers. Here they combine two of the Muslim's five daily prayers, the one for midday and afternoon. Virjee delivers one long sermon in English and later a short recitation in Arabic. The first, he explains, should concern how to improve the welfare of the community. "Every aspect of my life is for the sake of God. This is not a restrictive statement, but one that gives us freedom." He discusses success in its two forms. "If your target or focus is God, then you will have success. But if your idea of success is the kind that society values, which is materialism, you will fail." Here, Juma has a relaxed, genial atmosphere, that of a small group of people who are not worried about their needs or their place on this earth. The men sit on ground, or else lean back on their haunches.

Virjee completes his sermon, and then delivers a shorter, memorized sermon in Arabic. He invokes Shia's martyrs, Ali and Husain, whose violent deaths seem far from this peaceful redoubt in the suburban fields of upstate New York. He readies for prayers, holding a stick in his hand, just as the Prophet. The men line up on their two long prayer rugs. Several reposition the clay disc at the head of their rug section; Virjee, as the leader, uses two, one on the other. As the men complete one set of rakas and prayers, in the silence I hear the women on the far side of the partition finish theirs at a beat-slower pace.

Afterwards, we repair to the basement level for a simple lunch—several delivered pizzas and, to drink, tap water. I ask Imam about the day, and how its holiness is affected by the return to work. "In Islam, there is no free lunch. We cannot substitute supplication for work." He notes that they still pray five times a day on all days, work and free. "The idea in Islam is that Friday is another day in life, and in life we work. If you work for your children, to feed them and educate them, then your work can be a prayer." He reminds me of the importance of community. "The Prophet, blessed be his name, led prayers on Fridays. One day, he arrived late and they asked him 'Why were you late this day?' He said that he was walking to the prayers and he was behind an elderly woman. He didn't pass her, because she would have felt old, and that made him late." Imam cocks his head sideways at me. "You see the sensitivity he had," Imam says. "Anything you do on Friday, there's more reward. If people have charity to give," he says, pulling his hand out of his pocket and pretending to hand some money over, "then they may delay it until Friday. We get together, that's what is important. On Friday, Islam transcends all boundaries."

Allah's Hand: Azra and Despair

The Muslim's abiding faith is that Allah directs life. Having created the world and sent His Messenger to us, God is not pulling back, not now, not in

Colonie, New York in early spring on a Friday shortly before noon when Azra
prepares to leave her office for prayers. Perhaps God speaks through a colleague
who asks Azra, "Don't you have to go?" Azra nods as she sits and slips off her
sneakers, slips on her shoes. Though she never attended Juma as a child in
Pakistan, she goes every other week now. When the children were young, she
took them to Sunday school at the Islamic center and the family attended
Friday evening services together.

Today at the mosque, a visiting imam leads the prayers. He is an African
American convert, here for a tryout during the center's search for a new spiritual leader. His khutbah implores the faithful to fulfill their civic duty without
yielding their religious identity, especially in the fearful climate after 9/11.
"Most Muslims live [in America] not for the liberties but for the prosperity, the
comforts. . . . What good are freedoms if you don't use them? I was in the
Marines. I fought in the first Gulf War. I have the right to speak out." He tells
us that he understands the urge of Muslims in America to keep their heads
down, but also criticizes those who went so far as to campaign for George Bush.
He urges us to live confidently in faith. "That's why you will never see a Muslim
despair, because we know that all that happens is because Allah wishes it to."

On the ride back to the *Times Union*, Azra says that it is the American-born
imams who tackle current events and life in America, and that foreign-born
imams generally avoid those topics. We talk about the war in Iraq and the U.S.
soldiers, so young, coming under fire. (This conversation was in 2003.) "That's
why I feel for all those boys and girls over there that we've been seeing on television. What their parents must be thinking." Then she discusses her fears that
her husband Shamim, a doctor who serves in the reserves, may be called up for
duty. "They don't have another 100,000 troops as they said they need, so they
may have to use the reserves." (Shamim later served three months in Iraq.) She
drives in silence. The flat landscape of woods and fields and office parks slides
past. "But when the imam said that about despair, that helped me, oh yes it did.
Because I'm usually a pretty optimistic person, but I was pretty worried."

CHAPTER VI

Citizens and Sabbatarians:
1600 to 1890

It is easie to demonstrate by Scripture and argument as well as by experience that
Religion is just as the Sabbath is and decayes and growes as the Sabbath is esteemed.
THOMAS SHEPHARD, *THESES SABBATICAE: OR, THE DOCTRINE OF THE
SABBATH*, 1634

The Christian Sabbath shaped America as much as did the settlers' conviction
that God selected them to found a city on a hill. Indeed, the two concepts were
entwined. The Lord's Day made no sense "other than as a link in a perfect
chain."[1] The day embodied the faithful's relationship with God. During those
24 hours, all their hopes and wishes for salvation came to the fore. The Lord's
Day, as perfected in Puritan New England and other colonies also revealed
American attitudes toward work and play. Since the colonies used the state to
advance religion and ensure morality, Sabbatarianism invested politics and law
with theology and faith "with lasting consequences for American culture."[2]
Thirteen centuries after Ambrose, Bishop of Milan, had pulled apart church
and state, the Puritans yoked these together in the New World. In Europe,
many Christians reacted to the harshness of the Reformers and developed the
"continental Sunday" of church, relaxation, and entertainment. Through the
end of the nineteenth century, Americans pushed and pulled on the Lord's Day
with a fervor that proved Sunday's importance to all, be it a day for God or a
day off for working men and women. Given the lasting Puritan imprint on our
society, we can say that America was founded to keep and enforce the Lord's
Day. Unions and progressives drew on this legacy to justify an entirely secular
day off for workers. Even as the holy day became more private, the rituals show
communal and public results. That which we do on Juma, Shabbat, or Sunday

is part of public life. That which we do on the Sabbath shapes the other six days. Since our observance affects our work, our neighbors, and society, we are all the more citizens by being Sabbatarians. Neglect of the day bears results as well by subtly reshaping a country founded to keep the Christian Sabbath. In other lands, such neglect reverses centuries of habit and cycles of time. From the Puritans to the end of the nineteenth century, private devotion evolved in its use or rejection of social mores and civil sanction.

Our Lord's Day

In early November, we spend a Sunday on our legs: a day on foot and bicycle, no driving at all. Blessed be the land without motors. Madeleine and I walk to Mass ahead of Amy, Jeanne, and Mitchell. We discuss the private world we inhabit as we walk through our neighborhood, up Grove Avenue, left on Helderberg, eight blocks to Fairwood, right to New Scotland and St. Teresa of Avila. We see few others, and the birds chirp modestly from within their hedges. So too are we encased yet not enclosed in the Sunday spirit. Mass today is special because Jeanne for the first time helps Father Powers receive the bread and wine from the congregants who carried them up the aisle. She and her friend Molly Stenard bear the vessels from the aisle to the altar. Christ comes to us in the Gospel, in the consecrated bread and wine and in the communion of believers.

Afterwards, we dally with other parents as the older children climb up the magnolia tree and the toddlers hide under the drooping canopy of a blue spruce. Our social scene recalls Sunday as the day "when the disciples gathered" as recounted in the Acts of the Apostles. We walk home, eat bagels, laze about, then bicycle to a Girl Scout meeting and there deposit Madeleine. The rest of us pedal to Washington Park, visit the art gallery at the college—intricate black-and-white cutouts by Ugo Mochi—then to a playground where Mitchell and Jeanne clamber over the swings, slides, and monkey bars.

Back home, Dennis comes over with his daughter Sophia for two hours by the fire. Amy busies herself elsewhere. Mitchell and Sophia stay close. Outside, Madeleine and Jeanne gather fallen leaves of cherry crimson and cornbread gold with the Stenards and jump on and off the piles. After dinner, the children wrestle with me boisterously. They dress for bed and we watch old family movies before washing up. In our prayers, we bid adieu to holy time and ask its light be cast onto the time ahead. Be this not heaven, what could be closer?

Puritan America

On the eve of colonization, a new and powerful Sabbatarianism emerged in England in time to be carried off to America. The Puritans arrived bearing their conviction, like the Israelites with the ark of the covenant, that a well-kept Sunday ensured goodness on earth and salvation thereafter. On such biblical terms they sought to renew man and reorder society.

Though Virginia's Jamestown colony had the first Sunday law in 1610, America's Sunday was carved in New England. First to land were the Pilgrims, who quickly established the Sabbath in Plymouth in 1620. The larger Puritan contingent arrived in 1630 to begin the Massachusetts Bay Colony. Before landing, their leader John Winthrop announced that "we shall be as a City upon a Hill, the eyes of all people are upon us." In the next decade, 16,000 Puritans arrived. Guided by a crop of Puritan preachers educated at Cambridge and Oxford, they absorbed the Pilgrims, fixed New England's theology, and influenced American religious life till today.[3]

In sermons that were published in a 1649 book, Thomas Shephard summarized the prevailing doctrine: the Sabbath was a perpetual obligation involving a seventh day; Sunday was divinely inspired and ordained by Easter; it lasted from dusk to dusk and involved rest and works of necessity, such as cooking and dressing well; and a sin on Sunday, when blessings abound, was a double transgression.[4] Good Sabbaths would ensure survival and prosperity in the New World.

It came at a cost. The Puritans recoiled from the slack habits of medieval Europe. Now they could join state force to religious conviction. The Puritans adopted the strictures of Jewish law (that ironically led them away from the Protestant assurance of salvation as God's gift and toward rules to safeguard religion, which resembled the Catholic emphasis on good works). From 1630 to 1650, authorities in New England and Virginia levied fines, whipping, and the stocks on Sabbath breakers. As settlers moved west, leaders sought to ensure church attendance in these outlying areas as well.

If the Puritans were Israelites, the Dutch in New Amsterdam were the Greeks, hardworking but fun loving. A European observer contrasted the lawless people of Manhattan to the orderly Puritans marching to church on Sunday.[5] New England was founded to practice Puritanism and keep the Sabbath. New Amsterdam was established to make a profit. Nominally, the Dutch protected the Sabbath.

In 1641, William Kieft, the colony's director general, banned liquor sales on Sunday during church services. His successor, Peter Stuyvesant, further limited sales to between midafternoon and 9:00 PM. Stuyvesant ordered church attendance but failed to enforce it. Influenced by the Heidelberg Catechism of 1563, which spiritualized the fourth commandment and called all days holy—thus rendering none so—many Dutch settlers spent Sunday working, playing, and drinking. The English took over in 1664 and added more Sabbatarian regulations. But both colonial authorities found their zeal tempered by New Yorkers' resistance to moralizing.

The result was a classic American compromise. The 1695 Act against Profanation of the Lord's Day prohibited travel, labor, sports, and hunting, but did not require church attendance, nor did it apply to non-Christian Indians. Maryland and Rhode Island adopted similar measures.

While the modern mind imagines coerced observance to be the only kind, many or most colonists found rest and renewal on Sunday. Eventually, New England Puritans could congratulate themselves for keeping the best Sabbath in all Christendom. But change came. Puritan migration slowed after 1640 and the true believers were soon surrounded by less religious and more commercial parties.

Colonial authorities—embarrassed by the contrast between religion and the Age of Reason—eased their enforcement. Religious and other leaders responded with renewed zeal, though of a mixed sort. For instance, Connecticut stiffened its regulation of work on the Sabbath in 1676 while also curtailing the list of violations that merited death.[6] New codes protected freedom of conscience. Under one in Pennsylvania, the Seventh Day Baptists were the first group to demand the right to observe their beliefs.

The Lord's Day was observed, but variously. Virginians held horse races, slaves in North and South were freed to tend their own plots of land, and many Americans went to the tavern rather than church.[7] Puritan power began to decline in the late 1600s as a new generation began to value emotional preaching and conversions more than plain sermons and theological precision.[8]

During the mid-1700s, the people of Northampton, Massachusetts, swept their souls up toward God and kicked off the Great Awakening. Sunday meetings were central to the revival in this prosperous village. Their fervor was kindled by Jonathan Edwards, a Calvinist preacher and theologian who stressed the Christian Sabbath and crafted a systematic defense that endured for 200 years.

Edwards preached that it was the "mind and will of God" for Christians to observe the first day, when Christ rose and later appeared to the disciples, the Holy Spirit descended, and the disciples met weekly. Charity and mercy were proper works for the Sabbath, as shown by Jesus and the Jews as well.[9] Since the Old Testament so clearly mandated the Seventh Day, and since Christ said nothing about the first day, Edwards, as did his Reform forebears, offered a detailed if eccentric justification for Sunday.

He first suggests the Israelites lost track of days when they were slaves in Egypt, so which is truly the seventh? (I love this one; it is at once contrived and reasonable. As my wife said to me, "Who knows which was the first day anyway?") Then, Edwards argues, Sunday follows six days of labor so it is a seventh day for Christians. What's important is that we keep one in seven holy. Christ honored the first day, so that must be it.[10]

Jews: Persecution and Departure

As for the real Israelites, in the centuries since the destruction of the Temple they had spread into Mediterranean countries, becoming known as Sephardim—from the biblical Hebrew word for Spain—and into Europe, known as Ashkenazim—from the Hebrew word for Germany. During the eighteenth century in Europe, they achieved some civil equality and benefited from religious reform and the Haskalah, the Jewish Enlightenment. But through the nineteenth century, persecutions and other causes prompted both Sephardic and Ashkenazi Jews to leave for the Americas.

Some found a home in New Amsterdam when a group of refugees escaped there in 1654 from persecution in Catholic Brazil. They were allowed to settle and trade. At first they worshiped privately in small groups, for which Shabbat is eminently suitable. After 1700, they were able to gather publicly on Shabbat and other holy days and began to build synagogues.[11] Given the restriction on Sunday labor, observant Jews could only work five days a week. Nevertheless, some remained faithful to the law of God and man. Aaron Lopez, a wealthy trader, closed his business from Friday afternoon until Monday morning and did not allow any of his ships to leave port on Saturday.[12]

For Jews in tumult, as in Eastern Europe where pogroms and wars decimated their ranks, the Sabbath remained a delight. In eighteenth-century Russia, Hasidic leaders would gather their followers for the main meal after which they would lead listeners into the holy realm with lessons, song, and dance. Like the Sabbath, the ecstasy could only be experienced communally.[13]

The minority status and often private nature of Judaism moderated changes in that religion and spared it some of the public debates that entangled the more widespread Christianity. In both religions, ideals and popular appetites seesawed for centuries. Nevertheless, the Sabbath keepers maintained their hold until well after the American Revolution and, by social disapprobation, into the twentieth century.

Reacting to the Reformation: Europe and America

A reaction to Puritanism was building in both the New and Old Worlds. Both sides drew on the movement's founders. Martin Luther thought that the Jews, after a good start, went too far with the Sabbath and "restricted this too closely, and grossly abused it." Christ freed us from the need for holy days, but one day a week allows rest and worship, the true purpose of the fourth commandment.[14] Calvin was stricter and made the Lord's Day a 24-hour duty with a full checklist. Consequently, churchgoing became a legal obligation during the Reformation whereas it had been a religious one in all the centuries since Christ. Even Constantine, in 321, merely prohibited work. Clerics now reached for the whip.

In 1551, the British Act of Uniformity set fines for missing Sunday services and other jurisdictions, notably the Virginia and New England colonies, followed suit. On both sides of the Atlantic, it was not enough to rest; one now had to worship.[15] As debate swirled into the mid-seventeenth and eighteenth centuries, moderate scholars shrewdly associated Puritan Sabbatarianism with papist superstition. They said that the proliferating rules evoked the Catholic belief that believers earn salvation by deeds, rather than the Reformers' creed that salvation comes from God. These critics accused the Puritans of Judaizing the Lord's Day and making it more of a burden than it was to the Israelites under Moses.[16] Finally, this minority joked that, by Puritan standards, Jesus was a flagrant Sabbath breaker. So much conflict over the day of rest.

Toward the end of the Reformation, four positions emerged among Christians that persevere till today. First, some kept the seventh day holy. They felt that Christ fulfilled, not ended, the law, and we are thus able to observe the Sabbath, a sample of the eternal rest to come, as a joy rather than a necessity. These were a fervent minority.

Second, a small group held that all days were now holy. Converts may need special days as a temporary prop to their faith; real Christians serve God on all days. Despite the power of Paul's Epistles, this position is hard to sustain and has attracted the bold and brave few.

A third group believed that the Sabbath began at Creation and was renewed at Sinai. These Sabbatarians believed that since "seventh day" could mean "one day in seven," Christians could switch the moral obligation to Sunday. In 1707, John Samuel Stryk, a German jurist, felt free to admit that Christian practice was based not in Jewish law, but "rests entirely in a simple arrangement of the Church."[17] This remains the majority position by conviction or default. And fourth, the Dominicals—from the Latin for Lord's Day—believed the Sabbath began as a Jewish law at Sinai but did not oblige Christians. Since we need a day for rest and worship, Sunday will do. This popular but minority position breaks Sunday off most clearly from its Jewish roots.

From the Reformation till today, most Christians combine aspects of these four positions, especially the last two, which dominated the battlefield. The Sabbatarians accused the Dominicals of ignoring the Old Testament, especially the Creation account, and replacing a divine ordinance with a human one. Such would lead to careless frivolity, as it already had in France, Holland, Switzerland, and Germany. The Dominicals blamed the Sabbatarians for Judaizing the church with harsh measures that deflated the cheerful dispensation of Christianity.[18]

During the 1700s, there were shifting notions of rest, leisure, and recreation. The idea of rest was paramount and claimed the allegiance of most people. Leisure emerged as an activity somewhere between the solemn rest and profane recreation. Many English families began to favor sports, drink, and society on Sunday afternoon. They muddied the line King James I had drawn between healthy sports and dissipation.

The Puritans banned sport as a possible occasion for sin. If so, argued one wit, "We must also abolish going to church itself, in regard to which neither sex can pretend to be always actuated by spiritual considerations alone."[19] More importantly, said moderates, a life without pleasure deprives us of God's blessings. In America and continental Europe, they insisted on fun. By the early 1800s, a traveler to Geneva, once home to John Calvin, was astonished to find lifeless, half-empty Sunday services that contrasted with "the vigor and number of other enjoyments: boat rides, horse shows and coffee shops, with billiards, skittles and guns heard above the prayers."[20]

During the Restoration of the Stuart kings in England, from 1660 to 1685, even rest was neglected. More felt free to work, travel, and play. A new sect, the Quakers, repudiated the Sabbath as Jewish law and then, in a familiar pattern, adopted a familiar weekly cycle of six days hard work followed by one for rest and worship.[21] Persecuted in England, many left for America where they moderated Puritan excesses. In Pennsylvania, they passed a 1705 law prohibit-ing people from profaning Sunday while not requiring them to attend church. This shift was common in the colonies outside of New England.

The United States was embracing freedom of, and from, religion. The changing relation between religion and legal authority in the New World exemplified the perennial tension between faith and force, between the believer's free acceptance of God's love and the community's desire to preserve itself through obedience to God's commands.

Faith and Force

One Saturday evening while visiting relatives in the hills of New Hampshire, I take the air and stand at the edge of the forest. In the dusk of Sunday's vigil, when profane time blends into sacred time, the trees—white pine, hemlock, birch, oak, and maple—and plants—blackberry, blueberry, and ferns—melt into black globs against a grey background. The woods draw us toward obliv-ion or rebuke our domestic humanity entirely. With an ancient animal instinct we want to rush into nature's womb or dash from danger.

The Puritans, encamped on the small eastern edge of the New World, faced such a boundary between their tidy village and farm fields and the wilderness that stretched off toward an unknown distance. Standing here now, I fathom their compulsion to divide the two worlds. They chopped at the forest and spread their homestead, dividing light from dark and bringing order to the chaos as did God at Creation. So too they ordered their souls and society to keep God close and the devil away. On the Sabbath, they cleared a space in time and sanctified this 24 hours of what could easily slip into profane chaos. The calm repose of their Sunday was a joy unto itself that also secured the favor and protection of God. What seemed desirable in Europe was all the more necessary here when struggling to survive. God's law was to be enforced for the commonweal. Moot to them was the separation of church and state.

Still, we cannot separate the holy day from the world around it. Our Sabbath keeping engages us in public life. Never is our faith—as Jews, Christians, or Muslims—more apparent than when we refrain from labor or walk well dressed to services or congregate to pray as a group that stands, bows, kneels, and lies prostrate as one. In fact, these small actions prepare us to be citizens since we learn to act out religious beliefs in the public realm. (In *The Fall of Public Man*, Richard Sennett warned that citizens who cannot comport themselves publicly retreat to the private realm and let politics decay.[22]) For example, Jewish children who stroll to synagogue on Saturday grow comfortable demonstrating their faith in public. One day they will feel free to express opinions based on their beliefs. Such habits will also sustain more private acts as declining a play date that involves driving.

From the beginning, Americans valued religious liberty. They also felt, Alexis de Tocqueville observed, "the high necessity of imparting morality to democratic communities by men of religion."[23] While others are free to do as they wish, the believer feels that his practice helps all. Authority and oppression slip in under such a cloak. The seal of the Massachusetts Bay Colony, which sponsored the settlers, shows a pliant Indian saying, "Come over and help us." As for the Sabbath, the Puritans, like the Israelites, considered it part of the covenant with God that preserved their lives and souls. One person's neglect risked all of them. (In our own day, we ban or restrict hate speech, hate crimes, or suicide—acts that typically affect an individual but endanger all society by shredding a common value.) The wilderness at the door and the often-hostile Indians inspired them to faithfulness. From 1675 through 1676, the chief of the Wampanoag Indians, King Philip or Metacom, launched a war to stop English expansion. Before being defeated, the Indians killed hundreds of settlers, which some Puritans read as punishment for their Sabbath laxity.

Many Christians and others now keep a weekend of two Saturdays. They find in it a certain freedom, or at least more time for chores. To me, that's a nightmare. I like the holy day but also the division between times and tasks. The Puritans believed that good Sundays make good Christians. I say good Saturdays make for good Sundays. We often think the day of rest is God's gift. But his real gift is that he left the other six days to us. Who could bear seven holy days? On the other days we are left to our own devices. As for the holy day itself, it would be easier if more neighbors kept it holy and restful, but then they may be seized with Sabbatarian fever and ultimately impose their rules on us. So I wonder, can the Lord's Day, with its Christian message of liberation from sin and death and its older Judaic message of freedom and deliverance, come to embody Paul's vision of our liberation from religious law? Can a day that originates in a commandment now fulfill a new promise of salvation given rather than earned?

In our family the issue remains: how to institutionalize the Lord's Day habit—the prayers at start and end, the absence of chores, the joy and peace and play, the visits to the elderly—so that we do these without fuss or fail. One Saturday night in late summer, we forget the prayers as we attend "My Fair

Lady" in Washington Park and return late, straight to bed. The next day at a backyard dinner, Jeanne and Madeleine discuss God and whether we would follow a religion without God. Madeleine, the good-hearted skeptic, concludes, "I probably would go anyway because it's the right thing to do." Jeanne asks if I ever heard God talk. Through the Bible and other people, I say, and then Madeleine interjects, "and in your heart."

Compassionate Enforcement

Between the extremes of blind tribal obedience and sociable decay, the three religions showed common tendencies in encouraging, or mandating, the holy day.

The Sabbatarian crackdowns of the seventeenth century were followed by the reaction of the moderates and the hint of laxity and neglect to come. In this we see a common religious cycle: a joy becomes a burden that is then rejected and, finally, either neglected or rediscovered. These stages may repeat or short-circuit one another. Considered simply, the Sabbath in all three religions has been given a ride on this roller coaster. First it was a day of joy, a gift that expressed the original insight: God created and sustains us. Then the day became loaded with rules and regulations. After all, we want to do it right. In the third stage, believers rejected the rules and even the Sabbath altogether. God clearly did not intend what it had become. Finally, we forget the Sabbath, recalling it only in dim regret. Or we realize what has been lost and renew its practice with the original intent and, perhaps, modern modifications.

Early on, the Israelites marked Shabbat with the egalitarian and liberating spirit of the fourth commandment, best celebrated by Isaiah. One was allowed to advance the common good: Joshua brought down the walls of Jericho on the seventh day, and the priests conducted sacrifices and prayers then. But the rules multiplied. By the time of Jesus, the Pharisees wove a welter of obligation and duty. The sages elaborated on the rules but found room for creative exceptions while virtually mandating joy and celebration. Into the eighth century, however, some sages who relied only on scripture taught that not even childbirth would excuse building a fire on the Sabbath, the type of harsh measure seen centuries earlier in the ban, later overturned, on lovemaking. By the Middle Ages and beyond the Sabbath spirit of the Talmud prevailed. "In synagogal services the joyous note alone was heard. In fact, the life of the Jews is ample testimony that the Sabbath under the Law was anything but irksome, gloomy or fatal to spirituality." The literalism of earlier ages turned the day into a burden "but rabbinical legalism, with its legal fictions, avoided this . . . [and] accommodated itself to the demands of life."[24]

Truly, faith can rescue us from force. Our first epiphany and subsequent communion with God and others leads us, astray perhaps, to erect the "hedge about the law" that protects and promotes this experience. We do it first for ourselves, then unto others. It is always the eternal in the Sabbath, the ecstatic core of the experience, which inspires us.

Imagine the peaceful bliss of a girl standing in the outfield during a quiet spell in her softball game. She is in the game but also released from time. The clock slows. She stands deep in time's comforting current, a slow swollen stream on an August afternoon. We think the problem is to convert time into eternity, but time is already the start of the eternal. We seek eternity by filling time and space with things, which is the true heartbreak of life: an infinite appetite for the finite. But our outfielder has stumbled into the truth of time and wanders there free—until the batter smacks out a fly ball.

Another feature, compassion in enforcement, is strikingly common in all three religions. Throughout history, religious authorities prescribed punishment only after three violations of Shabbat, Sunday, or Juma. Hubris, not accidental neglect, is the real crime. Islam holds that skipping Juma without good cause is a grave sin. One tradition has it that Muhammad confessed an urge to burn the houses of slackers.[25] But his rule, commonly accepted today, was, "Whoever omits three Friday services making light of it, Allah sets a seal on his heart."[26]

Among the colonies, Virginia punished people after their third failure to observe the Sabbath. In Massachusetts, death was prescribed for a third Sunday robbery or burglary if committed "presumptuously." The New Haven code levied a fine or corporal punishment for working or playing; if done "proudly, presumptuously or with a high hand" death was prescribed.[27] Governor John Winthrop later struck this down, but not before a servant boy was executed for "buggery with a cow, upon the Lord's Day." He repented, but was hanged anyway.[28]

Woe could also come without human intervention. English preachers told of the man who drank at the St. Ives market during church services and later drowned in a river and of the vintner who stood in his doorway with a pot of wine on the Lord's Day and was carried away in a whirlwind. But the boom was not always lowered. In colonial America, Jewish synagogal courts, descended from the *kehillah* of medieval Europe, threatened to censure Sabbath violators but rarely did so.[29]

Theologians recognized the limits of force. Moderates in Scotland warned that strict Sunday laws encouraged extremism and hypocrisy. "A people thus constrained takes refuge in whisky," said one.[30] Coercion violated the elective nature of faith and often backfired. Laws that mandated church attendance left homes empty, prompting Sunday morning burglaries and fornication in some New England villages. Since fear works only so long, churchmen favored moral suasion. As Winton Solberg, the great historian of the New England Sabbath, concluded, "A free people united in the Sabbath had little need of superstition."[31]

Freedom of Religion and Freedom from Religion

From the Revolution through the Civil War, American leaders struggled to balance their urge to promote religion against the desire to avoid the sectarian oppression of Europe. No one was entirely free of religion's heritage. Early Jews, eager to embrace their new land, may have wished to transform themselves into pilgrims of a kind while Pilgrims and Puritans considered themselves New Israelites in a Promised Land where they could keep Sunday as the Jews kept Shabbat. Even the freethinking Ben Franklin proposed that the seal of the United States show Moses leading Israel across the Red Sea. The ancient covenantal language was used by George Washington in 1776 when he urged his officers and soldiers to be good Christians and thereby obtain "the blessing and protection of Heaven" during a time "of public distress and danger."[32]

Almost a hundred years later and during the Civil War, Abraham Lincoln—a careful nonpartisan when it came to religion—spoke similarly. "A due regard for the divine will demand that Sunday labor in the Army and Navy be reduced to the measure of strict necessity," Lincoln declared.[33] A mortal threat to the republic made Sabbath fidelity all the more important.

This approach allowed, as did the Maccabees, military acts of self-defense or even offense on the Sabbath. God could not have meant the day for self-sacrifice. But such exhortations were yielding to a consensus that while religion was desirable, our freedom to practice depended on the government's neutrality. In 1838, New York State legislators turned back a move to repeal bans on Sunday labor. They argued that while America had no established religion, it was a Christian nation, and that to allow Sunday's desecration by servile labor, sports or horse racing would violate the majority's freedom to worship. But the move to a less sectarian protection was afoot. By the mid-1800s, New York was one of five states with laws allowing Jews and Seventh-day Christians to work on Sunday, which indirectly enabled them to observe their Saturday Sabbath.[34]

America's religiosity and religious freedom routinely impressed visitors. In his 1835 report, *Democracy in America*, Tocqueville wrote that religion and freedom "marched in opposite directions" in France but "reigned in common" in the United States. Astonished, he asked many believers why. All to whom he spoke attributed "the peaceful dominion of religion in their country mainly to the separation of church and state."[35] Freedom of and from religion was already producing a very religious nation. A more direct effort to keep religion out of public life backfired in our revolutionary ally, France.

The French and American Revolutions and Afterward

The Age of Reason shocked the general consensus on religious practice, now seen by leaders as mere superstition that hindered progress. No longer was it safe to assume that most people wanted a holy Sunday.

The French rushed to rationalize every aspect of life such as the calendar. Stamping out superstitions and wasted time was part of the effort, so France abolished all religious feast days. No more Year of the Lord, or *anno Domini*; now the years dated from the revolution in 1792. Twelve months remained with new names and 30 days in each. The five leftover days were slotted to year's end for a public festival.[36] The French introduced a 10-day week to override the Lord's Day and thereby suppress religion entirely. Voltaire calmly predicted that it would be the death of Christianity. Churches could open only on the tenth day, one of rest, and people could not wear their finery on Sundays.[37]

Voltaire was wrong. Churches did not empty out, though believers may have been more private in their devotions. The mechanical ten-day *décade* lacked cultural roots and won few subscribers. After 14 years, Bonaparte canceled the experiment and restored the Gregorian calendar and the comfortable seven-day week.[38] Across the English Channel clerics contemplated the damage to French souls. "Ten years there without the Lord's Day and, it is to be feared, without the Lord."[39]

In America, the threats to the Sabbath were more personal and theological. German immigrants brought with them the Pietism that celebrated an intense personal encounter with God. Then, the Great Awakening further enshrined emotional revivals and conversions at the expense of doctrine and ritual.

The Unitarian holy man Joseph Priestley, in about 1790, taught that the Sabbath was not obligated. Services should be held in early morning or evening, so men could tend their fields and yet preserve Sunday's sanctity.[40] Meanwhile, Baptists were asking, with Paul, why Christians should observe the law if their hearts had been remade. They preached a Sabbath of the heart, plucking at the perennial religious tension between the mind and heart, between public practice and private emotions. Emerging was the American character, defiant of any intermediary between God and the believer. Once converted, the true Christian had no need of outside props such as Sunday rest. Observance and protections varied. While partisans of religion may think our founders lived in a profoundly religious society, church attendance in the colonial age was low, at least by today's standards and there was no national movement devoted to promoting religion in public life other than the Sunday blue laws.[41]

Jewish practice also fluctuated, due to the minority status of the people and the absence of a central authority. Hundreds of Jews served in the Revolutionary Army; at least one was reported excused from watch duty on Friday nights. After the American Revolution, many moved west to St. Louis and Cincinnati. These found comfort in the Puritan notion of a religious "errand unto the wilderness," which was, of course, derived from the Israelites.[42] Such ideals, and the portable habit of weekly holy day, sustained pioneers and stabilized their communities.

While never perfectly adherent to the Sabbath, Puritan New England was less and less so despite harsh religious laws. By 1776, only one in five residents had a religious affiliation.[43] But the Sabbath impulse survived the Revolution, at least for a time. In 1792, Massachusetts compelled its citizens to observe the Sabbath "as an affair of public interest" since neglect spreads "a taste for dissipation and dissolution." The law shut stores and businesses and banned entertainment, hunting, and unnecessary travel. Negative requirements were one thing, but the law also mandated worship. It fined those who neglected public worship for three months. New York had similar laws in its revised statutes of 1827 through 1828, though the tide was flowing away from the sharp rocks of coercion.[44]

Enforcement began to wane, as did laws governing morals generally. In Massachusetts during the late 1700s, only a small fraction of indictments were for moral and sexual crimes, which included profaning the Sabbath. In Virginia's Ohio County from 1801 to 1810, there were 242 indictments; only one was for breaking the Sabbath.[45]

Religious revolutions also affected Jews. Devotion was pumped up by the Protestant revival and reform encouraged by change in other religions. Synagogues added seating for women, who began attending in greater numbers, and even mixed the sexes. Shabbat continued in its domestic setting. One Chicago memoirist reported that most men and many women attended services on Saturday morning. Afterward men left for work while the women preserved the day's restful pattern. As so often, writes the historian Jonathan D. Sarna, women "kept the embers of Judaism glowing."[46]

Though sanctions lagged, the sentiment behind the blue laws was widespread. "Nothing strikes a foreigner on his arrival in America more forcibly than the regard paid to the Sabbath," Tocqueville observed in 1840. "Not only have all ceased to work, but they appear to have ceased to exist."[47] This rest made work possible in the heated economy of the New World. On Monday, the hubbub resumed as people rushed back to make and buy and sell. "A feverish activity succeeds to the lethargic stupor of yesterday; you might almost suppose that they had but one day to acquire wealth and to enjoy it."[48]

Europe and America by Midcentury

During the early 1700s, the Sabbath grew more relaxed in England before the evangelical revival led to renewed strictness. One change not to be reversed was the increased demand for something beyond rest, namely leisure and recreation. Habits of leisure once only for the rich spread among the middle class and workers.

Humane theologians argued that amusement fulfilled God's design for humans and for the Sabbath. "To fight against our nature is not to serve the course of piety and morals," one preacher declared.[49] God made us incapable of constant toil and with an appetite for recreation.

Alas, England at this time offered the poor nothing beyond the alehouse or gin palace. The commons and greens where they once played cricket or ran footraces had been enclosed for the pasturing of rich men's cattle. "The good country games of the times of our forefathers are forgotten," lamented one contemporary.[50] But the old censure held on. In 1781 a law banned public entertainments that charged for admission and as late as 1856, Sunday band concerts in London parks were canceled at the behest of Anglican bishops.[51]

Travelers praised the Seventh-day habits on the Continent. In German villages, families gathered at the inn and even the pastor would attend, which elevated the atmosphere. Musical classes and village bands edified people's Sunday afternoon. "Pleasure houses" with music and refreshments satisfied appetites for diversion and avoided the excess wrought by stricter regimes in England and Scotland.[52] In Germany and Switzerland, people walked along tree-lined promenades or sat in parks with their beer, coffee, and newspapers. Rich and poor mingled in their recreation, unlike England, where the only legal recreations were those of the gentry. While continental Protestants admired the strict Sundays of Britain, it was they who better achieved the original command for a day of rest for rich and poor alike.

America, with immigrants from both sides of the English Channel, merged Puritan and more moderate habits with a native orneriness. In his memoir of midcentury seafaring, *Two Years Before the Mast*, Richard Henry Dana reported, "The Catholics on shore have no trading and make no journeys on Sunday, but the American has no national religion, and likes to show his independence of priestcraft by doing as he chooses on the Lord's day."[53]

By 1838, the hold of Puritanism—and even organized religion—was waning in some corners. In the perennial rebellion of American believers, new avenues were being sought. Ralph Waldo Emerson lamented, while also extolling such brave individualism, that "It is already beginning to indicate character and religion to withdraw from the religious meetings. I have heard a devout person who prized the Sabbath say in bitterness of heart: 'On Sunday it seems wicked to go to church.' "[54] Despite exceptions, Sunday remained the nation's respite. On that day, Tocqueville observed, the American sets aside his petty concerns and interests and "strays at once into an ideal world, where all is great, eternal, and pure."[55]

As in the times of the Dutch in New Amsterdam, Sunday and abstinence were entwined in the minds of religious Europeans and their American descendants. But the weekly prohibitionists were often beaten back. In New York State, the legislature adopted an 1845 "local option" law that allowed towns to ban Sunday liquor sales; 80 percent did so. This was repealed two years later, only to be followed by a Prohibition Act in 1854 that was, in turn, ruled invalid by the New York State Court of Appeals in 1855.

Then in 1857, high-minded Republicans in the New York State legislature banned all liquor sales on Sunday and caused a Prohibition-style crime wave in Manhattan. In the 1890s, Police Commissioner Theodore Roosevelt raided saloons that kept Sunday hours and enforced other dormant blue laws. But his crackdown alienated German voters, who treasured their Sunday afternoons in the beer garden, and Jews who wanted to work on Sundays after keeping their own Sabbath on Saturday. (By 2003, New York had come full circle. When the legislature approved Sunday liquor sales that year, it limited hours to afternoon and early evening—the same retail window allowed in 1641.)

As in the early 1600s, advocates churned out tracts and magazines defending the Lord's Day. During the 1860s, *The Sabbath at Home: An Illustrated Magazine for the Family* exhorted readers monthly to keep the day holy with example and lessons. Sabbath fidelity elevated New England's moral and intellectual life, but adherents should avoid the Puritan gloom and sternness in favor of a Christian cheerfulness with a "suitable and profitable employment of the hours."[56] Writers emphasized the day's Jewish heritage and encouraged use of the word "Sabbath." A happy day with the family was another way to distinguish sober Protestants from over-the-top Roman Catholics with their popes and cardinals, incense and processions.[57] With father home from work and mother freed from chores, there was time for the family to learn about each other's inner life in the presence of God. Those who let it slip through their fingers should not be discouraged but instead turn to the Spirit for help.[58]

For Jews, the Sabbath often showcased change and adaptation. In the previous century, Jewish thinkers sought to regenerate traditional Judaism to accommodate lessons of the Enlightenment and, especially in America, new conditions of life. Organs were introduced in some synagogues, a violation of rabbinic rules. The Jewish organization B'nai B'rith launched a "peoplehood strategy" to enrich Jewish culture. Synagogue attendance suffered as interest shifted to ethics and community.[59]

During the mid-1800s, the Reform movement, now the third branch of Judaism, emerged and embodied the benefits and risks of accommodation. Some Reform congregations experimented with "second Sabbath" services on Sunday morning for those who had to work on Saturday. This was later rejected as nothing less than Christianizing Shabbat, a mirror image of the old charge that Puritans or Catholics Judaized Sunday.

Meanwhile, Jewish presence grew with immigration, from an estimated 3,000 in 1820 to 250,000 in the first Jewish census in 1877. Some worried that the refuge they found in America threatened traditional Judaism. But the prevailing religious moods in their new home could also help. The Second Great Awakening of the early 1800s, parallel to the evangelical revival in England, prompted many Jews to renew their Sabbath and other observances. In Philadelphia, women attended services Friday night and Saturday morning along with the men, using the native liberty of the New World to express a revived devotion.[60]

The Sunday Mails Controversy in the United States

As the energy of the Revolution waned and America settled down, many ministers grew alarmed at lax Sunday habits and fretted over a decline in American health and vitality. To fix one would repair the other. Their fears and hopes were joined in the fight to ban the Sunday mails.

When the United States Postal Service was established, Congress required mail delivery on all seven days. No one appeared to object. Then preachers renewed their attention to Sunday. Led by Timothy Dwight, the president of Yale and grandson of Jonathan Edwards, they taught that the Lord's Day was the Christian Sabbath and recommended its observance. Lay people agreed and sought to prohibit Sunday travel, work, and recreation.[61]

The fight turned to the Sunday mails in 1809. Hugh Wylie, a Pennsylvania postmaster and Presbyterian elder, obeyed the postmaster general's direction to open for business on the holy day. Each side dug in. Wylie was expelled by his church while the U.S. Congress soon required local post offices to open on Sundays, upsetting other postmasters who said it made them miss church.

The War of 1812 distracted the nation for a while. After 1820, the Second Great Awakening spread the New England Sabbath into the frontiers of upstate New York, Pennsylvania, Ohio, and Indiana. Church membership doubled and Sunday schools proliferated.[62] Religious leaders complained that the mail service profaned Sunday and detoured Christians. In many towns, post offices doubled as gathering places, notably for men, who collected their mail and lingered to talk, often diverted altogether from church.

The larger concern was the mail's role in promoting Sunday commerce. The debate raged elsewhere. Scotland ceased running a Sunday train between Edinburgh and Glasgow. New commercial centers such as Rochester and New Orleans chimed in for Sunday mail. Anti-Catholic forces found in Sabbatarianism a Rome-led plot to enslave Americans while moderate Protestants feared a fundamentalist conspiracy.[63]

A congressional committee labored over these issues and bravely concluded that the government should serve all—Christian, Jew, and pagan—on Sunday and all days.[64] Fervor grew during the 1840s. At the National Lord's Day Convention in Baltimore, former president John Quincy Adams pledged support for the "sacred observance of the Sabbath."[65] Advocates noted that almost all of Washington closed on Sunday and even London, center of world capitalism, refrained from the mails and most business.[66]

The debate continued for 84 years, but Sabbatarians slowly had their way. In 1912 Sabbath advocates finally convinced Congress to close all post offices on the first day of the week.[67] Most Americans may be surprised to find out that the government today does more to uphold this Christian practice than it did 200 years ago.

Industrial Revolution

After 1800, the pace of economic change accelerated, especially after midcentury when machines hastened factory production and the division of labor mechanized the worker's day. The Industrial Revolution colonized time and space, but religion preserved a sacred hamlet on Sunday. In the mid-1800s, some religious leaders reported that American Christians were most united on their observance of Sunday supported by laws in every state and many court rulings.[68] On both sides of the Atlantic, progressive preachers invoked the commandment's heritage. "We are no Judaizers, and yet we gratefully bless Judaism for our day of rest . . . an invaluable blessing to all the toiling multitudes of Christendom."[69] Instead of transporting us to heaven, one New York preacher taught, the day made this world better by bringing "heaven down to us."[70]

The weekend was emerging. By the early 1800s, British workers habitually took off on "Saint Monday" in order to recover from boisterous Sundays. At the core was the personal impulse to control one's leisure, preferably outside the bounds of doctrine. Thus did the notion of two days off evolve, once again from the grass roots up, into the weekend later advocated by social reformers. Interestingly, the Saint Monday habit continued into England's bank holidays, set for Mondays in 1871, and America's national holidays, most of which now fall on that day. Sabbath habits devolve but rarely die.

A way station was the half day on Saturdays, championed by such groups as the Metropolitan Early Closing Society in Britain, founded in 1842. The group's humane intent was balanced by its desire for well-rested workers to attend church on Sunday. The Young Men's Christian Association promoted healthful and proper sports suitable for Sunday after church, fulfilling with a twist the ancient ideal of a sound mind in a healthy body (*mens sana in corpore sano*).[71]

In Europe and America, many firms began to close at lunch on Saturday. Workers took up sports such as soccer, rowing, and bicycling; others shared a family meal and then cleaned the house and bathed for Sunday. Some spent Saturday night drinking. The contours of the weekend emerged with a clear divide between work and relaxation.[72]

Civil and religious leaders and lay people had long lamented that the only permissible recreations were those afforded the rich. Advocates supported opening museums and galleries and other noncommercial entertainments. But here was a tradeoff: these activities required clerks and guards and guides to work, often serving the middle and upper classes, an old problem. However, free entertainments also benefited most poor people and workers, whose other choices were limited. Sunday was emerging in a new public form with all people at rest, as was first ordered at Sinai.

Some happily blessed Sabbath rest as a support for hard work the other days. A French vicar, Abbe Guame, refuted his countrymen who opposed wasting one-seventh of life by pointing to England and the United States, where commerce and agriculture were not impaired by "a sacred day of repose."[73] Naturally, Americans saw a more practical side. Henry Ford became a weekend advocate when he realized it gave people more time to drive and more reason to buy cars. Within decades, the Sunday drive was an institution that lingers yet today.

Meanwhile Jews, guardians of the day's joyful rest, were rethinking restrictions at a time when leisure was becoming a right in itself rather than a support for worship. One writer in the late nineteenth century cited Maimonides to claim that the Pharisees were wrong in their debate with Jesus. To heal was allowable, just as it was to remove a burden from an animal or, more generally, relieve pain. Another, in London's *Jewish Chronicle* newspaper, reiterated the Sabbath guidelines of cessation from productive labor, recreation, and sanctification. Cessation does not amount to inactivity, so Jews could fulfill the other two by visiting gardens and museums. But commerce remained *verboten*. A Jewish business owner could allow his Gentile partner to open on Saturday, but he could not share in its profits.[74]

Religious Practices and Civic Engagement

The need for the community to reinforce Sabbath habits fired the debates of the seventeenth through nineteenth centuries. In all three religions, practice involves us in the world. Religion is not a private matter. In public we live by its morals and in public we practice its rituals. That which we do for God, we do for ourselves and others. Such has it been for Juma, Sunday, and Shabbat, with each sustained by a core belief despite vicissitudes of theology and practice.

The central idea of early Islamic teaching was the last judgment. Muslims thus concentrated on living out God's laws on earth in order to gain salvation. Rather than asceticism, the Muslim should live a full life as a believer, a family member, and a citizen of the nation and of the umma, the community of all believers and, ideally, all humanity. At times, God's message was subsumed under political or nationalistic creeds. But Islam returns to the taproot of God, aided by the conviction that we can know and do God's will. Despite competing schools of Islamic law (*sharia*) and other doctrinal disputes, the uniformity of Islamic culture and religious practice is one of the religion's most striking features. Earlier last century T. E. Lawrence, or Lawrence of Arabia, found among Muslims "a universal cleanness or hardness of belief. . . . They knew only truth and untruth, belief and unbelief."[75] Thus while accommodations for Juma varied, its basic doctrine was not debated in the way that Sunday was among Christians.

During the Abbasid dynasty, from 749 through 1258 and based in Baghdad, Friday became a day off for officials and students, making it easier for them to attend worship and maintain the day's spirit. The privilege eventually spread to other workers. But the presence of Jews and Christians in some Abbasid communities often meant that Saturday or Sunday became a general day of enjoyment. Rulers periodically sought to stamp out this practice by ordering stores to remain open on the Christian or Jewish Sabbath.[76] More recently, leaders in Basra, Iraq, took similar measures. It was the nature of the weekend that shifted with the fortunes of Islam. The religion came to Nigeria in the eleventh century and was still spreading in the seventeenth. Thus the earliest weekend was Thursday and Friday. British colonialists ended this arrangement and recognized Sunday. There was a similar pattern in other Islamic lands, and many have reverted to a weekend centered on the day of assembly.

The Christian Sunday has been grounds for working out our yearning for a better life. On that day, we live out an ideal in the real. The commandment's opening verb, "remember," may suggest that unlike the other nine commandments, it is not part of natural law and involves a departure from instinct. Paul and the reformers, of course, believed that we live in an ideal world every day thanks to Christ. But in recent centuries, the practical majority found in the weekly Lord's Day concrete results. Rest and worship make this world better. "Where this day is best kept, there all the other graces of Christianity are in most healthful exercise and preservation," declaimed one seventeenth-century preacher. Rather than a burden, "it is a day of holy and heavenly delight."[77]

For Jews, Shabbat has embodied some of these same tensions and differences. The first Sabbath meal begins with the Kiddush or sanctification said over the overflowing cup of wine. It begins with Genesis 2:1–3, the institution of Shabbat at Creation. It invokes the delight, and love and favor of God and recalls Creation and the Exodus from Egypt. The Kiddush prayer also reminds Jews that they are special. "For you have chosen us and sanctified us from among all the nations, and have allowed us to inherit your holy Sabbath in love and in favor."

Similar to Christians, Jews have debated the day's relation to the other six. Should it be a better version of other days or something entirely apart? The Talmud records different opinions. Shammai the Elder taught that one's efforts on other days should be directed toward the Sabbath, while Hillel reminded his followers of Psalm 68:20, "Blessed be the Lord each day."

The day blesses and sustains, gives and demands. The Zohar teaches the Sabbath is "a mirror of the world to come," but Jews also believe that the day is one of spiritual creativity that sustains them. These sensibilities are sorted through the filter of Jewish law, or *Halakhah*, the foundation of Jewish spirituality. The law and its requirements "bring an awareness of God into the details of daily life," writes Jossi Klein Halevi.[78] Jews must, he continues, renew the law without confusing the details for the goal—a temptation that plagued the other two religions as well. In this period, from 1600 through 1890, the Puritan regard for Sunday often slipped over into idolatry. Religion is not God; neither is religious law.

In the United States, there were periodic laments that Jewish observance was faltering. A visitor to San Francisco in 1877 reported that the men kept no Sabbath, only Rosh Hashanah and Yom Kippur. There was also fidelity amid difficulty: one report came of Jewish soldiers in the Union Army meeting for Sabbath services in the forests of Virginia.[79] The Jewish Sabbath, even if timeless, was affected by historical currents. A Jewish counterpart to the Protestant revivals was the Keyam Dishmaya movement in the late 1900s. Its major goal was to recreate the ancient Hebrew Sabbath as a first step to renewing Jewish practice and spirituality. This rejuvenation combined with the influx of Jews from Eastern Europe to transform American Jewry by the early 1900s.[80]

In the Breach: The Sabbath by 1900

The Sabbath endured to the end of the 1800s both in practice and consciousness. Sunday was a restful and restorative habit, even when not devoted to church and worship.

The English Sunday was part Sabbath, part festival.[81] Mainland Europe varied. Germany was judged better at rest than the French, though Paris officials
did suspend public works from "the Tuileries to the Louvre on that Holy
Day."[82] One British traveler reported that Paris "shows few signs of religion on
Sunday beyond the morning Mass" while "in Spain and Portugal, multitudes
rush on Sunday from the confessional to the bullfight." Geneva had plays and
in Sweden business was transacted, with even the national legislature meeting
on Sunday at the end of its session.[83] Clerics in France and Rome resisted the
intrusions of commerce, often for the humane reasons enunciated at Sinai.
French priests advocated Sundays as an antidote to dissipation or relentless toil.
In 1854, the pope weighed in with a letter promoting the Lord's Day.[84]

Time to rest could lead to time for worship, the Reformer's original impulse
for a Christian Sabbath. In Britain, employers and ministers speculated that
closing shops earlier on Saturday improved their workers' observance of Sunday.

Literature often acknowledged the day of rest through its profanation. In
The Merchant of Venice, Shylock swears by the Sabbath that he will have his
pound of flesh from Antonio. In *Hamlet*, Marcellus observes that Denmark's
preparation for war overrides sacred time.

Why such impress of shipwright, whose sore task
Does not divide the Sunday from the work.[85]

The mood of Sabbath observed in the breach is captured by Bret Harte in
one of his Western tales. A gambler steps onto Main Street in Poker Flat on a
Sunday and smells danger in the air. "Two or three man, conversing earnestly
together, ceased as he approached, and exchanged significant glances. There
was a Sabbath lull in the air, which, in a settlement unused to Sabbath
influences, looked ominous."[86]

In 1836 Charles Dickens urged a live-and-let-live approach in his polemic,
Sunday Under Three Heads. At a time when people were exercising new forms
of leisure and recreation, the bishop of London and other churchmen had
advocated a ban on most entertainments in order to promote "the true and sin-
cere worship" of God on the Lord's Day. But in these diversions, commoners
found respite and refreshment. Dickens depicts the happy faces of well-dressed
common folk on Sundays in London, out for their excursions, "joking and
laughing, eating and drinking, and admiring everything they see," much like
God finding Creation to be good. To Dickens, such is the real object and meaning of the Sabbath.

Dickens mocks "the idea of making a man truly moral through the ministry of constables," and warns against converting God's blessing into "a day of general gloom and austerity." Worst of all, the bill was cruel and unjust by banning only the chores and amusements of the poor. They could not work on their own behalf, but could as servants to their lords and ladies. Let the rich, Dickens concludes, fast on Sunday after their six days of pleasure, but let the working class, after their days of toil, have a Sabbath that was made for man.[87]

The Limits of Moderation

Exhausted by centuries of religious conflict, a quiet majority of Christians probably wanted to leave doctrine and theology aside. To these, the Sunday habit just made sense. In the mid-1600s, Peter Heylyn argued for a restful Lord's Day to serve humanitarian purposes. Two hundred years later, a leading light of the moderates, James Augustus Hessey, concluded his influential lectures of the mid-1800s on the subject with this mild peroration. "The day which draws us closest to God; but which at the same time reminds us that God is brought near to us in Christ . . . the day which, in our foolishness, we fancy we have adopted from expediency, or utility, or on political or sanitary grounds, or the like, but which we really owe to our moral wants, and to our moral sense, our moral wants discovered to us, our moral sense guided and directed by a particular issue, by the Holy Spirit, speaking in Scripture and by the Apostles."[88]

Terribly reasonable; I like it. But reasonable moderation rarely sustains religion over the long haul. Our Sabbath instinct, rooted in the desire to be with God, drives us over the centuries. We wield various arguments, many wrongheaded; with many self-righteous petitions; with some of God and much of man; with goodness and charity but often subsumed by our zeal and our fear that one violation will endanger the whole human enterprise.

There is another reason for regulating the holy day in all three religions: strictness pays. Since 1964, historians and economists theorized, with compelling data, that strict religions thrive because of their high demands on members. These demands or membership fees screen out freeloaders and ensure a congregation full of committed members who socialize with and support one another, participate in services and confirm one another's beliefs.

This conclusion may disquiet laity and clergy who try to boost membership by easing requirements (and calling it reform), an approach that has failed in

Christianity and Judaism alike. In Islam, one can only notice the success of orthodox sects. In any case, the theory helps explain the endurance of strict Sabbaths throughout the ages. When observance declines among believers generally, it thrives among the devout few. Then, when others call for its renewal, they can draw on the theology and example of the orthodox minority, such as Seventh-day Adventists or Hasidic Jews.

At dusk on a Saturday in November, I trot down the block to fetch some kindling from the curb. I wonder if the neighbors would heed Yahweh's mandate to Moses and stone me to death. Mitchell and I had a grand day together while my three dames were in Manhattan. After our meal for two, I light the candles, read a Psalm from the daily office and sing, "Come, thou almighty King." Mitchell sits on my lap and joins in the tune. As I wash dishes I realize that were we alone in the world I would still start the Lord's Day so. Steady habits of home have kept many an isolated explorer or missionary alert and alive in unknown lands. I think of the Amish elder who was quoted in a newspaper article on his community's refusal to change their traditional window size to meet a new building code. "If you break a tradition, where's the tradition?"[89]

At the sink I wonder if we should keep the Sabbath lest it vanish. Yes, millions of others may do so but one can't count on the habit of others. God spoke to each of us on Mount Sinai, as Christ did when he affirmed the day by saying, "The sabbath was made for man." But whether it serves man or God, faith can be a matter of life and death. It can save or condemn. The real impetus, however, always comes from faith—the joy of the experience, the sense of God's purpose —and not force. This conviction carried the Sabbath into the twentieth century.

Rabbi Silton

Sitting behind his massive desk in a book-lined study at Temple Israel, Rabbi Paul Silton lets on that despite his religion-teacher wife and their seven successful, shomer Shabbat children, and despite his genial but magisterial presence, he grew up in a nonobservant family. As a teen in West Roxbury, Massachusetts, Silton attended Saturday services "because I liked it. When I was 17 or 18, I began keeping Shabbat. My parents, very good people, thought I was crazy. 'What do you mean?' they asked me. My parents were good first-generation American Jews who were intent on not reflecting the Old World." (His grandparents, who were religious, came here from Belarus. And the rabbi notes "a history on my wife's side of complete adherence.")

Like a good teenager, Silton reacted to their shock by persisting. "I would go to synagogue and come home and study and read," he says, and then trails off. "It was wonderful. I was reestablishing ties with my God, and I was reestablishing ties with my people." On the Sabbath, he felt "a vertical connection with God and a horizontal connection with Jews all over the world."

Rabbi Silton says that Heschel, the great twentieth-century scholar who emphasized the Sabbath as a sanctification of time, "puts it in a proper perspective and makes it relevant to modern man." Silton smiles, then adds, "To put down the phone, turn off the computer—people *pay* to do that." As such, Shabbat can be a premonition of heaven. "If we theorize what the perfect life would be like, Shabbat can be that—you are at one with your self, with your family, and with your community."

And yet, Silton tells me, only a fraction of Temple Israel members keep the Sabbath as they should. "It's a big frustration. I would love to see the whole congregation do so." But Jews who want to take pride in their heritage must consider, he says at a different point, that "being Jewish means more than eating bagels and cream cheese."

Silton encourages observance by setting a good example. "I invite people to my home. People are very taken when they sit down to the meal," he says. "In those that are more deeply involved with Judaism, Shabbat becomes a major focus of their life." And one that will preserve the faith. "Jews from a Sabbath-observing community are going to cherish their Judaism." He offers his own family.

"We have seven grown kids and they are all Sabbath observing. It's a tremendous opportunity to strengthen the family, to see other people you don't see all week. If you pray in the synagogue as part of a community, it's guaranteed that your prayers are heard." (Islam offers a similar assurance.) The lesson sunk in.

Instead of growing up with Shabbat as a restrictive experience, Silton says, their children remember their parents at the dinner table, their father singing "these beautiful songs," and the good food, the light and warmth and togetherness. As the Silton children ventured into the world, some encountered skepticism from unlikely sources.

One son is a pediatrician, and after his residency he looked to join a practice. He was rejected by one because he kept the fourth commandment. "Who was it a problem for? The Jews. It was Jews in the practice who said, 'What, are you crazy? You're not going to work on Shabbat?'"

CHAPTER VII

The Sabbath Defeated, Reborn, Converted: 1890 to the Present

By the early twentieth century, the Sabbath was enshrined in civic culture as a day of rest. Social-minded clerics and union leaders drew on ancient and updated religious doctrine to secure the rights of workers. All three religions connect Sabbath teachings with human well-being. But stripped of its religious basis, the holy day lost some of its universal support. Meanwhile, theology shifted so that practices could survive or be adapted to modern times.

In passing the faith to children, the Sabbath can be a primary conduit. Even among the nonreligious, the day apart endures, even thrives. While religion has pulled back, in most lands, from dictating rules for all, governments have shielded individual observance. The Sabbath is not mandated, but it is protected. At the same time, the day illustrates enduring differences among Jews, Christians, and Muslims. For all people, the Sabbath anchors an institution loved by all—the weekend.

Saturday Afternoon

Shabbat blurts out moments of joy, happiness, and contentment. After the Torah reading and during the rabbi's homily at Temple Israel, and many synagogues, some of the men slip out for a drink. One Saturday at services, Tom beckons me and we meet six others in the small prayer area behind the main one. They smile like boys out for a clandestine fishing trip. One of them opened a cabinet tucked into the wall paneling, pulled out a bottle of rye, and poured seven small drinks, neat, into cocktail glasses. It seemed the most remarkable and natural thing in the world, albeit unsanctioned. The day ends in another happy interlude. Most weeks in fair weather, the Kligermans meet a dozen or more families at Albany's Buckingham Pond, about a mile northwest of Temple Israel. The pond is located in a residential neighborhood of large homes and a tidy apartment complex. A long, narrow park lies along the north shore. There is a small playground, benches, geese and ducks to feed or chase, a basketball court for pickup games, and a footpath that circles the water. The day's requirements push the faithful together.

"You're connected to this whole network of people who don't drive," says Tom. After their main meal, often eaten in groups, the families materialize at the pond. One large family lives nearby and people often repair there for the last hour and the Havdalah ceremony that closes the day. "We might spend eight or nine hours at the pond," says Tom. "It unites you. It's like, it's like a camping trip. You're marooned in this—I'm stealing from Heschel's book here—island of time. Even the ice cream truck guy knows. He comes around and goes right by because he knows he's not going to do any business."

I go there one Saturday in Indian summer. Darkness hesitates at the horizon. Bright by contrast, sunshine pops through the leaves. The scene is marvelously familiar, drawn from some primeval subconscious. Men and women, well dressed and relaxed, stand evenly spaced across the center of the park like angels on clouds. There is no cluster, no one place to be. Children slide, swing, run, toddle, and laugh. Twelve-year-olds help infants, toddlers walk up to the nearest adult for help or a lift. Relaxation washes over me. Such a state of repose must only be in heaven. An observant Jew on Shabbat is at home in the world. Their calm joy is palpable.

Judaism flexes and lives primarily in families and the doings of lay people. Joseph Braun, a dentist and father, talks to me quietly and emphatically about the scene. First he follows up on Tom, who mentioned—again—how today's prayers replaced the animal sacrifices of old. "What's interesting is that nineteen-hundred years ago they had the Temple and the priests did everything," Braun says. "Once the Temple was destroyed, the priests didn't matter anymore. The prayers and meals replaced the sacrifice." In effect, Shabbat became something for all Jews to do. Braun looked around at his fellows. "Here, the people range from the completely secular to the Orthodox." He ticks off five congregations within a mile or two of the pond. Members from each may join in the weekly outing. "Albany's completely unique in this regard," Braun continues. In other places where he has lived—Maryland, Florida, and New York—Jews from different traditions keep Shabbat apart. There is, however, a consistency to the day itself.

"The typical Saturday for us is to attend the service, have lunch with friends, relax and read, and then come here," says Braun. "It's very old-fashioned, like when people used to socialize by playing parlor games. You're not sitting alone in front of the computer or on the cell phone. Here, you have to socialize with people." Nearby a toddler stumbles and flops down. A boy of about ten steps in quickly and raises him, then sees me taking notes and volunteers, "I'll tell you one thing—it's a nice community."

This company of angels dwelling in the Sabbath illuminates my family's holy day, which is just beginning as the sun sets. After I return from Buckingham Pond, my family eats and then we begin Sunday with our prayers and a hymn. Madeleine had asked if we could resume this Saturday evening ritual, which had fallen away. So we do. She and Amy take more of a lead. The next day we stroll to Mass and home, eat waffles and hash, make a fire, go apple picking at Indian Ladder farms in Altamont. I bicycle home and then cook shish kebab. We eat dinner in the yard and then the children bounce upstairs to brush, wash, and dress for bed. Amy reads to them, the house dims. A week later Mitchell tells me, "Church day is my funnest play day."

Early Twentieth Century: Religion's Legacy

By the dawn of the twentieth century, Sunday fit into the cycle of work and rest. Begun in religion, it was sustained by social tradition and personal habit. In the public realm, people spoke more of the humane purpose of rest and recreation and less, if at all, of the religious intent.

Outside forces accommodated the demands for leisure in many nonreligious ways. The Sunday paper emerged in its bigger version for news-hungry readers during the Civil War. Publisher Joseph Pulitzer added Sunday sections that diverted and amused: comics, features, and book reviews. American and English Progressives campaigned to open libraries, museums, and concert halls to draw workers out from their squalid tenements and gin mills. Fairs and carnivals came next. Major league baseball played its first Sunday game in 1892.[1]

Be it religious, recreational, or both, the institution united many countries, notably Britain and the United States. American preachers celebrated it as an institution that helped assimilate immigrants; the English considered it part of their national character. They argued that good Sundays moralized society and rescued citizens, and especially the poor, from toil and squalor. On both sides of the Atlantic, people recognized weekly leisure as essential for the individual and society regardless of its religious content.

America began to recognize that others had different Sabbaths. In 1934 a New York judge ruled that a Muslim family in the Bronx could keep their children home from school on Friday in accordance with their religion, the same right granted Christians and Jews.[2] Across the globe, Turkey offered one interfaith model during the first decade of the twentieth century: all three sets of believers kept their respective holy days without a law suspending business on any of these.[3]

In Europe after the 1848 revolutions, authorities began to heed the needs and demands of workers for rest. Sunday was an easy first choice, though this attention transformed the holy day of rest to a day of rest. This shift in justification accelerated in the early twentieth century as workers' rights dovetailed with blue laws that would have otherwise faded into dust. Pope Leo XIII in his great defense of laborers, the 1891 encyclical *Rerum Novarum* (Of New Things), called Sunday rest a right that must be guaranteed by the state.

Stunned by the long hours and mechanical labor of nineteenth-century factories, unions and progressives in Germany, Austria, Switzerland, Denmark, Norway, Hungary, and Russia achieved laws that restricted employment or closed factories entirely on Sunday. The International Labour Organization, in 1899, 1921, and 1957, affirmed a weekly and uniform day of rest that coincided with the habit or custom of each country.[4] England banned Sunday factory work for women and children in 1901 and limited shop assistants to five and a half days in 1921. Reformers in the United States were on the same track.

Railroad and other unions supported Sunday rest, building on the Sunday closing and half-Saturday laws of the nineteenth century. They revived these issues during the Great Depression, when workers were most vulnerable. From his pulpit in the New York State capitol, Governor Al Smith thundered on behalf of a six-day work week by quoting the fourth commandment. He drolly confessed he found in scripture no exception for factories and canneries.[5] But commerce was a mighty and fluid force. By the 1920s, the weekly total hours of work had dropped but more Americans were working on Sundays.[6]

The secular utility of Sunday closing was confirmed when English munitions factories began to run seven days a week during World War I. Production suffered until government investigators concluded that a weekly rest was necessary for "maximum output." Later the Shops Act of 1936, without any reference to religion, imposed penalties on Sunday commerce that were stricter than those under the entirely religious Sunday laws of the seventeenth century.[7]

Even the Soviet Union found the Sabbath hard to override. In 1929, to boost production and curb religion, Joseph Stalin shuffled the calendar to 12 months of 30 days. Weeks were staggered, with four workdays followed by one of rest. Factories and farms operated constantly. Resentment and chaos ensued. Families rarely spent a day together due to different schedules; many Jews and Christians disliked losing their weekly holy day. Inefficiencies multiplied at offices, banks, and schools since the entire staff was rarely present. The Russian experiment lasted less than the French effort a century earlier; in 1940 they redeployed the seven-day week.[8]

Rest and religion could be uneasy bunkmates. In Spain, public outcry reversed a 1904 ban on Sunday bullfights. Portugal's Sunday closing law was largely ignored.[9] In the United States, the issue became political. New Jersey's governor declared in 1907 that Republicans stood "for righteousness in civic affairs and for morality and for the observance of the Sabbath Day." Democrats, by contrast, favored an "open Sunday" with legalized liquor sales.[10] In New York, leaders of the Congregational Church hotly debated a resolution in favor of Sunday newspapers and bicycling. An opponent defended the holy day as a "bulwark of our free institutions," and predicted that the United States would soon be worse than France in its profanation.[11] Echoing the ancient execution of the wood gatherer at Sinai, the death penalty was almost imposed during a 1909 raid on a Brooklyn textile factory. When workers who were violating the Sunday Observance law tried to flee, the patrolman threatened to shoot them.[12]

American Jews fought through a similar passage with this difference: Shabbat is even more central to Judaism while its observance was more difficult given the minority status of Jews. In his history of American Judaism, Jonathan D. Sarna shows how the Sabbath reflected the struggles of the Jews.[13]

Already in the 1890s, Reform rabbis held Sunday services for those who worked Saturday and even permitted smoking on Shabbat, contrary to the ban on kindling a fire. Some congregations added services late Friday or early Saturday so people could still put in their time at work. But many agonized over having to split the day between God and mammon. One wealthy builder told how he was paralyzed when leaving the synagogue for his office. He quit that job and pledged never to so desecrate the day again. Most had no such choice given the six-day workweeks.

In the first decades of the twentieth century, leaders feared a spiritual collapse among East European immigrants who could not refuse their bosses or were all too ready to drop old habits. Surveys found most neither had a synagogue nor lit Shabbat candles. In Manhattan's Lower East Side, a dense Jewish ghetto, 60 percent of stores opened on Saturdays. But many adults recited a Yiddish prayer that they prosper so that their children would not have to similarly desecrate the Sabbath. Jews formed employment bureaus to help each other find Shabbat-friendly work. At some Jewish-owned firms workers could take off Saturday and work Sunday.

During Orthodox and Conservative revivals, there were classes and workshops to promote Sabbath keeping. World War II and anti-Semitism led Jews to embrace religious identity and traditions. The popular guide *Jewish Home Beautiful* showcased holy day rituals, food, and decorations. During the Depression, Jewish officials in unions and Franklin D. Roosevelt's administration promoted the 40-hour work week for humanitarian and religious reasons. Labor and church leaders cooperated. By 1938, it was the law in most industries and spread by popular appeal and contracts to others. About this time, Reform synagogues dropped their Sunday services. Jews could now work and keep Shabbat.[14]

Late Twentieth Century:
Fluctuating Fortunes of the Holy Day

Wherever Jews lived over the centuries, the Sabbath reassured them that despite oppression they mattered and the world could someday be made whole and right. They recited Psalm 92 with its vision of a just universe where the evil were doomed and the good blessed. Even the poorest and most overworked gathered in good clothes to eat better foods and sing and dance. The day converted a vision of heaven into an alternate reality when Jews felt redeemed in this world. In the Nazi concentration camps, Jews risked death to hoard their meager portions of bread on Thursday so as to have the two required portions—recalling the double portion of manna in the desert—for the Shabbat meal.[15] In the face of destruction, they asserted their identity by keeping, as best they could, God's day of rest and worship.

Amid the secularization of American life, the holy day suffered but also endured and even thrived in new guises. The Jewish version, for instance, changed with the suburbanization of its adherents.

Between 1945 and 1965, more than 1,000 synagogues were built or rebuilt, most in the new subdivisions. In that time, one-third of Jews left cities and at a rate four times that of their neighbors.[16] Religious education, study, and theology all thrived. Suburban homes were signs of American success but also assimilation. But the new locations meant almost none could walk, in the ancient Sabbath habit. Outside of Jewish communities such as those on Long Island, northern New Jersey, and near Cleveland, Boston, and Los Angeles, families were more isolated. During the 1950s and beyond, many neglected the Sabbath, even shopping on that day, while they adapted Hanukkah to life in America. It was an easy ritual, close to Christmas, and involved gifts for children and the patriotic theme of freedom.[17] And it happened once a year rather than every week.

Seeking to help Jews keep the day in their new settings, Conservative rabbis ruled that people could drive but only to the synagogue. They also approved a limited use of lights, telephones, and even radio and televisions. This group grew the fastest in the 1950s and had a plurality of American Jews.

The 1960s and 1970s witnessed a revitalization movement led by a Holocaust survivor whose goal was to "teach our people to kindle the Sabbath lights."[18] Such revivals often bore fruit in the next generation, such as Tom Kligerman, Rabbi Silton, and many others whose parents were more concerned with assimilation and security in the aftermath of the Holocaust. By the turn of the century, however, once-small Jewish suburban outposts and city neighborhoods such as Brooklyn's Williamsburg were thriving as Jewish centers, often thanks to the influx and success of Hasidic and other Orthodox groups. The Chabad and other movements sought to revive Jewish practice and Shabbat was again a primary vehicle. Here in Albany, a family of Israeli missionaries hosts periodic Torah study and discussion at their home on Saturday afternoon.

Israel itself displays tensions among Jews. Shabbat is the law of the land and an unearthly calm descends in most quarters. But the ultra-Orthodox minority has twice brought down governments over Sabbath rules and some members throw stones at Seventh-day motorists. Many secular Jews go along begrudgingly; others shop at the hundreds of stores that open in malls that day, their busiest.[19] There are new challenges: when an Israeli astronaut was scheduled to fly into space on the shuttle *Columbia*, rabbis debated whether earthly rules would apply beyond earth's 24-hour orbit and seven-day cycle. In Israel, secular Jews are now trying "rescue" the Sabbath from its forbidding rules and regulations.

In predominantly Christian countries, Sunday observance was once a universal custom thanks to popular practice and civil regulation. This is no longer the case, at least religiously. As Pope John Paul II lamented, "changes in socioeconomic conditions have often led to profound modifications of social behavior and hence of the character of Sunday."[20]

A dramatic change in thinking that had occurred over the centuries was starkly revealed in 1961 when the United States Supreme Court upheld restrictions on Sunday retail sales as a legitimate government action that could be justified in secular terms. In *McGowan* v. *Maryland*, the justices concluded that Sunday transcended religion and had become a national day of rest kept by the nonreligious as well. The law's goal was to establish a common day of rest and recreation, not establish a religion.

In his mind, Chief Justice Earl Warren must have pictured the leafy Sundays of family picnics and boat trips when he wrote, "The state seeks to set one day apart from all others as a day of rest, repose, recreation and tranquility." But the day must be held in common for it to be useful, which requires government sanction, Warren continued. "People of all religions and people with no religion regard Sunday as a time for family activity, for visiting friends and relatives, for late sleeping, for passive and active entertainments, for dining out, and the like," he wrote. "Sunday is a day apart from all others. The cause is irrelevant; the fact exists."[21] The facts on the ground persuaded Warren's fellow justice, Felix Frankfurter, an active Jew. In a concurring and lengthy opinion, Frankfurter argued that the benefit of a government-enforced rest day outweighed any harm to non-Christians.

The hallowing of leisure represented a profound change in attitude. Whereas the Christians once ceased from labor in order to have time for worship, now society valued Sunday leisure in and of itself—more akin to the Jewish spirit of Shabbat. This legal shift began at least two centuries earlier, when both English and American laws and thinkers began to defend the day for promoting civility, personal regeneration, and fairness to laborers. Some laws referred to it as a "civil institution" rather than the "Lord's Day."[22]

British and American labor leaders developed and spread this reasoning as they pressed for Sunday legislation. By 1960, almost every state in the United States regulated Sunday commerce, 44 of them comprehensively. In these statutes, older religious justifications were increasingly subsumed by arguments both humane and civil.

Under the old religious justification, the blue laws had lasted for centuries. Maryland's 1692 ban on "bodily labor" on the Lord's Day remained intact in its

1957 statute. But once justified on humanitarian grounds, these statutes collapsed at an astonishing speed. The reason may have been an internal contradiction. One could not disconnect the tree from its root.

In a dissent to the 1961 ruling in *McGowan* v. *Maryland*, Justice William O. Douglas said that the issue was not the continuation of Sunday rest by force or custom. "The question is whether a State can impose criminal sanctions on those who, unlike the Christian majority that makes up our society, worship on a different day or do not share the religious scruples of the majority."[23] The weekly day of rest serves the common good, but government enforcement broaches religious freedom. In a free society, Jews, Adventists, or Muslims should not be forced to observe a second Sabbath.

The Sunday closing laws vanished, however, not for theological or constitutional causes so much as commercial ones. People wanted to shop. The mall, with its gleaming corridors of white marble and central fountains that baptized consumers with the sound of splashing water, now gathered believers who could transcend their lives by purchasing T-shirts, kitchen wares, and video games. The fellowship of the mall—the one place where most Americans can lose themselves in a crowd of their peers—confirms these habits. Meanwhile, more people displayed their sophistication by scorning "Puritanical blue laws" that, apparently, repressed their God-given liberties.

When New York allowed liquor stores to open on Sundays in 2003, clergy spoke up not at all. Big stores and distillers pushed for the change and predicted a boost in sales tax revenues. Sunday was a major shopping day and they wanted a share of that. Independent retailers protested, fearing that to compete they would have to open on Sundays and lose their day of rest or hire more help. They were ignored.

The scenario was reenacted in state after state. In 2004, Rhode Island became the thirty-second state with Sunday liquor sales.[24] But the demise of blue laws often increased protections for the religious practices of non-Christians. When Connecticut, for example, dropped its colonial restrictions, it stipulated that no one be forced to work on the day they considered their Sabbath.[25]

Among Christians, contradictions in the religious temperament make it hard to keep holy the Lord's Day. "It's absolutely essential theologically but it's not practice," David Roozen, director of the Hartford Institute for Religion Research tells me. "Generally, there's been a relaxation of practices even though the rhetoric has not changed. Americans are so individualistic and voluntary." He mentions the large, vibrant evangelical congregations that blossomed in suburbs across America in the 1980s and 1990s. "To me, one of the mysteries of the success of these megachurches is that they preach a serious religion, but [members] don't have to be serious about it." Indeed, while congregants may attend services religiously, the Lord's Day doctrine has yet to emerge as a primary teaching point among these Christians.

The devout minority treasures the holy day in various manners. Black Baptists often spend most of Sunday at church, with a morning service, a luncheon, and an evening prayer session. "We have a long service, with long sermons, and then we congregate at a member's home to eat," Ethel Hendricks of Albany's Mount Olive Southern Missionary Baptist Church tells me. People may go home, then return at dusk to end the day together. "We don't forsake the assembly," she adds. In Albany and many other American cities, Sunday transforms many a poor neighborhood, as church members, many of whom now live in the suburbs, promenade along the grey streets, the men in their dark suits and white shirts and the women in their dresses and upswept hats.

"The Sabbath has particular significance in the African-American community," the Reverend Wallace Smith of Shiloh Baptist Church in Washington, D.C., said in an interview. "During the week, someone may be at a job where they don't get the respect they feel they deserve, where they aren't valued. The church becomes a shelter, a place where they are empowered, and are given respect and identity."[26]

The Sabbath instinct, to observe a special day of withdrawal and repose, appears in many faiths. In the Hindu and Buddhist traditions, the days of the new moon and full moon are observed as times for fasting and self-sacrifice. Taoism celebrates the Sabbath spirit of full repose, of nonaction, in its central text, the Tao Te Ching. "When nothing is done, nothing is left undone."[27]

Mormons too keep Sunday holy, with worship and family. Thanks to their discipline and cohesion, they usually do so in a more unified manner than Catholics and other Christians. Keeping the Sabbath, said one Mormon elder, frees us to hear "the whispering of the Spirit." The Book of Mormon repeats the fourth commandment by example and teaching. In it, the Nephites, the fair-skinned Hebraic people who populated North America along with the dark-skinned Lamanites, the ancestors of American Indians, for 1,000 years "waxed strong in the land. They observed to keep the law of Moses and the sabbath day holy unto the Lord."[28] Later, the wise and holy Abinadi repeats the commandment as it is in Exodus 20. After the revelation of Jesus, Alma, who organized the "church of Christ," commanded his people "that they should observe the

Sabbath day, and keep it holy, and also every day they should give thanks to the Lord their God."[29]

Among Muslims since midcentury, the practice of Juma has grown with the boom in their numbers. The first mosques were built during the 1920s and 1930s in Massachusetts, New York, and the Midwest. There are now more than 1,300, with 80 percent of them constructed since 1980. As for the practice of Juma, any changes will be in terms of attendance, outside accommodations, and how Muslims use the rest of the day. The obligations and service, based on the unchanging word of Allah in the Quran and Muhammad's example, will remain as they have for centuries.

Fidelity Today

For decades if not centuries, we have lamented—or celebrated—the death of religion and ritual. To attend services and turn to God one day a week sounds nice but seems so sixteenth century. Still, we go.

As we entered the twenty-first century, one-third of Americans reported that they attend services at least weekly and 12 percent go almost every week, for a total of 45 percent.[30] These figures are higher than those reported by the congregations or sociologists, but they have remained relatively stable over recent decades and represent an increase from previous centuries.[31]

Keeping the Sabbath was strongly associated with religious commitment but varied widely and is often strongest in the denominations whose central doctrine involves the holy day. Today's Seventh-day Adventists and Seventh Day Baptists claim a long pedigree of Christians through history who kept Saturday holy, true to the fourth commandment. The Adventists, known for their successful door-to-door evangelization, have more than 2 million members worldwide, half in the United States; the Seventh Day Baptists report 5,000.[32]

We certainly preach better than we practice. Overall, about 47 percent of Christian, Jewish, and Muslim congregations placed a high emphasis on keeping the Sabbath. Among Catholic and Orthodox Christians, 84 percent placed a high emphasis on the Sabbath, which drops to 49 percent among Evangelicals, 36 percent among moderate Protestants, and 24 percent among liberal Protestants.[33] Seventy-two percent of Jewish congregations stressed Sabbath keeping; among Muslims, it was 87 percent.[34]

As with Christians, Jewish attendance lags behind these exhortations. Only about 15 to 19 percent of Jews said they attend synagogue services at least weekly.[35] The future may be better. In a sharp increase from the recent past, by 2000 to 2001 three-fourths of Jewish children received religious schooling and more than a third of Jewish college students had taken a class in Jewish studies.[36]

Among Muslims, the Mosque Study Project 2000 found that 17 percent of the 2 million associated with mosques attended Juma. (The portion among all American Muslims would be much smaller.) However, average attendance at Friday prayers nearly doubled to 292 between 1994 and 2000. Suburban mosques grew the most—typical for America but in conflict with Muhammad's teaching that it is a special grace to walk to Friday prayers. Nearly all mosques—90 percent—identified themselves as strict, adhering closely to the primary texts of the Quran and Sunna (practice) of the Prophet. Most reported teaching members to observe restrictions on the holy day.[37]

Perhaps the most enduring measure of Sabbath fidelity is our lament of its shoddy observance. Like candy-bar prices and good manners, holy days were more so when we were children or just before that. Today is ever given to hypocrisy and empty words. When the church was new, Clement of Alexandria lashed the "Sunday Christianity" of his time, from 150 to 215 CE. "After listening reverently to the word of God they leave what they have heard within the church itself, and go outside to amuse themselves in godless society."[38] In our own day, Pope John Paul II was more measured and positive. Sunday fellowship, he declared, could sustain "diaspora" Christians in a hostile world.[39]

Contemporary Theology and Reform

On the day apart we stop. On the other six days we are Abraham marching across Mesopotamia toward a Promised Land we never enter until we stop and wake up in Paradise—where we've been all along. The struggle may be the journey, but the journey may camouflage the truth of our location. To me Sunday often seems a mirage shimmering just beyond the horizon of Saturday afternoon. A gift it is and not our creation. Like the Jews, Christians could find in God's command to cease a joy, a light, a heaven here on earth. We act, not think, our way to it.

Unlike the more abstract realms of theology, that concerning the Sabbath is entirely bound up in concrete application. Our beliefs yield rules, and these rules result in practices that turn us toward God. The Jew wonders, "Will this act involve carrying from a private to a public domain? How soon must we finish cooking on Friday to be ready for sundown?" Similarly, the Muslim on Juma plans his day around congregational worship. Christians orient Sunday by following one major rule, attendance at the liturgy with the community of believers.

My family's attendance at Mass sets our sail for the day and week. We discuss the allowable, the binding, the helpful. Sometimes I ask Madeleine and Jeanne for their opinion, who may consider it carefully and deliver a child's fresh insight. We pray for a day of joy and family and charity, so we consider what actions or inactions promote those. If we break a minor rule, it matters not, for our eyes are still watching God.

The Catholic theology of the Lord's Day is spelled out simply in the church's 1992 catechism and elaborated in Pope John Paul II's letter, *Dies Domini.*[40] The major points resemble those of mainstream Protestantism and would, I believe, be acceptable to most Christians. It grounds Sunday in the Sabbath commandment, which recalls Creation and the Exodus and serves as a sign of God's covenant. God's rest, then, is a model for human action. Jesus respected the Sabbath's holiness while recalling its true spirit. Easter began the new creation, making Sunday the first of all days and giving the first Christians the right to transfer the meaning of the Sabbath to the Lord's Day. Sunday's ceremonial observance replaces that of the Jewish Sabbath, fulfilling its spiritual truth and heralding our eternal rest. Given Sunday's heritage, Catholic theology echoes aspects of Jewish tradition. For instance, John Paul II noted that the weekly return of Shabbat ensures that time never closes in on itself but "remains open to eternity."[41]

We rest to have time for worship, and also family, charity, and renewal, but also in the original spirit of liberation. The Second Vatican Council called it the original feast day, "a day of joy and freedom from work."[42] Sunday allows us to live in harmony with God's laws, our fellows, and nature.

Among Catholics, it is odd that amid the waves of spiritual renewals, little heed is paid to the Lord's Day. Some Presbyterians and many African American churches have been more attentive. Evangelicals have been oddly silent on the topic. Among a more diffuse set, there has been a Sabbath boomlet pervaded by flexibility rather than dogma.

In the lovely *Sabbath Keeping: Finding Freedom in the Rhythms of Rest,* Lynne M. Baab celebrates the growing number of people who take every seventh day to rest and develop intimacy with God; but she concedes people can choose the day and define its contours. Wayne Muller's popular *Sabbath: Finding Rest, Renewal, and Delight in Our Busy Lives* suggests traditional practices that readers can "play with, modify, edit, expand, or ignore" to find a Sabbath that "nourishes your heart and body."[43]

Another notable book, the meaty *Keeping the Sabbath Wholly: Ceasing, Resting, Embracing, Feasting*, by Marva Dawn, connects discipline and joy. She insists that people be adamant about the day, "that it *will* be set aside for ceasing, resting, embracing, and feasting." At the same time, Dawn warns against legalism. She encourages a Sabbath kept in response to God's grace and not as an obligation.[44] By contrast, Tilden Edwards' seminal 1982 book, *Sabbath Time*, emphasized the Christian's Sunday surrender to God's commandment. And Francine Klagsbrun's luminous book on the Jewish Sabbath, *The Fourth Commandment*, finds in the restrictions of rabbinic law a path to freedom.

Even the Catholic Church, which holds that skipping Sunday Mass without cause to be a mortal or serious sin, often encourages rather than demands a holy day. A 1949 *Handbook of Moral Theology* indicated all children over seven years, and even heretics, were obligated. But, it added, "transgressors are frequently excused from formal sin through ignorance."[45] The 1992 catechism states that Catholics can be excused from Sunday rest by family needs or "important social service."[46] (The Jewish Mishnah contains similar leniencies.[47]) Even Benedict XVI, once the stern guardian of doctrine, used a languid tone to tell German youths that Sunday is better with God. "Sometimes, our initial impression is that having to include time for Mass on a Sunday is rather inconvenient. But if you make the effort, you will realize that this is what gives a proper focus to your free time."[48] The church, above all, steers the believer to the act of attending Mass as a parish gathered by and in God. Beyond that, there are few rules.

In Jewish theology, Shabbat culminates Creation and memorializes the Exodus every week regardless of the calendar. Today, many Jews enliven the holy day with two ancient concepts, joy and restoration.

For many, oneg Shabbat, or Sabbath joy, dominates, such as through festive or casual get-togethers for unmarried Jews. As always, funerals are postponed a day and even those sitting *shivah*—the weeklong mourning—are to leave their homes for Shabbat services. Though a Jew "makes" Sabbath by preparing ahead of time and keeping the rules, the day is holy unto itself.[49] Jews who keep it help create harmony and repair the world, (*tikkun olam*). In this spirit, tradition prohibits cutting anything other than food, considered also an effort to restore creation to its natural state.[50] Tikkun olam permeates Judaism, and has been given new life by reformers who, for instance, emphasize the environmental benefit of Sabbath rest.

In all three religions, theology dictates one primary practice: communal worship or celebration. But in Islam, the umma is social and political as well as religious. Community is based on, and central to, individual faith. Yet there are tensions.

Muslims are encouraged to bring others to Allah, which has been exercised in extreme measure. Yet the Quran teaches, "There is no compulsion in religion" (2:256). Submission has its primary expression in Friday's public worship. Only when I went through the physical routines of Juma in martial intimacy, foot to foot and shoulder to shoulder, could I truly appreciate Islam's surrender to God. The experience drives home the lesson that, historically, the needs of the umma trump those of the individual. Muslims submit as one. The Friday ritual performed in unison reinforces the individual's obligation to live in accord with Allah's revelation and not one's whims and desires.

So too, Sunday is central to Christian identity and the Mass is central to Sunday. "Unfortunately, when Sunday loses its fundamental meaning and becomes merely part of a 'weekend,' it can happen that people stay locked within a horizon so limited that they can no longer see the heavens," John Paul II warned. "Hence, though ready to celebrate, they are really incapable of doing so."[51] He could have spoken similarly of Shabbat or Juma. We must come together. Faith makes sense only in the community of believers.

Sabbath Practices and Rituals

Practice reflects the theological elements of faith; it also strengthens that faith in Islam, Judaism, and Christianity alike. God is in the details; the details bring us to God.

Detail and simplicity mark Islam's Juma. Muslim prayer is not a personal appeal to God but worship, as Imam Sebkhaoui often reminded me. On Fridays, the umma gathers to recognize Allah's power and to place itself jointly under His dominion. The requirements and practice of the day of assembly have endured the centuries with few changes. A companion of Muhammad would likely be at ease in the Friday prayers at the Islamic Center or the chapel at Albany Medical Center.

As simplicity has preserved Juma, so has flexibility. People can be excused and just two worshippers can form a congregation. While Christianity does not have a required minimum for the Mass—a priest can say it alone—Christ encouraged group devotion. "For where two or three are gathered in my name,

I am there among them" (Matt. 18:20). Jews are stricter, and must have a *minyan* of ten men for Shabbat and other synagogue services.

All three religions share another element. Believers are encouraged to make the holy day special by doing things differently. Believers bathe, dress in special clothes, and often carry themselves with dignity. Jews clean and decorate the house to reinforce the day's character, and hurry to finish well before sacred time begins, as do many Christians for Sunday. Both groups may use special candles, table coverings, and dishes. In many American and European homes, religious or not, the wedding china comes out on Sunday. One set of Catholic instructions suggests that people attend cultural activities and even follow a different schedule for meals. Naturally, Judaism encourages the most comprehensive shift. The sages interpreted the Torah's ban on work to mean that Jews should walk, talk, and carry themselves differently on Shabbat. A farmer, for instance, may wave birds off from seeds if he or she does so differently from other days.

So do even people who are not religious live out the holy day. They too put aside material concerns and relax one day a week, often visiting a museum or concert. Their seemingly secular pattern reflects the deeper meaning of the Jewish restraint on work and related matters: to set down earthly concerns and concentrate on the beauty and joy of Shabbat and of God.

Sabbath rules leave room to breathe. One Shabbat, we meet at a late afternoon get-together at the home of an Israeli missionary. Earlier Tom took his son Eli to a Little League game that was outside the eruv, the perimeter beyond which carrying is not allowed.

"I didn't carry anything, he carried the glove," Tom says. Since Eli was under 13, the age of religious adulthood in Judaism, he was not obliged by rabbinic law. Baseball games are discouraged because, in running, a player may break a stick or compact dirt, which are prohibited agricultural activities. Basketball on a paved surface, which avoids those dangers, is okay. Games are different from working out or jogging, Tom says. "Exercise for the sake of exercise is work, especially because Shabbat should be different from other days."

After the game, Tom and Eli still managed to catch the end of the Saturday service as well. "If we do this once or twice a year, I still taught Eli that services are important to attend on Shabbat. Plus I got to spend a nice day with my son."

Though the synagogue service is important, the spirit of the day and the law lies in the home and family, the cessation of creative work, the blessings and prayers. This differs from Christian practice. Sunday liturgy is the centerpiece of the day and life. Beyond that, Catholic catechism situates Sunday rest as part of the rhythm of life. Holy unto itself, it also allows us time for family, culture, and society. By ceasing, we are free for God's blessings. "The faithful are to refrain from engaging in work or activities that hinder the worship owed to God, the joy proper to the Lord's Day, the performance of the works of mercy, and the appropriate relaxation of mind and body."[52]

For Catholics today, a threat to Sunday lurks in the vigil Mass held Saturday afternoon or evening. Permitted since the mid-1960s for those who had difficulty attending on Sunday, the vigil Mass has become the most popular at many parishes. Though better to have people at church than not, often the vigil allows some Catholics "get Mass over with." Then, efficiency overrides Sunday's holy leisure. More than one bishop, while not able to turn back the clock, has sought to persuade Catholics that regular use of the vigil Mass can erode Sunday's holy atmosphere.[53]

We Ringwalds have experienced this phenomenon. Sometimes we have attended the vigil Mass in order to leave early on a long hiking trip in the Adirondacks. Time in nature is certainly a good Sunday activity. Other times, attending the vigil Mass has been a guilty pleasure that converts Sunday into another Saturday. We sleep late, loll about, relax, dress casually—but the bloom is definitely off the day. No one puts on, spiritually or physically, their Sunday best. I'm wary of making it a habit.

Islam Endures in a New Generation

On a sloppy winter's day—snow yielding to rain under a grey coverlet—Naseem Haqqie waits for me outside the Islamic Center of the Capital District. He is home for the winter break from graduate studies in electrical engineering at the University of Southern California. Naseem is slim, of medium height, and has a shock of short black hair. Naseem's visage combines his father's thoughtfulness and his mother's friendly bemusement. We enter the mosque and store our shoes in the newly built vestibule, which now has separate rooms for the footwear of men and women. Naseem strides quickly and softly, like Shamim, into the main room and begins his private prayers. He bends, kneels, and prostrates himself. A hundred or so other men and boys, and a smaller number of women in the back, do the same as a man up front issues the Adhan, or call to prayer.

In his sermon, the day's leader spoke of limits to human endeavors, of Ramadan's call to improve ourselves, of Muhammad being unlike "Mark, or

Peter, or even John the Baptist" in that he was "a man of his community." As he spoke, about 200 people filled the main prayer room, with scores more in a room downstairs and a dozen teenagers perched on steps in the hallway. One tall youth, wearing baggy pants overlapped by his shirttails and a blue knit watch cap pulled down to his eyebrows, prostrates himself along the 10-inch width of one carpeted step.

The leader recalls Muhammad's time in the cave, and I compare that moment, when a solitary Arab merchant fasting in the darkness received Allah's revelation, to this overflowing mosque, already in need of another expansion. One man's glimpse of divinity became the religion of a billion Muslims, filling mosques around the world. Then in comes today: a camera man from a television news program, here for footage on the Muslim reaction to earthquakes in Iran. The center's president, dapper and capable, escorts him between the rows of supplicants as the service continues.

The leader speaks on, now about sacrifice and "building your inner self," perennial themes in Islam's core message of self-control and humility. He finishes and the congregation completes the midday salat of two communal rakas. Afterwards, I meet Naseem and his sister, Nadia, in the vestibule amid a stream of Muslims. Many are college students home from school for the Christmas break and eager to catch up with one another. In the congregation today, there is more than the usual mix of old and young, American and foreign born, dark and light skinned, prosperous and less so. At lunch, Naseem orders a club sandwich without realizing it has bacon, and abashedly reorders one without. He tells me that he attends prayers almost every Friday.

"Because it's a religious obligation, but more because it's a reminder of our faith, of the things we learned in weekend school." Nadia interjects. "I don't always go. Women don't have to go. I don't really think about it, but sometimes I would go mostly so Mom wouldn't yell at me. When we were growing up, Mom would always say, 'Try to learn at least one thing.' And I would have to have two things in case she asked Naseem first."

We discuss the special times of Islam, and the fact that the Day of Judgment is due to come on a Friday, another reason to attend prayers. "I try to avoid thinking about that," said Nadia. Naseem confirms that Ramadan has auspicious times to connect with Allah. "There are more opportunities for good deeds. We were told to think of it this way: Suppose there's a pair of shoes that costs $70, but during Ramadan they are on sale for $1. So you can buy 70 pairs at that time for the same price that one pair costs the rest of the time."

Nadia, in her charming and brisk irreverence, does not resent the gender disparity in the Friday obligation. "It's kind of good because I don't always want to go. It works for me since it gets me off the hook." She reconsiders, then trails off. "They teach that Islam offers equality for women, but . . ." Naseem picks up the grievance. "I always wonder why there never is a woman leading the prayers or leading the call to prayers, or why they always sit behind the men, why they're not alongside the men or in front of the men." Nadia says the seating "doesn't bother me because I grew up with it."

At school, Naseem often attends Juma at a mosque just outside the USC gates in Los Angeles. As for the daily prayers, they both admit to irregularity and occasional discomfort. "I do it in my room," Nadia says with toss of her head. "I won't break out and pray in the middle of the library." Naseem warily reminds her that some students use a certain stairwell in the library at RPI, where he also studied, and she nods back briskly.

Vestigial Sabbath

In the title of his novel *Saturday Night, Sunday Morning*, the British writer Alan Sillitoe captured the way working-class people prepare for the holy day with an evening of revelry in the pub or dancehall. In an ancient, intuitive way, we pair profane and sacred time or activity. Of course, for Sillitoe's protagonist, Sunday is the time he pays for his fun with a hangover and regret—some people's idea of religion's function.

Today among the secular, the Sabbath stamp lies most clearly upon Sunday morning, which people idle away at half speed over the newspaper and coffee. Others sleep late without fear of missing valuable work time. Unwittingly, they too abide by the spirit of the fourth commandment. In the post-dawn coolness, others take that long run or bicycle ride that is impractical other days. Many toddle off to a fancy restaurant for a midday meal. As a young man in Washington, D.C., I would periodically don jacket and tie on a Sunday and join my friends at a downtown hotel for a fancy brunch. Even when the champagne refills bubbled away the day's dignity, it was special and unlike the other six days.

Here at the Sage College of Albany, the local chapter of secular humanists meets on Sunday morning, a common time for such groups. Another venerable humanist organization, the Ethical Society (or Ethical Culture Society), holds Sunday "platform meetings" with ecclesiastical elements—uplifting music, readings, meditations, and a collection.[54] In Alcoholics Anonymous and other 12-step fellowships, meetings devoted to meditation, rather than discussion, are often held on Sunday, often with candles and time for silent contemplation.

All these groups, even those that have tossed the tethers of religion, find free time on the first day thanks to the once-lively hand of clerics and blue laws. No one escapes the past. These spiritual seekers simply fulfill under different guises God's command to cease. If nothing else, they value the day of rest preserved by religion and would complain if Sunday lost its character and protections, legal or social. God said rest, and we have ever since.

Religious or not, still we must settle on the appropriate form of ceasing. Christian leaders and writers encourage true rest and relaxation, not the busy leisure or hectic recreation that resembles work. Thus, writes one bishop, "leisure brings no re-creation from within but rather more tiredness of body, mind and soul. This is the 'weekend syndrome,' the 'Sunday neurosis' that have made leisure an exhausting problem for many who cannot remain still because they have to be enjoying themselves."[55]

This raises a perennial challenge. Can we find meaning in this world without reference to a transcendent power? Can free time release us from worldly concerns without that freedom being based in the assumptions and experience of faith? At best, I'd say, Sunday's atmosphere survives for all thanks to the care given it by those who based the weekly rest on God's example and command. And these faithful people, in modern times, must defend their Sabbath on their own terms while seeking the allowance of society, business, and government.

For my family, the hours outside of church orbit the one at Mass. The sacramental gathering illuminates those other hours fore and aft. A year into our heightened awareness, we have a perfect Sunday: a late breakfast with a sleep-over guest, James Doody, a ten-year-old friend to all our children, followed by a nice walk on a spectacular day—clear, 70 degrees, the green wave of spring upon us. Madeleine serves on the altar in her white robe and corded belt. Jeanne helps Father Powers carry up the bread and wine, I help give out communion with the other ministers. Outside we gab with Kathy, James's mom, and another family. At home we lounge about—coffee, newspapers, Leggos, scooters, sidewalk chalk—then bicycle to Washington Park to play tennis. Then off to the Kelly home for the end of Erin's birthday party. Our Jeanne is already there laughing and dashing with her gaggle of friends. We eat pizza and snacks and cake. Then we head home, where I read to the children on the back porch. We talk and pray. Our giant silver maple, the tips fringed in bright green buds, hovers over us protectively. I say that this may be where heaven begins. "Oh no," Madeleine interjects. "Then all the dead people would be here too."

A year later the pattern holds. Our Sundays do not develop in a linear fashion, constantly moving us up the escalator to heaven. Instead, the day of rest is a holy time that recurs cyclically, allowing us to be human. Each week we enter a day apart, a time that continues around and right through the other days. Sometimes on Saturday we prepare, unwittingly, for sacred time by flushing out the evil within. Our ids would emerge from the cave and roar or whine, then whimper and retreat to make room for our better selves. One could not be without the other.

Protection and Accommodation

Limits of Religion

The Sabbath question illustrates the larger debate over the limits of religion. If government cannot, or should not, make people observe the Sabbath, should it at least protect a person's choice of a holy day or a secular day of rest? Around the world, generally, nations no longer claim the right to mandate religious observance even though a fair number do forbid actions that violate religious law. In the United States, we struggle to balance the First Amendment's twin freedoms: to practice a religion and to be free of a state religion. A primary testing grounds has been the day of rest.

In 1829, during the Sunday mails controversy, Senator Richard M. Johnson divined the truth. A weekly respite made sense but should be freely chosen by individuals, especially if religious in nature, and not imposed by government.[56] For their part, religious people often recognize that they cannot impose their beliefs on all. In nineteenth-century Germany, modern Jewish Orthodoxy emerged among those who wanted to participate in secular life. They accepted that not all aspects of social or political life should have religious answers. As one thinker concluded, "a healthy spiritual existence often depends on the rigorous separation of the sacred from the mundane."[57] Such a distinction can be difficult or impossible for some to make.

Many Muslim reformers, and outsiders, argue that until Islam disengages mosque and state, political and economic progress and personal liberties will languish. While it is impossible to completely untangle the two in any society, the principle was established early on in Christianity by Jesus ("Render unto

Caesar . . ."). The persecutions of Christians in the first centuries and, later, their persecution of others, reinforced the separation at least as an ideal.

Legal Protections

In many Western countries, and notably the United States, religion remains enmeshed in government even as government tries to protect the free exercise thereof. We muddle along. Back in 1829, time off from work was already recognized as necessary for religious freedom. Though post offices at that time operated seven days, Jewish and Christian postal workers were not required to work on Shabbat or Sunday.[58]

Today protections vary. In 2000, the presidential primary for the western states was moved from a Saturday to a Friday to accommodate observant Jews. Muslims said the change was fine since they could vote before or after congregational prayers.[59] But protection can easily veer over the line toward government support for a religion.

For years in New York City, drivers could park for free on Sunday without having to feed quarters into the meters that line the curbs in crowded shopping areas, where many churches were also situated. During tight times in 2002, the city began charging again. In 2005, the city reversed itself to general relief. Advocates called the metered parking, which raised an estimated $14 million a year, a tax on worship and said that drivers deserved a day of rest.[60] Newspapers printed tales of worshipers who had to run out mid-liturgy to feed coins into the parking meters. However the free parking amounts to government support of one religion. And the Sunday treat ignores Muslims and Jews who have no such provision when they attend services on Friday or Saturday. (The city does, however, suspend other parking rules on various major religious holidays.)

Islamic countries often move from protecting religion to mandating it, and back. In 1977, Pakistan's rulers replaced the weekly Sunday holiday with Friday. The next year, businesses were allowed to choose their weekly holiday but still had to close for noon prayers on Friday. Then in 1979, authorities promulgated Islamic law and government chiefs had to lead even the daily prayers for their employees.[61]

The United States military, which has had Muslim chaplains since 1992, has stretched to ensure a person's ability to observe the holy day. During Shamim Haqqie's annual two-week stints in the Army Reserve, and even during longer deployments in Germany or Baghdad, commanders gave him and his fellow Muslims time to attend Friday worship. (In Iraq, Shamim attended Juma services inside a prison since that was closest, the holy day again joining people across lines of conflict.) Civil society has followed the military's lead. Through scattered court cases and negotiations, Muslim employees, some supported by the Equal Employment Opportunity Commission, have secured the right in many jurisdictions and firms to have time—usually 90 minutes—to attend Juma services. Advocates advise employers that an extended lunch hour should suffice, with the time made up before or after the usual shift.

Given the global spread of the Saturday-Sunday weekend, Muslims in many countries struggle to attend Friday services. In Nigeria, a 1990 survey found that half the Muslims cannot make it to the mosque.[62] Those that do, race from work, and "arrive sweaty and breathless" to hurry through the ablutions and miss the sermon. A 1992 ruling or *fatwa* favoring free Fridays by the country's imams had little effect. One writer described Friday as the Muslim Sabbath, which should be spent on matters of faith and charity, free from labor concerns. Instead, believers are forced to neglect the day, negating Islamic unity and losing the right of free association.[63]

Even in the United States, the right to a day off for religion is not guaranteed or even widely accepted. My workweek was changed to begin on Sundays after I had been working at one newspaper for several years. I objected. My editors, both Catholic, were dumbfounded. One asked me to write a memo laying out the reasons—a request that would have been incomprehensible a few decades earlier. To my shame, I agreed to a Sunday evening shift in order to preserve an assignment I valued. Years later, I told a prospective employer I could not work on Sunday for religious reasons. "What religion is that?" the person asked a colleague.

Around the country, legal protections vary and change. The general rule is that employers should accommodate a worker's request for time off on a religious holiday unless it would harm the company. Nevertheless, authorities often whittle away protections that they say promote religion.

In 1996 in Massachusetts, once home to the Puritans and their sacred Sabbath, the state's top court nullified a protection for employees who refused to work on religious holidays.[64] Since enforcement would require courts to determine the requirements of a particular religion, the judges reasoned, the law infringed on the separation of church and state. This is silly. A complex issue does not require the state to throw up its hands. In Colorado, an air traffic controller was dismissed for not working on Saturday, which the man's nondenominational Christian group considered the Sabbath. His boss dismissed this creed as "a religion of convenience." A federal jury waded into the thicket and agreed with the plaintiff, awarding him $2.25 million. The man called it a victory for someone who did not belong to a large denomination.[65]

Many states, such as New York, California, and Texas, protect the free exercise of religion by requiring that employers make reasonable accommodations, notably time off for religious holidays such as the Sabbath. In 2000, New York State's attorney general, Eliot Spitzer, settled a case with Sears Roebuck and Co. over Orthodox Jews or Seventh-day Adventist repairmen who could not work Saturdays. "People should not be forced to choose between worship and work," Spitzer said. But in 2004, Virginia, which had one of the first and strictest Sabbatarian laws as a colony, rushed to wipe out such protections.

After a legislative snafu eliminated an exemption to the "day of rest" rule for utilities, hospitals, hotels, and retailers, businesses howled that they would lose money and even go under if workers could take off on the Sabbath. Virginia's 116 state legislators rushed to a special summer session and reversed their mistake. The sole dissenter, Mitchell Van Yahres, castigated his colleagues for heeding bosses and ignoring workers. Observers treated the episode as a joke. One headline read, "Assembly fixes flub that gave day of rest." Religious leaders remained silent or said there were more important topics, such as gay marriage and abortion.[66]

Even the nation's highest tribunal has treated the topic lightly. In 1985, the United States Supreme Court struck down a Connecticut law that required companies to try to allow their workers to observe the Sabbath. Justice Sandra Day O'Connor dismissed the request as if a sneaky fifth grader were shirking homework. Observant Jews should not be given special privileges, she wrote, because all employees would like "the right to select the day of the week in which to refrain from labor."[67]

This approach, however, denies believers the right to define their beliefs and practices. In 2005, a man in Henrietta, New York, sued his employer, Home Depot, over its refusal to grant him Sunday off. The company, instead, said he could have Sunday morning and then report to work in the afternoon. In a brief supporting the Christian, the American Jewish Congress argued that, "Accommodation of the employer's concept of religious practice is not what a statute protecting employee observance compels."[68]

Protection may be uneven due to the lack of a national guideline. The Civil Rights Act of 1964 requires employers to respect the religious needs of workers; in 1977 the Supreme Court limited accommodations to those with a minimal cost to the employer. Given this uncertainty, politicians and religious groups have asked Congress to approve the Workplace Religious Freedom Act. The bill would require employers to accommodate religious practices of workers unless this caused an undue hardship or prevented the employer from fulfilling "essential functions." That is, a police department might refuse to hire a full staff of Orthodox Jews since it would have no one to patrol the streets on Saturdays.

Personal Accommodations

Regardless of the laws of the land, the believers are responsible for keeping the holy day holy. They must accommodate themselves and their lives to their God. In discussions of the Sabbath, the common refrain is, "I'd love to but," followed by a list of imposing factors. Most of these limits are self-imposed. People say life's too busy, the kids have sports and activities, when else can we shop or do chores, society has changed, it was easier 30, 50, 100, or 10,000 years ago when everyone kept the day holy.

Calm down. In most Western nations and many other countries, Jews and Christians, by and large, can avoid working on Saturday or Sunday. Most businesses close on weekends; at other businesses people can usually trade shifts. It may require sacrifice, but who said religion was easy? Muslims have it both harder and easier. In the West, at least, Friday is usually a work day; on the other hand, they only need one or two hours off, not the whole day. I suspect most can rearrange their workday. Shamim Haqqie, a busy doctor at a large hospital, starts early and works headlong before and after to be able to attend Juma at the chapel downstairs. Azra, an editorial assistant and staff writer at the newspaper, has less authority at her job but is still able, most weeks, to put in extra time and trade tasks with a colleague so as to be able to drive to the mosque.

Ah, you say, he has a chapel downstairs, she must have a nice boss. But each accommodation begins with a single person saying, "This I must do." And each assertion of belief makes it easier for the next person to have their rights and religion respected. Those with more power—lawyers, doctors, teachers— should pave the way, by example and by direction, so that people with less clout—janitors, waiters, clerks—will be excused without some boss saying, "What religion is that?" or calling it one of "convenience." Medical residencies are notorious for long hours and constant work. But a small group of observant medical students seek out Shabbat-friendly hospitals and the Association of Orthodox Jewish Scientists supports a fledgling clearinghouse. Through Shamim, I met Muslims who do the same.

During the race for president in 2000, the public was treated to an extended discussion of the ways a public figure can adjust his life to his religion's exacting holy day. An Orthodox Jew, Senator Joseph Lieberman of Connecticut, ran for vice president and had to explain his ability to fulfill his obligations. While in the Senate, he voted when necessary during the Sabbath, often walking several miles from home to the Capitol. With advice from his rabbis, Lieberman concluded he could act to protect human life and the greater good of the community. These two principles covered all the bases.[69] The greater good provision creates a loophole in the rule against a Jew asking a Gentile to complete a forbidden task. In this case, the Jew could direct the efforts of a non-Jew if these would help the largely non-Jewish community of America.

On the ground level, life goes on in the gaps. The Albany chapter of the Jewish fraternal order, the Knights of Pythias, for a time operated a Friday night bingo fund-raiser. And during the 1990s, the local Jewish Community Center upset some and pleased others by opening for business on Saturdays.

Technology has been harnessed for shomer Shabbat Jews who want to avoid breaking the many rules. In Israel, there are electronic milking machines that relieve the cows and special hotel elevators that stop at every floor to spare Jews from having to press an electronic button. As the folklorist Alan Dundes observed, finding loopholes actually perpetuates the rule and pays homage to its divine object. "Shabbat includes circumventions," he concluded.[70]

Still Fighting

As the observant struggle to preserve their holy days, the differences among Shabbat, Sunday, and Juma represents three religions that are still at odds. Christians and Muslims define themselves against the Jews. This is natural. Both religions arose within or near Judaism and broke away while retaining many of its teachings. Each became a new religion by replacing elements of Judaism. In rejection and innovation, the new faiths emerged. (And any religion can renew itself internally by the same process.)

Still, Muslims and Christians need Judaism in a way that Jews do not need them just as a parent can exist without a child but not the reverse. And as a son hates his father, at least for a time, in order to become his own man, so the children of Judaism often harbor hostility or bewilderment or defiance toward those who first came to know God. Centuries later, some offspring cannot accept, fully, the parents' intransigence in retaining the old faith and rejecting the new, improved versions. Orthodox Muslims or fundamentalist Christians sometimes express shock that any person is not of their faith.

One example is a visiting imam who preaches at the Islamic Center of the Capital District near Albany one Friday. An American convert, he is here for a job tryout, one that was unsuccessful, as it turns out.

Islam requires, he intones in measured syllables, "knowing who your Lord is." He dismisses other gods as tribal or otherwise limited. The world, he continues, "is divided between believers and disbelievers." He warns that "the people of the book" are jealous of Islam. "They see us standing in lines and they are jealous because they don't have those lines. They ask, 'What is this religion that is so beautiful and orderly?'" Like Muhammad, he laments the divisions among people of faith, who are always "separating themselves into new communities of believers." Among Muslims, he says, "our allegiance is to Allah and the Prophet." But then after all this religious saber rattling, he upends the formula and rejects earthly wisdom. "As I said before, we do not have victory by the strong but by the weak with their salat and their prayers."

Despite the common ground of a day of rest and worship among the three religions, differences beyond jump out. Compare the Christian and Muslim at prayers.

The Christian tends toward silence and with fewer body movements and those are at longer intervals. The Muslim follows a shorter, but quicker and almost athletic schedule: stand, bow, kneel, prostrate, sit back, and so on. The Christian thinks of herself as a child of God; the Muslim as a subject of God. Some say that Christian prayer develops spirituality while Muslim prayer fosters humanity. Finally, Christian prayer is supported by cultural or artistic aids such as hymns, statues, paintings, stained glass. While mosques can be architectural masterpieces, Muslims eschew icons and find in prayer itself sufficient inspiration.[71] Muslims share this use of a nonmaterial arena with Jews, who enter a holy time, rather than place, on the Sabbath and who also prefer spare sanctuaries and few if any icons.

Wherein arises another difference. On the holy day, the first duty of Christians and Muslims is to worship. They need time to do so, which justifies the day or hours off from work. For Jews, however, the day itself embodies their faith and God's covenant. The law (Halakhah) and lore (Haggadah) regarding Shabbat is the fruit of generations of spiritual labor, the equivalent of a great cathedral. Every detail and obligation elaborates and decorates the Sabbath edifice.[72]

Thus, as Tom Kligerman often tells me, Jews obey the law of Shabbat without struggling to rationalize it. If the Jew obeys only those commands that make sense, if his religious life expresses only his values and conscience, he serves only himself and rebels against God. Keeping the Sabbath turns believers toward God and away from their own inclinations. Hence, they rest because God, not man, says so. "The Sabbath loses all its pristine religious meaning should its laws be adjusted to human inclination and convenience."[73] The same holds for keeping kosher. Holiness through submission is the point.

Another gap yawns within Christianity. Catholics see the Mass as the central expression and exercise of their faith; they must attend. Thus the Catholic principle of *lex orandi, lex credendi*—the law of worship is the law of faith. In the Mass, Catholics believe they are united with God. Protestants, however, find the equivalent in scripture, the Word of God. "They can hear that anywhere, reading the Bible alone at home or even over the radio," David Roozen tells me. Protestants are not as driven to actually attend church, even if a significant portion does. The Reformation, after all, swept away those bothersome clerics and popes who stood between God and the believer. While this bolstered the individual's relation with God or Jesus, it inadvertently weakened his or her need for the congregation. This individualism dovetails neatly with the American temperament, which prefers the personal quest over the communal exercise.

Christians still justify the change to a first-day Sabbath in different ways, though they don't debate the topic as they once did. Protestants rely on their interpretation of scripture while Catholics claim the right as a church descended from the Apostles. In 1934, this distinction was made harshly by the editor of a Catholic magazine who declared that since scripture contains nothing about a change to Sunday, Protestants should return to the Saturday Sabbath, like the Seventh-day Adventists.[74]

Division plagues even that small portion of Christians, apart from the Adventists, who keep the Seventh-day Sabbath. One group, the Seventh Day Baptists, reportedly believe theirs is the true church and refuse to cooperate with other Christian Sabbath keepers. The president of the Bible Sabbath Association, an umbrella group, has cautioned against such disunity by pointing to Celtic Sabbath-keeping Christians whose divisions hastened their end, usually under siege by the Roman Empire.[75] (Despite dissension, their numbers impress: worldwide, the Bible Sabbath Association reports 400 Sabbatarian groups and 1,600 congregations.)

The Sabbath reveals different perspectives on the sacred and profane. Whereas Jews and Christians have an entire 24 hours of devotion, the partial nature of Juma represents Islam's integration of the divine and the temporal or material worlds. Muslims express their religion in politics; a disordered umma or Islamic community represents infidelity to God. Salvation comes through creation of a just society in which the believer is better able to submit to God.[76] It fits that many Muslims work before and after attending Friday prayers. "And when the Prayer is finished, then you may disperse through the land, and seek Bounty of Allah, and remember Allah frequently that you may prosper" (Sura 62:10). Allah blesses the believer in this world.

The mosque, to some degree, contains both sacred and secular as well. At the time of Muhammad, outside of prayers, business was conducted in the courtyard and people socialized throughout. At the mosques I visited, Muslims talk and laugh and trade stories with a vigor that reminds me of Jews at the synagogue. Catholics, once taught to revere God's presence in the consecrated bread stored in the tabernacle, generally speak in hushed tones within the church.

Juma also manifests some contradictory impulses within Islam. One of the two sermons typically comments on ethics or even politics and society. Today, fiery preachers in many lands inveigh at Juma against the West or corrupt Arab rulers or other enemies of the umma. Orthodox and moderates have even argued during such sermons. Media accounts of terrorist acts often trace a perpetrator's motivation back to a Friday sermon.

Ideally, Juma expresses the communal harmony at the heart of Islamic law and morals. It is also the occasion for reform, such as women pressing for equal space alongside or even with men rather than in the rear or on a balcony. In the United States, with Muslims from 80 countries, the congregation at Friday services may illustrate an emerging pluralism and religious diversity. One sees this at the Haqqies' mosque, the Islamic Center, with its moderate tone and diverse crowd. And after a long search, they eventually hired an imam, scholarly and dignified, who is known for his interfaith efforts and expertise.

Weekend Triumphant

Even where the Sabbath has shrunk, that which was established to allow and preserve it—the weekend—has flourished and endured. No one speaks of forsaking that. Even those who work 24/7 would be horrified if Saturday or Sunday lost its character.

Among Muslims, Juma led naturally to a two-day junction of the week. Muhammad instructed his followers to meet for prayers "on the day when the Jews prepared for their Sabbath." With Friday a special day, Thursday naturally developed an anticipatory air and became a market day throughout Islam, just as Friday was for the Jews.[77] However, Juma was emphatically not a day of rest. Indeed, Sura 62 directs people back to work and the Hadith teaches that rest was required of the Jews as punishment. In ancient times, some holy men disparaged fellow Muslims who followed the example of Jews and Christians by resting on the holy day.

During the rule of the Abbasid dynasty, which was based in Baghdad and endured from 749 to 1258, however, there were reports of government and school closings for Friday. A query to Maimonides, the medieval Jewish divine, mentions a jewelry workshop operated by Jewish and Muslim partners who took turns running the business on Friday and Saturday to allow the other their holy day apart.[78] There were similar tales involving a Jew and Gentile. In this way, when any two of the three religions are present, there is a natural support for the tradition of a holy day and an automatic endorsement of a second day to get ready.

By 1950, most of Islam observed Juma as a day of rest. Turkey chose Sunday as a day of rest, under the Westernizing influence of its leader, Atatürk. Pakistan made Friday a half day of rest and Sunday a full day, a legacy perhaps of British colonialism.[79] Muslim countries generally observe Friday as an official holiday, though the day is not ordained as one of rest. In Egypt, which has a large Christian minority, many private stores are open on Friday while government facilities and firms are closed. In Somalia, Saudi Arabia, and Jordan, a few shops may open on Friday morning. In Egypt, Saudi Arabia, Libya, and Sudan, the weekend consists of Thursday and Friday. People may work on Thursday but the evening is given over to family and even revelry. This pattern is ancient in religious history—the carousing just before the piety. Similarly, Americans and the English go out on the town Saturday before the holy day and in Latin nations, Mardi Gras gives vent to profane energies before the penitence of Lent. Perhaps we sin in order to be forgiven.

During a visit to Baghdad in 1999, on Thursday evenings I saw families strolling along the boulevards, groups of men walking or sitting as they talked and smoked, and carloads of youths careening along the avenues with music and horns blaring, a combined version of Friday and Saturday nights in the Americas. In many Islamic countries, however, taxis and buses run and newspapers are published on Juma—unlike the stricter cessation of most public activities on Shabbat in Israel.[80]

The day of rest and the day to get ready are natural mates. Similarly, sex and the Sabbath have long been mated, just as entirely secular weekends afford couples the time and inclination to conjugate. For married Muslim couples, the night before Juma is set aside for "fulfillment of matrimonial duties."[81] Jews are similarly encouraged, based on the Genesis teaching "to be fruitful and multiply." Some Orthodox rabbis encourage couples to mate three times during Shabbat. Catholic literature contains some oblique suggestions in this direction as well.

Though the Sabbath can be lost in the weekend, the day of preparation provides a useful buffer. To be in heaven, or somewhere close, on the holy day, we need the second day, a day for chores and market, for the mundane but satisfying activities that make possible the divine rest of the next day. Indeed, several Scandinavian countries still call the sixth day "laundry day." For Christians, Saturday can be a way station between the office and the church. We work five days, then have a lessened and domestic version of work—chores and errands—on Saturday. We are moving then from the profane world and time into the sacred realm. In each religion, then, Thursday, Friday, or Saturday can be the gateway to God's world.

CHAPTER VIII

The Window on Eternity

They get up and go inside to make havdalah. The Landauers get out the spice box and kiddush cup. Brocha holds the braided candle, and Isaac says the prayer marking the end of Shabbat. After he says the last words, *Hamavdil ben kodesh lihol*, Nina asks, "What do you think is the best translation for that?"

"Blessed be he who separates the holy from the profane," Isaac says.

"The sacred from the secular," puts in Elizabeth.

"The transcendent moment from the workaday world," suggests old Rabbi Sobel in his quavering voice.

"Mm." They pause around the smoking candle.

ALLEGRA GOODMAN, *KAATERSKILL FALLS*

In all three religions, the Sabbath embodies and evokes eternity and the after-life. The day apart—Juma, Shabbat, or the Lord's Day—brings forever into the now. We live in God's day, for it is the holiday He observed and then instituted on the seventh day of Creation. For Muslims, the world will end on Friday and Juma has them ready. Christians participate in the divine through a Mass or other liturgy and experience the peace and rest of heaven on Sunday. For Jews, Shabbat is a temporal oasis that evokes eternity and heaven. Abraham Heschel wrote that the Sabbath liberates and installs man "as a sovereign in the world of time."

The Sabbath recalls the first day of Creation when God separated light from dark. If one day is holy, we naturally think other days are less so, or not at all. Sabbath gives us a day, 24 hours, during which we access special privileges—forgiveness, blessings, God's attention. On this day, my family recalls our origin in Eden and hopes for the promise of heaven. Many envision a heaven that is the eternal Sabbath. Since the world's distractions drop away on the Sabbath, truth comes closer. We draw near to God and thus to ultimate reality and final judgment. In Islam, the Day of Judgment comes on a Friday. Man and woman were created on the sixth day, and they come to the end on that day, either to be with Allah or cast out.

For all three religions, and for the Kligermans, Ringwalds, and Haqqies, the Sabbath liberates us from the grip of space and material, of possessions and pride. The observant are freed from this world in order to more fully enter into it. Heaven and earth join. Yet the Sabbath remains holy with or without us. It is eternal. It is eternity.

Islam's Day of Judgment in the Month of Months

Since Muslims believe the world will end on Friday, keeping Juma keeps the person ready at the right time. "When I was young, they drummed it into us to do the Friday prayers because it will be in your favor," Azra tells me one day over the telephone. "I anticipate being judged and questioned, about my obligation to God and about my obligation to my fellow mankind and womankind. Not just my family, but my neighbors, my co-workers, the whole world."

This truth reveals itself when I attend Juma with Shamim during Ramadan. Here is the usual Friday mix of doctors, researchers, med students, janitors, and state workers. Given the holy season, there are 30 worshippers, more than usual. One man, in shirt and tie and shoeless, stands as he concludes the khutbah, or sermon. He implores the congregants to ask Allah to help them "do for the least among us as You did for me." He reminds them of the extra charity, self-denial, and prayers required during Ramadan. "All these are special ways of coming closer to Allah."

Afterwards, some rise and leave. Others stay and perform one or two more rakas. I wait for Shamim Haqqie and catch him at the door. In the doctor's lounge, an oasis of library-like stillness off the hospital's crowded main hallway, we sit and talk before he rushes off to see more patients. I ask about the special quality of the day.

"Friday is special anyway. During Ramadan, it's more special. I notice that more people come out on Friday. You try to become nice during Ramadan. All these things that you are supposed to do normally, you try to do more so during Ramadan. Now, with the prayers and breaking fast at the mosque—we go there almost every night—it's a long day. We get up at 4:00 AM for the first prayers and we don't get home until 10:00 PM." Shamim speaks in his usual clipped manner. A few words, stop. A tilt of the head, a few more words, stop. It's not that he's terse, or shy, or blunt, but just that he expresses the thought at hand and reaches for no other.

Shamim moves on to the duty of alms giving, or zakat, the third Pillar of Islam. The word is borrowed from the Hebrew, *zakut*, and the Arabic root *zaka* is connected to the concept of purity. For some, this means that by giving a portion of one's wealth to Allah, the Muslim purifies the remainder, which he or she can then use in good conscience. Technically, zakat is the official tax levied on the property of Muslims of means and given to the poor and the needy, and *sadaqa* refers to voluntary charity, but the two are used interchangeably.[1] In any case, one should give even more in this lunar month, since it is a special time.

"The Prophet was very generous anyway, but he was more generous in Ramadan. Allah is more forgiving than usual now. And who knows if you'll be here next Ramadan, so it is important to do these things. The last ten nights of Ramadan are special, and it could be one of them," he says, referring to the Night of Power or Laylat al-Qadr. One of the year's holiest moments, this falls on one of Ramadan's final ten nights, though no one knows which one.[2] On that night, all one's sins may be forgiven.

Shamim sees it this way, "If you catch that one night, it's better than if you prayed for a thousand nights." This echoes the teaching that an unknown hour on Juma is auspicious. So we have sheer chance combined with the divine interruption of earthly life, the intersection of the sacred and the mundane. I ask if the happenstance nature of maybe hitting the jackpot, so to speak, is unfair.

"Not really, since God will give you another chance." As with Azra, his wife, Shamim regards the existence of especially holy but unknown times as an aid to devotion. Then he waves toward the hubbub of the hospital and says, "Oh, we're practical, we pray on the run here." I ask about Allah's Day of Judgment, which will come at the same time for all the living and the dead. "I do believe that in the life after death we will be held accountable. With Allah's mercy, I'm pretty sure I will be forgiven. In Ramadan, that's what we pray for, is forgiveness."

We prepare to leave the sanctuary of the doctor's lounge. Shamim returns to the topic and observes that during Ramadan, the Haqqies and other Muslims try harder to be virtuous. He looks up at me with a fresh expression. "It's amazing to me, we all change then."

Time and Timing

If one day is holy, the others are less so. The Sabbath consecrates a portion of our week or recognizes God's consecration thereof. Sunday is special, Monday mundane. And so we divide and subdivide life into these categories, black and white, good and bad, so-so good and partly bad.

For Islam, perhaps more than the other two monotheisms, the special nature of their day apart, Juma, affects judgment, forgiveness, and grace. God listens better on that day. It affects the dead as well as the living. The torment of sinners abates on Friday and wandering souls return to their graves, making it a good time for Muslims to visit cemeteries (as do many Christians).[3]

The religious recognition of sacred time required a joint effort. The Sabbath requires a group. Time, law, and religion thus hold hands. "Over the long course of history, the law's endeavor to regulate the Sabbath has been the most striking legal effort to regulate time," one scholar observed.[4] Society must coordinate time or else chaos ensues. We agree that night is best for sleep and so we all get our eight hours. Many of us dine after work and so have evenings free for communal activities. We do in common or else we are alone. Without a shared timetable, we wither.

The laws of Sabbath in all three religions amount to a quarantine, the protective garments of emergency workers handling toxic chemicals or the stockade wall that keeps out the bandits. Though my family avoids shopping and most chores to keep the day special and fun, we may move the playing lines.

One weekend our daughter Jeanne is in Manhattan visiting her aunt and uncle. They plan to take her shopping for toys on Sunday after Mass. Amy and I wonder if we should we allow this. It seems okay given the special occasion. But it is as a child that we learn the habits that may save or destroy us. If a special occasion justifies a rip in the fabric, then soon there will be more holes than cloth. Nevertheless, Heschel assures us, "Even when men forsake the Sabbath, its holiness remains." So we relent. Jeanne receives without spending, just as we receive on Sunday and in all of life.

If God has divided space and matter, has He also split time into good and bad, holy and unholy? Was Eve and Adam's time in the garden better than their time outside? Is our time on earth less than our time in heaven? Is Sunday, or Shabbat, or Juma, a better day for believers than the others? Could all three be holy? If not, who's been wrong all these centuries?

We all realize, at some level, that time is more than the passage of seconds, minutes, hours, and days. The clock ticks each second in all its finality. It begins, occurs, and ends. Still we know there is a span beyond this small portion. Eternity grows out of this very moment despite its being hemmed in by the first and the sixtieth second of the minute we now inhabit.

Henri Bergson conceived time as duration rather than clock time. Time is always becoming, this second yielding or morphing into the next and creating a realm of new possibilities.[5] This approach is quintessentially Jewish, for Judaism is a religion of linear time. It was the first religion with a God who acted in and through history. As the Old Testament scholar Lawrence Boadt often told his students, the Bible shows us the "hand of God moving through time." The Hebrews broke free from the Greek cyclical notion of time and introduced a linear conception. Historical events such as the Exodus began to matter more than the seasons or other natural cycles.[6]

As a religion of time, Judaism sanctifies time. While finite-minded man may experience each moment the same as others, "the Bible senses the diversified character of time," Heschel observes. "There are no two hours alike."[7] Though each moment ends, eclipsed by the next, time endures pure, inviolate, and endless.

It may be easier to think of time in two senses as did the Greeks. There is *chronos*, clock time or transition, and kairos, holy time or opportunity. For the early Christians, kairos embodied their sense that God's eternity breaks in upon the present and endows it with its power. Similarly, Heschel considered time to be God's presence in the world of space.

For Jews, Christians, and Muslims, the holy day has times within it that are even more sacred. "The value of Juma is that there is a special time, a gift that God gave to the believers when their supplications are more acceptable to God," Imam Djafer Sebkhaoui says. The exact time is a matter of controversy. "Some say it is when the imam is in the pulpit. Others say it occurs after prayers. Or many say the time is not specified, and I believe that, so that people will spend most of their time on Friday in good works so their prayers will be answered."

One Friday after attending salat at the Islamic Center with Azra Haqqie, I ask about the exact time that the world will end on Friday. She begins to laugh. "I certainly hope it will be after prayers, and not before."

But could one's personal salvation depend on the slim matter of timing? Could she be doomed if she dies in the middle of sin after a lifetime of doing good? Could Allah be so set on a moment? Or in our prideful effort to control Creation do we create divisions? Time is as much a part of Creation as the land or water and then, perhaps, beyond our categories of good and evil. If so, what matters Friday, and the observance of Juma or Shabbat or the Lord's Day? For one day to be holy, must the six other days be profane? Can all seven be sacred and none set apart?

Then, does the profane side of life matter? If God's love is full and complete, what of our categories of good and bad? What good is love if it does not wipe away all sin, overcome all evil, redeem all people, and bring all Creation back to the Creator?

Despite the division of time, despite the hedge about the law, the Sabbath at its deepest evokes unity, not separation. The Jews consider Shabbat a small sample of the next world and imagine the next world to be an unending Sabbath. The day apart looks out from its island of holiness to a time when all Creation has been brought to God. At Creation, God created the heaven and the earth, and then separated the light from the dark, so as to have day and night. But in the very next line of Genesis 1:5, the order is reversed, "And there was evening and there was morning, a first day."

This is the basis for the Jewish Shabbat, and Catholic holy days, beginning the night before. Yet it is at odds with our experience of day and night, of the evening hours being a part of the day that preceded them. This counterintuitive demarcation, however, awakens us to time's flow. A day ends: we dine, relax, pay bills, do homework, play music, watch a video, attend a meeting. But rather than ending the day, we are already in tomorrow, which began at sunset.

Time ushers us relentlessly but easily on into the present that is forever. "Be here now," the Buddhists say. And thus all time, since it is of one nature—continuous and eternal—is holy. Time only appears stained by its association with aspects of matter and space, such as money and work and things. Time cannot be partitioned. On the Sabbath we exalt time, yet time flows on undivided. In time, there is no good nor bad, no holy and profane, for time is one with God in the world of space that He created. And in God there is no East or West, no day or night, but eternity only.

Sacred and Profane

We know, deep down, that each moment of life can be for good or naught; each decision for better or worse; each action for right or wrong. Thus all of life's parts click into one or the other category and nothing is neutral. We then divide all time and space into good or bad; helpful or indifferent; busy or boring; ours or theirs; sacred or profane. Now I am polite, but then I am rude. Now my thoughts are clear, later less so. You are a good person, he is bad. Sometimes the divides are more drastic: friend or foe, fellow human or alien monster with three heads, helper or hurter. Labels can harm but also make sense of the world.

Yes, in a world redeemed by God, all humans would be my brother or sister. But I can't know and love all earth's billions.

We do the same with time and place. This place, your favorite spot in the hills, inspires you to poetry. It becomes a good place. There you were robbed or your car overheated. It becomes an unlucky spot. And each spot acquires more power as we continue in our respective regard or disdain. The power is real because we have invested it so. So too with time, as Muslims make Juma more holy by their assembly. "Friday is a time of united zeal and the gathering of hearts in the soliciting of God's grace, which is one reason for the nobility of time."[8] Yet there remain, Islam teaches, other holy times we can never know—which only makes the times we know more worthy of our attention.

At the same time, Muslims are less likely to sanctify particular places other than their major shrines. A mosque is a meeting place, not a holy place. Friday is the day of assembly, but the assembly can take place anywhere. "Wherever the hour of prayer overtakes you, then shall you perform the prayers and that is a Masjid," Muhammad taught his followers.[9] (The Arabic word for mosque, masjid, means "place of assembly.")

We have always thought that some places, peoples and things were closer to the Divine. The tendency dates back, at least, to the ancient Greeks and is a universal religious phenomenon. Monotheism militates against these exclusionary claims by which we seek to tether God. Paul implored the Galatians in his Epistle, "Now that you have come to know God, or rather to be known by God, how can you turn back again to the weak and destitute elemental powers? Do you want to be slaves to them all over again?" (Gal. 4:9). But with our weak souls and limited minds, we can't help ourselves. Heaven doesn't seem here yet, so we divide time and space and matter. It makes life easier. "Order is Heaven's first law," Alexander Pope announces in *An Essay on Man*. Chaos is evil.

"Then God said, 'Let there be light'; and there was light. And God saw that the light was good; and God separated the light from the darkness. God called the light Day, and the darkness he called Night" (Gen. 1:3–5). From this separation come all others: water and land, Adam and Eve, the Garden of Eden and the land outside.

Paradise could only exist with its opposite. Perhaps God created each creature and element along with its negation. Yet when Moses comes to the burning bush near Horeb, God calls out, "Come no nearer! Remove the sandals from your feet, for the place where you stand is holy ground" (Exod. 3:5). Does this passage, one of earliest in the Bible, divide world into holy and not, or does it recognize all Creation as sacred, as God's? Perhaps the place is made holy by

God only for that moment. After all, God can use any and all times or things, high or low, for His purposes; in the Quran, we read that God made man from a clot of blood (Sura 96:2).

Jewish law, so full of distinctions, can tempt us to think that there is good and bad in space and time. But the prophet Isaiah insists that holiness resides in the person and not the Temple. And later Jesus lays holy claim to the entire world. Perhaps through these holy men God is saying that Creation is still His, holy and unsullied despite our subdivision and profanation. Nevertheless, all three religions recognize that there are good times and places for prayer, suggesting there may be less auspicious times and places. Take Islam.

"Definitely there are times when you cannot perform salat, for example, when the sun is rising," Imam Sebkhaoui tells me. "You have to wait 20 minutes until the sun is above the horizon. There are places where you cannot perform salat, where there is filth or urine, or in a graveyard. And salat must be performed in prescribed times. You cannot do it later or before. Prayer, or supplication, you can do anytime. There are times that are considered better times, such as Friday, or the last third of the night, before dawn. It's not that there are good or bad times, but that there are better and less good times. The best place is Mecca." So too with the Jews, for whom it always was and still is, "Next year in Jerusalem." These geographic longings bespeak our more deep-seated sense that we are meant for elsewhere and that this life is an exile. In the profane, we yearn for the sacred. Each reveals the other.

Many people suffer the blues, bouts of depression, on Sunday afternoon. In my late twenties, I often wandered through the deserted, quaint streets of Capitol Hill in Washington, D.C., feeling alone in the universe. Vacancy spread out around me. In 1910, the Hungarian psychiatrist Sandor Ferenczi identified a "Sunday neurosis" that plagued clients who were lost without the controls and limits of the other six days.[10] Throughout the Sabbath, people may miss the absorption of work. But at day's end we sense the return of formal obligations and the hassles of life. Our time in heaven is over and now we plummet back to earth.

Then back in profane time, we clutch at the sacred. We evoke and recall and make it real, as ever humans have yanked God into our midst. This can be religion's triumph, the artful and moving expression of the divine. The Christian Eucharist, a scandal in Paul's time and still shocking when we contemplate its reality, brings the divine presence into bread and wine that we then eat and drink.

But this tendency can also crush religion as surely as neglect. Johan Huizinga's comment on the Middle Ages still applies. "There is an unlimited desire to bestow form on everything that is sacred, to give any religious idea a material shape so that it exists in the mind like a crisply printed picture."[11] That sentiment produces great art. But the urge to sanctify all of life can drown the sacred in a profane mess or a false uniformity. Poets and writers from John Donne to Madeleine L'Engle depict dystopias where sameness is evil incarnate. What if the weekend was two Saturdays? What if all days were the same? Making sacred the profane robs us of the useful dualism that allows us to live in faith despite our sin.

But but but. The day I write this Imam Sebkhaoui and I talk briefly on the phone and I mention having been bogged down in the trivial. "There are no unimportant matters," he tells me in his rich, believing voice. "Nothing that God has created is trivial. It is all a matter of seeing things in their correct context. Something that seems unimportant and small today may be very important later on."

Indeed. The Sabbath contains its negation. We revel in this moment of eternity but also know it will end. Monday will come with the stern call of duty, the need to make a living and get the kids off to school and shovel the sidewalk and put away the laundry and feed the cat. In turn, each of these terribly finite moments suggests their infinite opposite. "If the life were good, the negation of it must be bad," William James wrote. "Yet the two are equally essential facts of existence; and all natural happiness thus seems infected with a contradiction."[12]

I ask Azra about the division between the sacred and profane. She reminds me that men leave their work, close their stores, and attend Juma. But then they return to those places. "In Islam, it is not one or the other. It's not that you give up the things of this world. In Islam, it is both this world and the afterlife. You do good deeds here that will carry you into the next world. You can live a good life in this world, within limits, but not forgetting that there is another life after this one."

We could call the history of the Sabbath a fight for peace. Julius Caesar said that the way to peace is by preparing for war. *Si vis pacem, para bellum.* One is always bound up in the other. At bedtime in our house, when it's my turn to read and pray with Madeleine, Jeanne, and Mitchell, I often suggest we sit or at least lie still and take a few deep breaths, maybe chant *om* in the manner of Buddhists. At ages ten, eight, and three, they often are like irreverent Zen monks and pray with one finger in their book to mark their place or fidget with a teddy bear or the pillow. Sometimes we do still ourselves with the pleasant vibration of our humming diaphragms. Other times they thrash, ask for cups of water, bounce in their bed, hyperventilate, and soon I am yelling, "Calm down and meditate." I don't feel too bad—Zen masters of old were known to club their students toward nirvana. *Si vis pacem, para bellum.*

Right Side, Left Side

In this life we live well by remembering the next. We have two worlds, then: this one and heaven. Such organization underlies much of human activity and learning. It begins with that first recognition in late infancy: I am me, not you. Biology confirms the instinct. "One of the main characteristics of life is discreteness. Unless a film of flesh envelops us, we die. Man exists only insofar as he is separated from his surroundings," Vladimir Nabokov writes. "Death is divestment, death is communion."[13]

The Sabbath combines a profound division—earth, heaven; man, God—with a practical split—Sunday versus the other days. Naturally, we shuffle these divisions down Jacob's ladder to the mundane level of daily life, such as the ancient preference for right over left.

When Nadia was a child, she says, "Mom always told us, 'The devil eats with his left hand.' There's a hadith that the Prophet would tie his right shoe first. A lot of Islam involves doing what the Prophet did." When Tom Kligerman and his family and guests wash their hands before partaking of the two loaves of challah at the Shabbat dinner on Friday, they pour the water from a two-handled pitcher over the right hand first, and then the left. The Catholic instructions for receiving Communion, revised in the twenty-first century, now direct communicants to accept the host into their left hand, then pick it up with their right to eat it. I suppose the bishops wanted uniformity and traded on the fact that most of us are right-handed, but it also reinforces the notion that one side is better. "The devil eats with his left hand!"

We all participate in such practices, which, to an outsider, seem superstitious. Small distinctions make life possible. We shake hands with the right one, presumably because this habit allowed our ancestors to show they were not holding a weapon. Yes, these habits and sentiments are born of the majority who are indeed right-handed, but the impulse is so deep-seated that it shapes our thinking. In their display rooms, funeral homes traditionally array the more expensive models on the right sides since people tend to walk in that direction once through the door. Most supermarkets arrange their floor plans to best use our tendency to enter and start shopping on the right. The next time you attend a buffet banquet with serving tables on either side, try the one on the left since it is likely to be less crowded.

After my time with the Muslims, I began thinking of my right foot and the left. One night in Troy, while leaving Imam Sebkhaoui's mosque I don my shoes in the vestibule. I open the door, say goodbye, and step out with my left foot into the night on Fifteenth Street. I did not act on a superstition, but on an awareness that led to a choice. I did not fear God's wrath or an unlucky mishap if I used the other foot. But the left foot, that bad one, returned me to the profane world. Did it confirm a negative impression of the world? Or did the action merely remind me of God and the things we do to recall him?

I carry a rosary. Most days I also carry a key ring, billfold, change, and a handkerchief. Habits save time. So when I dress, I tend to put the handkerchief in the right rear pocket and so on. I began putting my rosary in my right pocket. Soon it was automatic. And since one doesn't mix God and mammon, I began pocketing the money in the left. The preference for the right, the negation of the left, is universal. "If I forget you, O Jerusalem, let my right hand wither!" Psalm 137 declares. Teachers forced my father, a natural southpaw, to write with his right hand. If it wasn't the Sabbath that began us in these habits, every week it confirms the division between sacred and profane and therefore all other divisions.

At the same time, many religious rites have a purpose beyond the immediate. Muslims wash before salat in order to purify their inner selves more than to have clean hands, though that is a secondary goal. By being conscious of right foot, left foot, they remind themselves of Allah and his Messenger. Ritual order also promotes unity. Azra washes her right hand first on Juma along with millions of other Muslims around the world. So too in Judaism and Christianity. We choose right over left and the Sabbath over other days in the name of the divine unity and order that serve as the rungs of Jacob's ladder as we mount up from earth to heaven.

Truth

There are cracks in reality through which come angels. Throughout the Hebrew scriptures, there are times when ordinary reality and the supernatural overlap and truth reveals itself. James Kugel, a biblical scholar, calls these "moments of confusion." It is not so much that we see a different world, but that we see this one more clearly.

Normally we go about our lives vaguely conscious that just beyond our short horizons there are plains, valleys, mountains, other planets, and distant galaxies. God made all that is seen and unseen; we see only our small patch of ground. Then comes an angel to open our eyes.

On Sunday, the peace and contentment I know feels like a small glimpse of what is possible. By stopping a little, I sense the vast richness all around. By repeating God's rest after Creation, I give myself over to God.

Jeffrey Soleau, a friend and colleague, once defined art "as an event where truth happens, that is, where new ways of being are revealed." That's the Sabbath, when we glimpse the truth because we have given it an opportunity. We pause, drop our worries, and truth breaks out. We put down the umbrella and the sun emerges from behind the clouds of our fretful imaginations.

In the Book of Judges, the angel of the Lord appears and speaks to Gideon, whose awareness dawns in short dramatic burps. " 'The Lord is with you, you mighty warrior.' Gideon said to him, 'Excuse me, sir, but if the Lord is with us, why are we having all this trouble?' " At the end, Gideon awakens fully and despairs that he will die for having seen the angel of the Lord "face to face" (Judg. 6:12–12, 27). In Genesis, Abraham and Sarah are visited by three angels whose promise of a child in their dotage they refuse, at first, to believe. But even in their doubt, Gideon, Abraham, and Sarah are open to belief. Their faith makes sensible the revelation.

"The moment of recognition comes with some surprise, *but no incomprehension* on the part of human beings," writes Kugel. "They know, in other words, that the spiritual realm is always there, ready to intrude on the physical world."[14] In life and urban legends, we attribute divine aspect to passing strangers who deliver unexpected insights or assistance and then seem to vanish. We may miss these epiphanies and remain obtuse to the hints and signs of God that come like a spring breeze wrapped inside a winter's gust or a child taking your hand when you are lost in grief or fury. Rather than a remote God up in heaven, He is "just a blink of the eyes away."[15]

The ancient Greeks also saw the divine presence in our mundane world. In their myths, gods take on mortal guise and appear to men and women who slowly or quickly recognize their heavenly visitors. This theme continues from Homer through Plato and into the early Christian era.

In the Acts of the Apostles, Paul and Barnabas bring the message of Christ to Lystra, a Roman colony and Greek-speaking market town in Anatolia, in today's Turkey. After Paul announces to a crippled man that his faith has healed him, the residents acclaim the disciples, saying, "The gods have come down to us in human form." This greatly upsets the pair, who want the credit given to God. "We are of the same nature as you, human beings" (Acts 14:8–18).

Perhaps the truth is only partially revealed. Paul, Barnabas, and the man whose own faith cured his infirmity are not gods but they can work miracles with God's help. Their true nature, as humans, is to have been made in God's image. This we know on the Sabbath, when we do as God did.

Judgment

Truth comes at a cost. It is no wonder we dodge it. But on Sunday, it's there before me. The day apart opens a window onto our deepest concerns and onto religion's major issues. (Are there any minor issues in religion?) We stop long enough for these questions to present themselves to us, like specters emerging from the swampy mists. Naturally, on Sunday I occasionally experience fears, anxieties, black moods. I stop the labors that keep these at bay, the labors that maintain my sense of control, and here they come. But soon enough comes heaven too. We stop grasping, and gifts come without our reaching. But by this same beneficence, we are judged. The truth that saves must first expose its opposite if only to reconcile the two.

Exposed to God's light, our faults are revealed as the late afternoon sun lights up the clefts and ridges of a hillside. On our day of rest, or repose, or communal prayers, we expose ourselves to this light, this truth. The day's peace may clarify as we contemplate the judgment that will come with the eternal Sabbath or on Islam's Day of Judgment. Shabbat evokes heaven and, thus, death and judgment. In the "world to come," Jews anticipate the resurrection of the dead by the Messiah and restoration of Israel. God will judge all and Israel will restore the perfection of Eden.[16]

In his marvelous record of searching for God among the three religions in the Holy Land, Jossi Klein Halevi writes, "Shabbat is the time when I tried to forego ambition and anticipate my own death; I'd imagine those moments just before dying when you feel the shame of having consistently chosen the trivial over the eternal."[17] But perhaps Imam Sebkhaoui is right, that there is nothing in God's Creation that is trivial. Perhaps Halevi will see, on his deathbed, that our ideas of trivial and eternal are inadequate, even wrong, and that nothing has been in vain.

Muhammad taught that both the "blast of the trumpet" and "the thunderbolt" will be on the Day of Judgment. Another tradition has it that there will be two trumpet blasts, of destruction and of resurrection.[18] Just as Friday, the day Allah created man, is tied to Creation, so does it close the circle on Creation.

Ibn Khaldun, who died in 1406, summarized Muhammad's teaching on the next world, in this way, "[Allah] causes our resurrection after death. This constitutes the final touch to His concern with the first creation. If created things were destined to disappear completely, their creation would have been frivolous. They are destined for eternal existence after death."[19] Juma's connection to the judgment and resurrection cannot be overstated. Islam tilts relentlessly toward the afterlife. "The Koran almost might be called the Book of Resurrection, so certain was Muhammad that the Creation had not been frivolous."[20] Thus can Imam Sebkhaoui assure me that nothing in God's world is trivial, that today's small detail may be tomorrow's important truth.

We cannot always distinguish the minor from the major, the profane from the sacred. The way to heaven is through sin and begins here on earth.

Heaven and Eternity

The Sabbath inaugurates heaven here on earth. At times on Sunday I have the sense that what William James said may fill us "with that calm and strengthening certainty that our own life shares in the mysterious meaning of the world."[21] And on all days, we periodically suspect that life stretches beyond any minute that begins and ends with the second hand. Each moment emerges from the moment before. Each moment, each thing, contains the seed of its future shape. And so we are always becoming and nothing is finished. This moment that you read this sentence extends into forever.

Thus for a Muslim, every move he or she makes has an eternal as well as a temporal importance. In all religions, each prayer invokes transcendence. We stop in this life to connect to reality that lies behind and above and beneath and within the world we see. Hatim al-Asamm realized salat in stark existential terms. "I stand up, the *Kaaba* straight in front of them, the *sirat* [the bridge to Paradise that passes over hellfire] under my feet, paradise on my right, Hell on my left, and the Angel of Death behind me; and I think this salat is my last. I then stand wavering between hope and fear."[22]

One Sunday, I sit in what we call Mom's room for the time she lived with us. The clock on the wall ticked off a second. Meanwhile time swells out of the past and rolls forward into eternity. Just as light is both a wave and a particle, so is time finite and infinite. So on the Sabbath, confined between two sundowns, we sense eternity. By ceasing our labors we are in God's image and likeness. We walk into heaven, or as much of heaven as we can know on earth. I remember a reticent artist who, when pressed by an interviewer about why he paints, finally blurted out, approximately, "This world is a paradise. It may be the only paradise we will ever know."

The prospect of heaven can offend our love of life. On Sunday, this world is enough. I want no more, I want no other world. Once during Mass I heard a priest mistakenly ask God to "deliver us from eternity" (instead of "from all anxiety"). I like that. We're here now. I'll take the Sabbath.

When Worlds Unite

The righteous, according to the Quran, are "those who perform the salat and give the zakat, and who are certain in their faith in the Hereafter" (Sura 31:4). Since the final judgment will come on Friday, Juma stimulates a heightened state of readiness among faithful Muslims. (Likewise, my father encouraged us to remain in a state of grace since death may come suddenly.) And the grace of Juma, Shabbat, or Sunday glows on the other six days. The proof of this lies in our desire for more.

At the Havdalah service that ends Shabbat, Jews smell sweet spices and imprint the day's joy on their senses, a small deposit of the sacred they carry into the days ahead. There seems some tension between this extension of the sacred into the profane, for the service ends with a blessing of the separation between the holy and the profane. Yet we pray to carry the Sabbath peace into the days of work.

The Sabbath changes the other days by revealing their true nature. We do not escape the world on the Sabbath, but enter into it more fully. We do not leave the profane world, we merely realize the world is sacred and leads to heaven. The afterlife always bears on this one, in ways small and large. "The people will be seated on the day of resurrection according to how they came to the *salatul Jumu'ah*," Muhammad told his companions, referring to the Friday service.[23] Heaven taps on our door, even getting us to services on time.

As in Islam, much of Christianity seeks to transform the profane into the sacred through God's embrace and the application of His law. The ancient Jews, by some interpretations, helped collapse the divide between sacred and profane with a God who acted in history, in human time, rather than cosmic time. On the other hand, Jews continue to mark a sacred or cosmic time through their annual cycle of holidays and experience of God. Judaism's rich sense of a present that extends into past and future integrates cyclical and historical time.[24] This contradictory approach suggests the same end of making profane and sacred one.

Christianity, with a God made manifest in our midst through Jesus, further sanctified history and profane reality.[25] Catholicism, especially, joins the sacred and profane in one marvelous, messy embrace. As he regarded religion in nineteenth-century Europe, Ralph Waldo Emerson concluded that, "The Catholic Church, thrown on this toiling, serious people, has made in fourteen centuries a massive system, close fitted to the manners and genius of the country, at once domestical and stately. In the long time, it has blended with everything in heaven above and earth beneath it."[26]

The Sabbath may be a day for sin and then salvation. Sunday stirs our frustration at rampant imperfection in others and us. We come to God not perfect but in need. We say with the guilt-stricken King David, "Truly my sin is always before me" (Psalm 51:5). On the holy day, our driftwood washes up on shore, left behind by the receding tide of the other six days, and we can gather and burn it up.

Each second opens onto eternity, as an atom split yields a universe of energy. Now begins always. Always we start. Would I sense the deeper character of time without Sunday? For on Sunday time trips open to a dimension fuller, slower, more dignified because God has ordained it so and we treat it so. Sunday, begun at Creation and tilting toward heaven, compounds the dimensions of time, magnifies its elements as a prism divides sunlight into its many colors. Each Sunday moment opens to all other moments: past, present, and future. The Shabbat prayer states that "Eternity utters a day." I would say that on the Sabbath, on Sunday, a day utters eternity.

Salvation from the Finite

If God's presence in history conquers the profane, we can also consider another possibility, namely that on the Sabbath we enter into a sacred time that continues through secular, linear time. The Sabbath returns every week, week after week, as do other religious holidays. Mircea Eliade theorizes that these "insertions" of sacred time constitute another, continuous duration, as the Christian Mass is one with that of last Sunday and next Sunday. This sacred time is eternity and only appears to be interrupted by the intervals of profane time.[27]

In a mysterious way, God makes the profane sacred without changing its character. We finally see God in the profane—reversing all our expectations, crushing our delusions, and freeing us from the material constraints of the mind. Shusako Endo, the Japanese Catholic novelist, depicts such a moment beautifully in his novel *Silence*. A sixteenth-century Jesuit missionary gives in to torture and stamps on a holy image of the crucified Christ in order to satisfy his captors and obtain the release of his fellow prisoners, the peasants he helped to convert.

> He had lowered his foot on to the plaque, sticky with dirt and blood. His five toes had pressed upon the face of one he loved. Yet he could not understand the tremendous onrush of joy that came over him at that moment.
>
> No doubt his fellow priests would condemn his act as sacrilege; but even if he was betraying them, he was not betraying his Lord. He loved him now in a different way from before. Everything that had taken place until now had been necessary to bring him to this love. "Even now I am the last priest in this land. But Our Lord was not silent. Even if he had been silent, my life until this day would have spoken of him."[28]

God breaks through and emerges in the apostasy of the divine image. Just as the Sabbath remains holy regardless of our observance, God cannot be restrained or limited by our denial of Him. The act, the image, the priest—all shine in the light of heaven. There is no realm into which God cannot come, in which He is not present. The priest discovers that God urges him on in the apostasy. He presses his foot onto the image of Christ and joy comes into the torture chamber.

Similarly, Judaism envisions not a new world, but this world made whole. The prayer of mourning, the Kaddish, says, "May God's great name be exalted and sanctified in the world which will be renewed."

We are brought to these mysteries not by intellect but by experience, notably of the Sabbath. We must keep the holy day to enjoy its blessings. So many times on Sunday I have sensed my family poking its head into the clouds where God's peace touches us. The times I or my family spent with the Kligermans on Shabbat, or the Fridays I knelt and bowed with the Haqqies and their fellow Muslims, I felt as if I stepped into a special time and place, God's time and place.

Since the Sabbath puts God into our week, its influence is profound. Every land shaped by monotheism feels on the appointed day some period of unearthly relaxation or at least hears the call to such a promise. Even if a person shops at the mall, he either does so more calmly than usual, or with a sense of guilt, or with a vague wish that he had some better occupation.

One Wednesday the hours at work left me feeling blah, affectless, frustrated. On such days, I like to stop by my college office, my other workplace. Here I write this book and various pieces for newspapers and magazines. Here I have all my materials, my journals, and files. Here the mind wanders, rushes, lags, naps, and flies. My small office in West Hall looks out on a 200-yard stretch of lawn with maples, oaks, and a spruce scattered across it. A few Bibles, the Torah, and three translations of the Quran sit on the shelves, so here also is the mind of God. I do nothing, and the ideas jump through my mind, empty and at ease. The minutes here, before I head around the corner to home for dinner, put in perspective the parts of life high and low, fun and not, seeking God and paying bills.

Today, as I walk up the stairs, I wonder how the Sabbath graces the other days of the week. And this thought stops me in the hallway: the same way as stopping by this humble sanctuary. That is, the day apart reminds us of the big picture, of God, truth, eternity and heaven. On that day, we are placed in the big picture. We are godlike in our divine repose. Time is holy and touches us with a grace that is all around. We stop, we stop by, and we are recreated. We stand at the altar and sacrifice material, space, and all the finite limits on our souls. We jump into heaven. Or, perhaps we see heaven all around us. We jump into heaven without moving. After the journey we are where we started without making the journey. Heaven is here, now and always. Sabbath, the seventh day or one in seven, comes on and in all days. It is a day apart, every day, all days.

CHAPTER IX

Give Me a Break: Work, Rest, Equality, Play, and Place

Strenuous Sunday yesterday. The whole staff gave father notice.
FRANZ KAFKA, *DIARIES*

Come to the best work. (*Haiya ala khair al-amal.*)
FROM THE SHIITE ADHAN OR CALL TO PRAYER

And whoever enters into God's rest, rests from his own work as God did from his.
HEBREWS 4:9–10

Ending the Sabbath: The Jewish Minhah and Havdalah

On a late Saturday afternoon in November, twelve men and three women assemble in the small sanctuary at Temple Israel to close Shabbat. We are in the lee of Thanksgiving, which subdues the atmosphere even more. Jews are sad to see the seventh day end. They sing hymns in a minor key, a leitmotif for this Minhah service. The Minhah is the afternoon prayer service on all days. It dates back to Isaac, who in Genesis went out in the field at dusk to meditate. Jews today regard it as a replacement for the afternoon sacrifice at the Temple. At the end comes the Havdalah, one of the oldest rituals in Judaism. The Talmud dates it back to the Great Assembly of the Persian period (538–331 BCE) that was founded by Ezra, who revived Torah and Shabbat observance after Jews returned to Jerusalem from exile in Babylon.

From early on, ending the Sabbath acquired a melancholic air. A happy and holy interlude, often amid times of oppression, was ending. Rest was over, work was on its way. There is one comfort. The Messiah, whom Jews believe will not arrive on Shabbat when they are unable to greet him properly, may once again be on his way.

The service begins at 4:00 PM at this time of year. The sun has yet to set but darkness is creeping up the walls of the sky. Rabbi Silton and a cantor lead the group. The service typically includes the Ashrei, which includes passages from several Psalms, the Amidah, a set of blessings during which the believer imagines himself in God's presence, and the Aleinu, a prayer attributed to Joshua that notes Israel's special status and looks forward to God's kingdom.

The prayers are recited rapidly in Hebrew, which everyone seems to know. Rabbi Silton calls out page numbers to help us keep up. He walks over to a memorial plaque and prays for deceased members. Several people drape the scrolled Torah in a yellow-white embroidered silk cover and return it to the ark, its ornate cabinet.

As before, a member, Les Fisher, wanders over in the pew to ask if I'm new, guide me along and comment on the proceedings. He delivers useful footnotes in complete paragraphs. When they recite the Shema—"Hear, O Israel, the Lord our God, the Lord is one."—Les mentions some history, perhaps apocryphal. "During the Crusades, the Catholic Church made them change that to 'The Lord is *three*.'" (If so, this was due to the church's concept of God as a Trinity.) He peers at me through his round-framed eyeglasses with a smile. "The Jews couldn't say the prayer at the morning service, when the church sent a monitor to synagogues, so they switched it to the evening service when there wasn't any monitor."

On the Sabbath, the Minhah is followed by a small meal and lesson. We walk out to a terrazzo-floored reception area. A buffet lies spread on a table, with herring, gefilte fish, breads, snacks, and soda. We sit at a long table. The congregants sing a few hymns. One of Rabbi Silton's sons, home for Thanksgiving, sits ready to deliver a lesson, four thick volumes at his side. In quick, emphatic sentences, he details the history of the Shabbat candles. Early on, and in a rebuke to rigid doctrinists, Jews were encouraged to light a lamp since a dark house would mute the day's joy. After 1300, two candles were used, as today. Listeners butt in and the rabbi's son answers each, even contradicting his father at one point. Rabbi Silton smiles, his son continues; one snapshot of the great disputation that sustains Jewish thought and observance.

Done, we return to the sanctuary for the Havdalah. Rabbi Silton blesses the wine, a braided candle he then lights, and the elaborately worked silver spice box. Basically a fist-sized container with a handle, it typically contains cinnamon, cardamom, and cloves. Members pass it along, the top open, and each inhales deeply. Many believe the spices revive one's soul as the Sabbath angel departs. In ancient times, Erwin R. Goodenough writes, incense was burned to chase away demons. Jews continued the practice until the Greco-Roman period, and then relinquished it as too pagan or Christian.[1]

The Jews of Temple Israel recite a final prayer that thanks God for separating sacred from profane, light from darkness, Israel from others, and Shabbat from the other days. Technically, Sabbath ends once three stars have appeared in the night sky. Though the Minhah began before sunset, the meal afterwards puts us safely into the evening.

At the end, everyone wishes each other a good week. Les does so with me, then his face lights up as he remembers that as his holy day ends, mine begins. He leans in with a smile, "And you have a good Sabbath."

How Does the Sabbath Survive in the World?

As one looks across the earth, the universal phenomenon of a regular or recurring day for rest is striking. Many primitive societies have or had rest days, not necessarily periodic or religious but involving superstition and taboos on light, noise, food, or sex.[2] These days of solemn inactivity and abstinence were held after deaths or disasters, at changes of the moon, or at times of war, harvest, or planting. Irregular taboo or rest days usually became regular as priests sought to routinize religious calendars and, often, extend their control. The Hawaiian religion had four regular taboo periods every lunar month in honor of their four great gods. The Bontoc Igorot people of Luzon developed a Sabbath that happened, on average, every ten days.[3]

In many of these societies, the notion of taboo or forbidden activity, over time, yielded the familiar concepts of sacred and profane. The holy day could make observers holy, just as the impure could stain or doom them. Some early societies showed respect for the divine by enforced idleness, just as children are dressed up for a visit to a grandparent, then ushered in and told to remain silent and still. The urge to make burdensome rules, apparently, is as common as the instinct to stop working.

The Sabbath rest has been pushed underwater in Western lands only to bob back up repeatedly, often in secular garb. After nearly being crushed by commerce and industry during the final decades of the nineteenth century, in a remarkably short period, from 1890 to 1915, virtually every country passed laws to require a weekly day of rest.[4]

This ancient humanitarian impulse rescued Christianity from its tendency to spiritualize the Sabbath, which devalued rest and removed a protection for vulnerable people—servants, slaves, workers—the very people singled out in the original commandment. We humans need a real break from work, not a conceptual one.

In our age, the weekly rest day still thrusts a rhythm upon time such that all moments are not equal despite the modern economy's promise of constant choice and availability. The Internet may be open constantly for business or transactions; we are not so able. By invoking our origin and destiny, the Sabbath checks the pride or greed that often drives excessive work. At Creation, we were given time and the means to mark its passing, the seasons and days and years (Gen. 1:14). In each religion, believers give their time to God, whose it was all along. This obliges us to use our hours carefully. We always know when we are wasting time. Wrote William Penn, the Quaker leader, "Time is what we want most, but what, alas! we use worst . . . and for which God will certainly most strictly reckon with us, when Time shall be no more."[5] Yet we are hemmed in by society, which organizes and uses time in ways that often contradict personal conscience and divine dictates.[6]

The Sabbath survives thanks to its fruits, which sustain it from generation to generation. It sanctifies rest so that we indeed rest and become new people in God. The rabbis taught that the Sabbath delivers four blessings: equality in a special day free from the profane or mundane; freedom for all from giving or taking orders; a taste of heaven that renews and inspires; and the chance to end our work and call it "good," or not. This new perspective, given weekly, elevates us in a priceless manner. "If a seventh of every life is devoted to rest, then we have been given 52 days a year, or approximately 10 years of sabbath or rest or reflection in a lifetime," writes Joan Chittister, "to determine the meaning and substance, the purpose and direction of our lives."[7]

If Rest is Holy, What is Work?

The commandment is clear: don't work on the Sabbath. God created for six days, and then stopped on the seventh. So work and rest are inextricably bound together. One defines the other beyond merely being opposites. However, if rest is holy, does that make work profane? No. As we read in Genesis, it is by stopping that God completes His work. "On the seventh day God finished the work that He had been doing, and He ceased on the seventh day from all the work that He had done" (1:2). Work has no meaning without an end; it is only done when we cease. And though it seems obvious that we would simply stop when we are finished, this mindset actually prescribes an eternal jog on the treadmill. As God shows us, we stop and then the work is done, at least until next week. It's a mystery, but no less true for being so.

The reason for rest may differ between the monotheisms. Jews observe the Sabbath by resting or ceasing. Christians rest primarily to attend church but also to be renewed in Christ. Regardless, who has not felt the relief of having to stop work?

Years ago on my first day as a carpenter on a construction site, I was burning through the afternoon, eager to prove myself by finishing a complex doorway. I worked past several stages when I could have stopped. Then I picked up my circular saw for one more cut. The power was off. I stepped outside to see Glen, the foreman, winding up my electrical cord. "It's quitting time, let's go," he said. "We're done for the day." I still feel the relief of that moment. It comes every Saturday evening. (Yes, there should be a country-western song, "God is My Foreman.")

The entwined nature of work and rest emerged as thinkers contemplated the question of whether God truly ceased on the seventh day. The rest of God is not mere inactivity, according to Philo, the Greek Jewish philosopher of the first century. God's goodness is changeless and constant. Even when ceasing from Creation, God maintains the world.[8] Muslims, of course, went further and rejected the idea that God would ever rest or need to. God's work and rest, however, are both of a higher nature than ours. Some of the rabbis who compiled the Talmud said that on the Sabbath, God continues to sustain and judge the world.

The Gospel of John supports this interpretation with a verse that has often confounded Christians. In 5:17 Jesus tells the disciples, "My Father is still working, and I also am working." For our purposes, God can continue holding up the universe on the Sabbath, but we mere humans need to withdraw from earthly business if we are to enjoy a day of repose and worship.

Now back to Creation for a moment. Once God's work is complete and He declares it good and rests, the world is ready for human activity. And as the fourth commandment makes clear, we are to work the other six days. The sages who compiled the Talmud made this point repeatedly. And a person who does not work will not have food ready for a proper Sabbath. Even Torah study alone, unless combined with real work, will profane God and lead to sin.[9]

Work as Creation or as Servile Labor

So what is work? Jews took the story of Creation as their exemplar and defined work as creative activity, anything that changes the natural world. On this foundation, the rabbis elaborated the endless set of rules and guidelines for Sabbath rest. Work was not mere effort. For an act to be prohibited, the person involved had to intend the specific result and the result had to be personally advantageous. Thus if one went to gather grapes and collected dates instead, the act was not punishable. Similarly, if one destroyed his house there was no punishment unless the person did so in order to build a new one.[10]

Even early thinkers came close to violating the nature of the Sabbath in their interpretations. The Torah and Talmud relentlessly emphasize the divine nature of Sabbath. Jews are to keep it as a commandment, not because it serves their earthly purpose. But Aristobulus, an Egyptian Jew of the second century BCE, and later Philo demonstrated that Sabbath keeping made sense and paid off, so to speak. We still hear that a good Sabbath makes us better people and more productive workers. That sentiment strays into utilitarianism and away from the commandment's original spirit.

Early Christians, and in later years Catholics and some Protestants, defined the work that is banned on Sunday as "servile labor," a very different notion from the Jewish emphasis on creative work. Thus, for centuries physical labor was banned in Christendom while intellectual labor—reading, writing, and studying—was not. Dictated by the elites, the distinction discriminated. The work of slaves, servants, and the poor is so conveniently public and visible while that of the clerics, nobles, and officials is usually private and internal. Rest from servile labor signified not only the holy day but also which holy day. The Council of Laodicea in 364 declared that, "Christians shall not Judaize and be idle on Saturday, the Sabbath, but shall work on that day; but the Lord's day [Sunday] they shall honor, and as being Christians, shall, if possible, do no work on that day."[11]

Work as Divine Vocation

We find in Genesis a definition of work richer and deeper than mere effort. The world delights us, but it calls forth our talents for guarding, nurturing, growing, building, and making.[12] God makes humans co-creators, stewards of Creation with dominion over the earth and its lesser creatures. We are told to be fruitful and multiply. These thoughts were picked up by Reformers and, more recently, by Christians who advocate meaningful work.

By the Middle Ages, a vocation was the work fulfilled by monks, priests, and nuns. The rest of us wasted our days in servile labor. Some of this originated in the example of the disciples who abandoned their fishing nets and followed the Savior. Jesus himself tells us to imitate, by our trust in God, the birds "who neither sow nor reap" or the lilies "who neither toil nor spin," yet thrive and grow nonetheless (Matt. 6:23–33). In the 1500s, Martin Luther rescued the concept of work, and said our vocation was to be found in all we do in our jobs, families, and leisure. By these means are we to glorify God. Not everyone needs to burn incense and chant in cathedrals and monasteries.[13]

In 1633 the poet George Herbert asked,

Teach me, my God and King
In all things Thee to see,
And what I do in any thing
To do it as for Thee.[14]

A century later, Jonathan Edwards, the great New England preacher, turned this sentiment sternly, "Time is a talent given us by God; he hath set us our day; and it is not for nothing." Rest on Sunday, but be busy with God's work the other days. Sadly, Edwards reinforces the older Catholic prejudice against manual labor. "When we are most free from cares for the body, and business of an outward nature, a happy opportunity for the soul is afforded."[15] By this perspective, contemplating the divine is holy, growing food is not.

In 1891, Pope Leo XIII declared the church's concern for work and workers. The nature of work was further studied and developed. Since the 1960s, church statements have emphasized labor as the highest element in economic life since it comes from the person who endows it with his or her dignity and unique character. As such, the industrial sin was to fit people into factories and other schemes of production. Instead, work must fit the person. We should become neither slaves to the work nor to the products of our work—a growing danger in our technical, bureaucratic, and materialistic world. Indeed, many of us have been forced to adjust our work habits to a software program or corporate system requirement. More recently, John Paul II praised work as good for the individual because it is useful and enjoyable. More importantly, he wrote in his letter *Laborem Exercens*, work is "something that corresponds to man's dignity, that expresses this dignity and increases it."[16]

Today, a growing chorus of Christians sings the glory of work. Proponents of a "spirituality of work" say we should act out our faith on more than just Sunday. (The movement, of course, has members in other religions.) I'd say a Sunday, or Sabbath, well kept will help us follow God the other days. So much of what we do to earn our way can dehumanize and degrade us. Despite high earnings, numerous workers are unhappy; despite too much work and long hours for some, many others are unemployed. By drawing on the Genesis conception of work and rest entwined, the "spirituality of work" movement can revive the dignity of labor without romanticizing work or ignoring those who are without jobs.

The Sabbath spirit can inform and elevate the work we do the other days despite the danger of utilitarianism. "Have a good week," is the farewell issued by Jews and Christians alike after their weekly services. On the holy day, we remember the higher purpose of our labors. And until we rest in God, at least have a weekly rest. But if our hard work requires rest, does that rest require work?

No God but Work

We often forget that while the fourth commandment stipulates one day of rest, it directs us to work the rest of the week. Similarly, Saint Paul encourages Christians to "redeem the time" (Eph. 5:16). The Puritan Sabbath emerged during the early industrialization of English cities and villages when work was changing quickly. Luther had, already, developed a theology of daily work as a vocation by which the average believer served God on all days. Catholics still were divided, exalting the life of prayer and denigrating servile labor. But when Protestants joined these impulses, they also spiritualized economic processes.[17] As they reduced the feast days that clotted the Catholic calendar, it became the norm that "Six days shalt thou labor, and do all your work." Authorities were quick to cite this fourth commandment phrase to justify long hours for the common people.

Further, Sabbatarianism discouraged hindrances to worship, such as sports, gambling, and hunting, which were also distractions from work. And so the gospel of work emerged from Sabbatarianism and remained bound to it ever since. "Work hard, play hard" is still a popular notion, one that chains the two realms together.

Today, however, for many people it's only "work hard." For the world's poor, at least those with jobs, such is life and has long been so. Overwork, or at least long hours at something resembling work, is surprisingly common in rich lands. This contradicts predictions of the early twentieth century that technology and wealth would yield acres of leisure. Instead, jobs have become 24/7 obligations for many thanks to computers, cell phones, and a global market that is always open for business. These technologies and schedules intrude relentlessly on our time, our families, our communities, our psyches.

Though more connected, and therefore more productive, we feel more alone and vulnerable. We know that others across the world, similarly connected, could take our jobs. Out of fear we work harder. Thanks to modern marvels such as financial software, word processing, and e-mail, an individual often completes tasks once done by several people. Who dictates a letter anymore?

Honestly, we can't blame modern life. Man has always known that the primary ingredient of the Sabbath, time, can be converted to power and wealth. Driven by fear and greed, we work beyond reason. The Hebrew prophets declaimed this vice, the Talmud hedges it, and sixth-century Catholic bishops protested that people worked right through the Lord's Day. Today, more than ever, time is money. We certainly can't spare any for anachronisms like a holy day of rest. One contemporary executive dismissed the idea of Sunday morning at church, saying he had more economic uses for those hours.

The paradox lies in our growing discontent despite wealth and leisure. We work more and more in an almost spiritual quest for the fulfillment and meaning we may not find in our families, neighborhoods, or religion.[18] Work easily becomes the realm in which we feel omnipotent as we master complex tasks and achieve the heights of creativity. There we flex our hubris. With Ahab in *Moby Dick* we howl at the heavens and the seas, "Who's over me?"

The spirituality of work movement, replete with workbooks, Internet discussion groups and retreats, manifests a genuine desire to live out one's faith in the world. It also reflects a desire for personal transformation at the office. For some, therefore, the spirituality of work may further the abandonment of religion as the arena for conversion and fulfillment. Similarly, congregations may so embrace a "gospel of work" that labor intrudes on holy rest. Many churches stage job fairs and provide counselors and host support groups; all laudable, except when these happen on Sunday.[19]

However, a narrow religiosity that ignores the high calling of vocation hurts as well. Through work, we feed and house ourselves, serve others, and fulfill our potential. A balance between work and Sabbath should help. The day apart reminds us that all belongs to God. Once a week we turn to Him and are relieved from the burden of being beasts of burden or minigods of work. But often we stand in our own way.

"Modern non-religious man," Mircea Eliade observed, "regards himself solely as the subject and agent of history, and he refuses all appeal to transcendence. . . . Man *makes himself*," but only to the degree that he "desacralizes himself and the world. The sacred is the prime obstacle to his freedom. He will become himself only when he is totally demysticized. He will not be truly free until he has killed the last god."[20]

Nevertheless, we rarely toss off religion completely. We embrace new gods and new rituals as soon as we upend the old ones. New Year parties or house-warmings, for instance, resemble ancient rites of renewal.[21] Those who care to look will see religious structure to certain political ideologies. Personal lifestyles from "simple living" to excessive wealth often amount to faith-based creeds. Many people make a religion of parenting complete with gurus, fads, orthodoxies, and rebellions. During the 1980s, the insistence that bouts of "quality time" with children would make up for long hours at the office manifested the religious habit of using sacred time to ameliorate the harms of profane time.

Some of these counterfeit religions bear good results. Fundamentally, all of them reveal our yearning for Eden, for a time and place beyond this time and place, a time and place that is pure, eternal, and sacred, a time and place where we will be at peace and one with God.[22] Just like the Sabbath.

Equality: The Poor Most of All

The fourth commandment was revolutionary on two counts. It set aside one-seventh of time for rest and worship, and, by extending this to slaves, it demanded equal treatment for society's disadvantaged members. In Exodus and Deuteronomy, then, we have "the first appeals in world literature to treat slaves as human beings for their own sake and not just in the interests of their master."[23] Stimulated by this command, Hebrew law further limited an owner's power over slaves. Slaves usually can't decide when to rest, but the Sabbath restored this minimal dignity while reminding the Israelites that they were once in bondage and are now free.

Through the centuries Shabbat relieved even poor and oppressed Jews for a day from their burdens and offered them earthly delight and divine refreshment. The day, ideally, should do the same in Christianity and Islam. Little enforcement should be required beyond ensuring that rich and poor are treated alike in regard to a holy day of rest. Over the centuries Christianity in Europe "lived by the love of the people" because, in part, it freed peasants outright or at least from work on Sunday and other festivals. An English feudal lord who compelled his serf to work between sundown Saturday and sundown Sunday would forfeit him altogether.[24] This spirit reappeared during the Reformation. For John Calvin, the day of rest allowed worship and protected servants and laborers from endless toil.[25] In the next few centuries, government involvement cemented the liberating equality first heard at Sinai.

In 1679, the Rhode Island Assembly invoked this spirit by warning "that persons being evil minded, have presumed to employ in servile labor, more than necessity requireth, their servants . . . on the first day of the week."[26] Under the colony's new law these would now be penalized. The day of rest was already edging out the holy day in legal codes, often most helping those who had no other protection from the boss.

In 1885, the United States Supreme Court upheld a Sunday closing law in San Francisco. The law served not religion, but was to "to protect all persons from the physical and moral debasement which comes from uninterrupted labor." They declared that such laws are beneficial "especially to the poor and dependent, to the laborers in our factories and workshops and in the heated rooms of our cities."[27] Into the twentieth century, courts consistently ruled that legislatures could "secure the comfort, happiness and health of the people" by choosing the day "when all labor . . . works of necessity and charity excepted, should cease."[28]

Today, many educated people toss aside "blue laws" with legitimate concern about church-state conflicts, but without considering that these laws protect menial laborers. Ideally, each person should choose their own holy day. But choice is usually a privilege of the powerful and not of people cooking french fries or stocking shelves.

In the nineteenth and twentieth centuries, the very popularity of Sunday rest, perversely, threatened the Sabbath experience of the working class. Who works to make possible Sunday recreation? During the early 1800s, an English bill proposed in Parliament and backed by the bishop of London would have exempted "menial servants" from the ban on labor so as to not inconvenience the rich.[29] Today our Sunday pleasures may require museum guards, park attendants, or church sextons to be on duty. Though most of these workers should be able to switch shifts for religious reasons, people should consider the true costs of their leisure activities.

On the Sabbath we all are delivered from being slaves of time. "The Sabbath is a reminder that we are more than beasts of burden, more than cogs in a wheel, more than students or workers who are valued for our contributions," wrote Henry G. Brinton, a Virginia pastor.[30]

Nevertheless, we have long justified the weekly rest as good for the bottom line we serve the other six days, just as long-distance runners and swimmers know that the days of rest before a big meet can be as valuable as the weeks of workouts. In its 1956 report on the worldwide practice of weekly rest, the International Labour Organization recognized its purpose "in the light of the economic needs of modern society."[31] Though true, this reasoning shifts the focus of the Sabbath from God to man. The Catholic Church has tried to combine the two. In making laws regarding Sunday rest, "the Church has had in mind above all the work of servants and workers . . . because it needed greater regulation to lighten its burden and thus enable everyone to keep the Lord's Day holy."[32] When Pope Leo XIII demanded justice for workers in the nineteenth century, he said that the state must protect Sunday rest as a right. This spirit continues in current efforts by governments to require employers to release workers on their chosen holy day.

Finally, the Sabbath principle has been invoked on behalf of the over-worked, who yearn for free time, and of the underemployed or jobless. Labor unions have pressed companies to reduce mandatory overtime, which should appease some and create jobs for others.[33] The spirit of the Sabbath, then, could help more people make a living.

Women and the Chores of Sabbath

Women can have a very different holy day than men. The primary obligation, to cease, leaves many chores that are inescapable on any day. Meals have to be served, babies nursed, children chased, mittens picked up. This is true regardless of the amount of preparation.

"In most families, where the mother is the primary caregiver, the woman remains the primary caregiver on the Lord's Day unless her spouse makes a heroic effort," says Amy, my wife. "I couldn't take a Sabbath from being a mom."

We have had more than one tense moment sorting out these details. It was easy for me to sit and read the paper, semi-oblivious to her struggle to dress our five-year-old son Mitchell for Mass. Then later, with some hypocrisy and insensitivity, I would frown when she and the children would wander off to a tag sale next door. But after a week at home with the kids, especially before all were in school, Amy's idea of rest or recreation could contradict religious notions.

For instance, she finds tag sales a restful diversion, one that she can rarely attend on the six other days of the week. She doesn't drive to these, she doesn't spend much, she usually walks up to one or two she may see on our block a few times a year. Also during the at-home mom stage, she welcomed several invitations to give paid lectures on *Fritz Kreisler: Love's Sorrow, Love's Joy*, her biography of the Austrian violinist. "Any job I had was a diversion," Amy says. To our way of thinking these events, which often included musical accompaniment, fell under the "cultural activities" and "advancing the common good" clauses.

Here's the problem: women's work often makes possible a man's Sabbath. Rest from labor may be his prerogative most of all, especially with the advent of salaried jobs away from home. Dad can leave the office or factory behind; not so for Mom and the house. Before the Civil War, few people worked on Sunday. During and afterwards, industrialization led to longer workweeks and Sunday hours, often for husband and wife, which prompted religious leaders to resist. The push and pull was mirrored in homes. Wealthy households only required a half day of servants, but these still had to work that part to enable the leisure of their masters. In other homes, the longer workweek meant mother and often father had only Sunday to clean, wash, and cook.[34]

Though the Bible seems to assume a man's world, women were equally bound by the covenant at Sinai, including Shabbat. The fourth commandment and scripture generally emphasize social justice and protection of society's vulnerable members, even as women remained subordinate. The rabbis who wrote the Talmud increased the status of women and protected their rights in marriage.[35] For Jews, the domestic Sabbath duties were to be shared. The Talmud specifies that every Israelite, even if he has servants, should help prepare the meal, as Tom Kligerman does for his family.

To be sure, many Jewish mothers find Shabbat a gift. One, a mother of five, was the calmest among a group who met regularly for coffee in Park Slope, Brooklyn. When asked the reason by a mutual friend, she always smiled and replied, "Shabbat." Among the observant Jewish families I know, mothers of young children may still do the bulk of the parenting. But many fathers do more than the usual, often quite a bit more.

On many a Shabbat, Tom has taken his younger children to Buckingham Pond or on long walks and off Becky's hands. Several older Jews have told me that when they were young, they looked forward to Shabbat since it was the one day their father would be home all day to play with them. As often as I see Orthodox families with the mother tending the children as they walk to synagogue, I also see fathers by themselves with one or several young children, perhaps to give the mother a break. My own father gave my mother many

Sundays to herself when he took the five of us children out for the afternoon. I never found out what she did. I like to imagine her with a book, a Manhattan, and big smile.

There is no avoiding, however, the sense that once again in religion, men have made the rules and women have the hardest job keeping them. Says Amy, "It's that whole male-ordained Sunday where people with the paid job were resting, but people who are the caregivers were still doing it." More than one report from an Israel kibbutz, or agricultural commune, has it that, even during a careful observance of the Sabbath, there was work—tending chickens, setting out meals, chasing children—that usually fell to women.[36]

On the other hand, the gradual domestication of Shabbat after the dispersal of the Jews elevated the role of women. On Friday, women light the candles before sunset and usually say the initial blessing. The absence of the husband, who is often at the synagogue, confirms the centrality of the woman in what is essentially a domestic institution. It is their mother that children see starting Shabbat, week after week. The mystical traditions of the kabbalah further enhance the role of woman, placing them at the center of the Sabbath.[37]

Muslims avoid some of these problems since their "Day of Assembly" is not one of rest. However, the different role of women in Islam is obvious at Friday prayers, which are led and dominated by men. At Juma services in American mosques, on average, 78 percent of participants are men, 15 percent women, and 7 percent children.[38]

As we have seen, almost all mosques set women in a balcony or at the rear. While it makes sense to separate the sexes, given the physical intimacy and awkward postures of the service, some mosques divide the hall into two sections side-by-side. The Sunna reports that in Muhammad's time, women attended the mosque and prayed the Juma with him.[39] Today, Muslim feminists study the Quran and life of Muhammad for lessons that would help rescue women from subordinate roles while also advocating equal or different arrangements of space.

In mainstream Protestant churches over recent decades, female priests and ministers have multiplied. In other Christian denominations, women have assumed roles beyond just teaching Sunday school, itself a fundamental role. At Sunday Mass in many Catholic parishes, one sees on the altar a white-haired, aged priest surrounded by younger, vigorous women and girls serving as ministers, music directors, lectors, and altar servers. This picture speaks a truth often obscured by hoary notions of a sexist hierarchy. With women making up the majority of congregants in most churches, here too they fill up much of the center of the Lord's Day. If gender roles are to equalize, men will have to step up.

Fulfillment: Calling It a Day

The Sabbath, and not the making of man and woman, completes Creation. "And God blessed the seventh day and declared it holy, because on it God ceased from all the work of creation that He had done" (Gen. 2:3). The Sabbath, not Adam and Eve, is the only aspect of Creation that God blesses and sanctifies by His example and words. It is a "sphere of blessing" that we enter in order to discover our relationship with God.[40] For Jews, Shabbat rehearses the long-awaited messianic redemption by creating a space for joy and fulfillment. In this regard, the Sabbath continues and completes our real work on earth. "Man scatters himself in work, and therefore he must collect himself anew, and have seasons for so doing," wrote Richard Chenevix Trench, a nineteenth-century archbishop of Dublin.[41]

Our labors do not stretch on and on drearily before us. Instead, during the six days of work we, religious or atheist, look forward to our day of rest. Even before the Sabbath, we walk in that direction by preparing our hearts and homes in spiritual and practical ways. Thus we know that we move toward an ultimate goal, that our feeblest efforts have a purpose and an end.

God's gift of holy rest to humans distinguishes the Genesis story from other epics of the ancient Near East. In these, the gods make humans to run things on earth so that the deities can rest. Only Yahweh shares the break with us.[42] The Babylonian epic, *Enuma Elish*, features six days of creation followed by a seventh of rest that benefits the gods. In fact, man's making is really a "comic afterthought."[43]

When we rest from our own humble or egomaniacal world of work, we realize that the job is already done, at least for now. That's a lesson of faith. In more practical terms, we have three choices: the world is fine without us; the world needs us to complete or fix it; or the world is falling apart regardless of our acts. Most people seem to choose the second, a middle course that still requires a regular rest that reminds us of our source and end.

In Judaism, 9 of the 39 categories of prohibited work are agricultural. Fred Rheingold, a Jewish farmer who lives near Albany, says that these limits—no plowing, planting, harvesting, shearing—help him acknowledge that his control is not absolute. On Shabbat, even Fred's land, inherited from his father, belongs to God. The same is true during the Sabbatical year, when observant Jews in Israel let their fields lie fallow through the legal fiction of deeding these to a Gentile for the duration. The lesson, says Fred, "We don't own anything, even ourselves."

The week pivots on the weekend and Sunday. Now, on a Wednesday early in this project, I look ahead to the free time but also the time apart. If work exhilarates and fulfills us, perhaps a day off oppresses more than it does those who hate their job. Though the Sabbath anticipates eternal rest, it offers respite here and now. For Muslims, Juma is a day when Allah fulfills their needs and answers their prayers and requests in this world.

Calling it a day reassures us on the most fundamental level. We are relieved of having to work on and on, of having to make it perfect. We are relieved of being God.

During my childhood, after dinner we cleared the dining room and washed the dishes, upended the kitchen chairs on the table and swept the floor, sometimes washing it as well. My mother then turned out the ceiling light, a circular fluorescent bulb set in a chrome base, and announced, "The kitchen is closed." I remember the cool dim quiet of the kitchen then. The change in utility, the demarcation of time reassured me. The meal was over, and we shifted into evening when we would do homework or go to Boy Scout meetings and my parents would read or pay bills or attend civic or parish events.

Stopping is a sign of our godliness. Rest and repose requires and demonstrates reason, independence, dignity, and growth. Only machines and slaves cannot choose to stop. (When scientists finally "humanize" robots, I predict they will install a capacity to cease or rest.) I spent a year teaching carpentry in a mountain village in Peru where Father Carlos Iadicicco, an energetic Italian missionary, told me that he sought to impart one lesson above all to his parishioners: "I just want them to realize that they are not burros who have to work all the time."

Finally, the holiness of the day apart reminds us of the ideals we hold for all our days. One Monday morning at work I float through the peaceful void left by a Lord's Day well kept (odd that, since "to keep" implies a rigor opposite the peaceful languor of the day). I do not despise my weekday labor and I am well adjusted by the day before. But today it seems pedestrian. I have the urge for truly good and useful work. The Sabbath makes it harder for us to settle for less.

Work and Rest

The book of Exodus contains the Bible's most thorough picture of work. In it work and rest run together like "twin threads" in a tapestry. The Anglican scholars Ellen F. Davis and Samuel M. Garrett point out two sections on work, each of 13 chapters. One depicts bad or perverted work, that performed by the Hebrew slaves under the Pharaoh in Egypt. Its primary feature is relentless-ness—there is no break. The Pharaoh rebukes Moses and Aaron when they convey Yahweh's request for release. In the Bible's first use of the Hebrew word, the despot yells, "And you would give them sabbath from their loads?!" (Exodus 5:5 is also translated, "And yet you want them to stop working!")

The other 13-chapter section concerns holy work, that of building the sanctuary or tabernacle. This contains three restatements of the fourth com-mandment. The third occurs just before they start the actual work. Moses begins by ordering the Israelites to observe the Seventh-day Sabbath, an unusual stipulation for a construction superintendent.[44] All good work begins with a goal in mind, in this case, the holy rest at the end of six days. Few of us could start a project unless we knew it would someday end. The very idea of Sabbath renews our spirit.

Work and rest are as entwined as are a person and his or her beliefs. The 1981 film *Chariots of Fire* tells of a Scottish runner, the devout Eric Liddell, who refuses to run a race in the 1924 Olympics because it falls on a Sunday. Though a solution is found, several British noblemen first try to persuade him to com-promise his values for national honor. One eventually confides that he is glad they failed. "His speed is a mere extension of his life, its force. We sought to sever his running from himself."[45]

Work versus Rest

The Sabbath rest does not denigrate work. Rather, it elevates labor to godlike creation that is followed and completed by stopping as God stopped. Islam offers a counterpoint to the Judeo-Christian approach. The Muslim on Juma worships and works, a sign of Islam's mission to make holy the world. Coming full circle, Shiite Muslims make prayer and work one. When muezzin make the Adhan or call to prayer in Shiite lands, they add the words, "*haiya ala khair al-amal,* or "come to the best work." Conversely, when Muslims in the past heard this formula they knew a Sunni regime had been overthrown.

Of course, the other monotheisms look forward to the union of sacred and profane, and both ask believers to serve God in their work. More directly, Johan Huizinga observes, work can transform beliefs and emotions into visible signs. "Every profession has its relationship to the highest and holiest. The labor of the craftsman is the eternal generation and incarnation of the word and the alliance between God and the soul."[46] This message is often lost in the pious pronouncements of clerics. But on Juma, the Muslims join both realms in a world that is one.

In Christianity, rest emerged as a means to make time for worship. But joy preceded both. In the earliest days of Christianity, even before Sunday was proclaimed a day of rest by Constantine, it was primarily a time to rejoice. After all, their Savior had broken the chains of sin and death. The Didascalia, an early teaching text, insists, "On the first day of the week, you shall all rejoice." And the Maronite Catholic liturgy thanks God for raising "Sunday above all other days," an echo of Jewish prayers. Christians may be happy to rest on the Lord's Day, but the rest really follows the joy.[47]

It is easy to worry that rest will backfire. Taking a break seems the prerogative of the rich. Azra Haqqie recalls that back in Pakistan, when she was a child, her father opposed making Friday a full day of rest because it would retard the nation's developing economy either by adding a third day of rest or immobilizing workers on what was a workday in the West. "He said it would isolate the whole country from the rest of the world," Azra says.

In Islamic practice, Juma makes work better. The day beckons the Muslim to a sober contemplation of his destiny, which hinges on his effort and Allah's mercy. Juma is the day when the world will end and all people will be judged. Faith must show in works, and so it seems natural that the Muslim returns to work on his day apart, and that he returns with a renewed consciousness of Allah.

Imam Sebkhaoui elaborates. "In the Quran, we are told that the purpose of my community is to help us be a servant of God. To do this, we cannot do it on our own, or understand serving God as something we do only in the place of prayer. I'm going to be a servant of God 24 hours a day, 7 days a week, 60 minutes an hour, 60 seconds a minute. If I do a work that is prohibited by God, I cannot be a servant of God. If I do a work that is permitted by God, then I can be a servant of God. When I go to my lab, my factory, the office, I do so with a consciousness of God. When it is time for Juma, it's time for this kind of service, not that kind of service. It is not time to argue which is better, because if I do, then I am worshipping my desire. If I do the prayers, then I can go back to work and there is no discontinuity."

There is an even greater distance between Judaism and Islam on this topic. The Quran depicts the strict Jewish laws on diet and Sabbath as punishment for the Israelites' failure to keep the covenant, notably by working on Shabbat (Sura 16:124). The Quran in Sura 67:163 tells the story of a sea where the fish only appeared on the Sabbath and thus successfully tempted some Jews who lived nearby to transgress their holy day. Muslim tradition teaches that Moses had really meant to set aside Friday as a sacred day, and that the Jews mistakenly followed the example of God's rest after Creation. After all, Allah did not require a break after making the world, though three times in the Quran we read that God "settled [or established] Himself on the Throne" after Creation, suggesting He does rest even if He doesn't have to (Sura 7:54, 10:3, 32:4). However, as in Judaism and Christianity, Islam teaches that God continues to sustain the world, whose very order demonstrates His constant love and governance.

For Jews, the command to rest has endless implications for work. On a soft October Saturday afternoon, Tom Kligerman stops by our house on a long walk home with two of his children. I mention looking for a neighbor to help me carry ten sheets of wallboard from the driveway into our basement. "I'll do it," he says. I object, since it is Shabbat. But Tom points out that the carrying will take place within a private domain, not between public and private domains. To me, it still seems like work that violates the spirit of the day. "You have to change your conception of work," Tom says as we slide the 4-feet by 8-feet panels downstairs. "If you were having people for the Shabbat meal, you might have to carry some chairs up from the basement. But it's within your home so it's okay."

Reform Judaism ignores, for the most part, rules governing forbidden acts and considers just a person's regular employment to be off limits. Home rituals and synagogue services sufficiently generate, or recognize, the spiritual nature of Shabbat.[48] Other Jews, and the Talmud, cordon off a wider area. The Mishnah, or oral law, directs people to refrain from discussing or even contemplating workday matters. Though not work in itself, such talk or thought is prohibited just to be safe. Christians are similarly enjoined to not work, and also to avoid thinking or fretting over such affairs. As in Judaism, the safe zone of the Sabbath is extended by pushing away work. At the same time, such a division does nothing to disengage the intimate relation between creation and cessation.

Should Rest be Useful?

The Sabbath reveals our attitudes toward work. Perhaps we value the tasks that fill our weekends because we find little meaning in the jobs that use up the other five days. Or it may be that we treasure our weekends because it is then that we can play. "Play has no purpose, though it does have meaning," Kenneth

Woodward, a veteran religion writer, observes. "Play takes us out of time, which is what the ancient festivals and feast days used to do—and what the modern weekend struggles to preserve."[49] But work that fulfills and enriches, that completes a person, can also take us out of ourselves. Transcendence in either realm reinforces transcendence in the other. Good workweeks can make for good Sabbaths.

Rest can, however, become an end in itself with troubling implications for religion. Some judges have ruled it sufficiently valuable that protections in the form of blue laws can legitimately inconvenience the observance of non-Christian holy days, as in the 1961 case of *McGowan v. Maryland.*[50]

This sounds reasonable unless you are a Jew, Muslim, or Hindu. However, the courts have since moved away from this argument, sometimes to outright hostility toward rest-day protections. The more hopeful trend is toward protection of voluntary observance. In that case, believers assent to God's revelation rather than obey state law. Then is the liberation of the Sabbath boundless.

John Paul II argued that the Lord's Day had "a kind of fruitfulness," one that "is apparent above all in filling and, in a certain sense, 'multiplying' time itself, deepening in men and women the joy of living and the desire to foster and communicate life."[51] This fountain of time has a companion in Jewish thought that the Sabbath is a "time-out" for the imagination, which is the center of the calendar, itself a way of directing and regulating the imagination. All Jewish thought turns on the divine purpose of the Sabbath. "It introduces monotheism into the calendar, it subordinates the week to a creator who not only is unafraid to rest but consecrates that urge."[52]

More prosaically, rest ennobles. G. K. Chesterton, the English Catholic writer, thought that the highest and best form of leisure was the freedom to do absolutely nothing. Sadly, we tend to revert to defending the day of rest on narrow grounds of utility. In a typical comment, one prominent pastor writes that "if Christians carved out time for prayer on Sunday mornings and play on Sunday afternoon, they would be happier, healthier and more productive . . . from Monday through Friday."[53] That may be true. But soon some may say that good Sabbaths make for good gains.

In opposing the French suspension of Sundays in the nineteenth century, church leaders argued that the weekly rest in England and America had done little to impede the economic surge of those nations, in which they surpassed France. One French cleric pointed to the wharves of London. On Sunday, he observed with admiration, "all these workmen rest; and not a blow of the axe is given."[54] The implication was that a day of rest actually paid off. Maybe so, but that's a thin justification for the Sabbath by itself.

Worship and Play

Jews rest to observe the Sabbath; Christians rest to have time for worship on Sunday. Either way, both groups end up with free time. Once rituals are observed, communities gathered, and prayers said, what then? Over the centuries, free time on the Sabbath evolved to allow leisure and recreation. The debate over what and how has been more contentious in ages past but continues today.

In England during the late 1500s, entertainments such as plays by Shakespeare and others were often staged on Sundays. The Puritans protested; the Anglicans demurred. When they marched onto the battleground during the mid-1600s, one issue was King James' *Book of Sports* and its endorsement of Sunday games. The Puritans carried the day and the laws, for a time. In London they burned the king's heretical volume. The result, for many in the land, was a fierce ennui on Sundays after church. In his novel *Rob Roy*, set in the early 1700s, Sir Walter Scott depicts a family yawning and fidgeting away their time in their country home.

Boredom provoked its solution, as when English workers took off Saint Monday during the 1700s in order to enjoy the events and recreation that were banned on Sundays. Over the next two centuries, the tide shifted back, and museums, concerts, and other venues opened on the Lord's Day. Churchmen, despite rearguard actions, were mostly happy to have Sunday free of commerce.

Today leisure remains a challenge. People do not always know how to relax and enjoy themselves. Many people are fulfilled by their job but not other activities. Thus time off from their important careers may threaten their equilibrium. When we do play, we may bring a competitive, professional sensibility. Whereas we once muddled through skiing or a game of tennis, we now buy pricey equipment and apparel and concentrate on perfecting our step or stroke. By such means do we lose out on the fun and profane, or at least waste, holy rest. As Witold Rybczynski observes, "The lack of carelessness in our recreation, the sense of obligation to get things right, and the emphasis on protocol and decorum do represent an enslavement of a kind."[55] The "rest" of the Sabbath can rescue us from these instincts. We can relax and enjoy ourselves as amateurs, "lovers" in the word's original sense, in whatever recreation suits the day.

Today, Catholic and Protestant leaders occasionally remind believers that their priority is time to gather as a people of God. More often, they struggle to simply block the invasion of sports and commerce.

In some communities, ministers and parents have appealed to sports leagues not to schedule games on Sunday morning. John Cardinal O'Connor, the former Catholic prelate in New York, pleaded with families and coaches to stop encroaching on church time. "But why is it religion that must always accommodate?" he asked from the pulpit of St. Patrick's Cathedral.

Though many were relieved to hear someone defend the holy day, O'Connor was ridiculed in the press. Such campaigns often melt before the forces of busyness. One New Jersey league agreed, with considerable self-congratulation, to avoid scheduling team photos on Sundays when Catholic children were due to receive their First Communion, a major event in parish life. "We got a big thank you from the churches and the parents," said one coach.[56]

As did Eric Liddell during the 1924 Olympics, several Jewish ballplayers have inspired some fans and dispirited others when they chose observance over competition. In the 1934 World Series, Hank Greenberg of the Detroit Tigers refused to play on Yom Kippur, as did Sandy Koufax of the Los Angeles Dodgers in the 1965 series and Shawn Green, also of the Dodgers, in a 2001 pennant race. For these and other Jews and Christians, the Sabbath was generally another matter.

Professional baseball had already broached Sunday early in the century. Branch Rickey, a player and manager, was an exception during the first half of the twentieth century. Though most famous for integrating major league baseball by hiring Jackie Robinson for the Brooklyn Dodgers, Rickey also refused to play or manage on Sundays (though he let his teams go ahead).

Today, some Jewish athletes remain shomer Shabbat. In 2005, Tamir Goodman lost his college basketball scholarship when he refused to play Friday night or Saturday. He moved to Israel to play pro ball.[57] And Orthodox boxer Dmitriy Salita, a New York Golden Gloves champion, refuses to train or fight on the Sabbath.[58] For their children, Jews have organized baseball or soccer leagues that hold weekend games on Sunday. Among the ranks, interpretations vary. At my daughter's soccer game one Saturday, I see a friend refereeing, as he does week after week. I ask if his rabbi, who leads a Reform congregation, has approved. "She told me that it all depends on how you define 'rest,'" he replies with a wink before trotting off to call the game.

Restrictions meant to promote weekly rest linger in the law books, often newly justified by secular causes. One brand of recreation may compete against another, such as hikers versus hunters. As of 2005, 11 states, most in New England and the Northeast, still restricted Sunday hunting. Though the trend is toward liberalization; in 2002 West Virginia voters limited Sabbath shooting only months after their state legislature approved it and despite the potential loss of $42 million in hunting fees.[59] In Puritan-haunted Connecticut and Maine, efforts to allow Sunday hunting are being opposed by a new breed of Sabbatarians—wildlife protectors and conservationists. This accords with the Jewish doctrine that on the Sabbath, we should let nature return to its native state.

Some believers have shuffled a secular holiday to preserve the holy day. In 2000, Mormons in two Utah cities moved their New Year's Eve celebrations up a day, to Saturday, to spare members the danger of dancing and other inappropriate activities on Sunday. Church elders told members to have fun but be home by midnight, so as to spend Sunday quietly with their families and at services.[60]

God and Mammon Fight for Sabbath Time

The struggle to keep the Sabbath is fought on many fronts. We push and pull on the very minutes. During the week the load of work, commuting, and activities pushes domestic errands and hobbies from evenings toward the weekend. We spend Saturdays on these leftover chores, wishing-hoping-praying that soon we will have some time to ourselves. Soon enough domestic or paid work bleeds over into Sunday. It becomes a second Saturday and we lose one-seventh of our life.

Some surprising fronts open up in this war for holy time. The Christian debate over the nature of Sunday—Jewish-inspired Sabbath or Christian innovation?—can whittle down holy time. Protestants who sever Sunday from the fourth commandment reduce the obligation to the hour or so needed for worship.[61] We forget that the day of rest protects us from ourselves, from our avarice, our urge to always be doing, improving, earning, getting, spending, having, consuming—all the ways we hurry on toward death.

From the start, American believers worried that religious freedom would encourage license. In its laws of 1682, Pennsylvania declared tolerance for all who professed one God. "But to the end That Looseness, irreligion, and Atheism may not Creep in under pretense of Conscience," the authorities declared, the Lord's Day was still a mandated day of rest for all.[62]

Obviously, governments should not mandate a holy day for anyone. But protecting personal liberties can inadvertently set loose endless commerce. In the nineteenth and mid-twentieth centuries, labor reformers and individual merchants used holy time to protect personal time and dignity against industrialization. During a British debate in 1936, one member of Parliament warned darkly of the age we now inhabit, "Frankly, I am afraid of a seven-day week. I see it coming gradually, and a seven-day week means six days' pay for seven days' work."[63]

During the 1950s, these humanist Sabbatarians warned that Sunday openings would disrupt "community traditions" and "move labor and merchants a step back to a seven-day work week." A United States senator warned that Sunday sales would make it "the big bargain day of the week."[64] Notably, businesses that favored Sunday hours were not proposing a different day of rest. "All attacks upon these laws are in violation of the best interests and assail the health and manhood of the people," wrote one Christian scholar. "Such attacks are mainly commercial, aiming to destroy any rest day whatever, and never aim to substitute another day of rest for the Sunday day of rest."[65]

In recent decades, however, chain stores such as Kmart, Sears, and Home Depot financed campaigns, complete with ersatz grassroots support, which repealed blue laws in Texas in 1985 and Massachusetts in 1994. Remaining restrictions continued to fall away as religious and humanitarian concerns were swept aside. Stores needed to sell and shoppers buy, every day of the week.[66]

In Germany, shops once had to close by 2:00 PM Saturday in preparation for Sunday. Germans hustled through their morning errands and chores, like Jews on Friday afternoon. I remember watching the farmer's market in Waldkirch, my grandmother's native village, snap shut at noon. Under pressure from companies and shoppers, the deadline was changed to 4:00 PM in 1996, then 8:00 PM in 2003. Workers and unions opposed the change; 20,000 people in Berlin marched in protest to no avail. The government predicted a boost to the economy. "Consumers will now be able to fulfill their wishes without time pressure," a government minister predicted. Stores would still close Sunday, at least until that time was conquered by commerce.[67]

Sometimes secular Sabbatarians invoke religious doctrine to protect the rest day. The European Union favors a weekly day of rest that should, in member states, "coincide with the day recognised by tradition or custom in the country or region concerned as a day of rest."[68] This meant Sunday for most. In essence, modern Europe endorsed the Christian Sabbath long after many of its nations had canceled Sunday closing laws.

Admittedly, appeals for weekly peace and quiet appear differently to atheists and civil libertarians. They argue that when churches ask Little Leagues to skip games on Sunday, it imposes a religious schedule on nonbelievers. "Churches are already tax-exempt, and now they're enlisting government to make sure that there is no competition on Sunday," said Gil Lawrence of the American Atheists during a 1998 debate in Massachusetts. He said churches were assert-ing a monopoly in order to fill empty pews.[69] Perhaps. It's fairer to say that the churches were asking their members to observe their religion, for which no outside coercion should be necessary. But believers should realize that their efforts to reclaim Sabbath time can appear pushy to others.

To resolve the tension between sacred and secular time, some people favor more time for chores and preparation. In Israel, many work a half day on Friday, at least unofficially, to get ready for Shabbat. Secular Jews who favor a day of rest, if not necessarily worship, have proposed adding Sunday as a second day off. This would allow a day for shopping and entertainment, and reduce the need for these on Shabbat.

Invariably, the Sabbath instinct asserts itself, as it did against the schedules imposed by the French and Russian revolutionaries. Shortly after its revolution, China adopted a seven-day week. The days were numbered, not named, and the seventh was a civic holiday, Sun Day, a striking facsimile of the holy day.[70]

Holy Place, Safe Place

We worship in time but we live on earth. The Sabbath joins the two. We *shab-bat* in a place. We rest in God on the day apart in the place where we live. Aside from travel and migration, we are tied to home and we are tied to a community of faith. Jews are restricted to their home and neighborhood. All Christians are encouraged, in the Letter to the Hebrews, "not to neglect to meet together, as is the habit of some, but to encourage one another" (10:25). On the Sabbath we meet in a place that incarnates God.

The Bible relentlessly situates people in places good or bad, as the social geographer Jonathan Smith writes. In contrast to the biblical theme of exile, the ideal is being in one's proper place, the Promised Land, which fulfills the divine sense of order and stability.[71] Without such, we suffer or die.

Traditionally Catholics were obligated by canon law to belong to the parish where they live. Countries are divided geographically into dioceses and those are subdivided into parishes. In my childhood, people attended their parish church and few shopped around for a more congenial one. As an adult, I always joined the nearest church: in Washington, D.C., St. Augustine near Dupont

Circle and later St. Joseph on Capitol Hill and Our Lady of Victory up in Northwest D.C.; the adobe chapel in Huanroc, the Peruvian mountain village where I taught carpentry; in Manhattan, Corpus Christi, the high-church parish on a grey side street near Columbia University; and in Massena, N.Y., on the St. Lawrence River, the austere granite church two houses up from my apartment.

When I dressed up and walked to Mass on Sunday I announced to the world, such as cared to observe, my religious belief. Most of all, I announced it to myself. I kept the day, or at least the morning, holy and the day kept me. This was especially true in those wild, lost years just after college. St. Augustine's was a good ten-block walk. My passage to and from church seemed to sanctify the very sidewalks and streets. The pavement became that "holy ground" on which Moses stood when first addressed by Yahweh. One fellow who loitered on the corner called me "preacher man" after seeing me, pressed and presentable, make the trek every week. His nickname, uttered in a hoarse bark, made me want to live up to an ideal.

Before children, Amy and I attended here and there in Albany before settling on St. George's, home to the Black Catholic Apostolate, which serves minorities and others from throughout the region. We spent many happy Sunday mornings at the Gospel Mass, though the long service became difficult once our lively children came along. When our daughters began with religious education, the classes at St. Teresa of Avila were more practical for us. And I was strongly drawn to a local parish.

One steamy Sunday in August I was choking in my jacket and tie as we drove up the block like sardines in a can. I saw friends walking home from St. Teresa smiling, their children running and laughing. And I resolved to ask Amy to switch. I needed to walk, at least most Sundays. Periodically we visit the Black Apostolate, but a new location puts it a daunting 20-minute drive away.

The Sabbath makes neighborhoods. It anchors communities in time and place. It counters the fluid mechanics of consumer culture, where we are ready to move for a bigger home, another school, a larger yard, and fewer poor people nearby. Sabbath keeping pulls us back.

Catholic parishes, with their boundaries and schools and churches, embodied "the theological belief that the individual came to know God, and the community came to be church, within a particular, geographically defined space." The parish church is a shrine where you, your friends, your parents, and all those before and after met each other and God every day or week.[72] And you did it together in a place.

In an earlier age, churches and synagogues defined many city neighborhoods. As synagogues and many Protestant churches left, these neighborhoods
declined. In the decades after World War II, the Catholic hierarchy kept many
parishes open despite empty pews. These compounds of faith continued as
bulwarks in desperate areas, often serving food, shelter, and morale to non-
Catholic neighbors. "Protestant churches have long since abandoned the city,"
Leslie Woodcock Tentler told *Commonweal*, "Jewish [synagogues] move, usually
in advance of their congregations. And Catholics have just tended to stay
behind."[73] To be sure, in Albany and other cities some Catholic churches do close
and many synagogues and Protestant churches remain and stabilize their areas.

Today, in Catholic, Protestant, Jewish, and Muslim congregations generally,
many members live beyond the immediate neighborhood of their church,
synagogue, or mosque.[74] Even predominantly black churches located in
African American neighborhoods have many middle-class members who live
in suburbs. If members of these and other congregations relocated to within
walking distance, it would transform hundreds of neighborhoods. However
unlikely, "living the gospel means sharing in the suffering and pain of others,
and is most effectively witnessed when one lives among the poor."[75] This
uncomfortable truth, that helping is hard at a distance, undermines almost all
our do-good schemes. A return to Sabbath habits would mend the break.

If Sunday rest and worship shaped and sustained many villages and neighborhoods over the past 2,000 years, the Jewish institution of the eruv makes
communities in a way both concrete and transcendent.

From the original mandate to abstain from carrying a burden the rabbis
spun out three chapters in the Talmud tractate Shabbat that detail exactly how
much of what constitutes a burden. And based on the simple command, "Do
not leave your place on the seventh day," in Exodus 16:29, several chapters in
the tractate Eruvin define the limits of a person's place and explain how to
extend these boundaries.[76] The eruv in Albany uses wires, fences, and other lin-
eaments for a perimeter that converts a community to a private domain. As
Jacob Neusner explains, the household or private domain forms a mirror image
of the sanctuary or tabernacle, God's domain. And the Sabbath transforms this
private domain. "There, and only there, on the Sabbath, is life to be lived."[77]

While the eruv sounds restrictive to outsiders, to Jews it is a blessing. Within
it they are allowed to carry infants and certain objects or wheel baby strollers to
and from the synagogue, each other's homes, and other destinations without
violating the original biblical commands. The eruv allows them to "not leave
your place" by making their place so much larger. Conceivably, with an eruv
the Jews could make their whole world their home.

"It's one of the primary structures that give us comfort on the Sabbath," said Rabbi Moshe E. Bomzer, who oversees the Albany eruv and is rabbi at Beth Abraham Jacob, an Orthodox congregation near Temple Israel. Bomzer says that Israelites began to conceive of this solution while still in the desert. "The Jewish encampment was divided into four areas with three tribes each. We can only imagine that to increase the sense of community on Shabbat they had to have some common environment that was still acceptable as a private domain." In early stages, a series of houses or walls served as a perimeter to create a common "private domain." Later, the court of King Solomon "began using Talmudic logic to create an invisible wall," Bomzer continues.

The Albany eruv consists of three miles of fences that must be at least 40 inches tall and that contain about 300 to 400 invisible "doorways." Each "door image," or *tzuras hapesach*, consists of two side posts, usually a half-round plastic tube placed on the side of a telephone pole, with a connecting lintel, usually an overhead wire. The eruv contains Albany's six congregations and most of the city's Jewish families.

"It allows you to fully actualize Shabbat," says Bomzer, a bearded man whose energy balances a deep joy. "We would not want anyone to be held captive in their private domain, such as women or children. Now they are able to carry objects and experience the rest and comfort, to enjoy the gift of what these 25 hours are all about, which is the concept of sharing the day with other families and having a beautiful and warm sense of community."

This is one with the day's spirit. "If you walk into a synagogue, no one who wants to be connected on Shabbat will walk away without an invitation to someone's house for dinner," says Bomzer. "I wait for the hour of turning off my cell phone. I relish not driving. I relish being relieved of the technical world we have created."

As we spoke in the sanctuary—"You're not Jewish, you don't need a kipa in here," he tells me on the way in—a repairman outside wrestles with a cable connection. Bomzer jumps up to open a door, then returns, sits quickly, and turns to me. "Our Internet went down. *Nu*, what do I do? We still have the Talmud as the word that was gifted to us 4,000 years ago."

Doctor, Father, Muslim

Instead of creating another world, the Muslim experience of Juma occurs in the daily world of work and commitments. This I see most clearly when I meet Shamim one Friday at the hospital for late morning rounds and then midday prayer.

His day so far: 7:30 AM, visit patients on the dialysis unit; 8:30 AM, meet other patients for appointments; 10:00 AM, instruct medical students; 11:00 AM, visit other dialysis unit; 12:00 noon, grand rounds. "I don't have time for lunch," he says as we rush down a corridor and out an exit door—*clank, blam*—into a tiny parking lot between buildings and hop into his SUV. "I usually skip lunch, that way I can see more patients." We drive toward another dialysis unit, passing through the alleys of Albany Medical Center, across New Scotland Avenue and into the maze of the University Heights campus, shared by the hospital and four colleges. Shamim, talking quickly with a scientist's few words, tells me about his 15 years in the Army Reserve.

"It's been a good experience, traveling to Europe, Latin America, other places. Last year we went to El Salvador and Paraguay. Humanitarian missions, mostly. Other years it was Guatemala and Honduras, also for humanitarian missions. And it's good public relations." He pulls into a parking lot and looks up through the windshield at the sky. "America's doing good things."

Inside, he shakes hands with two patients in the waiting room. One he speaks to in Urdu. "This is Father Thomas. He's an archpriest in the Syrian Orthodox Church." We move on. Marybeth, the nurse supervisor, brings Shamim up to date on a boy who is also an avid baseball player. "We postponed his dialysis for a doubleheader," she says. The room is long and open, with four rows of ten recliners. There are televisions overhead and next to each seat, a dialysis machine with tubes that run into and out of each patient. "Yes, it is like a Laundromat for blood," he replies to my question. The machines remove phosphorus from the blood, which would otherwise accumulate and calcify in the lungs, kidneys, and heart, Shamim explains, and that the kidneys of these patients no longer remove. "These poor patients have a lot of restrictions on them." He continues down one aisle and back the other, checking charts and speaking with most patients.

As we drive back to the main hospital building, I ask why he picked this field. "I was originally fascinated with physiology. This body is so complicated that God has created, and we know not even a millionth of its operations. It is such a perfect organism. And we still don't always know why kidneys fail. Now, these days, 50 percent of the time it involves diabetes."

Today Shamim will lead the Friday service. We stop by a doctor's lounge for a cup of coffee, and hear about retired colleagues and their European vacation homes. Then by quick steps we head to the chapel. Shamim unfurls a small prayer rug that has a compass set in the middle, used to find qibla, the direction of Mecca. Another Muslim doctor leans over the rug, the two of them a white-coated huddle. "I think it's this way," Shamim says. We line up at a slight angle to the front wall. After opening prayers, Shamim speaks. "Today I am going to talk about the obligation of the Muslim, as a father, brother, citizen, child." He reads from Sura 17, which opens with the night journey of Muhammad to Jerusalem where he was shown the Signs of Allah. This story prefaces the journey of the human soul as it matures religiously, beginning with moral conduct.[78] Shamim reads verses 23 through 39. These direct the Muslim to worship Allah alone and trust Him fully, to care for parents and offspring ("Kill not your children for fear of want"), to respect all life, to be proper in business and clean in dress and habits and humble in bearing. Then he says, "I will outline some of these points."

Though he reads from a prepared sermon he found via the Internet, Shamim salts it with his own terse comments. "Be nice to your relatives and remember we have an obligation to society at large, but it begins with the family. . . . Allah says don't be too tight with your money. . . . We should have a good dress code for men as well as for women. . . . Remember the sanctity of life. Take care of orphans and be kind and compassionate even to the animals. . . . We should be humble, balanced, and not arrogant. The ultimate praise is due to Allah."

He pauses, then prays in quick, muted tones in Arabic, then English. (One translates as, "Do not lay on us as big a burden as you did on those who came before us." Amen to that in any religion.) At the end, some of the congregants remain to worship. Shamim performs two more rakas, then rises and steps out quickly, back to kidneys and people and the work of the world.

CHAPTER X

The Promise of Peace:
Sharing the Holy Day

But the present is a time of trial for [the Sabbath], partly from the overstatements and overstrictness of those who look at it solely on its Divine side, partly from the under-statements or laxity of those who look at it solely on its human side.
JAMES AUGUSTUS HESSEY, *SUNDAY*

Millions long for immortality who don't know what to do with themselves on a rainy Sunday afternoon.
SUSAN ERTZ, *ANGER IN THE SKY*

Sabbath Themes

In the history of Sabbath in Judaism, Christianity, and Islam, and in the lives of the Kligermans, the Haqqies, and the Ringwalds, several major themes stand out.

- The Sabbath was revealed at the beginning of time — or darn near—and has endured as a central teaching and practice in each religion. Sabbath practice is the benchmark of fidelity in all three; it sustains each religion and its community of believers to a degree beyond that of other religious habits, such as fasting or meditation or education.
- Practice leads to more. Practice builds faith that, in turn, renews commitment. Good Sabbaths make for good Jews, Christians, and Muslims.
- The Sabbath saves us from the abstraction that plagues all religions. Practice connects us to earth, ourselves, and each other.
- Community characterizes the Sabbath. We rest and worship together. All the rules push people together and the group confirms our practice. A

Muslim is never more a Muslim than when he or she bows before Allah and toward Mecca in the lines of believers at the mosque on Juma.

- Varying forms of Sabbath observance identify each religion and have allowed each to break away from other religions and peoples. Quite naturally, these conflicts continue.

- The Sabbath cycles through a common pattern in the three religions: a gift of joy becomes joyless; believers then reject or neglect it; then others finally rediscover and renew it.

- The Sabbath embodies the conflict between faith's liberation and its demands. The day releases us from anxiety and other profane concerns; but we best appreciate the day if we strive to leave those concerns behind. Joy emerges from restriction and limits, though we can go overboard and elevate the Sabbath into a golden calf. Wisely have prophets observed that what is in the heart matters more than procedure.

- Nevertheless, subjective arguments are not always useful. Yes, in keeping the Sabbath we know its blessings. But this emotional and intimate knowledge is, by itself, unstable ground for a foundation.

- In a variation on that tune, Christianity still struggles with the legacy of Paul, who celebrated our liberation from religious law including the Sabbath. For him and others, a regular day of rest and worship was a crutch. Real men of faith had no need of such any more. Yet, the Lord's Day is a tremendous aid to faith. Paul, of course, resolved the issue in Romans 14 by saying, basically, "So what?" Some keep one day and others keep all days, but all do it for the Lord.

- The Sabbath in all three religions conveys the presence and experience of God. Hence its profanation is an offense against God and duly censured.

- And yet the monotheisms preach and practice compassion regarding observance of the holy day. Three violations before punishment is a common rule. Even enforcement conveys the spirit of the Sabbath, God's love.

- As always, the Sabbath will survive, even thrive, on a grassroots level. By example, the Kligermans and Haqqies pass it on to their children. Today, the hunger of Catholics for the blessings of the Lord's Day will do more to reinvigorate it than the pronouncements of popes or theologians. The same goes for the deep urges of the secular simple-living crowd. Practice will follow.

Finally, the day apart spreads its spirit to all days, all life, all Creation. The day apart unlocks heaven and eternity. On it we do not escape this world so much as we truly enter it. By stopping, we realize that we really do have all the time in the world. All the world has this time only, this moment, this now that stretches back to the beginning and on into eternity. Each Sabbath connects with and continues the previous Sabbath in, through, and around ordinary time.

And so the day, so spiritual and graceful and calm, so aimed toward heaven, has enormous practical implications for life on earth. On Juma, Sunday, or Shabbat, we transform reality as we walk toward the ideal.

The Gift in Common

The day of rest has aroused argument and violence. Despite much in common among the Sabbath of the monotheisms, there are major differences in allowance and proscription, in justification and benefits.

The Muslim has his hour of worship on Friday. To him or her, all time is the same time, all time is Allah's. Ultimately, Jews and Christians believe the same though they do set aside one day as holy in a way the other six are not. Yet that day blesses the other days, and that day portends the time when all days are of the same kind in the world to come. This experience of holy time is cyclical and linear. The Sabbath folds both into itself.

Within a religion, other changes and conflicts have had nonreligious causes such as our shifting notions of work, rest, and recreation.[1] Between religions, legitimate differences can be inflamed by hatred.

When a minitheocracy emerged in Basra, Iraq, in mid-2005, reporters cited as evidence the switch of the weekend from Friday-Saturday to Thursday-Friday, done to avoid overlap with the Jewish Sabbath. This was blamed on rabid anti-Semitism. It may be more accurate to say that the Muslims were merely upholding their own holy day. And once a day is set aside, it is more practical to have a day for preparation before rather than after, much as Christians have Saturday and Jews, to some extent, have Friday afternoon. Further, when Friday was first used for group prayers by Muhammad, it enhanced religious coexistence since it was the time when the Jews were preparing for their Sabbath. Vitriol only came later and its resurgence in our own day should not obscure the more fundamental causes for religious decisions.

On the other hand, Sabbath observance can indicate tidal shifts. Many Islamists today, as in the past, call for life under sharia or Islamic law in order to create the umma that existed under the guidance of Muhammad.[2] Such a move would put Juma, with the faithful gathering to worship, at the pivot of the week. Leading Friday prayers was, arguably, Muhammad's most regular, public act of faith. Another tidal shift occurred a thousand years later in another land, when the Puritan Sunday inaugurated a Christian era in the New World.

Bridging the Divide

Common ground predominates. Each monotheism reveres one day in seven as a law instituted by God. They mark the day as holy time that invokes Creation and promotes recreation and re-creation. All three require communal worship and mandate or suggest measures to make the day special: good clothes, grooming, higher pursuits, family, meals, etc. Debates within religions over observance characterize Christianity most of all, Judaism to a lesser degree, and not so much Islam. Though Christians and Muslims had to displace their spiritual forebears via their new Sabbaths, these offspring cannot deny the singular contribution of Judaism to their religions. Any Jew can look around the world and see billions of people keeping Juma or the Lord's Day and know that this is the Sabbath that was first revealed to them.

As cultures mix and people intermarry, this common heritage can be used to build relationships and preserve religion. One-third of Jews already live in mixed homes and half the American Jews who marry do so with Gentiles. Of children raised by Jewish-Gentile couples, only a quarter become observant Jews. Among young Catholics, about half marry people of other faiths and even more Protestants do so.[3] A mixed couple eager to be religious could share many Sabbath beliefs and practices that support the religion of each or a shared faith to which one converts.

World peace via the Sabbath may be unlikely. But there is reason to hope. Religions can unite in their appreciation for the Sabbath. Christians could rethink issues that once divided them from Jews. For instance, they traditionally considered the Jewish Sabbath as a code of restrictions that contrasts with Sunday's message of salvation. But the Jewish Sabbath, in memorializing Creation and the Exodus, is also an enactment of salvation as well. Further, we can find common mystical ground in and through the Sabbath. Both Jews and Christians seek "the immediate intuition of God in the individual soul and conscience," James Parkes declared. To preserve that intuition, "each religion has 'hedged it round' with the discipline of a system and the humility of an authority."[4]

Different faiths can meet on the holy days. In early nineteenth-century Charlottesville, Virginia, the four dominant sects were without their own buildings, Thomas Jefferson wrote to a friend. "The courthouse is the common temple, one Sunday in the month to each. Here, Episcopalian and Presbyterian, Methodist and Baptist, meet together, join in hymning their Maker, listen with attention and devotion to each others' preachers, and all mix in society in perfect harmony."[5] Similarly, the three days for Jews, Christians, and Muslims offer a larger space to explore and share practice and beliefs.

A thousand years earlier, there was a larger experiment in respect and coexistence. In 711 the Moors invaded Spain and their first hundred years were anarchic, with a sorting out of relations between Muslims and their Christian and Jew subjects. These non-Muslim "people of the book" were made to pay a special tax, the *jizya*, but were exempted from other restrictions. Tolerance was embedded in Islam thanks to Muhammad's early praise and respect for the other people of Abraham. By the year 900, the capital of Cordoba was the world's second city, after Baghdad, "a luminous teeming metropolis of 100,000 . . . a fabulous polyglot of three continents and three faiths." Though many Christian churches were converted to mosques and no new ones were allowed to be built, church bells rang on Sundays and funeral processions allowed through Muslim neighborhoods.[6] Intellectually, the different worlds fed one another and science, medicine, and poetry flourished.

The respect for other faiths had a theological base. For Muslims, Islam culminated the religious development that began with Abraham and continued in Judaism and Christianity though these religions had lost their way. Muslims revered Moses and Jesus as prophets whose truths were fulfilled in Muhammad.[7] Along with the offer of protected status for Jews and Christians, and his belief in a common divine text from which all scriptures were derived, Muhammad's plans for a united umma joining the three religions of Abraham were "startlingly revolutionary ideas in an era in which religion literally created borders between peoples." While absorption into the umma may not be the dream of Jews and Christians, this original reverence for other religions is striking.[8]

One reason may be that while Christianity emerged in defiance of Judaism, Islam arose in defiance of paganism while identifying with the people of the book, that is, Jews and Christians. Many scholars and individual believers have noted, over the centuries, a deep sympathy in Islamic culture toward Judaism. Though hard to believe in today's heated climate, it is a fact that "from the rise of the Caliphate till the abolition of the ghettos in Europe the most flourishing centers of Jewish life were to be found in Muslim countries."[9]

At a certain point, Muhammad must have realized that Christians, like the Jews, were going to keep their religion. He would not force the issue; Allah would judge. That's not a full embrace, but it is a polite handshake. And as Azra Haqqie realized, Muslims often practice more in common with Jews than with Christians. The great Jewish sage Maimonides regarded Muslims as true followers of the original seven laws revealed to Adam and Noah. This "Noachide" code included the "one God" rule and anticipated the Ten Commandments. Jews considered this basic, ancient code to be obligatory for all, including Gentiles. Christians often disqualified themselves with the Trinitarian concept of God. However, Muslims qualified due to their strict monotheism. Maimonides concluded that such a righteous people would share in the world to come.[10]

In his book, *At the Entrance to the Garden of Eden*, Jossi Klein Halevi explores the unlikely prospect of peace among the three religions in the crucible of the Holy Land.[11] "Abraham is the root, Judaism the trunk, Christianity the branches, and Islam the beautiful fruit," one imam tells him. A rabbi prominent in interfaith work credits Islam with preserving the "mystical secrets" that Jews lost during their exile in Babylon, such as the immersion of the body in prayer and the ecstasy of the prophets.

Halevi finds Catholic monks and nuns who light Shabbat candles, say the prayers, and eat a meal on Friday evening. The Community of the Beatitudes has 1,500 members in 70 houses around the world who nurture the Jewish roots of Christianity. The Sabbath is the primary vehicle, notably because Jesus kept it. Halevi, a Jew, credits Jesus, who criticized the Pharisees on their Sabbath strictures, with trying to reinvigorate Judaism with the love and presence of God.

Since the ancient, and unlikely, prophecy that Jews would return to the Promised Land has materialized, it is also possible that Isaiah's vision of peace among religions can occur. As a friend in Israel says, there will be peace someday because there has to be peace. Despite all the contrary evidence, the rebirth of Israel recalls the promise that the ancient feud between Isaac and Ishmael will one day be healed.[12] But while the Sabbath offers a meeting place, its observance also distinguishes each religion.

The Litmus Test

When Rabbi Bomzer or a member of his congregation inspects the Albany eruv, they look to make sure that this perimeter is intact and ready for Shabbat. It's cut and dry: either it is or it is not. Similarly, a street or house is either within the eruv or not. Live outside the eruv and no pushing the stroller or carrying a dish to the synagogue. So too, a Jew is shomer Shabbat or not; a Christian keeps Sunday or not; a Muslim leaves work and joins the assembly on Juma. Or not.

The Sabbath is a litmus test. Our beliefs about the day, its obligations, and blessings, reveal our attitudes toward God, His intentions for us, the role of religion, the purpose of life. If we think religion is, as Alfred North Whitehead argued, what a person does with his solitude, then the Sabbath's communal obligation will annoy us and appear beside the point. Alas, it is true that our observance can become tedious to us and our children. That happened in the Middle Ages, when religion became largely externalized and daily life was only periodically interrupted by bouts of intense piety.[13] For many Christians in the centuries after the Reformation, Sunday degenerated into a list of restrictions, all duty and no gift.

We are commanded to rest, and we erect many rules regarding servile labor. Our prayers may follow exact directions on timing, direction, and movement. Some of this pattern is practical, some an effort to lasso the Lord with superstitions and human impositions. For Jews flexibility has worked. They make the Sabbath their own, which has preserved the habit these long millennia. Jews have considerable local autonomy in the spirit of the sages who first compiled and interpreted the Talmud. "Within each community the rabbi sets the rules for observance," Tom Kligerman says. "That's the age we live in; we don't hear the word of God directly."

So what to do? How to keep it fresh? If any religious observance bears within the seeds of renewal, it is the Sabbath. God rested from Creation and we rest from ours. By so doing, we re-create ourselves. We also remember that we earn salvation outside religion. The rites and rituals of institutional faith prepare us for life in the world, but do not replace that struggle to live well and decently.

The boundary of faith can set us against each other and society. We are within or without a religion's territory. Yet even here society can accommodate.

Orthodox Jews who want an eruv readily receive municipal permission to install or erect one, which is usually invisible to casual observers. Most major cities in the United States have one or several neighborhoods so encircled without much fuss, as do many smaller communities. In several New Jersey towns where the issue arose, non-Orthodox Jews and others argued that a religious perimeter would discourage non-Jews or create lopsided demographics or violate the church-state divide. Some call the eruv a religious symbol, as a crucifix, that should not be on public property. Generally, authorities have concluded that an eruv is not a symbol and does not intrude on anyone's life.

Politicians say the effect is usually minimal and some report an eruv attracted enough families to rejuvenate a depressed township or boost housing prices.[14]

Invariably, however, the Sabbath emphasis on community creates tensions with the state and society. As Christians long realized, the day of rest works best if kept in common. But any legislative mandate in this regard violates the freedom of non-Christians, as a California judge declared as early as 1858. "The truth is, however much it is disguised, that this one day of rest is a purely religious idea."[15]

Today we need only protection of the right to observe. "Christians will naturally strive to ensure that civil legislation respects their duty to keep Sunday holy," John Paul II asked in his encyclical.[16] This puts the burden, quite properly, on believers. They can choose to keep the day out of love rather than fear.

Thus kept, the day will foster a true sense of community. In all three religions, the day embodies egalitarianism. Pope John Paul II called Sunday "A Day of Solidarity." As such, it should be characterized by "works of mercy, charity and apostolate," much as the first Christians collected for the poor among them.[17] In their Epistles, the disciples Paul and James both demand equal treatment of rich and poor at the weekly assembly or Lord's Supper (1 Cor. 11:20–22, James 2:2–4). Christians should visit the sick, invite needy or lonesome guests to dinner, give food to yet others. Jews and Muslims teach similarly. In this way, the pope wrote, Sunday becomes "a great school of charity, justice and peace."[18]

In Israel, secular intellectuals who want to rescue the Sabbath from consumerism and Orthodoxy alike have sought to compromise on the laws governing stores, entertainment, and transit. Cultural opportunities would be enhanced in the interest of bolstering national identity.[19] As with the American move to justify the Sabbath in secular terms as one of rest, such a shift in Israel may raise some new issues while shifting the obligation onto the community of believers, where it belongs. But as so many Sabbatarians and their victims learned over the centuries, the state cannot and should not mandate belief and observance. That leaves people in a bind.

Without a religious justification, the day tends to collapse. Relaxation is a need, but not sufficient as a justification over the eons. The *McGowan* ruling was really the last stand for the holy day civilly upheld. In a way, this ruling was a logical extension of the spiritualized Sabbath. This doctrine, promulgated by Augustine and Luther alike, dissolves all distinctions and guidelines. All days become holy and all that matters is a state of mind and soul. Thomas Shephard, the seventeenth-century divine, countered that if the Sabbath were only an inward state and observance, "we may then bid *goodnight* to all the publike worship and glory of God in the world."[20] So again, the answer is faithful, voluntary observance. It's not easy but more people now find it possible and necessary despite distractions.

Resistance and Resurgence

One threat comes from within the pews and sanctuaries: the urge to cleave the material and spiritual into separate realms. The church, according to Dorothy Sayers, "has allowed work and religion to become separate departments, and is astonished to find that, as a result, the secular work of the world is turned to purely selfish and destructive ends."[21] Of course, this division is also central to the Sabbath, which sets holy time apart from profane time.

Even in keeping the day holy, people can pervert it. As the public Sabbath, notably Sunday, has shriveled, people have turned to personal outlets for this transcendent impulse and forsake the public realm as useless or bothersome in our quest for God. The Sabbath survives, then, in the moments of "quality time" we grab with ourselves or God, or that we buy through expensive retreats in converted monasteries or ecological encampments. We pray "in my own way" and find only the god in the mirror.

The outside world complicates Sabbath keeping. Commerce, from stock trading to clothes shopping, has spread into all hours thanks to the Internet. Cyberspace confronts us with many more chances to allot our time among religion, culture, family, and society, thus testing our fidelity to any and each.[22]

In the face of such threats, religious leaders often let people off the hook. They are too eager to accommodate the world, even if it degrades the lives of their congregants. One pastor who has preached and practiced a strict Sunday without shopping was philosophical about those who don't. "God understands the way society has gone. He understands we're at the mercy of the big corporations."[23] That's not exactly a prophetic pronouncement, but it is one you could hear from many pulpits. Likewise, many lay people say they would keep Sunday holy if, if, if.

We forget that religions are countercultural entities. By splitting the loyalty of their congregants, and giving them a moral code often at odds with social and government agendas, religions can promote freedom and check the tyranny of the majority.[24] The Sabbath is quintessentially countercultural, primarily because it contradicts economic laws and demands. Surely the Israelites, struggling to survive, resisted. But Judaism survived because a sufficient minority kept Shabbat against prevailing sense. All religions thrive, and best serve the greater good, by fidelity to their own beliefs. As David Tracy, the theologian, declares, "Religions live by resisting."[25] Deep in Nazi Germany, the Jesuit priest Josef Pieper spotted the deeply rebellious and protective nature of the Sabbath, especially in the fascist-industrial state when many, as today, regarded only paid activity as worthwhile.[26]

As environmentalists or neighborhood advocates have learned, the Sabbath heritage can be deployed to new uses. Cities and towns have resurrected blue laws or adopted variations to curb the chaos of modern suburbia. People walking to shops in a quaint village are one thing; thousands hurtling down the highways in their SUVs is another. In 1993, voters in Bergen County, New Jersey, an epicenter of malls west of New York City, voted to continue restricting Sunday sales to food, fuel, and drugs to alleviate traffic jams. At least one retail chain approved the ban so long as applied equitably. "Sunday is the only day that traffic doesn't wake me up," Paramus mayor Cliff Gennarelli said. Stores large and small approved the ban since it was applied equitably and across the county.[27]

Most people can keep their Sabbath without much ado, though support from their congregation would help. To do so, some people check their income or buck the prevailing tide. Truett Cathy, a Christian businessman, closes his 38-state chain of 1,200 Chick-Fil-A fast-food eateries on Sunday so that his workers can "worship, spend time with family and friends or just plain rest."[28] Such personal decisions and broader trends are giving the Sabbath a boost.

The resurgence in spirituality within Christianity, Judaism, Islam, and society may lead to a revived appreciation for the holy day. So could the renewed attention to worship, primarily Sunday services, that has helped evangelical churches to thrive. "It's the most striking change I've seen in the last 10 to 15 years," David Roozen of the Hartford Institute for Religion Research tells me.

Outside of the liturgy, the quotidian nature and ritual of Sabbath strengthens a people and their faith far more than intellectual propositions. I spent a year teaching carpentry in a Peruvian mountain village where the people had practiced their Catholicism during years without a priest or regular Masses. They sustained their faith through their religious fiestas and quiet Sundays, with the Lenten, Christmas, and other processions and their other popular pieties. Practice and habit does far more than creed and teaching. I remember the Sundays of my childhood; I can't recall what my father said about Catholic doctrine.

Surveying the field among Christians and Jews, David Klinghoffer predicted that America was due for a Sabbath revival, one that was already coming. Supporters range from conservative televangelist Pat Robertson to the liberal activist Jim Wallis, two very different clerics. Robertson condemned the modern neglect of the fourth commandment while Wallis predicted a comeback thanks to stress and overwork.[29]

Jews, from the progressive Reconstruction movement to the Orthodox Chabad evangelicals, campaign for the Sabbath. Thousands of Jewish college students have participated in programs to help them be shomer Shabbat in their dorm rooms and on campus. Other programs do the same for unaffiliated adults through synagogues and community centers.[30] Leaders in Conservative Judaism, caught in the middle, have veered from demanding that lay leaders meet certain levels of Shabbat and kosher keeping or attendance to lowering the bar to fortify current members and draw new ones.

The Kligermans have not launched any drive for Sabbath observance. They do more through their quiet, regular observance of Jewish law. Tom and Becky, who met as an unaffiliated Jew and a nominal Christian, have a family of six who keep Shabbat and share the day with dozens of others. Their friends Rich and Amy Drucker—she also a convert—developed their Sabbath habits through, in part, their friendship with the Kligermans. The Druckers are now expecting their fourth child, another six-member observant family. I kid Tom that the two families have their own Sabbath drive via repopulation. Even the dire demographics facing American Jews are not necessarily proof of decline. Judaism, sustained by the Sabbath, has weathered worse.

"A nation dying for thousands of years means a living nation," declared the Jewish philosopher Simon Rawidowicz. "Our incessant dying means uninterrupted living, rising, standing up, beginning anew."[31]

Liberation from the Self and Society

The Sabbath saves us from ourselves and society. For Jews and Christians, the Sabbath gives us freedom from work, worry, business, the making of a living and making in general. No one is a *macher*, Yiddish for bigshot, on Shabbat. Muslims, while they may work before and after prayers, are liberated from many earthly cares and, potentially, their sins. On the Sabbath, we are freed from ourselves. We are freed to see what we have done as good.

The Sabbath allows us to both secure and relinquish control. We grab back our time by giving it over. We say this day is not at the whim of my boss or the economy or my fears or my neighbors or my credit card debt. It is not even at the whim of our great expectations. We cede control to God as only free people can.

In all three religions, the communal aspect of the Sabbath counters the vague and individualistic spiritual tendencies of modern people. Private practice is inherently subjective; it complements any creed but by itself cannot sustain a community and its doctrine. If the ancient Israelites had rested on days of their personal choosing or in their own way, there would be no Sabbath left today.

We learn that we need not act like gods, always on duty spinning the globe. More fundamentally, God gives us not freedom from, but freedom to. We are freed by faith to be the persons He intended. On the Sabbath, we are free to be, to inhale and exhale, to do nothing. We drop our baggage; it's too big for carry-on. In his poem "Healing Leaves," Wendell Berry describes the gate into the Sabbath as narrow to ensure that we leave behind all that separates us from God. Paul tells Christians that by entering God's rest, we rest from our work just as He did (Heb. 4:9–10).

Unfortunately the long history of religion features a reversion to the self. Given its human element, faith frequently turns away from God and toward me, myself, and I. In Christianity, it was the Italian Renaissance that rediscovered the classical view of man and thereby shifted our attention from God in heaven to man on earth. Man became the measure of all things. And our hubris intensified from the fourteenth century on. Luther, in rejecting the corruption and sin of the church at the time, rejected the church as well. Conceptually, he had no place for the church as a community of believers united in God.[32] John Henry Newman, in his *Lectures on Justification,* warned us that Luther "released (Christians) by his doctrine of faith and then left them in bondage to their feelings."[33] Descartes, though Catholic, carried on this work when he made the individual knower as the basis of all reality, and later influenced Kant, whose "turn to the subject" relied so much on human reason.

Without ritual and order, religion becomes either too intellectual or too emotional. We need an anchor. When faith becomes too cerebral, we are unmoved and soon lose interest. When too emotional, we become exhausted. Then, disappointed by mundane results, we lose heart. We want to be moved, we wait to be moved, and then judge a doctrine false for its lack of payoff.

Many of the contemporary advocates of the Sabbath take this personal approach. They would fit the day to our convenience and find a time for God but on our schedule. Decide for yourself, alleluia. Turn off the computer and have a cup of tea. Be spiritual by brushing off from your shoulder—or from around your neck—the dead hand of religion. We would then have a billion Sabbaths, each person a celebrant at a private liturgy. At the other extreme, respite from work and worry should not dissolve into a painful ritual of emptiness that "earns" God's grace, nor into a vapid time-for-me vacation from life.

The Sabbath releases us from ourselves. Jews, Muslims, and Christians all anchor the day in communal prayer and worship. But here's a conundrum: if our allegiance is reinforced by the blessings we feel during observance, we cycle back toward the self. Harold Bloom observes, in his overheated way, "The God of the American Religion is an experiential God, so radically *within* our own being as to become a virtual identity with what is most authentic (oldest and best) in the self." He lets Emerson summarize the point. "It is God in you that responds to God without."[34]

Well, maybe. We are created in God's likeness and image, thus we recognize God in all—when we stop long enough to see, sense, and know. "It is not an issue of self-worship," Bloom continues, "it is an acquaintance with a God within the self." Well, yes and no. But the danger of self-worship creeps into the Sabbath, like the serpent in the Garden of Eden. It must be directed within and beyond, at once.

Liberation from Rationality and Abstraction

The Sabbath rescues religion from our urge to rationalize all and convert the experience of faith into abstract particles. The day apart produces results. While it may have been dictated from on high at Sinai as a one-way obligation of a divine covenant, believers ever since have found in it an earthly joy and satisfaction. It works. Witness the use of the Sabbath as a justification for "down time" regardless of belief or atheism. The Sabbath also saves us from a faith that devolves into abstract principals. It took the acute genius of Rudolf Otto to remind Christians that God was not an entirely rational proposition and that wonder and mystery lay at the heart of faith.[35]

We also like results because good outcomes appeal to our reason. Modern men and women can embrace the religious impulse since science announces, with increasing regularity and all due qualifiers, that faith makes one healthy. It drops blood pressure and hypertension, speeds convalescence from chemotherapy, and comforts patients before and after surgery. Religious involvement, we now know from scores of studies, improves mental health and helps alcoholics and addicts abstain and recover. And thank goodness! After dwelling these millennia in the dungeons and towers of impulse and fanaticism, believers now have a right and reason to practice their faith.

Religion always has had a purpose. We adhere for as long as it serves that purpose, primarily human survival. "By their fruits ye shall know them," it was said of the early Christians. Other religions have similar tests of fidelity. If faith is the first article of any religion, purpose is a second and results a third.

Liberation from the Irrational and an Anchor for the Mystical

The Sabbath saves us from irrationality while also giving the mystical elements of faith a foundation. From childhood and last week as well, I remember the formal comfort of Sunday. Though it is a day, utterly, for man we have it by the grace of God. As we have all days, every one.

Typically on Sunday by late morning, I am rested, serene, and magnanimous in my starched shirt and loosened-after-church tie. I beam at the world and receive back its glow (or is it the echo of my pious self-regard?). On Juma, Shamim Haqqie feels good for having prayed with his fellows in the chapel at Albany Medical Center. On Shabbat, the Kligermans smile calmly, even when the children run amok, during their luncheon with friends and in the peaceful island of their home, connected by a short walk to the oasis of Temple Israel. We keep the day and the day keeps us. Our happy experience reinforces our resolution to do so next week, and bolsters us when we think of skipping this or that Sabbath preparation or rite.

The day apart is a day in common. Its religious imagery—God in repose, humans at ease after six days of labor, the Queen of Shabbat approaching, the gates of heaven open, grace spilled on sinners—balances the individual with the communal. The concrete nature of observance has a balancing influence as well. Walking to the synagogue, not shopping, hiking in the hills, dining with friends and family, playing with children, being in time and not on the clock all draw the individual into his community. The individual is relieved of his or her burdens, and in turn relieves others of the burdens of selfishness, poor behavior, or greed that he or she imposes other days.

A Sabbath must be rooted in the world lest it end up someplace other than heaven. As early as 1600, some English and Continental Protestants found themselves led by their Sabbatarian logic to observance of the seventh day. Nearly a hundred years later, groups of German immigrants to Pennsylvania began keeping the Jewish Sabbath. Led by the charismatic Peter Beissel, one sect founded the Ephrata Cloister in 1735, on the Cocalico Creek near Germantown. Members worked at farming, crafts, and printing. The Saturday Sabbath, and their dunking method of baptism, bound them together. They despised outward institutions of religion. They believed themselves possessed by an "Inner Light," and eschewed formal prayers in favor of allowing the Holy Spirit to pour forth. They lived simply and sought to imitate the early church with foot washing, the kiss of peace, and midnight watches. But they never totaled more than 300 members. After Beissel died in 1768, the community dwindled away.[36]

Tradition and ritual can tether our light spirits even as the tension remains between grace and good works. In all three religions, will we keep a Sabbath as a joy and gift or because we were so commanded? Without public support and communal custom, how long will it last? Emotion and inspiration carried the Ephrata community, and thousands like it, only so long. By keeping our feet on earth, the Sabbath grants us the experience of a reality that transcends and affirms this life, here and now.

Forgiveness

The Sabbath forgives us for being human, for sinning, for failing, for trying and failing to be gods. Christians may wonder if, on Sunday, we are freed from sin by God's grace rather than our works. Yes, we observe the day, but we do not earn it. We keep the day by accepting the gift of the day, one day away from menial and material concerns. And in that deeper level of observance, which is really receiving, we feel saved. What person, religious or not, does not sense in their innermost being, a relief on Sunday? It is the day that most bears the stamp of the divine even in the most secular of settings.

Christians can escape that harsh choice, given by Paul and debated ever since, between salvation by works or by grace. Yes, Paul inveighed against Jewish law, which he said Christ had ended. Christians who kept the Sabbath, made Paul feel like a failure. Yet we muddled through to some happy compromise. Here we are now, with nearly 2,000 years of Sunday keeping in memory of Easter, in keeping with the Ten Commandments, and as an occasion for regular and communal celebration of the Lord's Supper.

The Sabbath is more than a rest stop. It sanctifies humans and the time in which we live our lives and it blesses the work of our other six days in the mystical relation between creation and cessation. With God, Archbishop Trench wrote, "The deepest rest is not excluded from the highest activity, nay, rather in God they are one and the same."[37]

By blessing all time and life, the Sabbath forgives our profanation of any part. The Sabbath relieves us from ourselves and from sin in particular.

Nature's Renewal

On the wall in the room next to my office hangs a reprint of Claude Monet's painting, "The Beach at Saint-Addresse." In it, men in dove-gray suits and floppy black bowties and women in flowing dresses and carrying parasols lounge on a rocky shore and watch a harbor freckled with sailboats. What is striking in the subjects is their utter ease. These gentlefolk do not earn their rest, they claim it.

Leisure comes naturally. Here our instinct is complemented by divine command. The Sabbath restores to humanity the natural rhythm of activity and rest. If the religious impulse is deeply human, the Sabbath instinct is deeper. Everyone needs to stop. With the Sabbath, we have an excuse. Plato gave thanks for such. "But the gods, taking pity on human beings—a race born to labor—gave them regularly recurring divine festivals, as a mean of refreshment from their fatigue."[38]

Rest has to happen regularly. If you doubt this, then work constantly. Work seven days, all day, never stop. Go ahead—your job really is that important, your home really needs all that attention, your cause is more than worthy. You will likely fall back into the ancient habit of weekly rest. The Sabbath is for us.

Interestingly, the religions that are thriving around the world meet basic human needs. The surging Christian sects in Africa succeed "because they help people survive, in all of the ways that people need to survive—social, spiritual, economic, finding a mate," Rosalind J. Hackett said in an interview. "People forget how critical that is." The Sabbath helps answer all those needs. Further, Hackett said, these new religious movements create transnational communities so that as people move for jobs they find a home and surrogate family in their new locale.[39] This is true too of older religions. When I travel or move, I am immensely reassured when Sunday comes with its familiar pattern and the local church where I gather with fellow believers.

On the day of eternity, we renew those ideals for which we strive the other days, the ideals that are unattainable but make life worthwhile. We may recall that outcomes are less important than simply doing what is right. As Dorothy Day, founder of the Catholic Worker movement, often asked, "Why must we see results?"

On the Sabbath, things fall into place and we see the world through new glasses. Spiritual truths replace material concerns. Gone is the pressure of work and school and the heartbreaking struggle to assert ourselves against others. We see each other as we are. And nature, no longer the object of our exploitation, can be rediscovered. "As the day on which man is at peace with God, with himself and with others, Sunday becomes a moment when people can look anew upon the wonders of nature."[40]

The weekly rest anchors the week itself. And the seven-day week has a counterpart in our internal *circaseptan* or weekly rhythms found in blood pressure, immune response, heartbeat, and levels of calcium and acid. Witold Rybczynski speculates that we matched the week to these patterns. I'd say it's more likely our biology has habituated itself to the way we spend the week.

The Sabbath helps the larger world of nature around us. Obviously, if we all spent a day without driving or jetting, the savings in gasoline and fresh air would be enormous. The Torah teaches that unless Israel grants the earth its sabbatical year of rest and lets the fields lie fallow, an equivalent rest would be imposed via drought or other desolation, just as the person who fails to rest collapses into the rest she or he needs. Today, pantheists and environmentalists adapt Sabbatarian teachings. They warn that unless we give the earth its rest, an ecological disaster will do that for us. For them it's nature, for the believer it's God, who thus responds to human greed and apostasy.

My Own Private Sabbath Work Experiment

One Sunday in winter I sleep late. Amy takes the girls to church while I stay home with my son Mitchell, who is ill. After breakfast, I experiment with the work-rest provision (really, the original point of the Sabbath and not an aspect). I had been painting the kitchen, and so today I prime a set of bifold closet doors to move things along. A great relief it has been to see more white and less dark red wood in this room that we use most of all. Mitchell naps and lies about on the couch. After my chore, I read him a few books. A favorite one tells of famous animals such as Koko, the gorilla who learned to communicate with her keeper. Amy, Jeanne, and Madeleine return. The day eases on in a frigid world: lunch, newspapers, Nok hockey. I attend the 5:00 PM Mass at the cathedral. A quiet pleasure it is to hear and pray and sit in silence without directing children hither and yon. At day's end, I can conclude little from the work experiment. A second Saturday beckons, with time for more chores and projects. The kitchen would be painted in half the time, the next project started and done within the same amount of time. Then what? Will I rest when it's all perfect? Or when the mood strikes me? I doubt mere whim can save us from a life of toil and gain. Once we put our shoulder to the wheel, would we ever stop unless we had to every seven days?

A year and a half later, I know better than even to experiment. I sit on the hacienda with the newspapers, coffee, and juice. I begin to lean over to pluck a weed from the vegetable garden at my feet. Nearby, an unintended morning glory supersedes a tomato plant—but no—or yes to Sunday. I hold back, I stop as God stopped. The weed will live another day, the flowering vine will mount further yet the air and prompt our smiles, and I will fall back from activity, back from creation, and into Creation. The joy comes only by ceasing.

God and Man Unite

The Sabbath offers participants their best experience of God. Few people escape entirely the suspicion that He is an illusion. We see the fruits of faith but not its object. Who has not doubted this deity who supposedly made the world and its inhabitants, who magically meets our needs, explains our purpose and redeems each of us? "The whole thing is so patently infantile," wrote Freud, "so foreign to reality, that to anyone with a friendly attitude to humanity it is painful think that the great majority of mortals will never be able to rise above this view of life."[41] He may be right, though my experience tells me otherwise. Yet the experience of faith is so powerful that it can seem godlike in itself. As Virgil asks in the *Aeneid*, "Is it the gods who put this fire in our minds? Or is it that each man's relentless longing becomes a god to him?" Can we separate one from the other?

Sabbath divides the sacred from the profane in order to, one day, convert all to holiness. The eighteenth-century Reformer, Johann Conrad Beisel, saw that this distinction, "between holy and unholy flows from God's love . . . and abides until the whole world is freed from sin."[42]

Yet I wonder. The divide between sacred and profane is ingrained in our minds and history. In a sense, the whole range of our notions of disgust, shame, and impropriety originate in our subconscious conviction that this earth is Eden, that the world truly is God's Creation, and that no stain shall be upon it. Always we are making God's world our own by our thoughts and labors. And like a parent who each evening gathers up his children's toys and trucks, God constantly steps in to set us right. Always He makes us His. The Sabbath is the weekly return of Creation to Creator.

We are freed from time on the Sabbath as well as from the chatter and bother and worries of life. This release suggests and rehearses the final release of death or salvation. All religions promise liberation from life and a return to God. In Sufism, a mystical branch of Islam, adherents study and practice various routes to *fana*, the final dissolution of the self into the religious experience. At death, mainstream Islam teaches, the soul or *nafs* is freed from physical constraints and moves onto another plane of existence.[43] We can also transcend material or profane concerns and limits in this life, which is the real secret of the Sabbath.

On the holy day, we so place ourselves in time and space as to be without direction or purpose. We lift our rudder out of the water and drift. Similarly, a fourteenth-century Christian mystic, Jan van Ruysbroek, described the "waylessness" of the soul in meeting God at the spiritual summit. There, all divisions yield to unity. The spiritual rest of Sunday is of the same substance of the eternal rest, and so moves us with all of Creation toward God's goal.

All religions promote this doctrine. In the scripture of Judaism, Christianity, and Islam, God speaks to us, personally and communally, in the most immediate way. In Sura 7:172 of the Quran, Allah asks, "Am I not your Lord?" Such a God loves us while seeking our entire consent. Comments one scholar, "Bare omnipotence does not speak this way. Love may and does."[44] In this spirit, some contemporary Islamic writers depict a divine engagement with humanity, rather than the exalted transcendence of earlier theologians. So too Christians strive to inject a transcendent reality into the hours and objects of life. Rather than turn from reality in denial and abstinence we can radiate divine love back into work and charity. This is the spirit and power of the Sabbath.

Consider the simple blessing of the bread at a Jewish meal on Friday evening. The two loaves of challah represent more than the double portion of manna given the Israelites on the sixth day. The kabbalah teaches that one loaf, the bread of luxury, is from heaven; the other, the bread of poverty, is from earth. Held together and blessed, heaven and earth are joined and the celestial Sabbath "flows forth and illumines all."[45]

Free to Be

Close to God is close to Creation. All three religions confess a God who is king of heaven and earth. Sabbath brings us near. God's commandments aim to transform believers inwardly through outward obedience. Jesus spoke for all the descendants of Abraham when he summarized the primary commandment, "You shall love the Lord your God with all your heart, and with all your soul, and with all your mind." That's what we do on the Sabbath, when we most explicitly give ourselves over to God.

Even the mystics of Judaism, Christianity, and Islam turn always to this earth. Even the whirling dervishes remain bound by gravity. Mystical union occurs in the midst of this life, not abandoning the world but transforming it.[46]

Today we are ever more removed from reality. Technology, wrote Max Frisch, the Swiss author and architect, is "the knack of so arranging the world that we don't have to experience it."[47] Sabbath connects us thereto. We leave off the implements of work, the tools by which we conquer Creation. Between us and the world stands nothing.

And so on the Sabbath we do not escape from reality, but fall back into it. Yet this is not death. I am left cold by those who foresee beyond the grave a happy dissolution into the godhead. Yuck. Did God really make each of us in his own image, but uniquely ourselves, in order to dump us all into some formless mass in the afterlife? Is the end of all our striving and all our resting nothingness? The Sabbath offers us an earthbound heaven. I'll take it.

As many of us have discovered, a desire for Sabbath rest can mutate into a lust for the country home, the perfect vacation, the tidy New England village, the Currier and Ives Christmas, the right décor, the California Closet, the writing-painting-pottery shed out back, the abundant vegetable garden, good health and low cholesterol. It's quite a spectacle: big bucks chasing simplicity and eternity. Doomed to fail it is when we try to satisfy an infinite urge with material goods.

All these are substitutes for the repose that God took after Creation and that God grants on Sabbath. As observant Jews discover every week, God grants repose through earthbound limits that liberate. In his sonnet, "Nuns Fret Not at Their Convent's Narrow Room," William Wordsworth contemplated the escape sought by those "who have felt the weight of too much liberty." Realizing the blessings of form and restriction, the poet concludes:

> In truth the prison, unto which we doom
> Ourselves no prison is.

True liberty never overwhelms.

On the Sabbath, there is a solution to two human limitations: our inability to bear too much of reality, as T. S. Eliot wrote, and our inability or unwillingness to stand too much divinity. Did not the Israelites plead with Moses to speak to Yahweh on their behalf? On the Sabbath we float in this water, freed from our fears of both reality and divinity and buoyed by a truth we only then realize through experience. The closer we are to truth the closer we come to God. Reality is divinity disguised.

It's what we want. In his poem, "Large Red Man Reading," Wallace Stevens tells of ghosts who return to earth from empty space and now relish, only indirectly, the common and beautiful and painful things of life that they failed to appreciate during their lives. For Stevens, poetry can save us from this fate.[48] For my part, good Sabbaths do the same. Sabbath puts us where we are.

It may be our limited notion of time that holds us back. In *The Last Unicorn* by Peter Beagle, a character describes how, when alive, "I lived in a house bricked up with second and minutes, weekends and New Year's Days, and I never went outside until I died, because there was no other door. Now I know that I could have walked through the walls."[49] Once a week there is a door through those walls.

Early in Heschel's book, *The Sabbath*, he tells us that, "The faith of the Jew is not a way out of this world, but a way of being within and above this world; not to reject but to surpass civilization." Our sense of the holy day being apart from life lies in the fact that it is, as Heschel continues, "the armistice in man's cruel struggle for existence, a truce in all conflicts, personal and social, peace between man and man, man and nature, peace within man." We are liberated and installed, perhaps as God meant us to be, "as a sovereign in the world of time."[50]

At Juma, Muslims are closer to Allah when they pray in a group and also during one unknown hour of the day, when He will answer their prayers. By keeping Shabbat, the Kligermans celebrate and preserve Judaism itself. On Sunday, I feel not removed but more deeply immersed in life, in its reality that so often lies hidden behind a film of distortion and distraction. That is our mission, to live fully. "If there is a sin against life," wrote Albert Camus, "it consists perhaps not so much in despairing of life as in hoping for another life and in eluding the implacable grandeur of this life."[51]

See? The other six days may be full of life's grand struggle, but the seventh gives us the time and opportunity to step back and see what it's all about. It is worthwhile in and of itself. Fully living brings us close to God, to truth, and back to a joyful life since joy grows with truth.

Each Sabbath bursts quietly from the last and flows into the next. These moments offer a window onto a "Great Time," Mircea Eliade argues. This "nostalgia for eternity" demonstrates our belief "that such a paradise can be won *here*, on earth, and *now*, in the present moment."[52] More accurately, sacred time presents us with the eternal present. For Christians, John Paul II wrote, the Lord's Day proclaims that time "is not the grace of our illusions but the cradle of an ever new future, an opportunity given to us to turn the fleeting moments of this life into seeds of eternity."[53] The Sabbath demonstrates that there is a realizable eternity. Once a week we walk into the eternal now.

Undone By Grace

The holy day proves itself in the riches unleashed. We turn a spigot and out floods Niagara Falls. One Epiphany Sunday, deep in snow, we attend St. Mary's, a baroque gem in downtown Albany. In his sermon, Father Robert Lefebvre enjoins us to be like the Three Kings and follow Jesus. What does it mean to follow Jesus? On other days, perhaps, there is a cross to pick up and bear. But as Easter follows Good Friday, so too does a life in Christ mean joy. So too does a weekly reorientation toward God shower blessings upon us. "Here, you drive," we say and slide over to the passenger seat.

Blessed for sure, but more so by the return on the small investment we made this Sunday to observe the Lord's Day. We work not, we attend more to the children, we go to Mass. After church and lunch, I take Mitchell out on his sled, twice around the block. I ask Madeleine about her Yugio cards, a complex Japanese card game. Jeanne I try to indulge, not correct or fix. And when they ask, I wrestle with the three children on the living room rug. I think with awe of the Jews, who are so observant and so aware of how to observe, and I think of them with thanks for preserving God's command—this day for Him and for us—over these thousands of years. I think too of the Muslims, so certain and calm and unified in their Friday rituals and assembly. Before toothpaste and pajamas, we repeat our little sundown ritual: the candles, the prayers, a hymn of thanks, the posture of belief. Afterwards, I read three books to my son, Mitchell, then age three. He goes to bed so willingly and contentedly, sweet beyond belief. My cup spills over.

The Sabbath is a moment of God come to all times, all people, and all places. It transforms all our life even as we continue living it. For in living the Sabbath, we sense life's richer, fuller possibilities.

"When we see all things in God, and refer all things to him, we read in common matters superior expressions of meaning," William James wrote. "The deadness with which custom invests the familiar vanishes, and existence as a whole appears transfigured."[54] On Sunday we change our perspective, see God in more, and do things differently. If we stop and see, then the Sabbath should never fall into stale weariness of bothersome ritual and devotion.

What do we see? Perhaps we see here on earth elements of Augustine's "Great Sabbath" that never ends. He predicted that for heaven. I say we need not wait. All the experience and theology of the Sabbath push us into a heaven on earth, if only for a day. "There we shall rest and see, see and love, love and praise," Augustine wrote in *The City of God*.[55]

On the holy day, fully realized, we will be free to do what is right because we so desire. "In the Perpetual Sabbath there will be felicity without taint of evil or lack of good which allows leisure for praise of God," Augustine continued. "We will not be idle. We will know all our parts and abilities as this worship involves all our faculties, so many of which we now are only dimly aware." Faith and reason will be joined. The discoveries of that time "shall kindle rational minds in praise of the great Artificer" and "there shall be the enjoyment of a beauty which appeals to the reason."

Sacred and profane will be joined. The body will be "wherever the spirit wills, and the spirit shall will nothing that is unbecoming either to the spirit or the body." True peace and true honor will be there, as will contentment. Striving and envy will be no more for God will be "all in all."[56]

****

One summer Sunday we enjoy a grand day of worship, rest, and recreation. We attend the 9:30 AM Mass at St. Teresa of Avila. I sit in on the children's liturgy of the word to assuage three-year-old Mitchell. After the opening prayers of the Mass, the priest calls up the teacher and children and blesses us before we troop off to the library. The mother leading the service reads a simplified version of the Bible passages. There is one from Genesis ("It is not good for a man to be alone. I will make a suitable partner for him.") and one from the Letter to the Hebrews about the human and divine nature of Jesus (2:9–11). Then we hear the Gospel, Mark's account of Jesus preaching the marital unity of a man and woman (10:2–16).

For the children, the teacher offers a lesson of friendship, of being lonely and of being a friend. When one boy asked, "Does God make mistakes?" she politely begs off and refers them to their parents on that. After Mass, we stop for bagels and visit a woman from the parish at a nursing home, the same one where my mother lived for a few years. We stop at another elder residence a block up Hackett Boulevard to see Sister Liquori. Back at home, I laze about while Amy wheels off on her bicycle. The children run back and forth with friends. Then the Stenards hold their annual ice cream social for the block. We play football, then soccer in the street, adults and children barreling back and forth, parents calming upset players and cheering on good kicks and catches. I cook dinner and we drive out to the theater to see an early showing of "School of Rock," a funny story about a burnt-out, head-banging rocker who fakes his way into substitute teaching at a prep school and then converts his class into a band with singers, roadies, and a manager. We leave the mall.

Driving home, I don't know how or why, my daughter makes a half-hearted sour comment. We overreact. Soon three of us are speaking loudly. I pull over on Western Avenue, put on the flashers and reprimand her too sternly. By the time we arrive home, Amy had calmed things down when came another barb; this time aimed at a sibling. My rebuke is harsh. And then we were off riding the mad tilt-a-whirl, both parents barking and someone storming off along the sidewalk. The other two children happily ignore the mayhem and dash about the front yard and sidewalk in their high-jinks sideshow.

We limp into the house, the adults mortified. I almost let the four of them pass upstairs, then on a whim I ask, "Does anyone want to end Sunday?" Yes, and Madeleine snaps to, takes charge, leans over the prayer book I have opened. She appears a different person: light, direct, unhindered, prayerful. She turns away from the profane and toward the sacred, and so helps us all to do so. I light the two candles, whose significance this time is in the extinguishing, and we sing the hymn, "Now Thank We All Our God," with which we usually conclude the Lord's Day.

Madeleine reads the Magnificat, the ancient prayer of Mary welcoming the Lord's favor from the Gospel of Luke. "My soul doth magnify the Lord, my spirit rejoiceth in God my Savior." Mitchell hurls droplets from the holy water flask at each of us and mutters in his toddler way, "Godblessyou weekahead." Jeanne, too tired, lounges dramatically on the staircase landing. We pass around the spice box, each sniffing to remind us of the sweetness of the Lord's Day in the week ahead. We then thank God for specific elements of the Sunday now ending—rest, friends, time together, "School of Rock," our home—and ask for His blessings in the days to come. As we do so, I stand behind Madeleine and hug her. We sway back and forth, a little, as I did with her in my arms when she was a baby. A sweet peace wafts over us like the first breeze of autumn that cuts through an August day's heat. In these few minutes our anger is long gone. God's peace beams down on our patch of earth and washes away worry, anxiety, harshness, and uncertainty.

Not an hour later, as I finish reading to the children and they turn in, I mention this miracle to Madeleine. "Isn't it amazing how we were all mad at one another and then we said the Sunday prayers and you took over and it changed our mood?" She stares at me. "I don't remember that," she says. I am speechless, and then recover with a recitation of the sequence of events. Madeleine nods, "Oh, okay," and turns to her book. Later, I tell Amy the story. I am still amazed Madeleine doesn't remember. Then I realize, "But she will, she will, they all will."

At about this same time, early in my four years studying and living the Sabbath, I attend Temple Israel on Saturday evening for the Minhah service that closes their holy day. After the main part of the service, we break for a small meal, followed by a lesson and a verbal quiz from Rabbi Silton. Afterward, the dozen or so people walk out the back door to bless the new moon, which floats halfway up in the southern sky. As a Catholic, I naturally recall St. Paul's injunction that followers of Christ have been freed from the law and should no longer observe special days and times and new moons. My thoughts are broken by a convivial air as the men and women of Temple Israel bid each other a good week. I walk toward home along New Scotland Avenue, contemplating the utter familiarity and strangeness of other monotheisms. I am in the crossover time that binds the three monotheisms. Juma was yesterday and the nightfall that now ends Shabbat marks the beginning of our Sunday vigil.

After ten minutes I am across the street from St. Teresa's, our parish church. I turn to face it; traditionally Catholics bless themselves when they pass a church to honor the divine presence within the tabernacle. Then I realize that Temple Israel is to my left about ten blocks. An almost equal distance to my right is Albany Medical Center, where I prayed in the chapel many times with the Muslim doctors and scientists and orderlies. I stand midway, at some holy pivot, a magical meridian among the three religions. All their billions are children of Abraham, who so long ago in the land of Ur heard God's call, "Go." And, miraculously, Abraham went, walking just as I walk this night, on a journey seeking the divine by following orders. God said "Go," and Abraham went. God said, "Remember the Sabbath," "Keep holy the Sabbath," and here we are, thousands of years later, keeping and remembering.

Appendix: Random Notes on Keeping the Sabbath

What to do? Though this is not a how-to book, you may like some suggestions. These are neither exhaustive nor sufficient for any of the three monotheisms. Islam, Christianity, and Judaism offer a wealth of requirements, rituals, prayers, services, and guidelines for members to follow on their respective holy days. My ideas here are more practical than theological, more general than denominational. These may also help people who are spiritual rather than religious, or who favor no faith whatsoever, but who still treasure a weekly day of rest. My suggestions may provoke further reflection on your part or give you some simple steps to take in order to understand and keep the Sabbath.

1. Keep it. Get started.
2. Keep it as a community; it is both easier and more meaningful. If you are a member of religion, follow its teachings. Study the theology and follow the guidelines of your denomination within that religion. If your neighbors in the pews or along the prayer line do not make holy the day, encourage them to. Even if alone, plunge in. Your example of joy may be the best means to attract others. And remember, solo or in a group, on the Sabbath you are joined across space to fellow believers near and far and you are joined across time to all who came before and all who are yet to come and keep the day.
3. Keep it regardless of the time and circumstances. Do not succumb to the "if only" syndrome. ("If only everyone kept the Sunday the way they

did when we were children." "If only we were in the old country, in Jerusalem, in Mecca, in heaven.") The commandment in each religion speaks to the believer here and now; the joy of the day is available to any who seek it.

4. Aim high. Accept that you will never exhaust nor completely gain the holy day. The theologian Karl Barth spoke of "the radical importance, the almost monstrous range of the sabbath commandment."[1] Keep looking for more; sink into the day; let go and let God. God gave the day to us.

5. Let the day shape you and your other days. If you learn to set aside worry and materialism once a week, you can do so in snippets other times. In my house, for example, we don't discuss money after 9:00 PM. It's a great relief. Develop that Sabbath instinct. Let your week lead up to and from the holy day.

6. Here's an insight for the Sabbath that counters stale rationalism. The Gnostic revelation of secret knowledge that saves us is really the revelation of God's love combined with our realization of God's complete otherness. Then we are shocked by God's simultaneous distance and intimacy. This we know on Sunday, Shabbat, Juma. So embrace that ennui, that panic. Hug that Sunday neurosis and doors to beyond will open.

7. Make it a day of culture, education, literature, arts, and renewal. Recreate and re-create. Appreciate and contemplate. Behold the world that we otherwise devour. Wander in your neighborhood, hike in the woods, attend concerts, visit museums. Be in the world.

8. Make it special in terms of dress, meals, bathing, activities, and your attitude.

9. Prepare ahead of time. For this reason Saturday is called, in most of Scandinavia, the day of washing and laundry (Laugardagur in Iceland, Lördag in Sweden, etc.) So too, Muslims and Jews may begin their arrangements days before. Appreciate that this effort turns your eyes to God.

10. Once the day arrives, draw a line. Say, "That's enough for now." If a mess remains but does not impede the day, step over it. Be relieved.

11. On the Sabbath, remember that we are not God. Learn to trust God and use the day to turn things over to Him. Let God complete our lives and work.

12. Perform acts of charity. Visit or help those in need: people who are sick, lonely, poor, troubled. Invite these people over for dinner along with your friends and relatives. Fulfill in your congregation the promise that Rabbi

Bomzer sketched for his synagogue: that no one who comes to services will have to eat alone that day.

13. Keep any other work to acts of necessity. Clean up the spilled milk but don't continue on to wax the kitchen floor. This vigilance calls for reflection and decision. On a Sunday Boston's Roman Catholic archbishop settled with lawyers representing hundreds of victims of sexual abuse by priests. Was it necessary to hold that last marathon session on the holy day? Or was it matter of saving lives, per Jewish teaching, or advancing the common good, as articulated in the seventeenth century? Remember that on the seventh day Joshua captured Jericho and Jesus healed the blind and the lame.

14. Try to relieve those people who help as a vocation, such as Catholic Workers who house the homeless and feed the hungry. After all, the need continues 24/7. Can we step in periodically to give these faithful servants a break? We also can fill in for people from other religions on their holy day, such as Jewish journalists who work on Christmas or synagogues that staff Catholic soup kitchens on Sundays.

15. Remember the second half of the traditional Christian rule: "to neither do, nor cause to be done, any servile labor." Your recreation may require others to work, such as museum guards, police officers, or lifeguards. See what you can do to ensure their day of rest as well.

16. Spouses, especially husbands, should remember that the day of rest may still involve many chores. Don't leave these to your wife or partner.

17. But be on guard. The demand is endless for the services of many people such as nurses, doctors, social workers, plumbers, firefighters, and others. The list can grow endlessly. Most of us believe or hope that our work makes the world better. Maybe it's our egos. Many of us could say the work must go on, even on Sunday. Where do we draw the line?

18. Shine the Sabbath spotlight on your other days. Does the Sabbath make good our labors? Is our work worthy? Can we look upon it, as did God at Creation, and call it good? The Anglican theologians Davis and Garrett offer three criteria for labor to deserve a Sabbath blessing: that it is done in remembrance and imitation of God's Creation; that it eschew excess in our investment of time and material; and that it elevates our hearts toward God.[2] We cease from work on the holy day, but the holy day can elevate the work we do the rest of the week.

19. Though the blue laws are gone, governments can protect the right of believers to their holy day. At the least, governments should require a

weekly day off for all workers. On a social basis, we can seek a common secular basis for the day of rest. In an 1858 case, a California judge said that laws upholding Sunday rest merely codified "a rule of conduct, which the entire civilized world recognizes as essential to the physical and moral well-being of society. . . . One day in seven is the rule, founded in experience and sustained by science."[3] We can work it out.

20. Religious leaders, laypeople, and congregations should speak up and proclaim their respective holy days. Too long they have acquiesced to the day's erosion. Each religion requires the holy day; each religion finds therein untold blessings and joys. If the Israelites in the desert could keep the day, so can any believer in the present age. Help is at hand in our communities, our scriptures, and our traditions.

21. From Nigeria, Is-haq Lakin Akintola suggests one solution: a three-day weekend that accommodates Muslims, Christians, and Jews as well as Seventh-day Christians. People would work longer days on the other four to make up the loss. While I am not sure this would work on a national level, it may help on a social or individual basis.

22. There are many thoughtful, practical guidebooks for Sabbath keeping. Christians may like Tilden Edwards' seminal 1982 book, *Sabbath Time*. More recently, there is *Sabbath Keeping* by Lynne M. Baab; *Keeping the Sabbath Wholly* by Marva J. Dawn; and *Receiving the Day* by Dorothy C. Bass. Wayne Muller's *Sabbath* will appeal also to nonreligious Sabbatarians. Among the numerous volumes for Jews, I found Francine Klagsbrun's *The Fourth Commandment* engaging and authoritative. Heschel's *The Sabbath* is, of course, intimate and majestic. There may be an equivalent for Muslims and Juma; I did not find it. Of course, the best guide to Juma rules and practices are Muhammad's examples and teachings as contained in the Hadith and Sunna.

23. In terms of research, readers can turn to Rybczynski's *Waiting for the Weekend* for an enjoyable account of the Saturday-Sunday evolution. For a marvelous cross-disciplinary piece of scholarship, there is *The Sabbath in Jewish and Christian Traditions*, edited by Eskenazi, Harrington, and Shea. I found nothing comparable for all three monotheisms, one reason I wrote this book.

24. Finally, learn from the other religions. Find out why those Jews down the block seem so content on Shabbat, or those Christians so joyful on Sunday, or those Muslims so certain on Juma. Each follows the same God; each has much to share with the others. Believers and nonbelievers can also learn

from each other. No one opposes, so far as I can tell, a weekly day of rest. Find out what others do and why. Tell them about your faith and practice.

25. Take that break, every week, for God, yourself and the world.

Notes

Chapter I

1. Earle, *The Sabbath in Puritan New England*, chap. XVII.
2. The joyful yet orthodox *Sabbath Time* by Tilden Edwards set the stage in 1982. More recently see Baab, *Sabbath Keeping*; Muller, *Sabbath*; Dawn, *Keeping the Sabbath Wholly*. Klagsbrun's *Fourth Commandment* covers the Jewish Sabbath.
3. Shulevitz, "Bring Back the Sabbath."
4. Baum, Dan, "Annals of War: Two Soldiers," *New Yorker*, August 9, 16, 2004.
5. Emerson, "Divinity Address," 1838.
6. See Nickels, "Benefits of the Sabbath."
7. See Otto, *The Idea of the Holy*.
8. Heschel, *Sabbath*, 6.
9. John Paul II, *Dies Domini*, §1.
10. Jerome, *In Die Dominica Paschae* II, 52: CCL 78, 550, cited in *Dies Domini*, §2.
11. Ali, *Holy Quran* (commentary), 1252, n. 5465.
12. Steinfels, Peter, "Beliefs," *New York Times*, June 7, 2003.
13. Rabbinical Assembly, *Etz Hayim*, 445, n. 8.
14. Ali, *Holy Quran* (commentary), 1251, n. 5462.
15. Kaufman, "Time," 983.
16. Bowker, *Oxford Dictionary of World Religions*, 978.
17. Haberman, Clyde, "Executed at Sundown 50 Years Ago," *New York Times*, June 19, 2003, B-1.
18. Anson and Anson, "Thank God it's Friday."
19. Huizinga, *Middle Ages*, 234.
20. Gordon, *Islam*, 63.
21. Leanman, *Islamic Philosophy*, 86.
22. Neusner, *Three Faiths*, 193.
23. Rahman, *Muhammad: Encyclopedia of Seerah*, 55.

24. *McGowan v. Maryland*, 366 U.S. 420 (1961).
25. Huizinga, *Middle Ages*, 235.
26. Geertz, *Interpretation of Culture*, 193.
27. Solberg, *Redeem the Time*, 154.

Chapter II

1. Redmount, "Bitter Lives," 106.
2. Greenberg, "Sabbath: In the Bible," 560; see also Soggin, "Sabbath."
3. Kafka, *Diaries*, 196–197.
4. Ibid.
5. Clifford and Murphy, "Genesis," 2:5.
6. Neusner, *Halakhah*, vol. IV, 1.
7. Greenstone, "Sabbath: Haggadic References."
8. Jacob, "The Sabbath: In Jewish Thought," 565.
9. Cited from Twisse, *Morality of the Fourth Commandment*, in Andrews, *History of the Sabbath*.
10. Andrews, *History*, chap. 1.
11. This summary primarily draws on Hasel, "Sabbath," in the *Anchor Bible Dictionary* and Bacchiocchi, "Remembering the Sabbath" in Eskenazi, *The Sabbath in Jewish and Christian Traditions*.
12. For this and following summary, see Hasel, "Sabbath."
13. Greenberg, "Sabbath: In the Bible," 562.
14. Solberg, *Redeem the Time*, 8.
15. See Zerubavel, *Seven Day Circle*, 9; and Campbell, *Churchhill's Nap*, 77–78.
16. Ibid. and Westby, "The Amazing 7-Day Cycle," 11–12.
17. Dostoyevsky, *The Grand Inquisitor*.
18. Buber, *Moses*, 80.
19. Hasel, "Sabbath," 852.
20. Philo, *On the Account Of the World's Creation Given by Moses*, chap. XXX. In *Philo*, trans. Colson and Whitaker.
21. Klagsbrun, *The Fourth Commandment*, 22–23.
22. Kugel, *The Bible*, 373.
23. Neusner, *Halakhah*, vol. IV, 1.
24. Greenberg, "Sabbath: In the Bible," 558.
25. Hasel, "Sabbath," 853.
26. Ibid.
27. Goodenough, *Jewish Symbols*, vol. I, 36; Philostratus, *Life of Appolonius of Tyana*, v, 33; cited in Goodenough, *Jewish Symbols*, vol. I, 37.
28. Plutarch, *Questiones Conviviales*, cited in Goodenough, *Jewish Symbols*, vol. VI, 133.
29. Ibid., 21–22.

Chapter III

1. Klagsbrun, *Fourth Commandment*, 133–134.
2. Neusner, "Oral Law," 673–675.
3. Moore, *Judaism*, 224. See also Klagsbrun, *The Fourth Commandment*, 69.
4. Klagsbrun, *The Fourth Commandment*, 156.
5. Solberg, *Redeem the Time*, 9.

6. Kugel, *Bible as It Was*, 8–9.

7. Leith, "Israel Among the Nations," 372–373.

8. See Ibid., though the inference is mine.

9. See Kugel, *Bible as It Was*, 385–389.

10. Ibid., 385–386.

11. Hastings, *Dictionary of the Bible*, 866.

12. Bacchiocchi, "Remembering the Sabbath," 74.

13. Tacitus, *The Histories*, cited in Regan, *Dies Dominica and Dies Solis*, 24.

14. Cited in Dundes, *Shabbat Elevator*, 19–20.

15. See Leith, "Israel Among the Nations."

16. Neusner, *Mishnah*, 164.

17. Ibid.

18. Potok, *Wanderings*, 149.

19. Slane, "Sabbath."

20. Lotz, "Sabbath," 136.

21. Ibid.

22. Hasel, "Sabbath," 854.

23. Goodenough, *Jewish Symbols*, vol. I, 39.

24. Ibid.

25. Ibid.

26. Charles, *Apocrypha and Pseudepigrapha*, chap. 1.

27. Solberg, *Redeem the Time*, 10.

28. In these I draw predominantly on Karris, "Luke," *NJBC*, 691.

29. Parkes, *Church and Synagogue*, 38–39.

30. Ibid., 694.

31. From the Midrash on Exodus, *The Mikhalta of Rabbi Ishmael*, cited in Greenstone, "Sabbath: Rest."

32. Nash and Cohon, "Sadducees."

33. Ibid.

34. See Kugel, *Bible as It Was*, 385–388.

35. Mishnah: Hagigah 1:8, cited in Kugel, *Bible as It Was*, 387.

36. Neusner, *The Halakhah*, vol. IV, 45.

37. See Rosen, *Talmud and the Internet*.

38. Neusner, "Sabbath," 539.

39. Neusner, *The Halakhah*, vol. IV, 6.

40. Kugel, *Bible as It Was*, 387.

41. Ibid.

42. Klagsbrun, *Fourth Commandment*.

43. Mishnah 2:25 cited in Neusner, *The Halakhah*, vol. IV, 6.

44. The tractate Shabbat cited in Ibid.

45. Hasel, "Sabbath," 854.

46. Shabbat 15:3, cited in Kehati, 2.

47. Josephus, *Antiquities*, vol. xvi, 2.3.

Chapter IV

1. John Paul II, *Dies Domini*, §52.

2. Complete story in Ringwald, *Faith in Words*, 97–108.

3. This summary draws on John Paul II's encyclical regarding the Lord's Day, *Dies Domini.*
4. Catechism of the Catholic Church, §349.
5. I am indebted for this and other ideas to the author of a monograph I read at Georgetown University Woodstock Theological Library without recording his name or the title. Neither I nor the librarian has been able to find it.
6. Ibid., §22.
7. Fox, *Pagans and Christians,* 480–482.
8. John Paul II, *Dies Domini,* §27.
9. Bercot, *Dictionary of Early Christian Beliefs,* 405.
10. Neusner, "Oral Law," 676.
11. Bacchiocchi, "Remember," 78.
12. John Paul II, *Dies Domini,* §18.
13. Ibid., §8.
14. Cited in Ibid., §19.
15. Justin Martyr, *Apologia Prima,* in Hessey, *Sunday,* 56–57.
16. Origen, *C. Celsum,* viii. 22f., cited in Glazebook, "Sunday," 105.
17. "Sunday," Oxford Dictionary of the Christian Church, 1558.
18. Ibid. Also see Hessey, *Sunday,* 64–65, and Bercot, *Dictionary of Early Christian Beliefs,* 405–407.
19. Cited in Hessey, *Sunday,* 64–65, and Bercot, *Dictionary of Early Christian Beliefs,* 405–407.
20. Cited in Bercot, *Dictionary of Early Christian Beliefs,* 406.
21. Glazebook, "Sunday," 105.
22. Cited in Bercot, *Dictionary of Early Christian Beliefs,* 572.
23. Cited in Hessey, *Sunday,* 64–65.
24. Glazebook, "Sunday," 105.
25. Cited in *Dies Domini,* §46.
26. Regan, *Dies Dominica and Dies Solis,* 145.
27. Eustache Deschamps, quoted in Huizinga, *Middle Ages,* 183.
28. Vatican II, 106.
29. Brown, Osiek, and Perkins, "The Early Church," 1340.
30. Ibid., 24.
31. John Paul II, *Dies Domini,* §32.
32. Ibid., §32–33.
33. *Catechism of the Catholic Church,* §1368.
34. Baldovin, "Sabbath Liturgy," 199–201.
35. Ibid., 202.
36. Justin Martyr, *Apology for the Christians to Antoninus Pius,* cited in Cox's *Literature of the Sabbath,* 4.
37. Ibid.
38. Cox, *Literature of the Sabbath,* vol. II, 4–5.
39. Bacchiocchi, "Remembering the Sabbath," 87.
40. Potok, *Wanderings,* 285.
41. Regan, *Dies Dominica and Dies Solis,* 77.
42. *Catechism of the Catholic Church,* §348–349.
43. See Glazebook, "Sunday," and Prime, "Sunday."
44. Justin, *Codex Justinian,* iii, 12, 1.3, cited in Hessey, *Sunday,* 77.
45. Augustine, *The City of God,* chap. 30.
46. Ibid.

47. See, among others, Glazebook, "Sunday," and Prime, "Sunday."
48. John Paul II, *Dies Domini*, §47.
49. Cited in Hessey, *Sunday*, 110.
50. Apostolical Constitutions, lib. viii, c. xxxiii, 419, cited in Hessey, *Sunday*, 102.
51. See Priebsch, *Letter from Heaven*, and Glazebook, "Sunday."
52. Conc. Matiscon II, canon 1; cited in Hessey, *Sunday*, 102.
53. Ibid.
54. Priebsch, *Letter from Heaven*, 7.
55. Ibid., 6.
56. Ibid., 28.
57. Ibid., 25.
58. Heylyn, *History*, 636.
59. MacDonald, "A Response," 60.
60. Parkes, *Church and the Synagogue*, 222.
61. Solberg, *Redeem the Time*, 15.
62. Ibid., 15–17.
63. Solberg, *Redeem the Time*, 14.
64. Spiro, "Meaning," 569.
65. Goldenberg, "Sabbath in Rabbinic Judaism," 34–36.
66. Ibid., 35.
67. Ibid., 36.
68. Hirsch, "Evolution of the Concept of Sabbath Rest."
69. Cited in Cox, *Literature of the Sabbath*, 446.
70. Solomon, *Historical Dictionary of Judaism*, 339.
71. Potok, *Wanderings*, 332.
72. Klagsbrun, *Fourth Commandment*, 166. See also Cantor, *Civilization of the Middle Ages*, 511–517.
73. Melammed, *Heretics or Daughters of Israel?* cited in Klagsbrun, 167.
74. Parkes, *Church and the Synagogue*, 319.
75. Pearce, "Sacred Time."
76. Solberg, *Redeem the Time*, 15.
77. Huizinga, *Autumn of the Middle Ages*, 182.
78. Quoted in Hessey, *Sunday*, 272.
79. Huizinga, *Middle Ages*, 203.
80. Hessey, *Sunday*, 279.
81. See *McGowan* v. *Maryland*, 366 U.S. 420 (1961).
82. Orr, "From Sunday to Sabbath."
83. Pearce, "Sacred Time."
84. Ibid.
85. Ibid.
86. See marvelous summary in Orr, "From Sunday to Sabbath."
87. Luther, *Treatise on Good Works*, (1520), cited in Bacchiocchi, "Remembering the Sabbath," 81.
88. Heylyn, *History of the Sabbath*, 300.
89. Orr, "From Sunday to Sabbath."
90. Ibid.
91. Bownd, *True Doctrine of the Sabbath*. I am indebted to Chris Coldwell's modern translation of an extract, "The Public Ordinances of Worship and the Lord's Day," and his notes.

92. Bownd, *True Doctrine of the Sabbath*, 18.
93. Ibid., 31, and Fuller, *Church History*, vol. 5, 212–214.
94. Coldwell, footnote 1.
95. Fuller, *Church History*, vol. 5, 214.
96. Hessey, *Sunday*, 279.
97. Orr, "From Sunday to Sabbath."
98. Ibid.
99. "Sunday," *Oxford Dictionary of the Christian Church*, 1558.
100. Coldwell, *Calvin in the Hands of the Philistines*. I found this a remarkable scholarly treatise.
101. Wells, *Practical Sabbatarian*, 28; cited in Coldwell, *Calvin*, 5.
102. Cited in Coldwell, *Calvin*, 5.
103. See Fuller, *Church History*, vol. 5, 212–214.
104. Disraeli, *Life and Reign of Charles*, vol. 3, 354–355; cited in Coldwell, *Calvin*, 15.

Chapter V

1. See preface for explanation of my participation.
2. Saabiq, *Fiqh-us-Sunnah*, vol. 2, *Salatul Jumu'ah*, 125a. This five-volume work was put together in the 1940s and is based on original collections. The Friday hadith also appears, for instance, in *Masabih ul-Sunnah*, compiled by Husain al-Baghawi in about 1100 CE.
3. Armstrong, *Muhammad*, 58.
4. Ibid., 63.
5. Ibid., 55–58.
6. Cited in Gibb and Kramer, *Encyclopedia*, 491.
7. Ibid., 148.
8. Ali, in *Holy Quran*, 29, footnote 67.
9. Muir, *Life of Mohammad*, 170.
10. Grant, *Oriental Philosophy*, 278.
11. Armstrong, *Islam*, 18.
12. Ibid.
13. Grant, *Oriental Philosophy*, 209.
14. Fluehr-Lobban, *Islamic Society*, 30.
15. Al-Bukhari, *Sahih*, 10.62.1.
16. Neusner, *Three Faiths*, 206.
17. Nanji, *The Muslim Almanac*, 14, and Gooch, *Godtalk*, 303–304.
18. Nanji, *The Muslim Almanac*, 13.
19. Siddiqi, "Salat," 20.
20. Al-Bukhari, *Sahih*, vol. 2, book 13, no. 19.
21. Ali, "Introduction to Surah Al-Kahf." In *Holy Quran*, 602.
22. Jeffrey, *Islam*, 180.
23. Goitein, "Djum'a," 37.
24. Ibid.
25. Ibn Saud, *Hadith*, in Goitein, "Djum'a."
26. Muir, *Life of Mohammad*, 195.
27. Thanawi, *Juma ke Khutba*, 7.
28. Ibid., 10.
29. Doi, *Principles*, 114.
30. Goitein, "Djum'a," 38.

31. Gaffney, *Prophet's Pulpit*.
32. Ibid., 16.
33. Saabiq, *Fiqh-us-Sunnah*, vol. 2, *Salatul Jumu'ah*, 131.
34. Jeffrey, *Islam*, 181.
35. Muir, *Life of Mohammad*, 188.
36. Ibid., 189.
37. Ibid., 200.
38. Mishnah, Berakhoth, iii, 3, cited in Margoliouth.
39. Lippman, *Understanding Islam*, 16.
40. Fluehr-Lobban, *Islamic Society*, 20.
41. Esposito, *History*, 95.
42. Bowker, *World Religions*, 46.
43. *The Holy Quran: Arabic Text and Translation*, 5th ed., trans. Muhammad Sarwar (Huntington Station, N.Y.: The Islamic Seminary, 2001).

Chapter VI

1. Solberg, *Redeem the Time*, 3.
2. Ibid.
3. Solberg, *Redeem the Time*, 126, and Carroll, *Routledge Historical Atlas*, 34–35.
4. Solberg, *Redeem the Time*, 154–157, and Shephard, *Theses Sabbaticae*.
5. Solberg, *Redeem the Time*, 204–205.
6. Ibid., 277.
7. McCrossen, *Holy Day, Holiday*, 12.
8. Carroll, *Routledge Historical Atlas*, 37.
9. Edwards, "The Perpetuity and Change of the Sabbath."
10. Ibid.
11. Sarna, *American Judaism*, 3, 11.
12. Ibid., 22–23.
13. Potok, *Wanderings*, 353–355.
14. Luther, *Large Catechism*, "Third Commandment."
15. Rybczynski, *Waiting for the Weekend*, 73.
16. Heylyn, *History of the Sabbath*, 27.
17. Cited in Cox, *Literature of the Sabbath*, vol. II, 134.
18. See Heylyn, *History of the Sabbath*, Cox, *Literature of the Sabbath*, and Hessey, *Sunday*.
19. Cited in Cox, *Literature of the Sabbath*, vol. II, 217.
20. Laing, *Notes of a Traveller*, 324–326.
21. Solberg, *Redeem the Time*, 228.
22. Sennett, *Fall of Public Man*, 3–6.
23. Tocqueville, *Democracy in America*, vol. II, 143.
24. Hirsch, "Sabbath Rest."
25. Saabiq, *Fiqh-us-Sunnah*, vol. 2, 131.
26. Ali, *A Manual of Hadith*, chap. XI.
27. Hessey, *Sunday*, 465 (fn. 39).
28. Solberg, *Redeem the Time*, 111.
29. Sarna, *American Judaism*, 17.
30. Hessey, *Sunday*, 473 (fn. 300).
31. Ibid.

32. Washington, *Writings*, vol. 5, 244–245.
33. Lincoln, "General Order Respecting the Observance of the Sabbath Day in the Army and Navy," November 15, 1862.
34. Cox, *Literature of the Sabbath*, vol. II, 433, 423.
35. Tocqueville, *Democracy in America*, vol. I, 308.
36. Rybczynski, *Waiting for the Weekend*, 44–45.
37. Zerubavel, *Seven Day Circle*, 29.
38. Ibid., 45–46.
39. Hessey, *Sunday*, 250.
40. Cox, *Literature of the Sabbath*, vol. II, 315.
41. See Feldman, *America's Church-State Problem*.
42. Sarna, *American Judaism*, 50, 71.
43. Finke and Stark, *The Churching of America*, 22.
44. Cited in Tocqueville, *Democracy in America*, vol. II, 341–342.
45. Friedman, *Crime and Punishment*, 128–129.
46. Sarna, *American Judaism*, 101.
47. Ibid., 343.
48. Ibid.
49. Channing, "Address on Temperance," cited in Cox, *Literature of the Sabbath*, vol. II, 314.
50. Cited in Cox, *Literature of the Sabbath*, vol. II, 314.
51. Rybczynski, *Waiting for the Weekend*, 73.
52. Cox, *Literature of the Sabbath*, vol. II, 311.
53. Dana, *Two Years Before the Mast*, XXIII, 14.
54. Emerson, "Divinity Address," 1838.
55. Tocqueville, *Democracy in America*, vol. II, 143. He refers to the "seventh day" but clearly means Sunday, the first day. He may have counted from Monday, as do many desk calendars today.
56. "The Sabbath at Home," *The Sabbath at Home*, January 1867, 2–3.
57. "How a Pope is Made," *The Sabbath at Home*, June 1867.
58. "The Sabbath at Home," *The Sabbath at Home*, January 1867, 3.
59. Sarna, *American Judaism*, 61–70.
60. Ibid., 68.
61. See Feldman, *America's Church-State Problem*, McCrossen, *Holy Day, Holiday*, and a masterful history by Richard R. John, "Taking Sabbatarianism Seriously."
62. McCrossen, *Holy Day, Holiday*, 28, and John, "Taking Sabbatarianism Seriously," 535–545.
63. John, "Taking Sabbatarianism Seriously," 545–555.
64. Cox, *Literature of the Sabbath*, vol. II, 413.
65. McCrossen, *Holy Day, Holiday*, 28.
66. Speech of M. Frelinghuysen, May 8, 1830, U.S. Congress.
67. Lynn, "The Sunday Mail Debate."
68. Stephenson, *Puritan Heritage*, 181.
69. Edward Higgins, a pamphleteer, cited in Cox, *Literature of the Sabbath*, 398.
70. Rev. Harvey D. Ganse, cited in Ibid., 437.
71. See summary in Rybczynski, *Waiting for the Weekend*, 121–135.
72. Ibid.
73. Hessey, *Sunday*, 251.
74. Cox, *Literature of the Sabbath*, 446, 444.
75. Lawrence, *Seven Pillars of Wisdom*, chap. 3.

76. Dunlop, *Arab Civilization*, 280.
77. Cited in Hessey, *Sunday*, 239–240.
78. Halevi, *At the Entrance to the Garden of Eden*, 125.
79. Sarna, *American Judaism*, 126, 119.
80. Ibid., 135–140.
81. *Times* of London, May 16, 1856. Quoted in Hessey, *Sunday*, 497.
82. Hessey, *Sunday*, 248.
83. Ibid., 252.
84. Ibid., 250–260.
85. *The Merchant of Venice*, IV, i, 40; *Hamlet*, I, i, 75–76.
86. Harte, *The Outcasts of Poker Flat*.
87. Dickens, *Sunday Under Three Heads*.
88. Hessey, *Sunday*, 342.
89. Foderaro, Lisa W., "No Wiggle Room in a Window War," *New York Times*, November 15, 2003.

Chapter VII

1. Gibbs, Nancy, "And on the Seventh Day we rested?" *Time*, August 2, 2004.
2. "Bronx Court Recognizes Moslem Sabbath; Rules Pupils Need Not Go to School Fridays," *New York Times*, February 9, 1934, 21.
3. Prime, "Sunday," 159.
4. *McGowan* v. *Maryland*, 366 U.S. 420 (1961), footnotes 30 and 40.
5. WNET, "New York: A Documentary Film, Episode 5: Cosmopolis (1914–1931)."
6. McCrossen, *Holy Day, Holiday*, 32.
7. Ibid., see also footnote 31.
8. Rybczynski, *Waiting for the Weekend*, 46–48.
9. Prime, "Sunday," 160.
10. "New Jersey Leaders Make Forecasts," *New York Times*, November 4, 1907, 3.
11. "Where Ministers Differ," *New York Times*, January 27, 1898.
12. "Raids Sunday Factory," *New York Times*, March 15, 1909.
13. See Sarna, *American Judaism*, 151–270.
14. Ibid., 257–258.
15. Gordis, *God Was Not in the Fire*, 117–120.
16. Sarna, 282–283.
17. Sarna, 284.
18. Sarna, 352.
19. Shulevitz, Judith, "The View from Sabbath," *Slate*, July 29, 2005.
20. John Paul II, *Dies Domini*, 4.
21. *McGowan* v. *Maryland*, 366 U.S. 420 (1961).
22. Ibid.
23. Ibid.
24. Gibbs, Nancy, "And on the Seventh Day we rested?" *Time*, August 2, 2004.
25. Rakoff, *A Time for Every Purpose*, 43.
26. McNichol, Tom, "The Seventh Day," *Washington Post Magazine*, August 1, 1993.
27. Cited in ibid.
28. Book of Mormon, Jarom 1:5.
29. Book of Mormon, Mosiah 13:15–18, 18:23.
30. *Gallup Poll Insights*, February 17–19, 2003.

31. Pew Forum on Religion and Public Life, "Religion and Public Life, August 3, 2005. See also NBC News/ *Wall Street Journal* Poll, May 19, 2005; and "Why Once a Week?" *Religion in the News*, Spring 2004, 13.
32. Lindner, *Yearbook 2005*, 376.
33. Dudley and Roozen, "Faith Communities Today," 42.
34. Bailey and Roozen, eds., Interfaith FACT's, 7 (derived from the data in ibid.).
35. Scripps Howard News Service and Ohio University survey, cited in *Jewish News of Arizona*, September 2000, available at www.jewishaz.com/jewishnews/971114/affiliat.shtml See also Roper Center Poll, *Los Angeles Times*, April 12, 1998.
36. National Jewish Population Survey, cited by Nacha Cattan, "New Population Survey Retracts Intermarriage Figure," *Forward*, September 13, 2003.
37. Bagby, Perl, and Froehle, "The Mosque in America."
38. Clement, *Paedagogus* III.xi.80, cited in Harnak, *Mission and Expansion of Christianity*, vol. 1, 309.
39. John Paul II, *Dies Domini*, §83.
40. See the *Catechism*, §2168–95 and John Paul II, *Dies Domini*.
41. John Paul II, *Dies Domini*, §60.
42. Constitution on the Liturgy, §106.
43. Muller, *Sabbath*, 12.
44. Dawn, *Keeping the Sabbath Wholly*, 205.
45. Prümmer, *Handbook of Moral Theology*, 193.
46. *Catechism*, §2184–5.
47. Neusner, *The Halakhah*, vol. IV, 50.
48. Benedict XVI, homily, August 21, 2005, Cologne, Germany.
49. See Robinson, *Essential Judaism*, 81–86.
50. Halevi, *At the Entrance to the Garden of Eden*, 190.
51. John Paul II, *Dies Domini*, §4.
52. *Catechism*, §2184–5.
53. Whealon, *Missal*, 679.
54. McNichol, "The Seventh Day."
55. Whealon, *Missal*, 677.
56. Currie, David P., "The Sunday Mails," *Green Bag*, Summer 1999.
57. Soskis, Benjamin, "Walking the Walk," *New Republic*, August 28, 2000, 50.
58. Currie, David P., "The Sunday Mails," *Green Bag*, Summer 1999.
59. D'Antuono, Dane, "Presidential primary may be rescheduled to avoid Sabbath," *Jewish News of Greater Phoenix*, January 8, 1999.
60. Caruso, David, "New York to Return to Days of Free Sunday Parking," *Associated Press*, October 11, 2005.
61. Esposito, "Pakistan," 151–153.
62. Akintola, *Friday Question*, 66.
63. See Akintola, *Friday Question*.
64. Ellement, John, "Law voided on days off for religion," *Boston Globe*, August 21, 1996.
65. "Worker Wins Sabbath Suit," *Business & Legal Reports*, July 20, 2001.
66. Hansen, Louis, "Assembly fixes flub that gave day of rest," *Virginian-Pilot*, July 14, 2004, D1.
67. *Estate of Thornton v. Caldor, Inc.*, 472 U.S. 703, 711 (1985), cited in Carter, *Disbelief*, 5–6.
68. "Jews support Sunday keeper," *Signs of the Times*, October 2005, 4.
69. Shulevitz, Judith, "The Orthodox Jew and the Vice Presidency," *Slate*, March 29, 2000.
70. Dundes, *Shabbat Elevator*, 172.

71. Maybaum, *Trialogue*, 71–72.
72. Hartman, "Imagination," 468–469.
73. Leibovitz, "Commandments," 73.
74. Letter from Peter R. Tramer, editor of *Catholic Extension Magazine*, 1934. Facsimile posted at www.remnantofgod/PiusAdmission.jpg
75. Nickels, Richard C., "Why the BSA?" in *Sabbath Sentinel*, Jan.-Feb. 2004.
76. See Armstrong, *Islam*.
77. See Goitein, "Djum'a."
78. Ibid., 37.
79. Ibid., 38.
80. Lippman, *Understanding Islam*, 17.
81. Ibid.

Chapter VIII

1. Bowker, *World Religions*, 1064.
2. Bukhari, *Hadith*, vol. 3, book 32, no. 233.
3. Al-Ghazali, *Death and the Afterlife*, 115.
4. Rakoff, *A Time for Every Purpose*, 35.
5. Kaufman, "Time," 983.
6. Ibid., 981.
7. Heschel, *Sabbath*, 8.
8. Al-Ghazali, *Death and the Afterlife*, 115.
9. From the Hadith of Muslim, cited in Doi, *Principles of Islam*, 126.
10. Rybczynski, *Waiting for the Weekend*, 210–211.
11. Huizinga, *Autumn*, 173.
12. James, *Varieties*, 137.
13. Nabokov, quoted in *New York Times*, April 9, 2001.
14. Kugel, *The God of Old*, 14.
15. Ibid., 196.
16. Neusner, *Three Faiths*, 257, provides a useful summary.
17. Halevi, *At the Entrance*, 86.
18. Jeffrey, *Islam*, 183.
19. In Bloom, *American Religion*, 261.
20. Ibid.
21. James, *Varieties*, 41.
22. Cited in von Grunebaum, *Medieval Islam*, 117.
23. Saabiq, *Fiqh-us-Sunnah*, vol. 2, 129.
24. Mendes-Flohr, "History," 376.
25. Eliade, *The Sacred and the Profane*, 110–112.
26. Emerson, *English Traits*, chap. XIII.
27. Eliade, *Comparative Religion*, 381–386.
28. Endo, *Silence*, 215.

Chapter IX

1. Goodenough, *Jewish Symbols*, vol. IV, 202–204.
2. See Webster, "Sabbath: Primitive," 885–889.

3. Ibid., 888.

4. Glazebrook, "Sunday," 109.

5. Penn, William, *A Collection of the Works of William Penn*, vol. 1, (London: 1726), 356. Cited in Solberg, *Redeem the Time*, 231.

6. See Rakoff, *A Time for Every Purpose*.

7. Chittister, Joan, "The Lost Sabbath," *The Tablet*, vol. 251, no. 8172 (1997), 374.

8. Philo as cited in Goodenough, *Jewish Symbols*, vol. IV, 131.

9. Klagsbrun, *The Fourth Commandment*, 138.

10. Hirsh, "Sabbath: Biblical Data."

11. Canon 29.

12. John Paul II, *Dies Domini*, §10.

13. See the excellent survey in Naylor, Willimon & Österberg, *The Search for Meaning in the Workplace*.

14. Herbert, George, "The Elixir," (1633) as it appears in Hymn #592 of *The Hymnal 1982* (U.S. Episcopal Church), available at http://www.oremus.org/hymnal/82.html

15. Edwards, "The Preciousness of Time," section IV, available at http://www.ccel.org/ccel/edwards/works2.vi.xiv.iv.html

16. *Laborem Exercens*, 3, cited in a very useful article by Batule, "Theology of Work."

17. Solberg, *Redeem the Time*, 43–46.

18. See excellent review in Tredget, "Contemporary Theology of Work."

19. Strugatch, Warren, "For High-Level Career Advice, Some Job Seekers Go to Church," *New York Times*, November 6, 2005.

20. Eliade, *Sacred and Profane*, 203.

21. Ibid., 206.

22. Ibid., 207.

23. Dandameyer, "Slavery in the Old Testament," 65.

24. Emerson, *English Traits*, chap. XIII.

25. Hessey, *Sunday*, 18–20.

26. *McGowan v. Maryland*, 366 U.S. 420, 491 (1961).

27. *Soon Hing v. Crowley*, 113 U.S. 703 (1885).

28. *Hennington v. State Of Georgia*, 163 U.S. 299 (1896).

29. Dickens, *Sunday Under Three Heads*.

30. Brinton, Henry G., "God Rested, And So Should We," *Washington Post*, August 8, 1999, B-2.

31. ILO, *Weekly Rest*, 26.

32. John Paul II, *Dies Domini*, §109.

33. Waskow, "Free Time for a Free People," 25.

34. McCrossen, *Holy Day, Holiday*, 30.

35. Hauptman, "Women," 1356–58.

36. MacDonald, "A Response to R. Goldenberg and D. J. Harrington," 58.

37. Klagsbrun, *The Fourth Commandment*, 102–130.

38. Bagby, Perl, and Froehle, "The Mosque in America."

39. Saabiq, *Fiqh-us-Sunnah*, vol. 2, 131a.

40. Davis and Garrett, "Slaves or Sabbath-Keepers?" 32.

41. Trench, *Notes on the Miracles of Our Lord*, 257.

42. Klagsbrun, *Fourth Commandment*, 31.

43. Armstrong, *History of God*, 63.

44. Davis and Garrett, "Slaves or Sabbath-Keepers?" 33.

45. Weatherby, *Chariots of Fire*, 142.
46. Huizinga, *Middle Ages*, 240.
47. Both cited in John Paul II, *Dies Domini*, §55.
48. Jacobs, "Shabbat," 191.
49. Woodward, "Leisure," *Newsweek*.
50. *McGowan v. Maryland*, 366 U.S. 420 (1961).
51. John Paul II, *Dies Domini*, §61.
52. Hartman, "Imagination," 469.
53. Brinton, Henry G., "God Rested, And So Should We," *Washington Post*, August 8, 1999, B-2.
54. Hessey, *Sunday*, 249.
55. Rybczynski, *Waiting for the Weekend*, 18.
56. Perry, Wayne, "Sports vs. Church," *Associated Press*, November 29, 2003.
57. Stratton, Ted. S., "Catching Up With Jewish Basketball Star," *Cleveland Jewish News*, November 8, 2005.
58. Shelly, Jared, "Orthodox Boxer's Story to be Subject of Movie," *Jewish News of Greater Phoenix*, August 26, 2006.
59. Arnold, Lee, "Sunday Hunting Stirs Debate," *Huntington (W.Va.) Herald-Dispatch*, October 23, 2002.
60. Ott, Matthew, "Some Utah Residents to Celebrate New Year's Eve Early," *Associated Press*, December 29, 2000.
61. Bacchiocchi, "Remembering the Sabbath," 86.
62. Pennsylvania Statutes 1682, cited in *McGowan v. Maryland*, 366 U.S. 420, footnote 51.
63. Cited in *McGowan v. Maryland*, 366 U.S. 420, 481 (1961).
64. "Sunday Business Embroils Stores," *New York Times*, May 20, 1956.
65. Prime, "Sunday," 150.
66. Rakoff, *A Time for Every Purpose*, 52.
67. McHugh, David, "Germans get Four More Shopping Hours Saturday as Government Eases Rules," *Associated Press*, June 6, 2003.
68. See background to Article 31, *European Union Charter of Fundamental Rights*, available at www.europarl.eu.int/comparl/libe/elsj/charter/art31/default_en.htm#3
69. "From Sunday Baseball and Soccer to the Art Gallery," *American Atheist*, May 18, 1998. Available at www.atheists.org/flash.line/bball2.htm
70. Rybczynski, *Waiting for the Weekend*, 43–44.
71. Smith, "Ramifications of Region and Senses of Place," 193–195.
72. McGreevy, *Parish Boundaries*, cited in Reidy, "Closing Catholic Parishes."
73. Ibid. See also Gamm, *Urban Exodus*.
74. See excellent discussion in Hugen, "Geography of Faith."
75. Ibid., 9.
76. Goldenberg, "Place of the Sabbath," 32.
77. Neusner, *Halakhah*, vol. IV, part A, 54.
78. Ali, Quran (commentary), 571.

Chapter X

1. See McCrossen, *Holy Day, Holiday*.
2. Leaman, *Islamic Philosophy*, 126.
3. Sarna, *American Judaism*, 360–364.

4. Parkes, *The Conflict of the Church and the Synagogue*, 77.
5. Jefferson, "Letter to Dr. Thomas Cooper," In *Writings*.
6. Reston, *Last Apocalypse*, 117–118.
7. Ibid., 207.
8. Aslan, Reza, "From Islam, Pluralist Democracies Will Surely Grow," *Chronicle of Higher Education*, March 11, 2005.
9. Gibb and Bowen, "Islamic Society," 218 and Rejwan, "Islam," 491.
10. "Noachide Laws," *Oxford Dictionary of World Religions*.
11. All persons cited in Halevi, *At the Entrance to the Garden of Eden*, 55–60, 190–210.
12. Halevi, *At the Entrance to the Garden of Eden*, 88.
13. Huizinga, *Middle Ages*, 203.
14. Twersky, David, "In N.J., Sabbath Fences Make Good Neighborhoods," *Forward*, May 2, 2002; and Klagsbrun, *Fourth Commandment*, 152.
15. *McGowan* v. *Maryland*, 366 U.S. 420, 509 (1961).
16. John Paul II, *Dies Domini*, §69–70.
17. Ibid., §69.
18. Ibid. §72–73.
19. Shulevitz, Judith, "The View from Saturday," *Slate*, July 29, 2005. Available at http://www.slate.com/id/2123283/
20. Cited in Solberg, *Redeem the Time*, 54.
21. Sayers, *Creed or Chaos*, 56.
22. Etzioni, Amitai, "The Internet versus the Sabbath," *Tikkun*, January 20, 2000.
23. Benson, David, "Some Would Like to See Most Sunday Working, Shopping Outlawed," *Mansfield (Ohio) News Journal*, September 7, 2003.
24. Carter, *Disbelief*, 37.
25. Tracy, *Plurality*, 83.
26. Pieper, *Leisure*, 47.
27. Ponessa, Jeanne, "New Reasons for Blue Sundays," *Governing Magazine*, April 1994, 24.
28. "Closed Sundays. It's part of the Chick-fil-A recipe." Corporate announcement available at http://www.chick-fil-a.com/Closed.asp
29. Klinghoffer, David, "If It's Saturday, This Must be America," *Forward*, March 4, 2005.
30. Keys, Lisa, "Psst . . . Guess What Students are Doing in Their Dorm Rooms," *Forward*, November 24, 2000.
31. In Sarna, *American Judaism*, 374.
32. I am indebted in this analysis, as in so many, to John Dwyer, theologian.
33. Oakes, Edward T., "The Great Awakener," *Commonweal*, June 6, 2003, 26.
34. Ibid., 259.
35. Otto, *Idea of the Holy*, 3.
36. Ibid., 258–262.
37. Trench, *Notes on the Miracles of Our Lord*, 257.
38. Cited in Pieper, *Leisure*, 2.
39. Quoted by Toby Lester, "Oh, Gods!" 45.
40. John Paul II, *Dies Domini*, §67.
41. Freud, *Civilization and its Discontents*, 21.
42. Cited in Solberg, *Redeem the Time*, 258–259.
43. Gordon, *Islam*, 92, and Leaman, *Islamic Philosophy*, 86.
44. Cragg, *The Pen and the Faith*, 172.
45. Cited in Goodenough, *Jewish Symbols*, vol. V, 94.

46. McGinn, "Comments," 193.
47. Frisch, "Second Stop," *Homo Faber.*
48. Vendler, "The Ocean, the Bird, and the Scholar."
49. Cited in Zerubavel, *The Seven Day Circle,* 141.
50. Heschel, *The Sabbath,* 27, 29.
51. Camus, cited in *New York Times,* June 12, 2000, E6.
52. Eliade, *Comparative Religion,* 391–408.
53. John Paul II, *Dies Domini,* §84.
54. James, *Varieties,* 465.
55. Augustine, *The City of God,* book 22, chap. 30.
56. Ibid.

Appendix: Random Notes on Keeping the Sabbath

1. In Primus, "Sunday," 119.
2. Davis and Garrett, "Slaves or Sabbath-Keepers?" 39.
3. *Ex parte Newman,* 9 California 502 (1858).

Bibliography

Scriptural excerpts: Most biblical quotes are from the *New Revised Standard Version Bible*: Anglicized Edition, copyright 1989, 1995, Division of Christian Education of the National Council of the Churches of Christ in the United States of America (available at www.ncccusa.org/welcome/sitemap.html). Several are from the *New American Bible*, Confraternity of Christian Doctrine, New York: Catholic Book Publishing Co., 1992, and from *Etz Hayim: Torah and Commentary*, ed. David L. Lieber. New York: The Rabbinical Assembly & the United Synagogue of Conservative Judaism, 2001. (The Kligermans and Temple Israel are Conservative Jews.)

Several quotes from the Quran are from A. Yusuf Ali, *Modern English Translation of the Holy Qur'an: Meanings and Commentary* (1934), Kansas City, Mo.: Manar International, 1998. (This is the version used by the Haqqies and the other Sunni Muslims such as Imam Djafer Sebkhaoui.)

Adang, Camilla. *Muslim Writers on Judaism and the Hebrew Bible: From Ibm Rabben to Ibm Hazum*. Leiden, Netherlands: Brill, 1996.

Akintola, Is-haq Lakin. *The Friday Question*. Lagos, Nigeria: Al-Tawheed Publishing, 1993.

Al-Ghazali. *The Remembrance of Death and the Afterlife*. (twelfth century) Trans., notes, and intro. T. J. Winter. London: Islamic Texts Society, 1989.

Ali, A. Jusuf. *Modern English Translation of the Holy Qur'an: Meaning and Commentary*. (1934) Kansas City, Mo.: Manar International, 1998.

Anderson, Erica. *The Schweitzer Album*. New York: Harper and Row, 1965.

Andrews, J. N. *History of the Sabbath and First Day of the Week*. (1873) Available at www.nisbett.com/sabbath/history/hos-preface.htm

Anson, Jon, and Ofra Anson. "Thank God it's Friday: The Weekly Cycle of Mortality in Israel." *Population Research and Policy Review* 19:2 (2000), 143–152.

Armstrong, Karen. *A History of God: The 4,000-Year Quest of Judaism, Christianity, and Islam*. New York: Ballantine Books, 1993.

Augustine, *The City of God*. Available at www.ccel.org/ccel/augustine/confess.html

Babb, Lynne M. *Sabbath Keeping: Finding Freedom in the Rhythms of Rest*. Downers Grove, Ill.: InterVarsity Press, 2005.

Bacchiocchi, Samuele. "Remembering the Sabbath: The Creation-Sabbath in Jewish and Christian History." In *The Sabbath in Jewish and Christian Traditions*, ed. Tamara C. Eskenazi, Daniel J. Harrington and William H. Shea, 69–97. New York: Crossroad, 1991.

Bagby, Ihsan, Paul M. Perl, and Bryan T. Froehle. "The Mosque in America: A Report from the Mosque Study Project." Washington, D.C.: Council on American-Islamic Relations, 2001.

Bailey, Martin and David A. Roozen, eds. "Interfaith FACT's: An Invitation to Dialogue." Hartford, Conn.: Hartford Institute for Religion Research, 2003.

Baldovin, John F. "Sabbath Liturgy: Celebrating Sunday as a Christian." In *The Sabbath in Jewish and Christian Traditions*, ed. Tamara C. Eskenazi, Daniel J. Harrington, and William H. Shea, 199–208. New York: Crossroad, 1991.

Barrow, Isaac. *A Brief Exposition of the Lord's Prayer and the Decalogue*. London, 1681.

Bass, Dorothy C. *Receiving the Day: Christian Practices for Opening the Gift of Time*. New York: Jossey-Bass, 2000.

Batule, Robert J. "Theology of Work." *Homiletic and Pastoral Review* 24–33. April 1996, 24–33.

Bercot, David, ed. *Dictionary of Early Christian Beliefs*. Peabody, Mass.: Hendrickson Publishers, 1998.

Boswell, James. *Life of Johnson*. (1791) Available at www.classic-literature.co.uk/authors/james-boswell/life-of-johnson-vol_05/ebook-page-20.asp

Bourke, Myles M. "The Epistle to the Hebrews." 60:24 In *The New Jerome Biblical Commentary*, ed. Raymond E. Brown, Joseph A. Fitzmeyer, and Roland E. Murphy, 920–941. Englewood Cliffs, N.J.: Prentice Hall, 1990.

Bowker, John. *God: A Brief History*. London: DK Publishing, 2000.

Bowker, John, ed. *The Oxford Dictionary of World Religions*. Oxford: Oxford University Press, 1997.

Bownd, Nicholas. *Sabbathum Veteris et Novi Testamenti: The True Doctrine of the Sabbath* (London, 1606). "The Public Ordinances of Worship and the Lord's Day." Extract trans. Chris Coldwell, 2000. In *The Blue Banner* (9) 1–3, January–March, 2000, 18–34. Available at www.fpcr.org/pdf/BlueBanner9-1&3.pdf

Brown, Raymond E., Joseph A. Fitzmeyer, and Roland E. Murphy, eds. *The New Jerome Biblical Commentary.* Englewood Cliffs, N.J.: Prentice Hall, 1990.

Brown, Raymond E., Carolyn Osiek, and Pheme Perkins. "The Early Church." In *The New Jerome Biblical Commentary,* ed. Raymond E. Brown, Joseph A. Fitzmeyer, and Roland E. Murphy. Englewood Cliffs, N.J.: Prentice Hall, 1990.

Buber, Martin. *Moses: The Revelation and the Covenant.* New York: Harper, 1958.

Bukhari, Sahih. *Hadith.* Vol. 3. Available at www.usc.edu/dept/MSA/fundamentals/hadithsunnah/bukhari/032.sbt.html

Busse, Heribert. *Islam, Judaism and Christianity: Theological and Historical Affiliations.* (1988) Princeton, N.J.: Markus Wiener, 1998.

Campbell, Jeremy. *Winston Churchill's Afternoon Nap.* New York: Simon & Schuster, 1986.

Cantor, Norman F. *Civilization of the Middle Ages.* New York: HarperCollins, 1993.

Carr, H. W. "Changing Background in Religion and Ethics." Cited in Sheen, *Religion Without God.* New York: Longmans, Green and Co., 1928.

Carter, Stephen L. *The Culture of Disbelief: How American Law and Politics Trivialize Religious Devotion.* New York: Basic Books, 1993.

Catechism of the Catholic Church. English trans., 2nd ed. Washington, D.C.: United States Conference of Catholic Bishops, April, 2000.

Charles, R. H. *The Apocrypha and Pseudepigrapha of the Old Testament.* Oxford: Clarendon Press, 1913. Scanned and edited by Joshua Williams, Northwest Nazarene College and available at www.ccel.org/c/charles/otpseudepig/jubilee/

Cheever, G. *Chronicles of the Pilgrim Fathers.* Glasgow and London: 1849.

Clifford, Richard J., and Roland E. Murphy. "Genesis." In Brown, Raymond E., Joseph A. Fitzmeyer, and Roland E. Murphy, eds. *The New Jerome Biblical Commentary.* Englewood Cliffs, N.J.: Prentice Hall, 1990.

Cohen, Arthur A., and Paul Mendes-Flohr, eds. *Contemporary Jewish Religious Thought.* New York: Free Press, 1987.

Coogan, Michael D., ed. *The Oxford History of the Biblical World.* New York: Oxford University Press, 1998.

Constitution on the Sacred Liturgy. (Second Vatican Council, 1963.) English trans., Washington, D.C.: United States Catholic Conference, 1993.

Cox, Harvey. *Common Prayers: Faith, Family, and a Christian's Journey Through the Jewish Year.* New York: Houghton Mifflin, 2001.

Cox, Robert. *The Literature of the Sabbath Question.* 2 vols. Edinburgh: MacLachlan and Stewart, 1865.

Cragg, Kenneth. *The Pen and the Faith: Eight Modern Muslim Writers and the Quran.* London: George Allen & Unwin, 1985.

Dana, Richard Henry, Jr. *Two Years before the Mast and Twenty-four Years After.* (1840) Vol. XXIII. The Harvard Classics. New York: P. F. Collier & Son, 1909–14; Bartleby.com, 2001. Available at www.bartleby.com/23/

Dandameyer, Muhammad A. "Slavery in the Old Testament." in David Noel Freedman, ed., *The Anchor Bible Dictionary*. Vol. 6, 62–65. New York: Doubleday, 1992.

Davis, Ellen F., and Samuel M. Garrett. "Slaves or Sabbbath-Keepers? A Biblical Perspective on Human Work." *Anglican Theological Review*, 25–41. Winter 2001, 83:1.

Dawn, Marva. *Keeping the Sabbath Wholly: Ceasing, Resting, Embracing, Feasting*. Grand Rapids, Mich.: William B. Eerdmans, 1989.

Dickens, Charles. *Sunday Under Three Heads*. (1836) Available at www.gutenberg. org/dirs/etext97/suths1oh.htm

Dix, Gregory. *The Shape of the Liturgy*. Westminster, England: Dacre Press, 1945.

Doi, A. Rahman E. *The Cardinal Principles of Islam*. Lagos, Nigeria: Islamic Publications Bureau, 1972.

Dostoevsky, Feodor. *The Grand Inquisitor*. (1881) Trans. H. P. Blavatsky. Available at www.ibiblio.org/gutenberg/etext05/inqus1o.txt

Dudley, Carl S., and David A. Roozen. "Faith Communities Today: A Report on Religion in the United States Today." Hartford, Conn.: Hartford Institute for Religion Research, 2001.

Dunlop, Douglas Morton. *Arab Civilization to A.D. 1500*. New York: Praeger, 1971.

Dundes, Alan. *The Shabbat Elevator and Other Sabbath Subterfuges*. Lanham, Maryland: Rowman & Littlefield, 2002.

Earle, Alice Morse. *The Sabbath in Puritan New England*. New York: Scribner's, 1909. Available at www.gutenberg.org/dirs/etext05/8sabb1oh.htm#06

Edwards, Jonathan. "The Perpetuity and Change of the Sabbath." Two sermons. (Undated) Available at www.jonathanedwards.com/sermons/Doctrine/Sabbath. htm

Edwards, Jonathan. *History of the Work of Redemption*. (1757) Period III, Part II available at www.jonathanedwards.com/text/Hist%20of%20Redemption/Hist%20% 20Period%203-2.htm

Edwards, Jonathan. *An Humble Inquiry into the Rules of the Word of God Concerning the Qualifications Requisite to a Complete Standing and Full Communion in The Visible Christian Church*. (1749) Available at: www.jonathanedwards.com/text/ Communion/Communion%20Outline.htm

Edwards, Tilden. *Sabbath Time: Understanding and Practice for Contemporary Christians*. New York: Seabury Press, 1982.

Eliade, Mircea. *The Sacred and the Profane: The Nature of Religion*. (1957) Trans. Willard R. Trask. New York: Harcourt Brace, 1959.

Eliade, Mircea. *Patterns in Comparative Religion*, trans. Rosemary Sheed. New York: Meridian, 1958.

Emerson, Ralph Waldo. "An Address delivered before the Senior Class in Divinity College," (1838) in *Essays and English Traits*. Cambridge, Mass.: The Harvard Classics (1909–14). Available at www.bartleby.com/5/102.html

Emerson, Ralph Waldo. "English Traits." In *Essays and English Traits*. Cambridge, Mass.: The Harvard Classics (1909–14). Available at www.bartleby.com/5/213.html

Endo, Shusako. *Silence*. Trans. William Johnston. Jersey City, N.J.: Parkwest Publications, 1980.

Eskenazi, Tamara C., Daniel J. Harrington, and William H. Shea, eds. *The Sabbath in Jewish and Christian Traditions*. New York: Crossroad, 1991.

Esposito, John L. "Pakistan: Questions for Islamic Identity." In *Islam and Development*, ed. John L. Esposito. Syracuse, N.Y.: Syracuse University Press, 1980.

Esposito, John L., ed. *The Oxford History of Islam*. Oxford: Oxford University Press, 1999.

Finke, Roger and Rodney Stark. *The Churching of America: 1776–1990*. New Brunswick, N.J.: Rutgers University Press, 1993.

Fluehr-Lobban, Carolyn. *Islamic Society in Practice*. Gainesville, Fl.: University Press of Florida, 1994.

Feldman, Noah. *America's Church-State Problem—And What We Should Do About It*. New York: Farrar Straus & Giroux, 2005.

Fox, Robin Lane. *Pagans and Christians*. New York: Knopf, 1987.

Frelinghuysen, Theodore. "Speech on the Subject of Sunday Mails." May 8, 1830. U.S. Congress, Senate, 21st Congress, 1st Session. *Gales & Seaton's Register of Debates in Congress*, Appendix, 1–4.

Freud, Sigmund. *Civilization and its Discontents*. (1930) Trans. James Strachey. New York: W. W. Norton, 1960.

Frisch, Max. *Homo Faber, a Report*. New York: Harcourt Brace Jovanovich, 1959.

Fuller, Thomas. *The Church History of Britain from the Birth of Jesus Christ until the Year MDCXLVIII*. London, 1655.

Gaffin, Richard. *Calvin and the Sabbath: The Controversy of Applying the Fourth Commandment*. Ross-shire, UK: Christian Focus Publications, 1998.

Gaffney, Patrick D. *The Prophet's Pulpit*. Berkeley, Ca.: University of California Press, 1994.

Gamm, Gerald. *Urban Exodus: Why the Jews Left Boston and the Catholics Stayed*. Cambridge, Mass.: Harvard University Press, 1999.

Geertz, Clifford. *The Interpretation of Culture*. New York: Basic Books, 1977.

Gibb, H.A.R., and J. H. Kramers. *Shorter Encyclopedia of Islam*. Leiden, Netherlands: Brill, 1953.

Gibb, H.A.R., and Harold Bowen. *Islamic Society and the West*. Vol. I, 2 parts. London: Oxford University Press, 1950–57.

Glazebook, M. G. "Sunday." In the *Encyclopedia of Religion and Ethics*, ed. James Hastings, John A. Selbie, and Louis H. Gray, 103–111. Edinburgh: T. & T. Clark, 1921.

Goitein, S. D. "Djum'a." In *Encyclopedia of Islam*, ed. Bernard Lewis, Charles Pellat, and J. Schacht, 37–38. Leiden, Netherlands: Brill, 1965.

Goldenberg, Robert. "The Place of the Sabbath in Rabbinic Judaism." In *The Sabbath in Jewish and Christian Traditions*, ed. Tamara C. Eskenazi, Daniel J. Harrington, and William H. Shea, 31–44. New York: Crossroad, 1991.

Gooch, Brad. *Godtalk: Travels in Spiritual America.* New York: Knopf, 2002.

Goodenough, Erwin R. *Jewish Symbols in the Graeco-Roman Period.* 13 vols. New York: Pantheon Books, 1953–68.

Goodman, Allegra. *Kaaterskill Falls.* New York: Dial Press, 1998.

Gordis, Daniel. *God Was Not in the Fire: The Search for a Spiritual Judaism.* New York: Scribner, 1995.

Gordon, Matthew S. *Islam.* New York: Oxford University Press, 2002.

Graham, Mark E. "Rethinking Morality's Relationship to Salvation: Josef Fuchs, S. J., on Moral Goodness." *Theological Studies* 64 (2003).

Grant, Francis. *Oriental Philosophy: The Story of the Teachers of the East.* New York: Dial Press, 1936.

Greenberg, Moshe. "Sabbath: In the Bible." In *Encyclopedia Judaica.* Vol. 14, 557–562. Jerusalem: Keter Publishing House, 1971.

Greenstone, Julius H. "Sabbath: Haggadic References." In *Jewish Encyclopedia* (1906, 2002). Available at www.JewishEncyclopedia.com

Greenstone, Julius H. "Sabbath: Evolution of the Conception of Sabbath Rest." In *Jewish Encyclopedia* (1906, 2002). Available at www.JewishEncyclopedia.com

Grunebaum, Gustave E. von. *Medieval Islam.* Chicago: University of Chicago, 1937.

Halevi, Jossi Klein. *At the Entrance to the Garden of Eden: A Jew's Search for God with Christians and Muslims in the Holy Land.* New York: William Morrow, 2001.

Harnak, A. *The Mission and Expansion of Christianity in the First Three Centuries.* 2 vols. Trans. T. Moffat. London: 1908.

Harte, Francis Bret. *The Luck of Roaring Camp, The Outcasts of Poker Flat & The Idyl of Red Gulch.* Cambridge, Mass.: Harvard Classics Shelf of Fiction, 1917.

Hartman, Geoffrey H. "Imagination." In *Contemporary Jewish Religious Thought*, ed. Arthur A. Cohen and Paul Mendes-Flohr, 451–471. New York: Free Press, 1987.

Hasel, Gerhard F. "Sabbath." In *The Anchor Bible Dictionary*, ed. David Noel Freedman, vol. 5:849–856. New York: Doubleday, 1992.

Hastings, James, ed. *A Dictionary of the Bible.* (1898–1902) Rev. ed. Frederick C. Grant and H. H. Howley, eds. New York: Scribner's, 1963.

Hauptman, Judith. "Women." In *Etz Hayim: Torah and Commentary*, ed. David L. Lieber, 1356–59. New York: The Rabbinical Assembly & the United Synagogue of Conservative Judaism, 2001.

Heschel, Abraham J. *The Sabbath.* New York: Farrar, Straus & Giroux, 1951.

Hessey, James Augustus. *Sunday: Its Origin, History and Present Obligation.* London: J. Murray, 1860.

Heylyn, Peter. *The History of the Sabbath.* (London, 1636) Amsterdam: Da Capo Press, 1969.

Hirsch, Emil G. "Sabbath: Evolution of the Concept of Sabbath Rest." In *Jewish Encyclopedia* (1906, 2002). Available at www.JewishEncyclopedia.com

Hugen, Beryl. "The Geography of Faith: Mapping the Features of Faith-Based Practice." *Social Work & Christianity.* 31:1, Spring 2004, 3–24.

Huizinga, Johan. *Autumn of the Middle Ages.* (1921) Trans. Rodney J. Payton and Ulrich Mammitzsch. Chicago: University of Chicago Press, 1996.

Iannaccone, Laurence R. "Why Strict Churches Are Strong." *American Journal of Sociology* 99 (5): 1180–1211, March 1994.

International Labor Organization. *Weekly Rest in Commerce and Offices,* Report VII (1). ILO, 39th Session. Geneva: ILO, 1956.

Jacobs, Louis. "Sabbath: In the Apocrypha; In Rabbinic Literature; In Jewish Thought; Laws and Customs of the Sabbath." In *Encyclopedia Judaica.* Jerusalem: Keter Publishing House, 1971.

Jeffrey, Arthur. *Islam: Muhammad and His Religion.* Indianapolis, Ind.: Liberal Arts Press, 1958.

John Paul II. *Dies Domini* (The Lord's Day). Rome: Vatican, 1998.

John, Richard R. "Taking Sabbatarianism Seriously." *Journal of the Early Republic* 10 (Winter 1990), 517–570.

Josephus, Flavius. *Antiquities of The Jews.* Available at www.earth-history.com/Judaism/Josephus/josephus-16.htm

Josephus, Flavius. *Life of Josephus.* Trans. and comm. Steve Mason. Leiden, Netherlands: Brill, 2001.

Kafka, Franz. *Diaries: 1910–1913.* Ed. Max Brod. New York: Shocken, 1948.

Kanof, Abram. "Sabbath." In *Encyclopedia Judaica.* Jerusalem: Keter Publishing House, 1971.

Karris, Robert J. "The Gospel According to Luke." In *The New Jerome Biblical Commentary,* ed. Raymond E. Brown, Joseph A. Fitzmyer, and Roland E. Murphy, 675–721. Englewood Cliffs, N.J.: Prentice Hall, 1990.

Kaufman, William E. "Time." In *Contemporary Jewish Religious Thought,* ed. Arthur A. Cohen and Paul Mendes-Flohr. New York: Free Press, 1987.

Kehati, Pinhas. *Mishnah: Seder Moed.* Vol. 1, *Shabbat.* Trans. Edward Levin. Jerusalem: Eliner, 1994.

Klagsbrun, Francine. *The Fourth Commandment.* New York: Harmony Books, 2002.

Kugel, James L. *The Bible as It Was.* Cambridge, Mass.: Belknap Press, 1997.

Kugel, James L. *The God of Old: Inside the Lost World of the Bible.* New York: Free Press, 2003.

Laing, Samuel. *Notes of a Traveller.* London: Longman, 1842.

Lammens, H. *Islam: Beliefs and Institutions.* London: Methuen, 1929.

Lawrence, T. E. *The Seven Pillars of Wisdom.* (1921) London: Jonathan Cape, 1935.

Leaman, Oliver. *A Brief Introduction to Islamic Philosophy.* Cambridge, Mass.: Polity Press, 1999.

Leibovitz, Yeshayahu. "Commandments." In *Contemporary Jewish Religious Thought*, ed. Arthur A. Cohen and Paul Mendes-Flohr, 67–80. New York: Free Press, 1987.

Leith, Mary Joan Winn. "Israel Among the Nations." In *The Oxford History of the Biblical World*, ed. Michael D. Coogan, 367–419. New York: Oxford University Press, 1998.

Lester, Toby. "Oh, Gods!" *Atlantic Monthly*. February 2002, 37–45.

Lincoln, Abraham. "General Order Respecting the Observance of the Sabbath Day in the Army and Navy." Executive Mansion, Washington, D.C., November 15, 1862. Available at www.wallbuilders.com/resources/search/detail.php?ResourceID=78

Lindner, Eileen W., ed. *Yearbook of American & Canadian Churches 2005*. Nashville: Abingdon Press, 2005.

Lippman, Thomas W. *Understanding Islam: An Introduction to the Muslim World*. 2nd rev. ed. New York: Meridian, 1995.

Lotz, W. "Sabbath." In *The New Schaff-Herzog Encyclopedia of Religious Knowledge*, ed. Samuel Macauley Jackson. Grand Rapids, Mich.: Baker Book House, 1952.

Luther, Martin. "The Large Catechism." (1530) In *Triglot Concordia: The Symbolical Books of the Evangelical Lutheran Church*, 565–773. St. Louis: Concordia, 1921. Available at www.sacred-texts.com/chr/luther/largecat.htm

Lynn, Ken. "The Sunday Mail Debate." *Freethought Today*. October 1997.

MacDonald, Dennis. "A Response to R. Goldenberg and D. J. Harrington." In *The Sabbath in Jewish and Christian Traditions*, ed. Tamara C. Eskenazi, Daniel J. Harrington, and William H. Shea, 57–66. New York: Crossroad, 1991.

Margoliouth, G. "Sabbath (Muhammadan)." In Hastings, James, ed. *A Dictionary of the Bible*. (1898–1902) Rev. ed. Frederick C. Grant and H. H. Howley, eds. New York: Scribner's, 1963.

Martin, R. H. *The Day: A Manual on the Christian Sabbath*. Pittsburgh, Pa.: The National Reform Association, 1933.

Maybaum, Ignaz. *Trialogue between Jew, Christian and Muslim*. London: Routledge & Kegan Paul, 1973.

McClay, Wilfred M. "Two Concepts of Secularism." *The Wilson Quarterly* 25 (Summer 2000):54–71.

McCrossen, Alexis. *Holy Day, Holiday: The American Sunday*. Ithaca, N.Y.: Cornell University Press, 2000.

McGinn, Bernard. "Comments." In *Mystical Union in Judaism, Christianity, and Islam*, ed. Moshe Idel and Bernard McGinn. New York: Continuum, 1999.

McGreevy, John T. *Parish Boundaries*. Chicago: University of Chicago Press, 1997.

McKay, Heather A. "New Moon or Sabbath." In *The Sabbath in Jewish and Christian Traditions*, ed. Tamara C. Eskenazi, Daniel J. Harrington, and William H. Shea, 12–27. New York: Crossroad, 1991.

Melammed, Renee Levine. *Heretics or Daughters of Israel? The Crypto-Jewish Women of Castile*. New York: Oxford University Press, 1999.

Mendes-Flohr, Paul. "History." In *Contemporary Jewish Religious Thought*, ed. Arthur A. Cohen and Paul Mendes-Flohr, 371–387. New York: Free Press, 1987.

Moore, George Foot. *Judaism.* Cambridge, Mass.: Harvard University Press, 1946.

Morgan, Lewis Henry. *League of the Iroquois.* (1851) Secaucus, N.J.: Citadel Press, 1962.

Muir, William. *The Life of Mohammad.* (1876) Rev. ed., T. H. Weir. Edinburgh: John Grant, 1912.

Muller, Wayne. *Sabbath: Finding Rest, Renewal, and Delight in Our Busy Lives.* New York: Bantam Books, 1999.

Nanji, Azim. *The Muslim Almanac.* Detroit: Gale Research Inc., 1996.

Nash, Henry S., and Samuel S. Cohon. "Pharisees." In Hastings, James, ed., *A Dictionary of the Bible.* (1898–1902) Rev. ed. Frederick C. Grant and H. H. Howley, eds. New York: Scribner's, 1963.

Nash, Henry S., and Samuel S. Cohon. "Sadducees." In Hastings, James, ed. *A Dictionary of the Bible.* (1898–1902) Rev. ed. Frederick C. Grant and H. H. Howley, eds. New York: Scribner's, 1963.

Naylor, Thomas H., William H. Willimon, and Rolf Österberg. *The Search for Meaning in the Workplace.* Nashville: Abingdon Press, 1989.

Neusner, Jacob. "Oral Law." In *Contemporary Jewish Religious Thought*, ed. Arthur A. Cohen and Paul Mendes-Flohr, 673–677. New York: Free Press, 1987.

Neusner, Jacob. *The Mishnah: A New Translation.* New Haven: Yale University Press, 1991.

Neusner, Jacob. "Sabbath." In *Dictionary of Judaism in the Biblical Period*, ed. Neusner and William Scott Green. New York: Macmillan, 1996.

Neusner, Jacob. *The Halakhah: An Encyclopaedia of the Law of Judaism.* Vol. 1, *Inside the Walls of the Israelite Household*, Part A. Leiden, Netherlands: Brill, 2000.

Neusner, Jacob, Bruce Chilton, and William Graham. *Three Faiths, One God: The Formative Faith and Practice of Judaism, Christianity, and Islam.* Boston: Brill Academic Publishers, 2002.

Nickels, Richard C. "Benefits of the Sabbath." In *The Sabbath Sentinel*, 4–19. March–April 2004.

Orr, Ralph. "From Sunday to Sabbath: The Puritan Origins of Modern Seventh-day Sabbatarianism." Worldwide Church of God, 1994. Available at www.wcg.org/lit/law/sabbath/sun-sab1.htm

Otto, Rudolf. *The Idea of the Holy.* (1923) Trans. John W. Harvey. London: Oxford University Press, 1950.

Parkes, James. *The Conflict of the Church and the Synagogue.* (1934) Reprint, New York: Hermon Press, 1974.

Paul, Gregory S. "Cross-National Correlations of Quantifiable Societal Health with Popular Religiosity and Secularism in the Prosperous Democracies." *Journal of Religion & Society*, vol. 7 (2005). Available at moses.creighton.edu/JRS/2005/2005-11.html

Pearce, Augur. "Sacred Time (1): Times Past—An Historical Perspective." A paper presented at conference on Law and the Sacred: Legal Problems of Time and Space, November, 2000. Newcastle Law School Working Papers.

Peterson, Merrill D., ed. *Thomas Jefferson Writings*. New York: The Library of America, 1984.

Pew Forum on Religion and Public Life / Princeton Survey Research Associates International. "Religion And Public Life Survey." Washington, D.C.: Pew Research Center, August 3, 2005.

Philo. "On the Account of the World's Creation Given by Moses," chap. XXX. In *Philo*, trans. F. H. Colson and G. H. Whitaker. Cambridge, Mass.: Harvard University Press, 1929.

Pieper, Josef. *Leisure: The Basis of Culture*. (1948) Trans. Gerald Malsbary. South Bend, Ind.: St. Augustine's Press, 1998.

Pope, Alexander. *An Essay On Man*. Epistle 1. London: 1733–34.

Potok, Chaim. *Wanderings: History of the Jews*. New York: Knopf, 1978.

Prideaux, B. *Oratio Septima, De Sabbato*. 2nd ed. London: 1634.

Priebsch, Robert. *Letter from Heaven on the Observance of the Lord's Day*. Oxford: B. Blackwell, 1936.

Prime, Ralph E. "Sunday." In *The New Schaff-Herzog Encyclopedia of Religious Knowledge*, ed. Samuel Macauley Jackson. Grand Rapids, Mich.: Baker Book House, 1952.

Prümmer, Dominic M. *Handbook of Moral Theology*. (1949) Trans. Gerald W. Shelton. New York: P. J. Kennedy & Sons, 1957.

Rahman, Afzahur. *Muhammad: Encyclopedia of Seerah*. Vol. I. London: Muslim Scholars Trust, 1981.

Rakoff, Todd D. *A Time for Every Purpose: Law and the Balance of Life*. Cambridge, Mass.: Harvard University Press, 2001.

Redmount, Carol A. "Bitter Lives: Israel in and out of Egypt." In *The Oxford History of the Biblical World*, Michael D. Coogan, ed., 79–121. New York: Oxford University Press, 1998.

Regan, Francis A. *Dies Dominica and Dies Solis: The Beginnings of the Lord's Day in Christian Antiquity*. Washington, D.C.: Catholic University Press, 1961.

Reidy, Maurice Timothy. "Closing Catholic Parishes." *Commonweal*, 11–17. September 10, 2004.

Rejwan, Nissim. "Islam." In *Contemporary Jewish Religious Thought*, ed. Arthur A. Cohen and Paul Mendes-Flohr, 487–493. New York: Free Press, 1987.

Reston, James Jr. *The Last Apocalypse: Europe at the Year 1000 A.D.* New York: Doubleday, 1998.

Ringwald, Christopher D. *Faith in Words*. Chicago: ACTA Publications, 1997.

Ringwald, Christopher D. *The Soul of Recovery: Uncovering the Spiritual Dimension in the Treatment of Addictions*. New York: Oxford University Press, 2002.

Robinson, George. *Essential Judaism: A Complete Guide to Beliefs, Customs, and Rituals.* New York: Pocket Books, 2000.

Rosen, Jonathan. *The Talmud and the Internet: A Journey Between Worlds.* New York: Farrar, Straus & Giroux, 2000.

Carroll, Bret E. *Routledge Historical Atlas of Religion in America.* New York: Routledge, 2000.

Rybczynski, Witold. *Waiting for the Weekend.* New York: Penguin, 1991.

Saabiq, Sayyid. *Fiqh-us-Sunnah.* Vol. 2, *Salatul Jumu'ah.* Trans. Muhammad Sa'eed Dabas, Jamal al-Din M. Zarabozo, Abdul-Majid Khokhar, and M. S. Kayani. Indianapolis, Ind.: American Trust Publications, 1995. Available at www.usc.edu/ dept/MSA/law/fiqhussunnah/fusintro.html

Sarna, Jonathan D. *American Judaism: A History.* New Haven: Yale, 2004.

Sayers, Dorothy. *Creed or Chaos.* New York: Harcourt, Brace & Co., 1949.

Scholem, Gershom. "Kabbalah and Myth." In *On the Kabbalah and Its Symbolism.* Gershom Scholem, trans. Ralph Manheim, 87–117. New York: Schocken Books, 1965.

Sennett, Richard. *The Fall of Public Man.* New York: Knopf, 1977.

Sheen, Fulton J. *Religion without God.* New York: Longmans, Green and Co., 1928.

Shephard, Thomas. *Theses Sabbaticae: Or, the Doctrine of the Sabbath.* (1634) London: 1649.

Shulevitz, Judith. "Bring Back the Sabbath." *New York Times Magazine.* March 2, 2003.

Siddiqi, Muzzamil H. "Salat." In *The Encyclopedia of Religion,* ed. Mircea Eliade. Vol. 13, 20–23. New York: MacMillan, 1987.

Skinner, James, and James Muilenburg. "Sabbath." In Hastings, James, ed. *A Dictionary of the Bible.* (1898–1902) Rev. ed. Frederick C. Grant and H. H. Howley, eds. New York: Scribner's, 1963.

Second Vatican Ecumenical Council. *Constitution on the Sacred Liturgy (Sacrosanctum Concilium).* Rome: Vatican, 1963. Available at www.vatican.va/archive/hist_councils/ ii_vatican_council/documents/vat-ii_const_19631204_sacrosanctum-concilium_en. html

Slane, Craig J. "Sabbath." In *Baker's Evangelical Dictionary of Biblical Theology,* ed. Walter A. Elwell. Grand Rapids, Mich.: Baker Books, 1996. Available at bible.crosswalk.com/Dictionaries/BakersEvangelicalDictionary/bed.cgi?number =T619

Smith, Jane I. *Islam in America.* New York: Columbia University Press, 1999.

Smith, Jonathan M. "Ramifications of Region and Senses of Place." In *Concepts in Human Geography,* ed. Carville Earle, Kent Mathewson, and Martin S. Kenzer, 189–211. Lanham, Md.: Rowman & Littlefield, 1996.

Smith, Wilfred Cantwell. *Islam in Modern History.* Princeton, N.J.: Princeton University Press, 1957.

Soggin, J. A. "Sabbath." In *The Oxford Companion to the Bible*, ed., Bruce M. Metzger and Michael D. Coogan, 665–666. New York: Oxford University Press, 1993.

Solberg, Winton U. *Redeem the Time: The Puritan Sabbath in Early America*. Cambridge, Mass.: Harvard University Press, 1977.

Solomon, Norman. *Historical Dictionary of Judaism*. London: Scarecrow Press, 1998.

Spiro, Jack D., "Meaning." In *Contemporary Jewish Religious Thought*, ed. Arthur A. Cohen and Paul Mendes-Flohr, 565–571. New York: Free Press, 1987.

Stark, Rodney. "Why Gods Matter in Social Science." *The Chronicle of Higher Education*. June, 6, 2003.

Stephenson, George M. *The Puritan Heritage*. New York: MacMillan, 1952.

Thanawi, Ashraf Ali. *Juma ke Khutba: A Collection of Sacred Congregational Sermons Delivered on the Eve of Fridays and Eidain including Sermons of Holy Prophet*. New Delhi: Saeed International, 1995.

Tillich, Paul. *A History of Christian Thought: From its Judaic and Hellenistic Origins to Existentialism*. Ed. Carl E. Braaten. New York: Simon & Schuster, 1968.

Tocqueville, Alexis de. *Democracy in America*. Vols. I & II. (1835, 1840) New York: Knopf, 1994.

Tracy, David. *Plurality and Ambiguity: Hermeneutics, Religion, Hope*. Chicago: University of Chicago Press, 1987.

Tredget, Dermot. "Can the Rule of St. Benedict Provide an Ethical Framework for a Contemporary Theology of Work?" Paper delivered at the Monastic Theology Commission. Belmont Abbey, Hereford, UK, June 4–7, 2002. Available at www.benedictines.org.uk/theology/2002/dermot_tredget.pdf

Trench, Richard Chenevix. *Notes on the Miracles of Our Lord*. London: John W. Parker, 1846.

Twisse, William. *Morality of the Fourth Commandment*. London: 1641.

Vendler, Helen. "The Ocean, the Bird, and the Scholar." 33rd Jefferson Lecture in the Humanities, National Endowment for the Humanities. May 6, 2004. Available at www.neh.gov/whoweare/vendler/lecture.html

Washington, George. *The Writings of George Washington*. Ed. John C. Fitzpatrick. Washington, D.C.: Government Printing Office, 1932.

Waskow, Arthur, "Free Time for a Free People." *Nation*, 22–26. January, 1, 2001.

Weatherby, W. J. *Chariots of Fire*. New York: Dell, 1981.

Webster, Hutton. "Sabbath: Primitive." In *Encyclopedia of Religion and Ethics*, ed. James Hastings, John A. Selbie, and Louis H. Gray, 103–111. Edinburgh: T. & T. Clark, 1921.

Westby, Kenneth. "The Amazing 7-Day Cycle." *Sabbath Sentinel*. July–August 2004, 11–16.

Whealon, John F. "Instructive Material." In *The Vatican II Weekday Missal for Spiritual Growth*, ed. The Daughters of St. Paul. Boston: St. Paul Editions, 1975.

Whitehead, Alfred North. *Religion in the Making* (series of four lectures delivered during February 1926, at the King's Chapel, Boston, Mass.). Available at www. darktreasures.com/Strangelore/Stuff/Religioninthemaking.pdf

Wilken, Robert Louis. "Keeping the Commandments." *First Things*, 33–37. November 2003.

Woodward, Kenneth L. "What is Leisure Anyhow." *Newsweek*, August 26, 1991.

Zerubavel, Evitar. *The Seven Day Circle: The History and Meaning of the Week.* New York: Free Press, 1985.

Index

9 780195 370195

Printed in the United States
By Bookmasters